The Making of the University of Michigan

University of Michigan

175th Anniversary Edition

THE MAKING OF

THE UNIVERSITY OF MICHIGAN

1817﹡1992

BY

HOWARD H. PECKHAM

EDITED AND UPDATED BY

MARGARET L. STENECK
NICHOLAS H. STENECK

UNIVERSITY OF MICHIGAN
BENTLEY HISTORICAL LIBRARY
ANN ARBOR, MI

175TH ANNIVERSARY EDITION

ISBN 0-472-06594-7

Library of Congress Catalog Card No. 94-061108

Published in the United States of America by the Bentley Library of the University of Michigan

Distributed by the University of Michigan Press

Manufactured in the United States of America

1997   1996   1995   1994   4   3   2   1

Cover design, Liene Karels. Photography, formatting, and composition by Margaret and Nicholas Steneck using Kodak Photo CD™, Adobe Photoshop™, and Aldus Pagemaker™ electronic technology.

FORWARD

As one of America's leading universities for almost two centuries, the University of Michigan has a rich and well-documented history of considerable interest to scholars. Howard Peckham's book, *The Making of the University of Michigan*, has long provided a popular account of this history for students, alumni, and friends of the University.

As one component of the celebration of the 175th anniversary of the University, its History and Traditions Committee, chaired by Dean Emeritus Robert Warner, recommended that the Peckham book be updated through the 1980s. With the approval and financial support of the Office of the President, the Committee commissioned Dr. Margaret and Professor Nicholas Steneck to carry out this revision. The Stenecks were particularly well-qualified, since they have developed and teach an exceptionally popular course for undergraduates on the history of the University. They were assisted in this task by the oral histories provided by former presidents and first ladies of the University, including Harlan and Anne Hatcher, Robben and Sally Fleming, Allan and Alene Smith, and Harold and Vivian Shapiro, to whom we are indebted for their participation.

This new edition of the Peckham book makes it clear that the past twenty-five years have been just as exciting and challenging as any period in the University's history. Due to the talents, efforts, and commitment of countless students, faculty, staff, alumni, friends, and Regents, and due as well to the strong leadership provided by the exceptional university presidents of the 1970s and 1980s, the University of Michigan has emerged from this period better, stronger, and more exciting than perhaps at any time in its long history.

We are indebted to Margaret and Nicholas Steneck for their efforts in revising and updating Howard Peckham's 150th anniversary history of the University. We are grateful as well to the University History and Traditions Committee for recommending this project along with many others aimed at providing links between the past and the future of the University of Michigan.

James D. Duderstadt, President

CONTENTS

PREFACE TO THE 175TH ANNIVERSARY EDITION

The years between the University's 150th and 175th anniversaries have been filled by three presidents, two acting presidents, economic crises, fund-raising campaigns, activists, demonstrations, eleven Rose Bowl appearances, and much more. With each passing year, the University has also grown more complex, adding new administrative offices, programs, business ventures, and research areas. We have attempted to summarize the developments of these years in a style that is compatible with Howard Peckham's earlier work while endeavoring to bring some order to the confusing array of activities that comprise the modern public research university. For the 1970s and 1980s in particular, it can be difficult to see beyond the seemingly annual economic crises that have captured and required so much attention to the general path the University has taken. That path will no doubt be far more clear in 2017 when the University celebrates its bicentennial and, hopefully, updates "Peckham" once again.

There are many people whose contributions to the work of updating this history we wish to acknowledge. From the conception of the project to its completion, technology changed rapidly, enabling us to integrate many more pictures into the text than originally anticipated. The staff of the Bentley Historical Library deserve our special thanks for cheerfully handling our requests in the last weeks for ever more boxes and folders as we sought photos to enhance the text. The History and Traditions Committee has provided encouragement and guidance throughout the publication process. We learned a good deal more about the history of the University from our discussions--in person, via phone, and over e-mail--with Presidents Fleming, Shapiro, and Duderstadt as they commented on our drafts. Many present and former members of the faculty, administration, and students talked patiently and with candor about events and policy that enhanced our understanding of events. We are grateful to all these people, who make the University of Michigan "the leader and best," for their assistance. Interpretation of these years since 1967 remains our own.

Margaret L. Steneck
Nicholas H. Steneck
July, 1994

ix

PREFACE TO THE
SESQUICENTENNIAL EDITION

This narrative account of the University of Michigan was written for Michigan residents, for alumni and students, and for parents of students. It was not produced for my faculty colleagues.

The University has not lacked for historians, as may be seen in the Bibliography. The aim of this work is to relate in chronological order the intertwined developments of the Board of Regents' autonomy, state financial aid, academic programs and faculty, campus expansion, and student interests and activities, in order to produce a composite and moving picture of institutional history. At the same time, occasional reference to higher education elsewhere in the United States hopefully allows some perspective on the process.

In such a highly selective history, difficult choices prevailed, and many names and incidents had to be omitted. I am quite aware that another author might well have selected different events and other names by which to relate his history of the University. I take comfort, however, in the existence of the *Encyclopedic Survey* of the University in four large volumes, wherein each department and all its faculty receive their due.

The frailty of memory is nowhere better evinced than in our faith in giants of the past, in a lost Golden Age. Not now, but *then* great and good men directed University affairs and taught its courses, while earnest and hardworking students sat at their feet. It is a pleasant myth, despite its implication of a declining institution. Upon examination the truth is that there were little men in the past as well as big ones, delinquent students as well as serious ones, and nothing new has been added to University problems since 1850. The University of Michigan has flourished because there have always been a majority of men of vision and wisdom to project its potential steadily toward the high goal of excellence in teaching and learning, which in itself attracted a preponderance of students avid to secure the advantages of varied opportunities. Insofar as success is a secret, this is it.

On the eve of our Sesquicentennial observance, I cannot do better than repeat Andrew Ten Brook's final admonition in his first history of the University, 1875: "May those who have its management never allow it to lose its prestige by standing still to contemplate and proclaim the wonderful successes which it has already achieved."

Howard H. Peckham

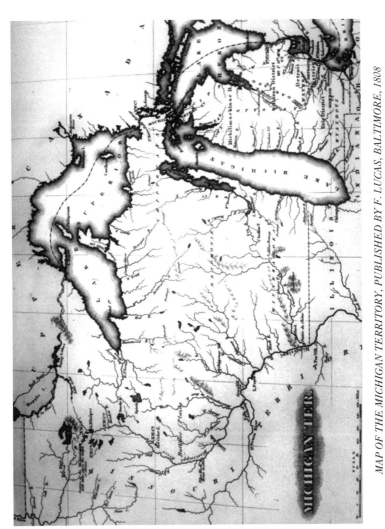

MAP OF THE MICHIGAN TERRITORY, PUBLISHED BY F. LUCAS, BALTIMORE, 1808

CHAPTER ONE

FOUNDING IN
DETROIT

THROUGHOUT THE LONG HISTORY of The University of Michigan runs a cord that thickens as time passes. First, there was only a single strand representing the University's aim to disseminate knowledge. As a Territorial institution it tried to embrace all education by instructing young people in a continuous program at elementary, secondary, and collegiate levels. After statehood, the University concentrated on higher education, not for an elite who paid its cost as in the East, but free for all men who could qualify and afford board and room. As it grew the State entered into support by providing a fraction of the property tax revenue. Women were admitted, then all graduates from approved high schools. The emphasis was still on good teaching. Michigan was in the front rank of the assault on the traditional classical curriculum; it added to recitations and lectures the seminar method of critical research and, finally, the honors program for exceptional students.

JOHN MONTIETH

Meanwhile, a second strand was turned around this first line. By the 1890's the University saw it must contribute additions to knowledge, which was not a static, fully known body of facts and accepted interpretations. The University had a duty to do research in its laboratories, libraries, and museums. Graduate students must be encouraged and directed in their searches. Scientific expeditions ventured forth, rare book collections were gathered, a Department of Engineering Research was organized. Sabbatical leaves encouraged faculty investigations and a University Press was established. Knowledge was to be expanded as well as disseminated.

Now there is a third strand wound with the other two. The University touches more than just its young students and faculty. It gives services to the State that help maintain it; it aids citizens who never enroll. These services began when its hospitals received perplexing cases from all over the State. It continued with the upgrading of high schools, the testing of municipal water supplies, with experiments in reforestation, testing programs for state highways. It supplied reading lists for club programs, lecture series for enlightenment, and musical concerts for entertainment. It expanded to research contracts for Michigan industries, development of new products for manufacture in Michigan, seminars for business executives, realtors and assessors, state college presidents, and refresher demonstrations for physicians and dentists. It provided radio and TV educational programs for all.

Teaching—research—and service. These are the warp and woof of the University today. The following pages show how one grew out of the other, how each reinforced the others, and how all together have made the institution effective and large. These fundamentals, shaped with durable skill and experience by scholars, give the University of Michigan the reputation it proudly upholds.

1. Michigan Territory: The Frontier Years

When the Territory of Michigan was set off from Indiana Territory in 1805 and allowed a government of its own, the population amounted to less than 4000, and the capital town of Detroit probably held about 700 inhabitants. The old French families, who were in the majority, had been apathetic about schooling for a century; the few families who cared sent their children to one of the Catholic schools in Montreal. The British, who had succeeded to the command of Fort Detroit in 1760, did nothing because the garrison soldiers and the fur traders were generally without children. The first recorded efforts at education were provided by occasional English and French schoolmasters, male and female, who conducted private classes from time to time in the 1790s.

Detroit did not pass into American hands until 1796, after British-allied Native Americans had been subdued and American troops appeared at the gates. In the same year Levadoux was assigned to Detroit, and began utilizing a *chantre* to teach the Catholic French their catechism. Gabriel Richard assumed this duty when he arrived to assist in 1798. Four years later he succeeded Levadoux as pastor, but did not give up his interest in education. In 1804 he organized the first parochial school to prepare nine Detroit boys for entrance to the Catholic seminary in Baltimore. The school lasted one year.

Then came the great Detroit fire of June 1, 1805. Ste. Anne's Church, the shops, dwellings, in fact the entire town within the old picket stockade was destroyed. Houses up and down the river bank, and the fort on the north side of town, were spared, and no one was killed. But blackened ruins greeted the new governor and judges who constituted the appointed Territorial government. Judge Augustus B. Woodward, fresh from Washington and a friend of that city's architect, set about immediately planning a town of geometric hexagons radiating from a couple of half-hubs on the river bank. It looked fascinating on paper. Congress allowed each inhabitant a frontage equal to his former holdings and gave a lot to everyone seventeen years of age or older. Other lots were to be sold and the revenue used for erecting public buildings. Rebuilding began in earnest. Woodward's paper plan was soon modified, and a series of long spokes extended from a half-hub on the river.

Richard persevered, too, and trained four local young women to be teachers. In 1806 he opened a school for girls. The next year he established a school at Springwells, three miles south of town, primarily for Native American children.   By 1808 he reported that he had eight schools operating in the area and petitioned for a school building. Then he went East and brought back an organ, a piano, a printing press, and a printer to publish bilingual textbooks of his own selection. By 1816 this press had produced fifty-two imprints. Richard also possessed the largest library in the Territory. A native of France, he was a graduate of the Sulpician Seminary at Angers who had come to the United States in 1792 to escape the French Revolution. He was forty in 1817.

Again education was interrupted, this time by the War of 1812 and the British capture of Detroit. Although the town was recovered in 1813, war swirled around it for another year. With news of the peace treaty in 1815, immigration from New York and New England picked up. Fire and war had stunted the growth of Michigan Territory, but the new Yankee arrivals agitated for schools as a public responsibility. Richard had never ceased his efforts and now was abetted by the young John Monteith, who came to Detroit in the middle of 1816 at the call of the Protestant residents. Incidentally, these Protestants, to whom Richard had preached occasionally, held their first services in the new Ste Anne's Church; at the invitation of the priest! Monteith, twenty-nine years of age, was a graduate of Jefferson College in western Pennsylvania and of the new Princeton Seminary.

The Territorial government agreed in 1817 that a town of 1200 and other villages at Frenchtown, Sault Ste. Marie, and Mackinac Island should enjoy a system of public schools. The governor at this time was Lewis Cass, thirty-five, originally from New Hampshire, a graduate of Philips Exeter Academy who had read law and practiced in Ohio, and a major general in the late war. He was later to be secretary of war, United States senator, minister to France, secretary of state, and the Democratic candidate for President in 1848. The secretary of Michigan Territory was William Woodbridge, thrity-seven, a graduate of the famous Litchfield Law School in Connecticut, and later a governor and U. S. senator. Judge Woodward, forty-three, a graduate of Columbia College, a lawyer and former teacher,

DETROIT IN 1820, WITH THE STEAMSHIP WALK-IN-THE-WATER

was appointed to his position by his friend Thomas Jefferson. Judge John Griffin, forty-six, of Virginia, was an alumnus of the College of William and Mary. Woodward and Griffin, incidentally, were fluent in French. Judge James Witherell, fifty-eight, was a former Vermont physician and member of Congress; he played no active part in the educational movement until later. With Richard and Monteith, these were the men who talked of an educational plan for Michigan in 1817, and they had vision as well as background.

Alexander Macomb, newly stationed in Detroit, gave his impression of the place in a letter of March 14, 1817, a crucial year in the history of the University: "Our population is a mixture of French & Yankees, and considering this is a frontier province, the society is wonderfully good. We are not much troubled with politicks because the people generally think one way, most of them being appendages of the government. No elections take place here. . . . We only want a few New England families to set an example in industry and in the true mode of farming. The French people are of the times of Louis the 14th, without any of the changes or improvements of the present day. The other part of the population is engaged in trade or official duties under the government."

Elsewhere what sort of a year was 1817? There were signs of change: the Native Americans still resident in Ohio were about to give up the last of their land there; Indiana had just entered the Union, and Illinois was filling up; the first steamship had appeared on the Mississippi; and the New York legislature authorized the start of the Erie Canal. And signs of stability: James Monroe had just started eight years in the presidency; and the New York Stock Exchange was organized.

In Michigan educational concerns moved toward a climax in August

1817, but were overshadowed for the moment by the visit of President Monroe to Detroit on his national tour. He arrived on August 13 and stayed five days. Frenchtown was renamed Monroe in his honor. Then Governor Cass accompanied him across Ohio and as far east as Pittsburgh, from which place Cass returned to Fort Meigs, Ohio, to conduct a treaty with the Native Americans. If President Monroe's visit awakened pride, there were other stimulants toward self-improvement. A weekly newspaper, the *Detroit Gazette*, had begun publication on July 25. At the same time the first shipment of books, selected by Monteith during a trip east, had arrived for the new Detroit Library, organized by stockholders, of which Monteith was secretary. The publishers of the *Gazette* likewise acquired a stock of books and school texts for sale.

Secretary Woodbridge served as acting governor in Cass's absence. The actual drafting of an education law was left to the eager hands of Woodward. These two men, in addition to Richard and Monteith, were the architects of the measure. What did they have for models? Indiana had established a university at Vincennes which was operating only a secondary school so far. The Regents of the State of New York had been created, but were only a state agency for chartering colleges and academies. Ohio had chartered a university that opened in 1809 at Athens, but had granted its first degrees only a year ago. Foremost in the minds of Woodward and Richard, however, was none of these neighboring precedents or the British universities which had so influenced the older seaboard colleges. Their model was the imperial University of France founded by Napoleon a decade earlier. It was not a university at all, but a centralized system of state supported schools throughout the country under the direction of a minister of public instruction.

2. Founding the University of Michigania

The product in Michigan was stamped with Woodward's far-ranging and individual mind. He was not much to look at: a very tall, stooped man of narrow face and large nose. A bachelor, he lived in untidy rooms and dressed carelessly. He had no church affiliation, but no one could recall the slightest immoral act or even a word of profanity from him. He interested himself in everything about Detroit and became a kind of eccentric uncle to everyone. It was he who stood up to the British during their year of occupation during the war and earned the admiration and gratitude of all the inhabitants, who felt deserted by the governor. By 1817 he was well loved, his foibles familiar and tolerated. A conscious intellectual, he had just published A *System of Universal Science* (Philadelphia, 1816), a classification of all knowledge by departments, classes, orders, and specifics, to each of which he gave original names. The nomenclature he would use in creating a university might have been predicted. The subjects themselves were drawn heavily from the Napoleonic concept of a university.

The education act Woodward drafted was adopted by himself, Griffin, and Secretary Woodbridge, which made it a Territorial law, on August 26, 1817. It is to this date that the University of Michigan traces its origins. There was created a *"Catholepistemiad,* (Cath-o-lep-is-STEEM-i-ad), or university, of Michigania." The University of Michigan was born. It was to be composed of "thirteen *didaxiim* or professorships." His listing of these drew on his earlier classification of knowledge:

1. *Catholepistemia,* or universal science. (The *didactor* or professor of this subject was to be president.)
2. *Anthropoglossica,* or literature and languages.
3. *Mathematica,* or mathematics.
4. *Physiognostica,* or natural history, or what we include under biology and mineralogy.
5. *Physiosophica,* or philosophy.
6. *Astronomia,* or astronomy.
7. *Chymia,* or chemistry.
8. *Iatrica,* or medical sciences.
9. *Oeconomica,* or economics.
10. *Ethica,* or ethics.
11. *Polemitactica,* or military science.
12. *Diegetica,* or history.
13. *Ennoeica,* or intellectual sciences, including psychology and religion. (The professor in this field was to be vice-president of the institution.)

Much more than eccentric intellectualism was at work here. At a time when Eastern universities were heavy with ancient languages and literature, with religion and philosophy, and with mathematics and a nod to ancient history—the classical curriculum—Woodward had boldly emphasized science and introduced economics for the University of Michigania. He was cracking an old and powerful tradition. If *Ennoeica* appears particularly exotic, let it be said that in the 1960's a group of "supercyberneticists" took on the study of interactions between computers and human intellects and found the word *Ennoetics* the only adequate term to describe their field.

Second, this degree-granting university was not to be an isolated tower of learning, but the capstone of a statewide educational system which it would supervise. The president and didactors, or professors, were given power "to establish colleges, academies, schools, libraries, museums, athenaeums, botanic gardens, laboratories . . . and to appoint instructors and instructrices in, among, and throughout the various counties, cities, towns, townships, and other geographical divisions of Michigan." This power was much broader than New York's Regents possessed. Here was the French idea of achieving a single and high set of standards for all schools by centering control in the university.

Third, the professors themselves were to run the university. No supervisory board was mentioned. While at the outset more than one professorship might be conferred on the same person, this faculty control made the university nonsectarian and oriented to scholarship. Other colleges and universities to this time were under boards of churchmen and often received part of their financial support from denominations. Michigan launched a radical departure that was to arouse criticism for several decades thereafter.

Finally, this educational system was to be supported by taxation. The primary schools should be free to all, and higher education should be available at low tuition. The acting governor and judges increased existing taxes in the territory by 15 percent and appropriated that percentage for the university. It was easier declared than actually levied and collected.

In subsequent acts passed that day and later, the tongue-fluttering *Catholepistemiad* was omitted and "University" or "University of Michigania" was used. Annual salaries were set as follows: president, $25; vice-president, $18.75; professor, $12.50; instructor, $25. The sum of $181.25 was appropriated for initial salaries of professors, and $200 for instructors.

Two weeks after the establishment of the University, the Territorial government appointed the Reverend John Monteith as president and gave him seven professorships, or courses. Richard was named vice-president and was given the other six professorships. A few days later "the university" (Monteith and Richard) established public primary schools in Detroit, Monroe, and Mackinac Island and named some of the textbooks to be used. They also established a Classical Academy in Detroit and listed the courses to be taught. These were not free schools; a small fee was charged, although poor children could attend at public expense—presumably after declaring their poverty. A board of trustees and visitors for each school was named. Then the University appointed a treasurer and register and arranged to receive private contributions.

The *Detroit Gazette* published the appointments of Monteith and Richard, and their subsequent actions, but it never printed the Organic Act creating the University. A reader complained of this omission, but it wasn't rectified. The first subscribers (donors) were listed in the issue of September 19 and showed $180 pledged from the Territory, $250 from the Masonic Lodge, $200 from Woodbridge personally payable over four years; $180 from James Conner payable over three years; and $250 from merchant James Abbott spread over ten years; all for a grand total of $1060. A twenty-four by fifty foot building was started immediately on Bates Street near the

ORIGINAL UNIVERSITY BUILDING ON BATES STREET, DETROIT

corner of Congress Street. A month later donations and pledges totaled more than $3000. Private support for the state institution thus began at once. The Territorial government allowed the University treasurer to have the money raised in Montreal and Mackinac for sufferers in the Detroit fire of 1805 but not paid out for "want of some principle on which payments can be made." It amounted to $940.

On October 3 the University bravely established—or, more accurately, called for the establishment of—a college in Detroit, which was also to have a board of trustees and visitors. Unfortunately, no student was sufficiently prepared to enter it. The action probably was for the purpose of becoming eligible to receive land offered by the Native Americans "to the college." At the Treaty of Fort Meigs which Governor Cass was conducting while the University got under way, he persuaded the chiefs, who still owned most of Michigan, to grant six sections—3840 acres—half to Ste Anne's Church and half for the new "college at Detroit."

The vision of Woodward, who drew the plan, and of the young minister and the older priest was remarkable. They had given substance to the clause in the Northwest Ordinance of 1787 that read: "Religion, morality, and knowledge being necessary to good government and the happiness of mankind, schools and the means of education shall forever be encouraged." They had energized the Jeffersonian ideal of education for all to the extent of the individual's capacity, for without an educated citizenry democracy would fumble and fail. Since society benefitted, education was logically a responsibility of the territory or state to be exercised through its taxing power. The countervailing idea, that since the individual would profit personally from his subsequent vocation he ought to pay for his college education, is a new and aristocratic notion that would not crop up until the middle of the twentieth century.

The creation of a university and the call for a college were bold. Any young men of Michigan who might be qualified and desired to go to college in 1817 had to look east or southeast. The closest college was Ohio University at Athens, not ten years old. Farther south was Transylvania University at Lexington, Kentucky, the oldest educational institution west of the Alleghenies. To the southeast were Jefferson and Washington colleges (later combined) in western Pennsylvania. New York state offered nothing until one traveled beyond Syracuse to Hamilton College at Clinton, or to Union College at Schenectady. Such were the nearest degree-granting institutions.

President Monteith submitted his first annual report as University president to the governor and judges in November 1818. He took note of the opening of the three primary schools and the Classical Academy, for which instructors had been engaged. A university building was still going up, largely from private contributions. Other schools were needed, he said, particularly the collegiate institution already projected on paper.

Financial problems continued. The higher tax rate seems not to have been enforced. A township of land had been granted to Michigan Territory by the federal government in 1804, but it could only be leased, not sold. So far it had not even been located because southeastern Michigan had not been surveyed. The three sections given by the Native Americans had not been located either. Potential assets existed, not actual resources.

Meanwhile, also in 1818, Illinois had been admitted to the Union, and the territory lying north of it (modern Wisconsin and part of Minnesota) was attached to Michigan Territory. This addition and immigration had pushed the population well above 5000, the number necessary to permit Michigan to enter the second stage of territorial government and to elect a general assembly and a delegate to Congress. Cass therefore put the question to the voters, and to his surprise they voted against a change! Apparently, the French majority did not want to assume political responsibilities and feared more taxes. Nevertheless, Congress in July 1819 extended to Michigan the privilege of sending a delegate to the House of Representatives. Woodbridge was elected, but after one year of criticism for his attempt to hold two political offices he resigned. Attorney Solomon Sibley, a graduate of Brown University, was elected in his place. Michigan was growing, albeit slowly. Pontiac and Mt. Clemens were laid out and promoted. Cass purchased a huge tract of land from the Native Americans in order to open it for settlement: it embraced the Saginaw Bay area and part of central Michigan.

3. Reorganization in 1821

The University entered a second phase of its life when the governor and judges on April 30, 1821, without stating their reasons, adopted a new law that reorganized the university. It was to be managed by a Board of Trustees numbering twenty and the governor.

The Board was required to appoint a treasurer and secretary and to render an annual report to the government; it had power to appoint a president and professors and to confer degrees. Also the trustees "may from time to time establish such colleges, academies and schools, depending upon the said University, as they may think proper, and as the funds of the corporation will permit." The unified educational system was retained. In a notable section it was stated that no trustee, professor, or student should be barred from appointment or admission because of religious beliefs. To the Board was granted control of the township of land promised in 1804 and the three sections allowed by the Native Americans in 1817. Similarly, all properties, credits, and debts of the University were transferred to the successor board. Since the governor and judges could never enact original legislation, it was solemnly declared that this act was adopted from laws of Massachusetts, New York, and Ohio. It was signed by Cass, Griffin, and Witherell. Concurrrence of Judge Woodward was not needed, and omission of his name may mean that he objected or was not consulted, although Griffin was regarded as his friend and even was accused of being his tool. Woodward was not appointed to the new Board of Trustees, and with the expiration of his judicial term the Detroit Bar petitioned against his reappointment because "of his entire want of practical knowledge." Although this action reflects no credit on the local attorneys, President Monroe omitted Woodward's name for the Michigan court in January 1824. Detroit citizens gave him a testimonial banquet before he departed for Washington, where President Monroe, convinced of his mistake, appointed him to the federal court in Florida Territory. The loss to Michigan culture was serious. Detroit's principal business street bears his name.

As for the University Act of 1821, the biggest change was not the omission of Woodward's pedantic verbiage, but the transfer of management from the faculty to a board of public-spirited citizens outside the University, possibly to arouse public support. Monteith and Richard lost their administrative titles of president and vice-president but were named to the Board of Trustees. The change may or may not have disappointed Monteith. He had secured the building of an interdenominational Protestant church and in the summer of 1821 he left Detroit for a professorship at Hamilton College.

The other trustees named besides Cass, Richard, and Monteith were as follows: William Woodbridge, secretary of the Territory; Solomon Sibley, attorney, judge, and later Territorial delegate to Congress; John

Biddle, register of the land office and later delegate to Congress; John R. Williams, half-French merchant and soon to be Detroit's first mayor and president of the Bank of Michigan; Dr. William Brown, one of the earliest Americans in Detroit and director of the Bank of Michigan; John Leib, chief justice of the Wayne County court; Charles Larned, Williams '06, and veteran officer of the War of 1812; Philip Lecuyer, justice of the Wayne County court and director of the Bank of Michigan; Austin Wing, Williams '14, sheriff of Monroe County and later delegate to Congress; Henry Hunt, second mayor of Detroit; John Hunt, later a Territorial judge; Peter Denoyers French silversmith and county treasurer; Benjamin Stead, a Detroit tailor; Daniel Le Roy, Pontiac lawyer and later the state's first attorney general; Nicholas Boilvin, Native American agent in Wisconsin; Christian Clemens, founder of Mt. Clemens, militia colonel, and first probate judge of Macomb County; John Anderson, Monroe merchant and district judge; and William Puthuff, War of 1812 officer, former Native American agent at Mackinac Island, then a merchant there.

The Board of Trustees met frequently at the Classical Academy for the next seventeen years. They organized themselves with a chairman or president, a secretary, and a treasurer. Cass presided from 1821 until he left the Territory in 1831 to join President Jackson's cabinet. Charles C. Trowbridge, later president of the Bank of Michigan and mayor of Detroit, acted as secretary from 1821 to 1835. Treasurer from 1823 to 1837 was De Garmo Jones, merchant and later mayor. Their first duty was to employ teachers for the Academy and the primary school, and to maintain the Bates Street School.

Harmony on the Board appears doubtful. After Sibley succeeded as territorial judge in 1824, the office of delegate to Congress was fiercely contested by John Biddle, Austin Wing, and Richard. Richard won. These same three men were pitted against one another in 1825, and in a rigged election Wing emerged with a narrow lead. Biddle finally won in 1829.

Meanwhile, in 1823 Congress permitted Michigan to elect a slate of eighteen men from which the President would select nine to serve as a Legislative Council and relieve the governor and judges of law making. In 1827 the voters of Michigan were allowed to elect the Legislative Council, now thirteen in number, and a unicameral assembly continued until statehood.

The Legislative Council stepped into the education picture in 1826 by authorizing all townships containing fifty or more families to employ a schoolmaster for six months each year. Two years later the Council decreed that the costs of maintaining schools should be paid by the parents of pupils, although poor children must be instructed at township expense. At the same time the Board of Trustees gave up supervision of primary schools, and the unity of education envisioned by Judge Woodward was lost.

The University Board of Trustees petitioned Congress about the township of land it had never received. The Secretary of the Treasury now authorized Cass to locate the six sections of land granted by the Native Americans in 1817 to Ste Anne's Church and the University. A section was a square mile of land containing 640 acres. Since a township was thirty-six square miles, it had thirty-six sections—23,040 acres. Thus, the University had as a potential resource this acreage plus 1920 acres from the Native Americans, or almost 25,000 acres to sell. Depending on the quality of the soil and desirability of location, these lands were worth from $30,000 to more than $150,000.

The three sections given by the Native Americans were located in 1824 on the Detroit River and in Oakland County, but their ultimate disposition is not clear. In June 1825 the Board decided to sell one section, which bordered on the Detroit River, at public auction, setting an ambitious minimum price of $6 an acre. After one postponement of the auction, how much was sold is not known, or what the University netted. The sale was advertised in the *Detroit Gazette*, but the results were not reported; neither do the minutes of the Board mention receipts.

The Congress in May 1826 passed an act setting aside two townships of land in Michigan Territory to be leased or sold for support of a "seminary of learning." This act meant two townships in addition to the one granted in 1804. The Board took notice of this grant and asked for a few sections on the Maumee River, the boundary of Ohio being in dispute. Then interested individuals proposed swapping certain University claims for others. Squatters in other desirable sections asserted preemption rights and delayed sales. Title was not cleared up for several years; not until 1834 was the University credited with two sections of land near Perrysburg, Ohio. By that time only forty-one other sections, in Michigan Territory, had been located, leaving twenty-nine sections not yet staked out, even though the Board had appointed John Mullet in 1830 to locate all the proffered seventy-two sections of land. This kind of muddling kept the Board largely without funds.

As for education itself, the Board appointed a committee of three members to superintend the Classical Academy and primary schools by visiting them at least once a month and submitting recommendations about teachers. The Board also repaired the Bates Street building, ordered maps, mathematical instruments, and laboratory apparatus, and even built a stage for the Academy. It also adopted a University seal in 1825, and ordered a die cut for use by the secretary. No impression of this seal remains today.

The University stumbled along. Late in 1827 the Board gave up support of the Classical Academy and asked the teacher to continue "provided he be willing to accept in full of his compensation such sums as he may be able to procure by individual subscription." In 1831 the use of the building was granted to the City of Detroit for a common school until wanted again by the Trustees. Apparently, they got it back late in 1833, after Detroit had passed an ordinance permitting taxation for school sites and buildings, while teachers' salaries continued to be met by pupil tuition. Public, but not free, education in the Territory was inching forward, but not collegiate learning.

The cholera epidemic of 1832 had taken its toll and disrupted community life. One of the victims was the venerable Richard, who for thirty-four years had been a force for education in Detroit. His purposeful energy would be missed.

In 1834 the Board rented the Bates Street building to two schoolmasters for a "high school" at $180 a year. The cholera returned that summer. In the same year the Board finally sold 767 acres (but counted as two sections) on the Maumee River for $5000 and wisely put the money aside as a general fund for The University of Michigan. The other Native American gift section was held until 1849. In 1932 the Regents of the University, recollecting this grant, made available five scholarships for Native Americans.

Young Stevens T. Mason, acting governor, began presiding over the Board in 1834. By this time Michigan Territory was in political turmoil over forming a state, writing a constitution, and getting admitted to the Union. The latter step turned out to be an ordeal.

4. Statehood and State Education

Michigan's population had grown slowly and numbered 31,000 in 1830, with Detroit holding about 3000. Despite the cholera epidemics, immigrants then began pouring into southern Michigan, chiefly from New York and New England via the Erie Canal and Lake Erie steamboats. Hundreds were arriving every week. By late 1834 the population was believed to be 85,000, or 25,000 in excess of the number needed for statehood. So the Legislative Council issued a call for a state constitutional convention, which met at Detroit in May and June of 1835. In six weeks it turned out an excellent constitution.

Two men from the town of Marshall were most influential in writing the educational provisions. John D. Pierce, a graduate of Brown University who had also attended Princeton Seminary, served as a missionary preacher in the small community. He was thirty-eight years old. Isaac E. Crary was a graduate of Trinity College and a lawyer who had lived with Pierce and his wife when he first went to Marshall to practice. He was thirty-one years old and a delegate to the Constitutional Convention, at which he became chairman of the committee on education. The two friends had discussed

ISAAC CRARY

education in the new state as a result of reading M. Victor Cousin's *Report on the State* of *Public Instruction in Prussia* (Paris, 1831; English translation, 1835). It was an elucidation of the system of primary and secondary schools and universities supported and supervised by the state.

It is not surprising to find that Article 10 of the new constitution incorporated the Prussian idea, which was derived from the Napoleonic concept that had appealed to Woodward. The first section declared that the governor, with the consent of the legislature, should appoint a superintendent of public instruction, whose duties would be prescribed. Second, the legislature should encourage intellectual, scientific, and agricultural improvement; the obligation was definite. Proceeds from the sale of school lands granted by Congress should be held inviolable for support of schools. Third, the legislature should provide a system of common schools, with one in every school district. Fourth, the legislature should, when conditions warranted, provide for libraries, at least one to a township. The fifth and last section read: "The legislature shall take measures for the protection, improvement or other disposition of such lands as have been or may hereafter be, reserved or granted by the United States to the State, for support of a University; and the funds accruing . . . shall be and remain a permanent fund for the support of said University, with such branches as the public convenience may hereafter demand . . . ." The reference to support of a university indicates that the delegates felt it was already in existence.

The new constitution was ratified by Michigan voters in October 1835, and they immediately elected Mason the first state governor and chose a legislature. Crary was elected representative to Congress, and the state legislature elected Lucius Lyon of Kalamazoo and John Norvell of Detroit as United States senators. The three men went to Washington, but Congress refused to seat them because it had not yet taken Michigan into the Union.

Michigan's application for admission to the Union had brought to a head an old quarrel with Ohio about their common boundary. The southern line of Michigan had been determined by the Northwest Ordinance of 1787 and reaffirmed by Congress in 1805; it touched Lake Erie at Maumee Bay. Ohio had objected strongly because it wanted all of Maumee Bay, where Toledo was developing. Ohio was taken into the Union in 1803 without this northern boundary finally determined. Legal and moral right in 1835 were still clearly on the side of Michigan, as the U. S. attorney general advised President Jackson; however, Jackson recommended that Michigan wait until December and let Congress settle the matter. This was politically naive, since Ohio was represented in Congress and Michigan was not. Mason rejected the proposal and called out the militia. Jackson thereupon removed his appointee from office as Territorial governor at the end of August 1835, but he was promptly elected governor under the new state constitution.

During 1836 the United States Senate sought to break the deadlock by establishing Wisconsin Territory and detaching the northeastern portion as compensation to Michigan—the present Upper Peninsula. In brief, the state was offered 22,600 square miles of timber, copper, and iron lands in exchange for 468 square miles of flat land around Toledo and west to the Indiana line. The "consolation" prize, or bribe, was added to the bill to admit Michigan, provided that a special convention of the people would accept the Ohio boundary as decreed by Ohio. Michigan citizens objected furiously to both clauses: the southern area wanted the Toledo strip, and Sault St. Marie hoped to belong to a separate and new Territory of Huron, embracing the Upper Peninsula. A special convention met in Ann Arbor in September 1836 and rejected the proposal from Congress, even though Governor Mason and Senator Lyon reluctantly changed their minds and advised acceptance.

Since matters continued at an impasse, a second convention, also held in Ann Arbor, was called by Jacksonian Democrats in December 1836, no doubt without legal sanction, and dubbed the "Frostbitten Convention" by its opponents. This convention assented to the boundaries prescribed by Congress. Unnoted by anyone was a phrase that Isaac Crary had slipped into the act of admission: sale of the lands set aside for public schools as well as those for the University was put in the hands of the state, not the townships or counties which might dissipate the money improperly.

Meanwhile, at a special convention of the legislature in July 1836, Governor Mason appointed John D. Pierce, with legislative consent, to be superintendent of public instruction—a constitutional office new in state government. He was directed to submit a plan for common schools and for a university with branches at the next session. Pierce sold his house in Marshall and spent several weeks in the East studying education systems.

On January 26, 1837, Michigan was formally and belatedly admitted to the Union by a relieved Congress as the twenty-sixth state. It now had a population of 175,000—twenty-two counties were organized, and Detroit was a city of 10,000. The time was overdue to provide for higher education, in fulfillment of Woodward's grand design.

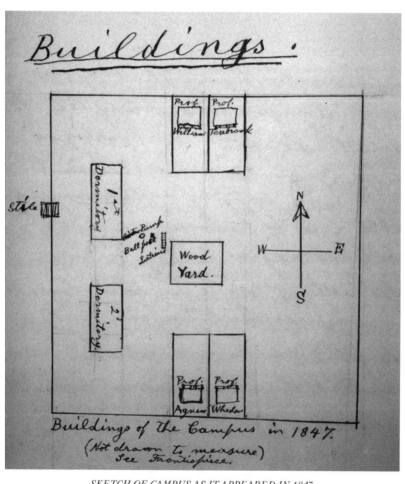

SKETCH OF CAMPUS AS IT APPEARED IN 1847

CHAPTER TWO

FULFILLMENT
IN ANN ARBOR

SUPERINTENDENT OF PUBLIC Instruction Pierce presented his comprehensive plan for public education to the state legislature in January 1837. There was no precedent in the United States to guide him, yet he devised a system that marked a new step in educational progress. State supervision of all education was revived in a pattern modeled on the Prussian system. No longer were common schools to be under the jurisdiction of the University. They were placed directly under the state superintendent's office. His ex-

JOHN D. PIERCE

tensive report need not be detailed here, except to say that his plan for primary education was adopted and except for minor changes is still in operation.

Secondary education was to be provided through county branches of the University, each of which was to have its own board of trustees responsible to the state superintendent. Each branch was to offer three courses of instruction: for future teachers of the primary schools, for students preparing for college, and for students who expected to terminate their schooling. The county was to contribute support equal to that received from the University fund, and tuition would be charged. As for higher education to be offered by the University, Pierce called for three departments: literature, science, and the arts; medicine; and law. Professorships were specified, as Judge Woodward had done; however, they need not be established all at once, but only as warranted. More interesting is the resemblance of the thirteen professorships in the Literary Department to the thirteen called for by Woodward in the University of 1817. Superintendent Pierce added only rhetoric and oration, fine arts and civil engineering and architecture, then omitted astronomy and military science; and separated medical science.

Control of the University was vested in a Board of Regents of eighteen members, six ex officio and twelve appointed by the governor for staggered terms. They had power to grant degrees, regulate courses, and prescribe textbooks; they could appoint and remove professors and erect buildings; and they could recommend to the superintendent and legislature the branches that should be established in the counties. Entering students, coming for the most part from these branches, would be charged an initial fee of ten dollars. Pierce himself retained control of all University lands and would apportion the income from invested sales revenue between the branches and the University. Clearly, the Board of Regents was the executive and administrative head of this University, and just as clearly it was subject to the direction of the state government.

Pierce was openly opposed to encouraging private schools, such as flourished in the East, and to chartering private colleges; but his position being regarded as somewhat autocratic, he did not win the legislature to his view. Private colleges were granted charters, but at the secondary level the University branches developed so well as to discourage private academies. Outside of parochial high schools, Michigan has had very few private academies.

The idea of education from first grade to University degree as a continuous flow of public instruction under public responsibility came out of the Old Northwest, and Michigan was its prime demonstrator.

1. Reorganization as a State University

The state legislature accepted Pierce's report on March 18, 1837, thus beginning the third phase in the life of the University of Michigan. He was authorized to sell at auction thirty-two sections of University land (20,500 acres) at a minimum price of twenty dollars an acre so as to raise half a million dollars. A group of enterprising citizens forming the Ann Arbor Land Company promptly offered forty acres of land in the thriving town of Ann Arbor, seat of Washtenaw County, as a site for the University. Two days later, on March 20, the offer was approved by the legislature. The town had been planned in 1824 and now contained about 2000 people, including several German families. There were four churches, two newspapers, two banks, eight mills and factories, numerous stores, eleven lawyers, and nine physicians. Yet it was still frontier enough that neighboring Native Americans came into town to trade. Railroad connection with Detroit was made two years later.

1837 was a year of signs, auspicious and ominous. Michigan had entered the Union as a free state, but in Alton, Illinois, editor Elijah Lovejoy was killed by a proslavery mob. The Republic of Texas was recognized as independent from Mexico, and Martin Van Buren was inaugurated as President. When New York banks suspended specie payments panic set in that caused 618 banks to fail, and business depression followed. Mount Holyoke Female Seminary, for the exclusive education of women, opened in Massachusetts, and Ralph Waldo Emerson delivered a Phi Beta Kappa address at Harvard calling for American independence from Europe in intellectual matters. Yet, like Michigan, Massachusetts and Ohio were adopting public school systems drawn from the Prussian plan.

The new Board of Regents for the University was appointed in the spring of 1837. Members were Senators Lyon and Norvell; Representative Crary; U. S. District Court Judge Wilkins, Dickinson '21, of Detroit; Dr. Zina Pitcher of Detroit; U. S. Indian Agent Henry R. Schoolcraft, of Middlebury College, geologist and ethnologist of Sault Ste Marie; Secretary of the Senate John J. Adam, University of Glasgow '26, of Tecumseh; Dr. Samuel Denton of Ann Arbor, Judge Gideon O. Whittemore of Pontiac; Attorney Robert McClelland, Dickinson '29, future governor and secretary of the interior; Attorney Michael Hoffman of the Saginaw Land Office; and John F. Porter of St. Joseph. The latter three resigned in the next nine months and were succeeded by Major Jonathan Kearsley, Washington College '11, testy veteran of the War of 1812; Banker Gurdon C. Leech of Utica; and Seba Murphy of Monroe. Norvell, Wilkins, and Kearsley had served on the old Board of Trustees. The ex officio members were the governor, lieutenant governor, three judges, and the state chancellor (an office shortly abolished).

2. Faculty, campus, and buildings

The Regents held their first meeting, lasting three days, in Ann Arbor, June 5-7. Governor Mason was elected president of the Board, and several standing committees were appointed. Charles W. Whipple of Detroit was chosen as secretary, and C. C. Trowbridge, secretary of the old University Trustees, was named treasurer, but he declined and John Norton was appointed. Four professorships were agreed upon but no appointments were made; salaries were fixed at between $1200 and $2200. The only University appointment was of the Reverend Henry Colclazer, Methodist minister of Ann Arbor, as librarian, his salary to begin when some books were accumulated.

The main business was selection of a campus, since two sites had been offered. The Regents chose the flat tract lying east of State Street rather than the hills to the north overlooking the Huron River. The forty-acre tract selected was part of the Rumsey-Nowland farm, and it was well cleared of forest trees. Part of it was a wheat field, part a peach orchard, and the rest pasture.

At another meeting later in the same month, the Board of Regents established a University branch (high school) at Pontiac and appointed the Reverend George Palmer Williams, Vermont '25, who had taught at

Kenyoll College, as principal. It opened in the fall of 1837. Other counties were now seeking branches. The old Academy building in Detroit served as the branch there. Subsequently branches were organized in Monroe, Kalamazoo, Niles, and Tecumseh, and the Regents adopted elaborate regulations about admission, courses of study, textbooks, fees, and student conduct.

Construction of a University building was stalled by lack of money, yet the Regents decided early in 1838 to buy the 2600 geological specimens collected in Europe by Baron Lederer, Austrian consul in New York City, for $4000. (It was said to surpass Yale's collection.) Then the Regents purchased a copy of J. J. Audubon's monumental *Birds of America* and C. C. Rafn's *Antiquitates Americanae*, the Scandinavian sagas of early discovery. It is one of the glories of The University of Michigan that this first Board recognized the value of Audubon's work and ordered it despite the considerable cost of $970, for the five elephant-folio volumes are still in fine condition in the University Library. Museum and library resources preceded both faculty and classes.

It was a wonder that the Regents accomplished anything in 1837 or 1838. After New York banks suspended specie payments in May 1837, the Michigan legislature allowed state banks the same relief from paying out coins for bank notes. As a result forty-nine new banks were organized in the state, in addition to the existing fifteen, and they all began issuing paper currency that was not redeemable in cash. With such easy money, speculation was rife. State bank inspectors began catching up with wildcat institutions in 1839, and others closed from their own folly. By 1845 Michigan had only three banks, and losses were widespread.

At the same time the state was in process of borrowing five million dollars for a program of internal improvements involving canals, roads, and railroads. On top of all this financial juggling, a rebellion broke out in Canada at the end of 1837, and the rebels found sympathy, arms, and a launching ground in Michigan throughout 1838, while the Canadian government complained bitterly over Governor Mason's feeble counteractions. With land sales dwindling, internal improvement stopping, and banks failing, a less auspicious time for moving a University to a new location and attempting to expand its facilities can hardly be imagined.

Nevertheless, the Board of Regents appealed to the state legislature in the spring of 1838 for a loan so as to operate the six branches and to begin the University buildings. Perhaps more surprising, a loan was granted, to be drawn as needed, to the amount of $100,000. The Regents now called in a New York architect of reputation, Alexander J. Davis, to plan a building. They also made their first appointment of a professor Dr. Asa Gray, a young physician of New York who was turning to botany, as professor of botany and zoology. Because he was going to Europe, they gave him $5000 to spend on books for the University library.

Mr. Davis prepared plans for an elaborate Gothic building with wings. It was U-shaped, with a tall central entrance like the facade of a cathedral. (The original drawing is in the Metropolitan Museum.) Because it would have used up all the state loan, Superintendent Pierce vetoed the plan near the end of the year. He was more concerned about collecting payments on the $150,000 worth of University lands he had succeeded in selling.

The year 1839 opened with a clamor from illegal squatters occupying University lands around the state to be allowed to buy them by right of preemption at the old federal price of $1.25 an acre. Other citizens were muttering about the University claiming some of the best acreage in the state. In this year of depression the legislature abjectly favored the squatters, and over protests from the Board of Regents passed a bill to let them stay put for only $1.25 an acre. In April the Regents prepared to close the seven branches (another had just been authorized at White Pigeon) when Governor Mason, who was still president of the Board of Regents, courageously vetoed the bill and saved the University lands from outrageous political spoliation. A crisis was passed.

The dormant building program was now revived, and the Regents authorized the erection and furnishing of four houses for professors, anticipating that one or two might be used first to house the museum, library, and laboratory equipment. Two of these houses were to be in the middle of the campus tract on the south side (South University Avenue) and two on the north side (North University Avenue), and all would face toward the center. It was decided later in the year to finish them with stucco, the newest vogue.

In October 1839 the Board appointed as professor of geology, mineralogy, chemistry, and pharmacy Dr. Douglass Houghton, the state geologist. He was a graduate of Rensselaer Polytechnic Institute and a physician who had accompanied Henry Schoolcraft around the state and gathered a local mineral collection that was promised to the University. His salary would begin when he entered on his teaching duties, but that would be delayed by his election as mayor of Detroit.

As the year ended the Board was gratified by an enrollment of 218 students, male and female, in the six branches (the one at Kalamazoo was temporarily suspended). Monroe and White Pigeon with seventy students each far outranked the Detroit branch that had only twenty-eight. But the Regents were concerned that the branches by their very success were taking up too much of the University's income. They decided to ask the legislature to eliminate the superintendent's power over establishing branches and over dividing funds between them and the University proper.

PRESIDENT'S HOUSE, SKETCHED IN
1855 BY J. F. CROPSEY

The four professors' houses were finished in March of 1840 at a cost in excess of $30,000. Fences and outbuildings were added. One of these houses, altered and enlarged, on South University Avenue, is the home of the University president and the oldest building on campus. Dr. Houghton was given $200 with which to plant trees on campus. The Board now took up the necessity of a college building and rather quickly adopted plans of a contractor, Haspier Lum, who had built the professors' houses, for a rectangular structure 42 by 110 feet and four stories high. It was to be of brick construction faced with stucco and stand between the two pairs of houses. The first floor was to contain classrooms, a library and museum, and a chapel, the essentials of any college, and the upper floors were a dormitory consisting of three-room suites, each with two bedrooms connected to a study having a fireplace. The estimated cost was $16,000. Such spacious quarters for students were not to be seen again until 1924, when the Lawyers Club (a gift from a New York alumnus) was built with similar suites.

Professor Gray returned from Europe that summer and shipped to Ann Arbor 3707 volumes of history, philosophy, classical literature, science, art, jurisprudence, and other subjects. With perhaps a few dozen books acquired by the library committee of the Regents, the University had a respectable resource for learning. But for lack of a building teaching was not to begin yet, and Professor Gray agreed to a suspension of his salary for the ensuing year.

The state legislature came back in 1841 with a different bill to relieve squatters and settlers, cutting in half the price they need pay for University lands. This time there was no Governor Mason to veto it. He had not run for reelection, and William Woodbridge, former Territorial secretary and trustee of the University, was now governor. With less backbone, he signed the bill. The University had to return to the purchasers money received in excess of the new maximum. Despite this raw and dishonest political interference (it was legal because the legislature could overrule the Regents), it must be said that Michigan yet obtained more out of its federal grant of land for university education than any of the older states and some of the younger ones. By 1881, when all the University lands in Michigan had been sold, the average price per acre realized was $11.87—more than twice the price received for educational lands elsewhere in the Old Northwest. Altogether the University eventually obtained some $547,000, a healthy sum, but more than a million dollars had been anticipated by the superintendent from the federal gift. The imagination is dazzled by what could have been done with that amount of money.

ORIGINAL CLASSROOM BUILDING (1841), LATER CALLED MASON HALL (LEFT) AND SOUTH COLLEGE (1847)

It was the summer of 1841 before the Main Building was finished, including furniture, a wood yard, and a cistern. The library and museum collections were moved into it. Reluctantly, the Regents had had to decide that they must limit their support of the branches to $500 each annually in order to finance higher education adequately. Although the seven of them enrolled 247 students, three closed at the end of the term. Three principals were thrown out of work. The Regents capitalized on this opportunity by appointing two of them to the University faculty. The Reverend George Palmer Williams, head of the Pontiac branch, was made professor of mathematics and science. He was to get a salary of $500, free house rent, and half the tuition fees of a preparatory school that was to open in Ann Arbor—virtually another University branch. The Reverend Joseph Whiting, Yale '23, head of the Niles branch, was named professor of Greek and Latin under the same terms. Although these were appointments of convenience, Williams and Whiting were actually splendid teachers and scholarly men. The Regents felt unwilling to bring other professors into the state when the financial outlook was so uncertain. Williams was destined to remain for thirty-four years, as Whiting might have but for his untimely death in 1845. The University now had a faculty of five on paper, although Houghton was not available, Colclazer did not teach, and Gray was not called, an unfortunate decision.

3. The first university students, 1841

At last courses at the collegiate level were offered beginning on September 25, 1841, with six freshmen and one sophomore, and twenty-three in the preparatory school. The ratio of one professor to 3.5 students was never achieved again. The freshmen had been examined for admission in mathematics, geography, Latin, and Greek and made to "furnish satisfactory testimonials of good moral character." Each had paid an entrance fee of $10.

All the boys were easily housed in the Main Building with room to spare. After the death of former Governor Mason early in 1843, it was named Mason Hall; sturdy and hallowed it stood until 1950; today a new building bearing the name occupies the old site. The boys led a Spartan existence. They paid $7.50 a term for their room, $2.50 for incidentals, and another $1.25 to $1.50 for firewood—which they had to split in the adjoining woodyard and carry up to their rooms. They also carried up water from the pump for washing and furnished their own candles. Each living room contained a study table, two chairs, a stove, and a wood closet. The adjoining small bedrooms each had a bed, chest, and closet.

They were awakened at 5 A.M. by a clanging bell; compulsory chapel was held at 5: 30 A.M. in fall and spring, and 6:30 in the winter. One recitation class followed at 6:00 before the boys were dismissed for breakfast to their private boarding houses outside the campus, where the weekly board bill came to $1.50 or $2.00. A second class was held before a break for lunch, and studying might be done in the library before the afternoon class. A second chapel service was held in late afternoon, then supper and freedom until 9 P.M. after which no one could leave the campus.

The boys took care of their own rooms. They swept dirt and ashes into the hall for the janitor to collect. He was one Patrick Kelly, inevitably dubbed "Professor of Dust and Ashes." He was also the first in the string of "characters" inhabiting this and every other college campus. For a time he lived in the basement of one of the unoccupied faculty houses. He rang the bell for rising or shouted up the stairways, cleaned the classrooms, kept the wood-yard filled with firewood, shoveled paths in winter, and kept an eye on student behavior. He also enjoyed the privilege of planting wheat on the far east side of the campus and pasturing some cows to keep the grass down. For some discrepancy in accounts he was dismissed in 1847 and replaced by George Allmendinger.

The freshmen were enrolled in a curriculum that included rhetoric, grammar, Latin literature and Roman antiquities, Greek literature and antiquities, algebra, geometry, and natural science. The lone sophomore faced a program of advanced mathematics, surveying, rhetoric, logic, ancient history, and Greek philosophy. The classical tradition was respected, although questions were being raised about it in a few places. The national spirit that infected the country after 1815 introduced a new goal in education that inevitably conflicted with the original ends of intellectual learning. The new stimulus was toward making the colleges more popular, in order to educate the electorate and reinforce democracy. This goal was at variance with the older aristocratic concept that colleges were for perfecting an intellectual elite. It would alter the requirements for admission and for graduation, it would add new courses to the curriculum, it would reduce the prevalent religiosity and paternalism, and it would emphasize useful knowledge.

Besides daily chapel Michigan students were required to attend one of the town's churches every Sunday. This decidedly Christian stance of a nonsectarian, government-supported institution was defended in the Regents' report to the superintendent in 1841. "Whatever varieties of sect exist in these United States, the great mass of the population profess an attachment to Christianity and, as a people, avow themselves to be Christian. There is common ground occupied by them, all-sufficient for cooperation in an institution of learning, and for the presence of a religious influence. . . . Attempts made to exclude all religious influence whatever from the colleges, have only rendered them the sectarian of an atheistical or infidel party or faction, and so offended and disgusted the majority of the population agreeing in their respect for a common Christianity, that they have withdrawn their support. . . ." Clearly, "nonsectarian" meant no favoritism toward any denomination, not religious indifference. This statement was drafted by Regent Reverend George Duffield, Pennsylvania '11, of Detroit. It is all the more noteworthy when regarded in the light of religious squabbles then arising in college administrations and supporters that finally erupted at Columbia, 1853, and South Carolina, 1855.

University enrollment swelled quickly. In 1842 the six freshmen became ten sophomores, and a new class of fifteen freshmen entered. All were from Michigan towns. Asa Gray now asked the University to release him because he had an opportunity of going to Harvard, and Michigan lost a botanist who was to gain national fame. As a replacement Dr. Abram Sager, another graduate of Rensselaer and Castleton Medical College '35, and former assistant to Douglass Houghton, was appointed professor of botany and zoology, but teaching was not yet ready to be started in this field. He remained practicing as a physician in Jackson until 1845.

The University was operating on three terms throughout the year. One term ran from January to mid-April; the next from mid-May to early August; the third from mid-September to Christmas. In the year 1964-65 the University returned to the trimester schedule. On August 10, 1843, the first "class exhibition" was held at the Presbyterian Church, with every member of the sophomore class participating by an oration, an essay, or a poem. This marked the start of a tradition that continued until 1870.

What was student life like in the 1840's? Two literary societies were organized: Phi Phi Alpha in 1842, and Alpha Nu the next year. They held weekly meetings and debated serious and frivolous questions. Pranks were prevalent as always, among themselves, against their teachers, and against the town. They built bonfires in the streets, they piled hay in the chapel one day, they locked the monitor in his Mason Hall room one night, they stole fruit from faculty gardens. The excessive paternalism of the faculty and the piety of the times had by no means suppressed the old Adam. One of the chief attractions of Ann Arbor for University students was the presence of the Misses Clark's boarding school for girls.

Consider the diary of George W. Pray, '45, during his junior year. Of church on June 2, 1844, he wrote: "The girls possessed as many witching and enticing ways as usual—they hitched and twitched and showed their huge bustles as much as ever. The students rather more attentive than usual because a professor preached; notwithstanding their eyes often wandered in the direction of some fair object. . . . In the evening I went to the burial ground, which seems to be the fashionable or rather common resort on Sabbath evening. You may see the pert misses going from one tombstone to another reading the inscriptions as if they cared for them and as if they had not read them a thousand times before. They are very ready to catch an ogle from any gentleman who will favor them with one."

How current the entry for June 27 sounds, following the surprise nomination of James K. Polk for President: "Politics begins to rage among the students. Heard several chats among the students who spoke and disputed with as much energy as if the fate of the Republic depended upon the result of their dispute." Then he recorded that Alpha Nu literary society debated a resolution that the Military Academy at West Point should be abolished. It was decided in the affirmative!

In the fall of 1843 there were fifty-three students in three classes. Four came from outside the state, and one from Canada—the beginning of the growing out-of-state and foreign student attendance that quickly gave reputation and financial stability to the young institution. At the same time the state seemed to ignore its welfare. Bank failures and hard times had piled up overdue interest on University lands already sold to nearly $60,000, and the legislature extended the time for payment. Only four of the original Regents were still on the Board, although the return of Lewis Cass to the state had led to his reappointment for a year. The Regents needed the interest on that uncollected money so as to operate and to repay the earlier loan from the state. Their gloom and fears were not abated by a petition from the citizens of Berrien County to the legislature to close the University and transfer its property to the state primary school fund. The petition declared that the University was of little benefit to the state anyway; what were fifty students compared to thousands of children in the elementary grades?

Early in 1844, however, the legislators enacted a relief measure, possibly from a lingering feeling of guilt over their depressing the value of University lands. The state accepted the depreciated bank notes it had received in payment for University lands at face value, thus raising the interest available to the University. Thus, the amount the University must repay the state on its loan no longer absorbed two thirds of income. The Regents were cheered.

4. *A decade of growth and crisis*

In the fall of 1844 two new professors were added to the faculty to accommodate the four classes now enrolled. Dr. Silas H. Douglas, Maryland '42, came as assistant to the absent Dr. Houghton in geology and chemistry. The Reverend Andrew Ten Brook, Madison College '39, was appointed professor of moral and intellectual philosophy. There was no University president, just a presiding officer elected annually by the faculty members from their own number. Directives came from the Board of Regents.

Under this resident active faculty of four, with a tutor and a librarian, the senior class of eleven was moved toward graduation on August 6, 1845. The University's first Commencement exercises were held in the Presbyterian Church. Each student gave a short oration—one was in Latin—and Professor Ten Brook addressed the audience. That very afternoon the proud graduates met and formed an alumni society, open to all college graduates in Michigan.

As an indication of what kind of young men the University was attracting, it is instructive to list what happened to the eleven first graduates of 1845. Several died young. Paul Rawles served as a lieutenant in the Mexican War, returned home ill, and died in 1849. (The Mexican War was the first national conflict in the life of the University. Five graduates and former students served in the armed forces.) Judson Collins went to China in 1847 as the first Methodist missionary there and died in 1852. Charles Clark became principal of the Monroe branch until it closed in 1849; then he studied law and practiced until his death in 1854. Thomas Cuming served as sergeant in the Mexican War, was afterward appointed secretary of Nebraska Territory. He was briefly acting governor before his death in 1858. John MacKay of Maine, the only out-of-state graduate, took only his senior year at the University. He became an attorney and editor in Illinois. At the outbreak of the Civil War he was revealed to be an ardent secessionist and had to leave town. He turned up in St. Louis, where he was regarded as decidedly eccentric before his death in 1874. Edwin Lawrence remained in Ann Arbor to become a judge, but migrated to San Francisco after the Civil War, where he practiced law, supported and led the local

YMCA, and served in the state senate. He died in 1886. George Pray, already quoted, studied medicine at Western Reserve University and practiced in Ionia County, Michigan. He served in the Michigan legislature before his death in 1890. Merchant Goodrich studied law at Harvard, practiced in Ann Arbor, and died in 1892. Fletcher Marsh became principal of the Tecumseh branch, then professor and acting president of Denison University until 1875. After several years in business in Chicago, he joined the faculty of Leland University in New Orleans and died in 1893. George Parmelee died in San Francisco in 1898; he was reputed to have been a businessman in New York City. Edmond Fish became a teacher, was one of the organizers of the Republican party at Jackson in 1854, moved to Kansas and served in the constitutional convention as an antislavery delegate, then settled in Illinois, where he acted as county surveyor and farmer until his death in 1904, the oldest of his class. Michigan was embarked on providing leadership for the development of the West.

The University now called on Dr. Houghton to teach, but in October 1845 while exploring Lake Superior he was accidentally drowned. Professor Whiting also died in 1845, and the Regents appointed John H. Agnew, Dickinson '23, to succeed him as professor of Greek and Latin. A new field was opened with the appointment of the Reverend Daniel B. Whedon, Hamilton '08, who had taught at Wesleyan for ten years, as professor of logic, rhetoric, and the philosophy of history. He was a Methodist and became an outspoken abolitionist.

Professor Ten Brook, who taught philosophy, was a Baptist. He succeeded in converting six of his students to his church. Of course, they had to be baptized by extramural immersion. He announced the date of the ceremony, to take place in the Huron River. On the appointed day a crowd of two hundred townspeople and students gathered on the bridge to watch the immersion. The bridge collapsed. Fortunately, no one was injured, but a theological debate was precipitated. What was the significance of this happening? The Methodists declared that it displayed the wrath of God against a foolish ritual. Nonsense, retorted the Baptists, it demonstrated His approval of immersion for all!

A new element entered student life at this time—the secret societies, or Greek-letter fraternities, as distinguished from the literary societies. They had started at Union College in 1825 and spread. Subtly they ushered in a new social system. Unlike the literary societies, their aims were strictly social. They substituted for home and family and afforded an escape from the grind of study, recitation, chapel, and church. They institutionalized drinking, smoking, card playing, singing, and athletic teams. From their fathers they borrowed the secrecy of lodges. They were antidemocratic yet they emphasized the secular values of sophistication, organizational fellowship, good manners, and leadership training, which were important in expanding America. They were not opposed to literary societies, but they helped dispel them—with unconscious help from the colleges as the latter gradually took over their functions with libraries, lectures, and debates.

Beta Theta Pi established a chapter at Michigan in 1845. In December some other boys were taken into Chi Psi. A third group was initiated into Alpha Delta Phi in August 1846. It was then that the faculty first took notice of their existence in the student body of seventy. There was an old rule forbidding students from joining any society which had not first submitted its constitution to the faculty for approval. Rumblings and warnings caused Alpha Delta Phi to submit its constitution to the faculty in 1847, whereupon the faculty replied that "it had no authority to legalize them as a society." The student reaction was that if the faculty could not legalize a fraternity, then it could not forbid it.

Clearly, there was disagreement among the professors, and in 1848 they appealed to the Regents and even to the presidents of several eastern colleges for their views on suppressing fraternities. The replies from the latter were not encouraging, and on the question of exempting fraternity members from punishment the vote of the Regents was a tie. The three societies at Michigan also argued that they were not University organizations, but rather clubs in Ann Arbor because one of them had a few members who were not students—including, incidentally, one Regent.

In the fall term of 1849 the faculty felt free to issue an ultimatum, and at the end of it on December 18 refused to readmit those boys who had not withdrawn from Chi Psi and Alpha Delta Phi. A large number were suspended. Beta Theta Pi was temporarily spared on a technicality that its constitution had not been signed. But the University was not going to get off so easily. After all, the Masons and Odd Fellows were secret organizations, and the townspeople of Ann Arbor convened in an indignation meeting on December 20. They called for reinstatement of the fraternities and expulsion of the faculty!

The rift between town and gown was not healed at once. The faculty submitted a long report to the Regents justifying its action on the ground that the fraternities were not only defying a rule, but were irresponsible, exclusive, expensive, convivial, and intriguing. The Regents took no action. In September 1850 the faculty axe fell on Beta Theta Pi. But after a series of meetings in October the faculty by a vote of four to two reinstated the three fraternities under conditions that each should furnish the names of its members to the faculty, all meetings should be held in the college building at times announced, and other regulations to which the fraternities had no objection. The damage in lost students and unfavorable publicity remained. Whereas the graduating class in August 1849 numbered twenty-three, the next four Commencements saw only ten to twelve graduate. It was a foolish episode, exposing the need for a University president.

Meanwhile, the Regents, having determined to devote their slim resources to the University, had felt obliged to discontinue all financial aid to the branches. Some continued as private academies or became town or union high schools. The preparatory school in Ann Arbor was dropped as a University function in 1848.

The faculty was rounded out by the appointment of a professor of modern languages: Louis Fasquelle, a graduate of the École Polytechnique, Paris, who had taught in England before migrating to Ann Arbor in 1832 and settling on a farm. He never thoroughly conquered the English language, and his cadence and accent were imitated by his amused students, but in the next decade he wrote a series of textbooks for the teaching of French that became widely used throughout the country and spread the name of the University.

Back in January 1847 the Board of Regents had received a petition from a number of physicians and surgeons in the state reminding it that a Medical Department, as called for in 1837, had not been organized and estimating that seventy Michigan boys were attending medical schools outside the state. The petition was tabled. Instead, the Board appropriated $5000 toward erecting a second college building to match Mason Hall, part of which would be used for a chemical laboratory and part as a dormitory to accommodate increased enrollment. As work progressed, the investment increased until the building cost $13,000.

MEDICAL BUILDING, COMPLETED IN 1850

Regent Kearsley was appointed to superintend the building of the new structure and received pay at the rate of $500 a year. It was finished in the summer of 1848, and although the Regents considered naming it Pitcher Hall in honor of Regent Dr. Zina Pitcher it was known simply as South College because it was located south of Mason Hall and in line with it. Meanwhile, Dr. Pitcher had pressed the issue of a Medical Department, and the Regents now ordered a third building to be constructed as a medical laboratory. Drs. Douglas and Sager were given additional appointments in the future Medical Department. Dr. Moses Gunn, Geneva Medical College '46, was appointed professor of anatomy in 1849, and in January 1850 Dr. Samuel Denton of Ann Arbor, former Regent who had trained under Dr. Pitcher, was made professor of physics, and Dr. J. Adams Allen, Middlebury '45, Castleton Medical College '46, professor of pathology and physiology. The Medical Department with its own building, costing $9000, on the east side of the campus, opened in the fall of 1850 with ninety-one students, twenty-one from out of state. Made of sandstone in the style of a Greek temple with columns and portico, the building was by far the handsomest on campus.

The University budget for the year 1850-51 was based on an income of $17,088—$15,088 from the interest on the University land sales and $2000 from student fees and room rents. Expenses were set at $16,263, comprising $6010 as payment on the $100,000 loan, $8000 for salaries of ten professors, and $2253 for operations, insurance, the library, and Regental expenses.

None of the existing Regents was elected to the new Board in the spring of 1851. Clearly, there was no enthusiasm for them or their accomplishments. The strongest personality on the old Board was Major Kearsley, who put much time and exertion into his position, but saw no distinction between executive and administrative functions and no conflicts of interest. He enjoyed looking into what the faculty was doing and teaching, and at examination time he would appear to put oral questions to the students. They called him "Major Tormentum." Since 1838 he had been stubbornly trying to collect from the Board a fee of $1000 for having "negotiated" the $100,000 loan voted by the state legislature. Finally, the other Board members summoned up enough courage to refuse him irrevocably.

The faculty had disagreed over the fraternity situation, and they were at variance on matters of education. A sad want of strong central authority was evident, both to regulate themselves and to stand up to the Regents on educational policy. In 1851 the faculty was in dispute again, this time about relative teaching loads, out of which Professor Ten Brook resigned. Then in a spiteful mood disguised as the offer of a free hand to the new Board, the old Regents by a vote of seven to two terminated the contracts of three other professors. This was Major Kearsley's last motion before he disappeared from the scene. Dismissed were Professor Williams, the oldest in service and the most popular with students; Professor Agnew, for no expressed reason; and Professor Whedon, because he was active in antislavery speaking.

Let it only be remarked here that by 1851 the University had experienced all the troubles that were to occur again and again, until it seems as though they must be endogenous to the nature of a university. In brief these cyclical ailments were: (1) political meddling by the state legislature, (2) financial squeezing until a crisis is reached, (3) intrusion of the Board of Regents into educational operations that are of faculty concern, (4) factionalism among the faculty, (5) rowdy or lawless student behavior outside of class, and (6) irritations between town and gown. Almost nothing new can be added to this list of recurrent maladies since that time; neither have permanent solutions been found.

UNIVERSITY OF MICHIGAN.
1855

CAMPUS, VIEWED FROM THE NORTHEAST, AFTER AN 1855 PAINTING
BY J. F. CROPSEY

CHAPTER THREE

TAPPAN AND THE MODERN UNIVERSITY

THE PEOPLE OF MICHIGAN voted in 1849 to call a constitutional convention, and the delegates met at Lansing, the new capital, in June 1850. The new constitution was twice as long as the old one, exhibiting a distrust of politics after sore experience. More offices were made elective, salaries were specified, conflict of interest for officeholders was defined, and laws allowing banks to suspend specie payments were prohibited. Not least among other changes was the popular election of University regents, one from each of the judicial districts, which then numbered eight. The terms of all ran for six years concurrently.

HENRY P. TAPPAN

1. Reorganization in 1851

More significantly, the Board was not only separated from the superintendent of public instruction, but from the legislature itself. It was authorized to "have the general supervision of the university and the direction and control of all expenditures from the university funds." Created by the constitution, the Board of Regents of the University was as firmly founded as the legislature, the governor, or the judiciary, and was equal in its power over its designated field of state endeavor. It was a coordinate branch of state government, and unique among state universities. The stage was set for greatness as the University entered another phase of growth.

It was difficult for future state legislatures to comprehend what the constitutional convention had done and what the people of Michigan had approved. Several court tests were necessary before the independence and autonomy of the corporate Board of Regents of The University of Michigan were recognized. With its constitutional power and its own funds, the Board of Regents was free to develop the best university it could visualize and afford.

The first legislative session under the new constitution felt that it had to remodel the act of 1837 defining the University. The statute enacted on April 8, 1851, was short and general. It did not attempt to list the professorships, but it did say that the University should consist of at least three departments (Literary, Medical, and Law) and such other departments as the Regents should deem necessary and University funds permit. Tuition was not to be charged to Michigan residents. The idea of University branches was revived, but they were to be established only as income from the University interest fund permitted. But to check dissipation of the latter revenue, no buildings were to be constructed from this source. The Regents were to submit an annual report to the superintendent, the only public record of their duties. However, the state Supreme Court eventually made clear that even this statute was invalid, because the Board of Regents derived from the constitution all the power necessary to govern internal affairs of the University and required no directives from the legislature.

Implicit in the new constitution was a certain public dissatisfaction with how the Regents had been selected and how they had conducted University affairs. At their first annual meeting the Board must elect a president of the University who should preside, without a vote, at all their meetings. Since he was obviously the executive officer of the University, the Regents were slyly relieved of administration; they need only determine policy.

The Democrats made a clean sweep of the election, and the new Regents were Dr. Michael A. Patterson of Tecumseh; Senator Edward S. Moore of Three Rivers; former Senator Judge James Kingsley of Ann Arbor; former Representative Elisha Ely of Allegan (who died in 1854 and was not replaced); Charles H. Palmer, Union '37, former principal of the Romeo branch; Dr. William Upjohn of Hastings, who was born and educated in England; and Lieutenant-Governor Andrew Parsons of Corunna, who resigned in 1853 to become governor and was replaced by the Reverend Henry H. Northrop, Union '34, of Flint. The eighth man was former Regent Elon Farnsworth of Detroit, former attorney general.

One of their first actions after they convened in January 1852 was to invite the three faculty members who had been dismissed to rejoin the University. Two declined, but Professor Williams accepted and remained the rest of his life. To succeed Professor Agnew in Greek and Latin, James R. Boise, Brown '40 and a Brown faculty member, was appointed. The Board elected one of its own members, Mr. Palmer, to serve as secretary. It then named a committee to find a president for the burgeoning University. Palmer even made a trip east on this quest. He interviewed George Bancroft, former secretary of war and noted historian, and asked if his name could be presented to the Board. Bancroft refused but recommended Henry Philip Tappan, former professor of philosophy at New York University, who was living in Europe and had just written a notable criticism of higher education in America.

Upon his return to Michigan, Palmer found that the other Regents had come up with other candidates. A formal offer of the presidency was made to Henry Barnard, widely known New England educator who was later to be chancellor of the University of Wisconsin and first U.S. Commissioner of Education. Barnard declined. The Board then turned to the Reverend Dr. William Adams of the Madison Square Presbyterian Church, New York City. He too refused and later became president of Union Theological Seminary. In August the Board then elected Palmer's candidate, reinforced as the nomination was by President Eliphalet Nott of Union College, probably the foremost educator in the country, who had known Tappan ever since his student days.

2. Years of Growth

Tappan accepted the call because he was fired by an idea—several ideas—and he regarded the University of Michigan as one of the few institutions in which they could be realized. A native of Rhinebeck, New York, a Dutch settlement, he graduated from Union College in 1825 and from Auburn Theological Seminary two years later. After a brief period as a minister, he became professor of philosophy at New York University in 1832. In a faculty-administration quarrel five years later he was dismissed with several other professors. In the next seven years he published four notable works on philosophy, showing the influence of Victor Cousin, the same French philosopher whose work on Prussian education had influenced the University of Michigan plan of 1837. Tappan lived abroad part of the time, where he became enamored of the German universities. In 1851 he published *University Education*, wherein he set forth his ideas with vigor.

Tappan had not sought popular approval in his book, for he made a disturbing indictment: "In our country we have no Universities. Whatever may be the names by which we choose to call our institutions of learning, still they are not Universities. They have neither libraries and material of learning, generally, nor the large and free organization which go to make up Universities."

As he saw it, "A University is literally a Cyclopedia where are collected books on every subject of human knowledge, cabinets and apparatus of every description that can aid learned investigation and philosophical experiment, and amply qualified professors and teachers to assist the student in his studies, by rules and directions gathered after long experience, and by lectures which treat of every subject with the freshness of thought not yet taking its final repose in authorship, and which often presents discoveries and views in advance of what has yet been given to the world . . . where, in libraries, cabinets, apparatus, and professors, provision is made for carrying forward all scientific investigation; where study may be extended without limit, where the mind may be cultivated according to its wants, and where, in the lofty enthusiasm of growing knowledge and ripening scholarship, the bauble of an academic diploma is forgotten . . . ." These were strong words.

"Universities," he said, "may, indeed, make learned men; but their best commendation is given when it can be said of them, that furnishing the material and appliances of learning, setting the examples in their professors and graduates, breathing the spirit of scholarship in all that pertains to them, they inspire men, by the self-creative force of study and thought, to make themselves both learned and wise, and thus ready to put their hand to every great and good work, whether of science, of religion, or of the state."

A controversy was going on in American higher education, and sides were chosen. On one side were Yale, Princeton, Harvard, and several small eastern colleges upholding the classical curriculum for selected young men pursuing old learning. On the other side were Brown, Union, and Antioch arguing for popular education. Was higher education going to serve learning, or was it going to serve the people? President Francis Wayland of Brown, indicting the traditional curriculum, wrote in 1850: "We have produced an article for which the demand is diminishing. We sell it at less than cost, and the deficiency is made up by charity. We give it away, and still the demand diminishes. Is it not time to inquire whether we cannot furnish an article for which the demand will be, at least, somewhat more remunerative?"

Wayland conceived of higher education as a democratic need, a social agency. He wanted more flexible entrance requirements and more useful courses. So over faculty objection he augmented the classical curriculum with modern languages, history, economics, and natural sciences. Brown University did not have the resources to carry out all his plans.

Stepping into the middle of this controversy, Tappan could see values and limitations in both camps. He felt that Yale, for instance, stopped short of giving its students the satisfaction and distinction of a thorough education; while Brown sought to prepare young men for commercial and political success, yet the country's business and political spirit—the Jacksonian elevation of the self-made man—placed no value on formal education. Tappan was concerned primarily with the former group: "After the college course is completed with all its advantages, the student who wishes to pursue his studies still further will look in vain for an Institution to receive him." He aimed to develop that institution, which would cultivate the originality and genius of the talented few. For the other group, such a university would stand as "a powerful counter influence against the excessive commercial spirit, and against the chicanery and selfishness of demogogueism."

What Tappan was talking about, fundamentally, was a graduate school in which diligent and responsible students could pursue their studies and research under the eye of learned scholars in an environment of enormous resources in books, laboratories, and museums. Since the University of Michigan had begun with Woodward's French plan and been carried forward more or less on the Prussian system, Tappan thought he saw an opportunity to develop a true university on the German model. If that opportunity did exist in Michigan in 1852, it would have required a superman to raise the money for it and to impose it on a faculty of collegiate limitations to say nothing of a democratic people who were caught up in the practical concerns of settling half a continent, achieving livelihoods from the land, trades, or manufacturing, and trying to hold a constitutional government together that was being torn apart by the absolutism of slaveholders.

However clearly Tappan perceived his educational ideal, he did not adequately examine the soil in which it must be nurtured. Consequently, he had no idea how long the growth would take. He was ahead of his time, but he gave the University of Michigan a conception of what it could be. The "idea of Michigan," planted by Judge Woodward, watered by Super-intendent Pierce, burst into bud with Tappan. In 1902, one of his Michigan faculty who subsequently became a university president and ambassador, Andrew D. White, said of Tappan: "To him, more than to any other, is due the fact that, about the year 1850, out of the old system of sectarian instruction, mainly in petty colleges obedient to deteriorated traditions of English methods, there began to be developed universities—drawing their ideals and methods largely from Germany."

Henry Philip Tappan arrived in Ann Arbor with his wife, son, and daughter, in the summer of 1852, fresh from Europe. He was forty-seven years old, six feet tall and handsome, with side and under-chin whiskers. In the semirural, parochial town of Ann Arbor, he was unmistakable. There was an urbane, cosmopolitan air about him, along with an intellectual and slightly condescending manner. Outdoors he carried a cane and was invariably accompanied by one of his huge St. Bernards, Buff or Leo. In a day of stovepipe hats, he wore a felt hat tipped to one side. He walked briskly among the stores not unlike the lord of the manor in the market-place of the peasants.

He looked and acted like a university president. The students were not merely impressed, they were almost overwhelmed. Some of them more than fifty years later remembered him with awe. Their comments paint him best:

"He was an immense personality. It was a liberal education even for the stupid to be slightly acquainted with him."

"Dr. Tappan seemed to me about the acme of human perfection."

"He walked with vigor, like a great commander, and when with other men he impressed me that he was a born leader."

"Whether his chapel prayers were answered or not, they were well worth listening to either in heaven or on earth; they were divine classics."

"It was especially in extempore speech, and when moved as only powerful natures can be moved, that he made his grandest appeals to conviction and feeling."

To achieve his ideal university Tappan had ample work waiting for him. He indicated his program in an inaugural speech in December 1852. He would bring distinguished scholars to the faculty. He would enlarge the library and laboratory, and establish an art gallery. He would open the University to persons who already had earned a bachelor's degree. He recommended the lecture system as more appropriate to a university than a textbook-recitation procedure. And he would institute a scientific curriculum to compete with the hallowed classical curriculum and lead to a bachelor of science degree. His aim was not to appeal to students tired of Greek and Latin but to broaden the field of learning that a university should make available.

Tappan advocated that a university professor should engage in research as well as teaching, and indeed that his students should participate to some degree in his research. He wanted to swing the University from dissemination of learning (teaching) to advancement of knowledge (research). In brief, the University should be an investigating institution that maintained the excitement of learning.

Further, partly because increased enrollment required more classrooms, Tappan moved all the students out of Mason Hall and South College. No doubt he was aware that his friend President Wayland of Brown, blamed dormitories for most of the evils of college life: temptations to vice from evil student leaders, the costs of building that should go into libraries and laboratories, danger of epidemics from contagious diseases, and imposition on the college of responsibilities it could not carry out effectively. Tappan not only wanted to get away from the English system of housing students, but also to end their institutional isolation and make them community citizens. Henceforth, they would room as well as board around the town, starting a new local industry. One bonus was that morning chapel was delayed until after breakfast—7:45.

Tappan himself assumed the chair of philosophy left vacant by Whedon's departure. Professor Boise's double duties in Greek and Latin were cut in half by the appointment of the Reverend Erastus O. Haven,

Wesleyan '42, to teach the Latin language and literature. When he was shifted two years later to history and rhetoric, Henry Simmons Frieze, Brown '41, took over Latin and began his long and illustrious career at the University. Alvah Bradish, Detroit artist, was hired to give lectures in fine arts. Alexander Winchell, Wesleyan '47, was appointed professor of physics and civil engineering, but not succeeding in those fields was transferred to geology, zoology, and botany. William G. Peck, U. S. Military Academy '44, was then appointed professor of physics and civil engineering. Another West Point graduate, William P. Trowbridge, was brought in to teach mathematics. These men were to carry the weight of the scientific curriculum, which was modeled after that of West Point.

Two men were added to the Medical Department: Dr. Corydon L. Ford, Geneva Medical College '42, as professor of anatomy in place of Dr. Gunn, who became professor of surgery, and Dr. Alonzo B. Palmer, city physician of Chicago, as professor of materia medica and diseases of women and children. At the same time the Board of Regents and president resisted a directive from the state legislature to appoint a professor of homeopathic medicine, a recurring demand.

The president's son John was eventually appointed librarian and secretary to the Regents. When Haven left in 1856 to edit a Methodist paper, Andrew D. White, Yale '53, was made professor of history and English literature, commencing a distinguished career that led him to be first president of Cornell and ambassador to Germany and then Russia. In 1857 young DeVolson Wood, Rensselaer '57, succeeded Peck, and engineering at Michigan had found its crusader and great teacher.

CHEMICAL LABORATORY

In the realm of equipment President Tappan at once set about enlarging the meager Library by soliciting funds among the citizens of Ann Arbor. The sum of $1500 was raised, and some 1200 volumes were purchased. The total number of books jumped to nearly 6000, and annual appropriations by the Regents to the Library were begun. The University's first microscope was ordered. New chemistry supplies were bought, and a special Chemical Laboratory built in 1856. It stood about halfway between Mason Hall and the Medical Building.

Tappan's greatest achievement, however, was an astronomical observatory, called the Detroit Observatory because the bulk of the money

DETROIT OBSERVATORY

for it was raised in Detroit. To the $15,000 contributed there the Regents added another $1000. The small building with its great dome was erected on a hill northeast of the campus, where it still stands. The 12-inch telescope was ordered, and on a trip to Berlin in the summer of 1853 Tappan himself selected the transit instrument and astronomical clock. The Observatory was soon regarded as one of the three best in the world, and represented the fulfillment of Judge Woodward's recommendation in 1817. Tappan also met Franz Brünnow, PhD Berlin '43, and asked him to become director. The German scholar, the first PhD on the Michigan faculty, won an international name and married Tappan's daughter in 1856. His discoveries were chronicled in *Astronomical Notes*, begun in 1858, the University's first scholarly journal. Brünnow also joined Professor Frieze and Mrs. Andrew D. White in a chamber music trio.

As projected, Tappan instituted his scientific curriculum that eliminated Latin and Greek, and the first bachelor of science degrees were awarded to two Ohio boys in June 1855. Michigan was the second school in the country to grant such degrees. The curriculum attracted more and more students who disliked the classical studies and were vocationally oriented.

Late in 1855 the Regents paid the landscape painter J. F. Cropsey $25 to make a drawing of the campus as seen in perspective from the northeast corner. Then they had it engraved and copies struck off at an additional cost of $538, which may have been recovered through sales. The University had sat for its first portrait.

Enrollment in the University mounted swiftly. In Tappan's first year there were 60 students in the Literary Department and 162 in the Medical

Department, a total of 222. Five years later the whole enrollment was 460, with 287 in the Literary Department and 173 in the Medical Department. Growing dissatisfaction with pure classical studies was channeled into science, although the number of classical students increased after it was no longer compulsory. An "optional course" was made available to those who lacked the prerequisites for either of the other courses, or who aimed at special acquirements. The calendar was altered in 1856 so that the year's studies consisted of two longer semesters, beginning October 1 and concluding in late June. Professors now had a three-months' vacation in summer for research and travel. This calendar lasted 108 years.

Speakers of national prominence were now appearing in Ann Arbor under the auspices of the Students' Lecture Association. Ralph Waldo Emerson first spoke in 1856, Edward Everett the next year, and Bayard Taylor in 1859.

Financially, the University had managed to pay off the $100,000 loan just as Tappan arrived and now was receiving from the state interest on this money because of criticism of the way the state had handled sales of federal land donated to the University. The mortgage on income was gone, total income had increased considerably, and there were still University lands unsold. The Board of Regents was immensely pleased with its choice for president, and in their final report of December 1857 they testified their approval of his services: "Believing that his views of a proper University Education are liberal, progressive, and adapted to the present age, we have sustained him to the extent of our ability in all measures for the advancement of the University, and it gives us pleasure to add that we have rarely disagreed with him as to its true interests during the period we have been associated in charge of the Institution." Their virtue was that having recognized an able president, they supported him.

The wide growth of common schools created a demand for more teachers. To meet this need the state legislature had established in 1849 the Michigan State Normal School at Ypsilanti. It was left to local residents to provide a building, and classes did not begin until 1853. This precedent emboldened Tappan to ask the legislature to provide for expansion of the University, which was also training teachers. Although he was well received before the legislature, no appropriation resulted. Instead, at the urging of the Michigan Agricultural Society, the legislature established the Michigan Agricultural College in the country outside Lansing. It was the first state college of agriculture in the United States. Three brick buildings were completed and classes began in 1857. Students were required to work on the college farm three or four hours a day, for pay. Although the legislature subsequently neglected the institution, another precedent for state aid to higher education was visible. President Tappan did not let the legislators forget it and addressed them at almost every session.

3. Phase Two, the Years of Controversy

Tappan might have maintained the same accelerated pace of scholarly progress under the new Board of Regents if they had been as perceptive and intelligent as the old Board, but he was to encounter personal antagonism immediately and a struggle for power. All new members took office on January 1, 1858. There were ten Regents now because two new judicial districts had been established. Politically, the new Republican party dominated the Board, but party politics played no part in their view or votes. The leaders soon proved to be Attorney Levi Bishop of Detroit; Banker Donald McIntyre of Ann Arbor; E. Lakin Brown, Schoolcraft merchant; and Benjamin Baxter, former principal of the Tecumseh branch. They set out to operate the University down to the last detail, even to telling the librarian "the manner and form" by which he should catalogue the books. In their view the president was merely another employee of the Board.

Tappan had not progressed this far without making some enemies, chiefly of men lacking his broad vision. This is not to say that Tappan was free of faults. He had a superior intellect—and he knew it. He was farsighted, but not nearsighted; in close relations with people he could not perceive the effect he had on them or discern their sensitivities. He lacked a sense of humor about himself. He was not adept at settling disagreements among faculty members. His condescension, which the students expected, sometimes irritated his faculty colleagues, particularly those who were not sure of themselves. Tappan did not hesitate to reprove them like students and in front of others. Moreover, his fondness for German universities and his admiration of things Prussian, while it did not bother the Germans of Ann Arbor, rankled most of the democratically oriented and self-conscious citizens of the state. Because he used the title of chancellor as often as president (indeed he had been installed with both titles), he was accused of aristocratic leanings. Some Michigan residents were even annoyed by his Eastern accent.

Certain of his virtues and tastes were held against him. Tappan had always been used to wine with his meals and was indifferent whether students drank beer. Although he spoke out against the use of distilled liquor, this was not enough for the state prohibition forces which had succeeded in passing a temperance law in 1855. Regent McIntyre was an ardent prohibitionist. Then, although Tappan was an ordained minister, he considered that as University president he ought to attend the various Protestant churches in Ann Arbor instead of associating himself exclusively with the Presbyterian. Such tolerance pleased neither the Presbyterians, who thought he was dissatisfied with them, nor the other denominations, who regarded his circulation as indifference to any creed.

His efforts to select faculty members for their scholarship and not their church affiliations, in short to make the University genuinely nonsectarian, was interpreted by the denominations of the state as evidence that the University was a "godless" institution, undeserving of the legislative support it sought and which they hoped to procure for their own colleges.

There were persons and incidents that worked actively against Tappan. Foremost, was the editor of the *Detroit Free Press*, W. F. Storey. A self-made man, a printer who had established the *Jackson Patriot* as a raucous Democratic organ, he bought the *Free Press* in 1853. Vitriolic and ruthless in all his writings, he attacked the abolitionists, denounced the Republican party, asserted the right of the South to secede, and even threatened the federal government if it should attempt to coerce the South. Since Storey respected no man's opinions but his own, President Tappan loomed as a ready-made contender to take on. He began in December 1853 by ridiculing his title of chancellor, his admiration for German universities, his salary because it was twice that of the professors, and his idea that the University should be more than a vocational college. Intelligence was equated with snobbery, and cosmopolitanism with un-Americanism. Brünnow was another target simply because he was a German scientist. Unfortunately, more than twenty other Democratic papers in small Michigan towns looked to the *Detroit Free Press* to identify objects for attack and to define the party line.

(Happily for Michigan, Storey sold the *Free Press* in 1861, bought the Chicago *Times*, continued to favor the South throughout the Civil War, and died rich and despised.)

Regent Bishop came on the Board in 1858 imbued with the *Free Press* attitude toward President Tappan. The minutes reveal him to be a frequent maker of motions. Ill-tempered and venomous, he set out to oppose every plan to "Prussianize" the University, as he termed it. Another self-made man, he worked in the leather trade until he lost an arm; then he studied law and served on the Detroit school board. He was a leader in whittling away the executive power of the president in order that the Board could administer the University through committees. Worst of all, Bishop began writing pseudonymous letters to the *Detroit Free Press* criticizing Tappan, revealing confidential matters, calling the new Observatory useless, and uttering other malicious charges. When the Board in 1859 condemned the series of newspaper letters, the author was still unknown. Bishop also asked for presentation to the Board of all the regulations governing the University and began a long fight to revise these internal rules. Tappan countered by getting Bishop's new code refered to the faculty, but their recommendations were not allowed by the Regents. Tappan then lectured the Regents on the proper organization of a university. His logic and persuasion prevailed over Bishop's scathing denunciation, but the victory was temporary.

Student behavior at this time aroused the town. The so-called "Dutch War" occurred in 1856. Two German-owned eating places down town became favorite student hangouts. One was Hangsterfer's on the corner of Main and Washington streets; the other was Binder's Hotel and Saloon farther north on Detroit and Fuller streets. One night two noisy students, becoming obnoxious, were thrown out of Hangsterfer's by the proprietor. Next night they returned with a gang of students and demanded a treat for all or "take the consequences." Hangsterfer refused, and a fight followed. Clubs and even knives were used, kegs and barrels were broken open, glass and furniture were damaged. The police intervened and herded the students back to campus.

Soon afterward, following an Alpha Nu Literary Society "spread" at Hangsterfer's, six students went over to Binder's where a dance was in progress. The students climbed in a window and helped themselves to the unguarded refreshments. Discovered, five escaped and one was captured. The escapees soon roused a student mob that returned and demanded release of the prisoner. Binder made the mistake of demanding $10 ransom. The students prepared to assault the place. They collected three big timbers as battering rams and even produced muskets. The party guests were terrified, and Binder gave up his prisoner. Next day he swore out warrants against six, whom he could identify, but they were kept hidden while an old charge of selling liquor to minors was raised against Binder. He quashed the warrants.

In 1857 the lamentable death of a student from drunkenness during a fraternity initiation gave the University further unpleasant publicity. Although eight students were expelled or suspended for the semester in consequence, and although others formed a temperance society on campus, the Methodists passed resolutions condemning the moral conditions of the University. President Tappan joined in a faculty petition to the Ann Arbor city council complaining of the "wanton violations" by local residents of a city ordinance forbidding sale of liquor to minors. As one result the town and University came to an agreement, much later enacted into an ordinance, that no liquor licenses would be granted to places of business east of Division Street.

Tappan presented to the Regents a report on the moral conduct of the students. He called attention to daily chapel, Sunday church attendance, Sunday afternoon lectures, weekly student prayer meetings, and meetings of the Society for Missionary Inquiry. More revealing, perhaps, the professors at Michigan who came from Eastern institutions testified that Michigan students were more religious than those in Eastern colleges.

By 1860 Regent Bishop was asserting openly that he intended to get President Tappan fired. Meetings of the Board were opened to the public,

COMPOSITE "PHOTO"OF THE CLASS OF 1858

chiefly for publicity purposes, while the real business had to be transacted in private meetings, to which Tappan was not invited.

The faculty was drawn into the controversy, but not all supported the president. Professors Winchell, Boise, and Fasquelle disliked Tappan, possibly for personal reasons. Winchell's diary reveals that he was the instigator of the resolution of censure passed by the Methodists and intended Tappan to be named in it and that he became a confidant and informer of Regent Bishop. As early as 1859 Winchell hoped to see Tappan replaced by former Professor Haven. Several colleagues wished that Winchell could be replaced.

Regent McIntyre's bank office in Ann Arbor was a favorite gathering place for the Regents, and he made himself available to faculty members with complaints. Besides being a prohibitionist he was a Presbyterian. When some trouble arose over money belonging to Mrs. Tappan's deceased mother, which he had loaned to the church, and McIntyre could have clarified the original transaction, he refrained from explaining. In the cooling church atmosphere toward the Tappans they gave up attending services there. A petty matter to be sure, but bound to affect connections of the president with the Regent.

Despite the strained relations between Board and president, and the appearance of factions in the faculty, the University continued to develop. The perennial tree planting went on—Professor White was the enthusiast now—until the campus must have become an impenatrable forest had the trees all lived. White also graveled the paths and laid out the main diagonal walks.

Planning for a Law Department got under way early in 1859, a fulfillment of Superintendent Pierce's plan. Agreement on the law professors came easily; the three to be appointed were James V. Campbell, justice of Michigan's Supreme Court; Charles T. Walker, Detroit lawyer, former state legislator, and student of Michigan history; and Thomas M. Cooley, Adrian attorney and official reporter of state Supreme Court cases. The latter was also to be elected to the Supreme Court, to become a great authority on constitutional law, and to be appointed first chairman of the Interstate Commerce Commission.

The course in law was to run for two terms of six months each and lead to a bachlelor of laws degree; law was also a one-year course at Harvard. Opening of the new department was set for October 1, 1859, amid doubts whether the teaching of law would ever draw students from the time-honored reading of law in an attorney's office. The Regents ordered the opening to be advertised in newspapers in Detroit, Chicago, St. Louis, Cincinnati, New York, and Washington. Probably as a result, ninety students presented themselves and matriculated. A law library was quickly assembled, and the chapel was made the chief classroom. Space was now a problem, and plans were made for the state bar to take the lead in raising money in Ann Arbor, Detroit, and elsewhere in the state for a building— a dream that never materialized.

Meanwhile, President Tappan continued to mold the University according to his vision. The old-style master's degree that had been awarded to alumni on a purely honorary basis was superseded by a graduate program of study and examination that led to an earned degree of master of arts or master of science, first granted in 1859 to De Volson Wood and James C. Watson. In other words, a graduate curriculum was casting the shadow of a future graduate school. And years before Harvard shocked the academic world by allowing classes above the freshman level to select some of their own courses, Tappan began to let seniors have a choice. Further, a degree in civil engineering, growing out of the scientific curriculum, was first awarded in June 1860.

Professor White instituted the first scholarships by offering jointly with the Regents four grants of $50 each. They were awarded as prizes that stimulated all the students in the Literary Department. White was distinguishing his instruction in history by introducing directed reading periods, the use of interleaved syllabi, and by meetings of his students at his house one evening a week (a colloquium).

Increasing enrollment naturally produced more student activity — organized and unorganized. Besides three literary societies, there were two chess clubs, a Shakespearean Club, a University Choir, an Amateur Music Club, and a Senior Society. The Students' Lecture Association continued to bring outstanding speakers to Ann Arbor for an audience of faculty, townspeople, and students. The Students' Christian Association (not a YMCA) was organized early in 1858, the first of its kind in any college.

Prayer meetings and religious discussions were held in South College; the members were also interested in mission work. A monthly periodical, the *Peninsular Phoenix*, was started by the three literary societies.

Four new fraternities appeared on campus, bringing the total to seven. They were Delta Kappa Epsilon and Delta Phi, organized in 1855, and Sigma Phi and Zeta Psi, in 1858. Altogether they enrolled about two-thirds of the student body, a high proportion. The student body was referred to as "Wolverines" as early as 1861.

The Pioneer Cricket Club was formed in 1860, with thirty-three members, the first organized sport on campus. Wickets were set up on State Street, and play went on between the passing of buggies and wagons. Finally, the Regents appropriated $50 for maintenance of nearby grounds. An elementary kind of football, or soccer, with an unlimited number of players on either side and much kicking of the ball, was played between freshmen and sophomores in 1862. Although the town of Ann Arbor had baseball teams as early as 1860, the game seems not to have been taken up by student teams until 1863, when a diamond was laid out at the northeast corner of the campus.

Left to themselves the students carried on the immemorial pranks of collegians. Public signs possessed an irresistible attraction as room decorations. Once again they filled the chapel with hay from the cuttings standing in cocks on the campus. Another time a calf was let into a classroom. Almost every winter someone thought of turning the college bell upside down, pouring water in it, and leaving it to freeze. But the bell being the only "clock" on campus, it was too useful to be silenced. The boys were seldom quiet or orderly when they gathered for daily chapel— apple cores and even hymn books being thrown at one another, and there was disturbance at times during the services. Class rivalries existed, especially between freshmen and sophomores. School rivalries arose between "Medics" and "Lits" and grew more lively after "Laws" appeared. The Lits resented the fact that chapel remained compulsory for them, while the other schools were excused because the room would not hold them too.

Certain difficult courses were personified as enemies and at the end of the semester had to be disposed of. So there came to be the "burning of Mechanics" and the "hanging of Physics." Beginning in 1860 and probably earlier, the custom continued with lapses and variations until 1900. The ceremony involved a procession of several classes, the "corpse" with perhaps a skull borrowed from the medical laboratory borne on a bier to a place of judgment. There the victim was tried before a *Pontifex Maximus*, with an *Advocatus Pro* and an *Advocatus Con*. Then came the execution amid cheering around a bonfire. Sometimes the festivities ran far into the night, and the whole affair was accompanied by a printed program that frequently exceeded the bounds of propriety and good taste.

Both President Tappan and Professor White encouraged the students to take an interest in current events. They debated tariffs, the Kansas-Nebraska Act of 1854, the Dred Scott decision in 1857, John Brown's execution in 1859, and the presidential campaign of 1860. Of course, they debated other weighty issues too, such as: do brutes reason? or, do the benefits of novel reading compensate for its injuries? or, should students form matrimonial engagements while in college?

In his annual report of December 1860, Tappan spoke out sagely on the subject of student discipline. "From year to year there has been a manifest advance in scholarly, manly, and moral deportment. . . . This is to be attributed in part to the fact that a large proportion of our students are young men who have to rely altogether or chiefly upon their exertions to gain an education. They are drawn here by the love of knowledge, and an education to them is a prize to be won and not a penance imposed by authority. Much also is due to the system of discipline which the President and Faculty have from the beginning of their appointment carried out. This is based on two cardinal principles:

"First, that of regulating the conduct of the students through the requirements of our course of education. Each student is required to pursue studies sufficient to occupy his whole time. . . . A multitude of laws might be enacted defining and enjoining proprieties or conduct that would only serve to awaken opposition, inspire the students to practice stratagems to elude vigilance, and cause infinite perplexity in their execution. The single regulation . . . makes an appeal to his sense of obligation which he cannot gainsay, encourages him to honorable exertion, binds him to habits of diligence, imposes the necessity of avoiding places of dissipation and evil company, and when he is dismissed leaves him without excuse . . . .

"The second principle is that of teaching the student that in order to become a scholar and a man he must assume the responsibilities of thought and self government. . . . He is taught that he cannot be absolutely shielded against temptations to vice, that he lives in a world where evil besets him, and that he possesses within himself a weak and erring nature . . . and that he must apply himself to the battle of life and acquit himself as becomes a man. In carrying out this principle, experience has taught us that much more can be done in restraining youth from vice or, when they have gone astray, in winning them back to virtue, by private, affectionate, and paternal admonition and advice, by appealing to their inward sense of truth, honor, and rectitude, by addressing their manly fears and hopes, than by threats of enforcing statutes or the infliction of public disgrace."

4. Civil War and the end of Tappan's Presidency

Ann Arbor grew to a population of 5000 in 1860, much of the growth being from more German immigrants as well as from Yankees and New Yorkers. They were proud of the University and recognized it also as an economic asset. Most of the inhabitants were church oriented and business minded. The new Republican party had absorbed some of the Whigs and some of the Democrats opposed to slavery. Washtenaw County voted for Lincoln in November 1860. Ann Arbor had three weekly papers, representing the three parties; the Whig paper thought the differences between North and South not worth a war; the Democratic paper, although disgusted with President Buchanan, hoped that political leaders would achieve some compromise; only the Republican paper on January 1, 1861, prophesied war.

Ann Arbor had an abolitionist society, and there was also a secret one on campus. They helped slaves who passed through town along the "underground railroad" to Canada. There were also antiabolitionists who, although opposed to slavery, feared war so much that they would not provoke the Southerners. When Boston abolitionist Parker Pillsbury came to town late in January 1861, his advance handbills proclaimed "No Union with Slaveholders Religiously or Politically." He spoke at the Free Church on North State Street and because his talk of disunion sounded treasonable, students interrupted him with jeers and began smashing furniture. The speaker had to jump out a rear window. Next morning, Sunday, other students helped clear up the damage so that Pillsbury could preach again.

CAPTAINS OF THE STUDENT COMPANIES: ADAMS, ELLIOTT, AND NYE

Regardless of student opinion, war came. Word of South Carolina's attack on Fort Sumter reached Ann Arbor on Saturday, April 13, 1861. News of the fort's surrender followed late Sunday. The bewildered and anxious students looked to their president on Monday morning. He knew what to do: there should be a civic rally at the courthouse and he would speak. At 2:00 P.M. Tappan addressed an overflow crowd of townspeople and students. He declared that the government had borne with secessionists and traitors until forbearance was no longer a virtue. Now an overt hostile act had been committed, and the government must respond or fall to pieces. The seceders must be conquered and the flag restored. The unhappy editor of the Democratic paper was elected secretary of the meeting and had to record resolutions to stand by President Lincoln and to organize citizens into military companies to be ready to meet a draft.

Ann Arbor already had a militia company called the Steuben Guards. It was called into service on April 29 and became part of the Regiment of Michigan Volunteers, enlisted for three months. The excited students promptly formed themselves into three companies. The Chancellor Greys were captained by Isaac H. Elliott, '61; the University Guards, by Charles K. Adams, '61, a lad who was headwaiter in one of the boarding houses and would one day be a professor and university president; and the Ellsworth Zouaves, captained by Albert Nye, '62, the only one of the three to be killed in action. They drilled in South College and outdoors under Joseph H. Vance, the law librarian. At noon they paraded north on State Street singing as they marched.

President Tappan, who had enrolled in a home guard unit for men over forty-five called the Silver Greys, advised against immediate enlistment, as Commencement was so near, but after that day thirty-two of the sixty-two Literary graduates, thirty of the forty-four new physicians, and seventeen of the forty-four graduating lawyers signed up. George P. Sanford, '61, raised a company in the summer of 1861 for the reorganized 1st Regiment, enlisted for three years. Dr. Palmer served six months as a regimental surgeon, and Dr. Gunn eleven months.

The war's effect on enrollment was predictable. From a total of 674 in 1860-61, it dropped to 614 in the fall of 1861. The three student companies were not revived, as the Board of Regents asked the legislature for money to establish a military engineering school. Although the state adjutant general endorsed the idea, nothing was forthcoming. Professor DeVolson Wood instituted a series of lectures on military engineering and tactics in February 1862. Sentiment on slavery remained divided. When Wendell Phillips came to Ann Arbor in April 1862 to speak in behalf of immediate emancipation, the seniors with clubs ringed the Congregational Church sanctuary to protect him from any violence.

Through the minutes of Literary Adelphi Society (founded in 1857) can be seen frequent debates on war issues, after which members voted for one side or the other. They had a hard time making up their minds about freeing the slaves. In the spring of 1861 they favored General Fremont's action in freeing the slaves of disloyal citizens of Missouri, although President Lincoln repudiated it. In August, however, they disapproved of general emancipation, and did not favor it until April 1863, four months after Lincoln's proclamation had taken effect. In 1862 they debated the military competence of General George B. McClellan, but decided against requesting the President to remove him.

A good many students joined the 20th Regiment in the summer of 1862. The annual *Palladium*, published in December 1862, aware that enrollment was rising, was somewhat self-conscious about the relative safety of the students. Proud of those who had joined the army, it apologetically commented: "A less warlike, perchance less patriotic and ambitious class, still remain at the University."

War or no war, relations between the Regents and the president deteriorated. Apart from this feud, the Regents took some pride in the University they insisted on operating. Annually, the Board reminded the state legislature that University income was inadequate for continued growth and ought to be supplemented by a direct appropriation. It bravely supported its own medical faculty and resisted the appeal of petitioners and an order from the legislature to establish a professor of homeopathy. On the other hand it disagreed with the medical faculty by refusing to consider moving the Medical Department to Detroit, where there was a hospital. When the state bar failed to raise money for a law building, the Board pushed ahead and erected a building anyway out of its own meager funds. It also ordered an addition to the Chemical Laboratory. In 1860, recognizing their earlier unfamiliarity with the University, the Regents asked the state legislature to amend the constitution in order to stagger the terms of office so that after the next election the Board would never have all new members at one time.

That the Regents favored a national university is indicated in their report of December 1860, wherein they pointed "with a pardonable partiality" to the "list of foreign students drawn thither from every section of our country" (46 percent from other states and foreign countries). Three years later in their swan song they called attention to the fact that the Law Department had the largest enrollment of any law school in the country, and that the enlarged laboratory was the biggest chemical laboratory in the land.

Minutes of the Board meetings do not mention the acrimonious debates or the embarrassments of Tappan over certain motions. Tensions increased. By revising the bylaws, or University code, the Regents drew more and more executive power into their own hands, leaving the president with only clerical and ceremonial duties. The center of University authority shifted subtly from the president's office to the office of the local regent. The faculty tried to ameliorate the differences. Tappan remained firm, sustained by alumni, students, local friends, and a few newspapers. To his relief, the new Board of Regents, elected in the spring of 1863 and limited to eight, contained all new faces save one: J. Eastman Johnson, lawyer from St. Joseph. A new day was coming.

But Tappan and outsiders generally underestimated the vindictive-ness of the old Board. One member had died in 1862; two of the more enlightened ones—Oliver Spaulding and William M. Ferry—were army officers away at war. The seven remaining could see that their time was running out. On the night of June 24, 1863, they held a secret meeting in a hotel room. Next day, after Commencement, they met in regular session with the president. Regent Brown presented a resolution obviously composed and agreed upon earlier.

"Whereas, it is deemed expedient and for the interest of the University that sundry changes be made in its officers and corps of professors, therefore Resolved, That Dr. Henry P. Tappan be and he is hereby removed from the office and duties of President of the University of Michigan and Professor of Philosophy therein."

Tappan rose and replied briefly. He said this was the first intimation he had had of their intention. "I cannot but regard it as an extraordinary proceeding. Of its constitutionality I have some doubts; of its impropriety I have no doubt." He reminded them that they had been repudiated by the people and a new Board elected to which the matter ought to be referred. "But, gentlemen, you will act your pleasure." He professed one consola-tion: "The pen of history is held by the hand of Almighty Justice, and I fear not the record it will make of my conduct." He then walked out.

Regent Baxter was called to the chair. The resolution was put to a vote and adopted by the other six: Bishop (his threat fulfilled), Brown, McIntyre, Johnson, Whiting, and Bradley. Baxter did not vote. They then proceeded to dismiss John Tappan as librarian, no reason given, knowing that they could count also on the resignation of Brünnow. They elected the local Presbyterian minister as professor of philosophy and just as quickly named the Reverend Erastus O. Haven, editor and former professor, as president of the University. Thus, they hamstrung their successors.

Tappan's reaction was much more mild than that of anyone else. Students and local alumni held an impromptu meeting and adopted a resolution of protest. Later that night they serenaded Tappan at his home, then threw stones at Regent McIntyre's house and burned him in effigy. Citizens of Ann Arbor again called a protest meeting on June 26 and condemned the Regents as "jackasses." As word spread southward among soldier alumni, a protest meeting was even held at Union headquarters before Vicksburg! A call went out to alumni to meet at the University chapel on July 9. A large number did turn up, but found the chapel securely locked against them. They moved down to Hangsterfer's, condemned the Regents, and urged Dr. Haven to reconsider his acceptance of their offer.

The *Detroit Free Press*, now in friendlier hands, joined the *Detroit Advertiser and Tribune* in castigating the dismissal. Henry Barnard, as editor of the *Journal of Education*, called it an "act of savage, unmitigated barbarism." The last report of the Board of Visitors to the Superintendent of Public Instruction at the end of 1863 condemned the Regents for interfering in "the interior management of our beloved and honored university," and characterized the dismissal of Tappan as the "fit termination of the disorganizing and revolutionary measures which they undertook to introduce."

Still, there were religious groups unsympathetic to Tappan. The Methodists in particular were pleased to have a clergyman of their own persuasion in the presidential chair.

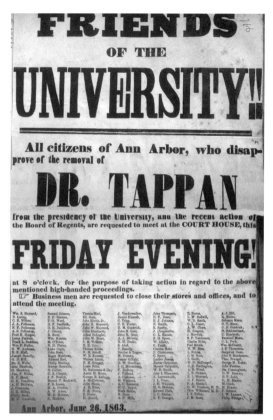

BROADSIDE CALLING FOR A RALLY TO PROTEST THE FIRING OF PRESIDENT TAPPAN

The faculty was divided, since Tappan had wounded the feelings of many. So sure was he of the correctness of his views that he attributed opposition either to a want of understanding or to a personal grievance. Contrary opinion, faculty felt, could not be discussed objectively on its merits. They also feared that an open fight now over an alleged injustice might injure the University irreparably, so they acted upon expediency. After denying that there had been any interference internally by the Board of Regents (!), on July 6 the faculty extended to Haven a pledge of cooperation.

Certain other circumstances favored the Regents, too. The students had dispersed for the summer, and some professors were gone, too. The battle of Gettysburg riveted everyone's attention early in July, and on July 17 news of Ann Arbor's casualties burned in on the wires. Many houses were saddened and shuttered, and a series of memorial services in the churches was set in motion. The University quarrel seemed of much less importance.

Professor Brünnow resigned as expected, and in September the Tappans began packing. A large body of citizens headed by the mayor called on the president and presented a service of silver plate. The Tappans set out for Europe again and never returned to this country. Brünnow had no trouble getting another observatory appointment. Tappan never felt it financially necessary to secure another position. He corresponded with friends in Ann Arbor and probably hoped to be recalled. He was much cheered in 1869 to be offered the presidency of the University of Minnesota, although he declined it. He did, however, sell his library, left in Ann Arbor, to Minnesota. Three years later he was much bereaved by the death of his son John. With Mrs. Tappan he then settled in Switzerland. In 1875 he was invited by the Regents to be an honored guest at Commencement, but his health would not permit it. He was gratified more by their resolution erasing all criticism of him from the records. This action was taken at a time when all but one of the Regents who fired him were still living. Tappan died suddenly in 1881.

Many years afterward President James B. Angell delivered himself of his opinion. "Tappan," he said, "was the largest figure of a man that ever appeared on the Michigan campus. And he was stung to death by gnats!" Tappan was the first and last University president to be dismissed by a Board of Regents. Further, he suffered more open abuse and underhanded sniping from the Regents than any other president. Because of their bad taste, he was attacked also in the party-oriented newspapers and personal journalism of the 1850's more often and more scathingly than any other president.

Yet he left his stamp on the University. He raised a banner around which the liberal in the state and the intellectual in the faculty could rally— few as they were. He antedated the founders of Johns Hopkins University by more than twenty years in acknowledging the German universities as a model. His idea of what a university could be and should be might be obscured from time to time as other goals attracted temporary attention, but it was never forgotten. The University has moved, albeit slowly, in the direction he indicated ever since.

His other great contribution was to reveal to the people of Michigan the kind of university which they had brought into being. It had been declared to be nonsectarian, and at a time when sectarianism was rampant Tappan proceeded to clarify what its absence meant and to channel the freedom that was thereby released. The prospect was frightening to most people because it was outside their experience. They were not ready to accept the University for what it was. In spite of the fact that various churches had established their own colleges (the Congregationalists at Olivet, the Methodists at Albion, the Baptists at Kalamazoo and Hillsdale), they could not keep their hands off the University. Their trouble was they could not conceive of education without strong religious coloring or proselytizing opportunity, and they were even jealous among themselves about the rightful representation of their denominations on the faculty. A president who did not believe that religious indoctrination was paramount and who was tolerant rather than denominationally committed was regarded as profane or weak.

Further, the University now was imbedded in the state constitution, and Tappan accurately foresaw that the original federal grant of lands would not long support a growing institution. Therefore, he argued, the legislature must appropriate tax revenues to the Board of Regents for expansion. This standing notion of continuing financial responsibility was unwelcome. It was bound to increase taxes, and it aroused the jealousy of the private colleges. Little thought was given to Judge Woodward's axiomatic assumption that Michigan society would benefit from educating each youth to his utmost capacity. That democracy might depend for its success upon an educated electorate smacked of unegalitarian philosophy.

In brief, in the University of Michigan the people had a better instrument than they yet knew how to use. It was Tappan who revealed its potential.

CAMPUS IN 1865, VIEWED FROM STATE STREET AND NORTH UNIVERSITY

CHAPTER FOUR

THE BIGGEST IN THE LAND

IN OCTOBER 1863 when the University recon-
vened, President Haven was inaugurated at the
new Presbyterian Church. Regent McIntyre spoke
and displayed the monumental bad taste to defend the outgoing Board of Regents by making
public its charges against Tappan. When he was
roundly hissed and booed, he turned to berating
the audience. Such an introduction to the ceremonies could only embarrass Haven, but his
inaugural address was conciliatory. The new
president was adept and possessed a quiet sense

ERASTUS O. HAVEN

of humor; he was patient and knew how to get along with people. Even so,
many local citizens refused to speak to him, and the students regarded him
with suspicion or indifference. With his chief supporters about to go out of
office, his position would become almost impossible. There was no other
course for him than to announce that he would not stay unless the new
Board reelected him.

Before the new Regents met in January 1864, the board of state
canvassers had classified by lot the terms of each member. Two were to
hold office for two years, two for four years, two for six, and two for eight.
Thus, there might be two new faces every second year, but no sweeping
change. These staggered terms remain in force today. Half of the new
Regents were college graduates; half were lawyers. The leaders were
Edwin C. Walker, Detroit attorney; Thomas D. Gilbert, Grand Rapids
lumberman; and George Willard, Latin professor at Kalamazoo College,
state legislator, and later newspaper editor in Battle Creek. They promptly
resolved themselves into eight committees: one each for the Law and
Medical departments, and two for the Literary Department (classical and
scientific courses); a library committee, museum committee, financial
committee, and executive committee.

The first Board meeting faced a student petition asking that Tappan be restored to his position as president. After long deliberation and probably explanations by holdover Regent Johnson, the petition was rejected. The Board met again in February to consider six more memorials favorable to Tappan. Meanwhile, Tappan had allowed to be published locally a pamphlet giving his view of his differences with Regents and faculty members. Acrimonious in tone, sardonic in style, it spared no one who had crossed him and even embarrassed his friends. The result was that any serious attempt to restore him to the presidency would have provoked several faculty resignations and a fresh uproar in the state. The Regents adopted a resolution excusing themselves from sitting in judgment on their predecessors and accepting the University as they found it. It went on to say that it was "impracticable" to recall Tappan and "would prove injurious" to the University. Such was the Board's meager endorsement of President Haven. Further, the Regents declared that the powers seized by the former Board from the faculty were relinquished. The faculty would have more authority over courses and degree requirements, although the Board continued to administer many details.

1. Haven takes control

The new administration pulled together, and the University regained public support. What had accrued from the Tappan days was something neither Haven nor the Regents identified. It was momentum, a forward thrust, and the recent upheaval could not deflect its course. Haven had no reforms to offer; rather he continued the policies of Tappan with quiet competence and diplomacy. The faculty found him considerate.

In the spring of 1863 the students formed a battalion of infantry (four companies of thirty to fifty boys each) for voluntary training, but they represented less than a quarter of the student body. Not everyone was eager for war and the Union. There were nonconformists then as now. Such students could find support in the *Detroit Free Press's* frequent criticism of the war and of President Lincoln. A group of them organized an excursion to Windsor, Ontario, on Saturday, November 14, 1863 (five days before Lincoln's address at Gettysburg), to sit at the feet of exiled Clement L. Vallandigham, antiwar Democrat from Ohio who had been banished to the Confederacy for sedition and had then fled to Canada.

The students greeted him with a prepared speech of sympathy and admiration for "a noble martyr in the cause of Liberty and Union." He opposed the war because it freed the slaves rather than preserved the Union and because it would lead to military despotism. He may have disappointed the students in his reply, for he urged them simply to study hard, especially in the classics, and to avoid following "demagogues in political life." He recommended "patriotism" over loyalty to a particular leader, by whom he meant Lincoln. How many of the students understood the implications of Vallandigham's role, or were merely "demonstrating" cannot be determined today. The *Free Press* published Vallandigham's speech, and it appeared also in pamphlet form. In April 1864 the Literary Adelphi debated the arrest and banishment of Vallandigham and decided it was justified. About the same time the affirmative side won in arguing that "the Administration is sometimes justified in limiting freedom of the press."

Enrollment in the fall of 1863 was bigger than ever: 871. Although there was only a 13 percent increase in the Literary Department, the Medical and Law Departments leaped ahead. The draft law of 1863 did not apply to men under twenty, nor to those who could find a substitute or provide $300 for one. It certainly did not diminish the enrollment, whatever the reason. Each year the annual *Palladium* took note of the war and the students who had been killed or who had enlisted (201 from the four classes of the Literary Department by the end of 1864), but its focus was primarily on the campus itself. The issue for 1864-65 was happy to publish two college songs, specially composed for Michigan. One, by Arthur H. Snow, '65, was entitled simply "Song for the University" set to the tune of the "Marseillaise." The other, by James K. Blish, '66, was called "Our College Home" and was set to the music of something called "Upidee."

The U. S. Christian Commission provided kits of handy articles for the soldiers and sent unpaid civilian agents into camps and hospitals to minister to the soldiers physically and spiritually. Each agent must serve for six weeks. During 1864 both Andrew Ten Brook, who had just returned to the University as librarian, and Instructor C. K. Adams, ex-student captain, served one mission. Ann Arbor citizens raised money to send five senior medics as volunteers to army hospitals; they were soon made assistant surgeons.

Although the state of Michigan again voted for Lincoln in the election of 1864, ten counties, including Wayne and Washtenaw, gave majorities to General McClellan, the Democratic candidate—a fact they would just as soon not recall today.

The total number of alumni and students who served in the Union forces was not compiled until much later, but eventually numbered more than 1800. Of this total, 61 were killed, 48 died of disease, and 181 were discharged as disabled; 431 served as surgeons, 435 as lieutenants and captains, 31 as majors, 60 as lieutenant colonels and colonels, and 2 as brigadier generals.

News of Lee's surrender was announced by the clanging of the courthouse bell early on the morning of April 10, 1865. After various cheers, stores were closed, and the students were addressed at chapel by President

Haven, who drew more cheers by dismissing classes for the day. Only five days later followed the shocking news of President Lincoln's assassination. It was a Saturday, and the next afternoon special union services were held at the Presbyterian Church at which President Haven, Professor Cooley, and others spoke. On the day of Lincoln's funeral, April 19, Haven gave a eulogy of Lincoln again at the Presbyterian Church. The faculty met later and expelled a freshman "for repeatedly expressing gratification at the assassination."

In June 1865 the Alumni Association voted to erect a memorial chapel to those who had given their lives. The alumni pledged themselves to raise $50,000, and the Regents promised a plot of ground when it should be needed. No one then anticipated that the building, named Alumni Memorial Hall, was forty-five years away.

Inevitably, there were changes in academic personnel. When the Reverend Mr. Chapin gave up teaching philosophy in 1867, this duty was added to Haven's work load. Professor Fasquelle and Dr. Samuel Denton died. Brünnow's place in astronomy was awarded to his best student, James C. Watson, MS '59, whom Tappan had castigated in his pamphlet. But the young man began immediately building a distinguished reputation in his field by discovering new asteroids.

When Professor Boise moved to the first University of Chicago in 1868, his place was taken by Martin Luther D'Ooge, '62, PhD Leipzig '72, who was to remain in charge of the department of Greek for nearly forty-five years. Edward Olney, a self-educated mathematician, author of textbooks in algebra and geometry, and exacting teacher, was appointed in 1867.

The most serious loss was the resignation of the brilliant Andrew D. White after his leave to pursue a brief career in politics. He had been elected to the New York state senate and was helping Ezra Cornell organize a new university; indeed, White was named first president of Cornell University in 1867. His place in history at Michigan was taken by the hardworking C. K. Adams, '61, AM '62, who had been held on as an assistant professor. He was made full professor in 1867. After a year's leave in Europe he introduced the German seminar method of teaching in 1869. The seating in such classes was rearranged in a circle. Each student prepared an independent research paper and read it in class, where it was criticized by his classmates and Adams. The seminar approach caught on slowly in other universities.

One of Haven's finest appointments was that of Moses Coit Tyler, Yale '57, as professor of rhetoric and English literature in 1867, the first time this important subject was given one professor's undivided attention. More than any other person Tyler is credited with awakening this country to a study of its own literature. His biographers regard him as having "inaugurated the heroic age of scholarship in American literary history." Tyler had spent his freshman year at Michigan before finishing at Yale and studying theology at Andover. Then he lived for three years in Europe. He gave his students the example of an indefatiguable scholar as he labored over his monumental *History of American Literature 1607-1765* (2 vols., 1878).

2. Post-war growth, expansion, and diversification

The University experienced its first "postwar bulge" in 1865-66, when 1205 students enrolled, many of them veterans. With this number Michigan edged out Harvard and became the largest university in the country. No one was more impressed than Professor F. H. Hedge of Harvard who (calculating the University's founding date from its opening in Ann Arbor) wrote in the *Atlantic Monthly* for July 1866:

". . . look at the State University of Michigan. Here is an institution but twenty-five years old, already numbering thirty-two professors and over twelve hundred students, having public buildings equal in extent to those which two centuries have given to Cambridge, and all the apparatus of a well-established, thoroughly furnished university. All this within twenty-five years! The State itself which has generated this wonderful growth had no place in the Union until after Harvard had celebrated her two-hundredth birthday. In twenty-five years, in a country five hundred miles from the seaboard—a country which fifty years ago was known only to the fur trade—a university has sprung up, to which students flock from all parts of the land, and which offers to thousands, free of expense, the best education this continent affords."

In the following year enrollment reached a peak of 1255. Medicine attracted the most: 525, a figure not reached again until after 1900. The Law Department swelled to 395, fell off for a decade, then advanced again. The Literary Department rose to 335 and continued to move steadily upward. On the other hand, the faculty increased only from 30 in 1863 to 33. Although enrollment declined, Michigan remained the largest university for four years. A new dimension was added to its growing reputation.

Size alone registered the University of Michigan in the minds of everyone who professed to know something about higher education in the country. 837 students in 1866-67—two-thirds—came from twenty-eight other states, chiefly Ohio, Indiana, Illinois, and New York, and forty-one came from Canada and four other foreign countries. Michigan was not merely a national university but an international one.

When certain legislators objected to giving support to the University because two-thirds of its students came from outside of Michigan, President Haven reminded them that the University had not been founded by state money, but by a grant of land from the United States Congress, which support rendered its obligations national. Further, the larger fees from out-of-state students provided most of the University's income from student sources. Many out-of-state students, he added, stayed in Michigan and raised its education level. Finally, no beneficial result would come from excluding nonresidents; such a prohibition would only degrade the University. His arguments resolved the matter for the moment, but it will be revisited many times under subsequent presidents.

Equally interesting is the fact that in 1868 two African-American students entered the University, the first of their race. Both were from Michigan, their entrance caused no headlines, and the University did not bother to record that they were African-Americans. They qualified for admission and were registered as a matter of course. One, John Summerfield Davidson, stayed one year; the other, Gabriel Franklin Hargo, graduated from the Law Department in 1870.

ANATOMY LECTURE, 1865

To accommodate the increasing enrollment, plant extension was unavoidable. A large and much-needed addition to the Medical Building was made in 1864, half financed by Ann Arbor citizens who raised $10,000. Although it ruined the proportions of the Greek-style building, it was ready for the influx of postwar students. An addition was made to the Chemical Laboratory in 1867. Then came a bold new idea. In 1869 one of the four professor's houses, the northeast one, was fitted up for a University Hospital, so that students could actually see patients, examine them, and observe the diagnosis and treatment. It was not a charity ward, but a hospital charging modest fees in return for permission from the patients to let themselves be studied by students under professor physicians. It was a small teaching hospital, the first university hospital in the country.

The Observatory came under criticism: it was not open enough hours, it was too small, it was hard to get to, and Detroit made a bid for it. To keep it, the city of Ann Arbor promised to spend $3,000 if a matching sum was raised. The Regents met this challenge by sending young Watson to Detroit to find the money. Living quarters for the director were added to the building, and the road up the hill was improved. President Haven also sought a separate library building and an auditorium that would seat all the students, but on these two projects he failed.

There was a broadening of the curriculum. Mining engineering was offered in 1864. Mechanical engineering was added in 1868, but omitted two years later. At the same time a course of study in pharmacy was authorized in the Literary Department by the appointment of Dr. Albert B. Prescott, '64*m* who had returned from a post as military surgeon during the Civil War. The degree of pharmaceutical chemist was awarded. This was a radical undertaking because the curriculum included much basic science not of use in the average drugstore, and because it ignored the traditional apprenticeship system of pharmacy training. Of course, it

SURVEYING CLASS ON THE DIAG IN THE 1860s

succeeded and became a separate school in 1876.

President Haven proudly announced that students in the Literary Department now had a choice of six courses of study: classical, scientific, Latin and scientific, civil engineering, mining engineering, and pharmacy. Such a wide choice was not available in more than a few other universities. The degree of bachelor of arts was conferred on graduates of the classical course, bachelor of philosophy on the scientific and Latin and scientific courses, and bachelor of science on the engineering courses.

In 1866 the Regents decided to allow themselves the right of granting honorary degrees, thus marking a few persons with distinction and reflecting honor on the University by its recognition of these persons. Two years and several degrees later, the Board voted the degree of doctor of laws (LLD) to the minister from Argentina, Sr. Domingo F. Sarmiento. Shortly afterward he became president of his country. In 1951 one of the University professorships was designated by his name.

President Haven would have appreciated that. In his annual report for 1866 he remarked that students were not encouraged to study by means of prizes, medals, or rank in their classes. The proper stimulant for excelling "is the gratification produced by an enlarged acquaintance with truth, and by the greater influence for good thereby produced." Therefore, he did not want contributions for prizes and scholarships, but for endowment of professorships and for the library, museum, and observatory. Although Michigan now awards thousands of scholarships, they are usually tied to need not to grades alone.

The other effect of higher enrollment was to arouse the Regents to exert themselves for state aid and not leave the matter entirely to the president's efforts. Early in 1867 the Board formally requested financial aid from the state legislature, which also was impressed by the postwar appetite for degrees. The request was not startling, for President Tappan had gotten the legislature used to hearing of their responsibility for helping higher education. Now they acted, granting to the University one-twentieth of a mill on every dollar of state property tax—provided that a professor of homeopathy be added to the Medical Department. The old ghost had risen again.

The unwilling Regents countered by offering to establish a School of Homeopathy in any community other than Ann Arbor or which would offer buildings and endowment for such a University branch. But the millage money was not surrendered to the University, and on appeal the state Supreme Court ruled that since the Board of Regents was not complying with the clear stipulation of the appropriation, it was not entitled to the money. The victory of the homeopathic lobby was not popular, however, and eventually this court decision was overturned.

When the legislature convened again early in 1869, Haven appeared before it and pleaded for removal of the homeopathic proviso from the act. Courageously, he told the legislature that the University had never in its Medical Department taught any exclusive theory of medicine (which homeopathy was) and should not do so. Further, he remarked that the Board of Regents had always enjoyed full freedom to decide which courses should be taught, just as they appointed those professors they deemed best. A vital constitutional question was at stake, aside from scientific policy, about whether the legislature could dictate University courses through acts of appropriation.

After debate it was recommended by ex-Regent Benjamin Baxter, now a legislator, that the homeopathic stipulation be stricken out, and the majority agreed. The University then received approximately $15,000, a boost of 25 percent in its total income. The legislature also allowed a similar amount that had accumulated in 1868 from the tax. Haven's victory was a tremendous gain for the University. The principle of state aid had been accepted, but the flexible method of the mill tax was not allowed to work. A ceiling of $15,000 annually was placed on the appropriation, regardless of how much money the tax produced.

If the legislature of 1867 first showed some qualified liberality with tax revenues, it displayed even more social liberality in recommending to the Board of Regents that the University admit women. The Regents and President Haven recoiled like true men and said no. Foreigners and African-American, yes; but not women of any origin. "Youth is a transitional period," Haven wrote, "when passion is strong and restraint is feeble, and if, just at this period, multitudes of both sexes are massed together, not in families and not restrained by the discipline of the home circle, consequences anomalous and not to be cultivated by an Institution supported by the State are likely to ensue." He recommended that women students, like the homeopathic physicians, should have a separate college of their own. However, women were a permanent fact, not a transient theory like homeopathy. A year later President Haven confessed to a change of mind and was willing to enroll women students, although more money would be needed. The Regents were made of sterner stuff, however, and refused.

3. Campus life in the 1860s

Possibly, Haven was moved by the hope that women students might improve the manners of the men students. The postwar student was serious, but he could also be belligerent and destructive. Class loyalties and antagonisms were so peculiarly intense that frequent fights broke out whenever groups met. Bonfire celebrations took a toll of the town's wooden sidewalks. Then there were actual fires in town. A student reported in 1865: "Our town was thrown into as much excitement the other evening by the burning of a barn as New York would have been by the destruction of a whole Square. It was the first fire of the winter & students worked side by side with the 'roughs' on the engines, and drank out of the same whiskey barrel. After the fire was partially extinguished and a neighboring block of houses secured from danger—all hands indulged in the luxury of a free fight, which I did not remain to witness, as I escorted a lady to the scene."

Chapel disturbances discouraged faculty attendance, and their absence led to greater disturbances. When the Junior Class held its annual exhibition in 1868, certain students published a "vile burlesque" of the proceedings. The faculty was so aroused that it urged the poor president to discover and punish the authors. Privately, Haven wished that the faculty had ignored the whole thing.

Rules were not lacking to combat misconduct. Every entering student received a list of "laws and by-laws" of the University that delineated faculty responsibilities, financial arrangements, and student regulations. Fundamentally, the students "must at all times obey the direction of the President or any of the Professors of the department to which they belong, pertaining to good order in the University." Further, they could not petition the Regents in regard to the government of the University or their professors, and they were not allowed to hold meetings to criticize the University.

Specifically, "no student shall be allowed to frequent gaming houses, play at cards, or practice any species of gambling, or attend gaming or drinking saloons, or be guilty of profaneness, or any act of violence, or keep the company of persons of ill repute, or be guilty of any other vice; and the use of intoxicating drinks is prohibited." Drinking remained a continual problem. There were six breweries in Ann Arbor and an astonishing number of retail outlets. A student in 1867 reported a revival of temperance societies in town which "are going to shut up all the whiskey cellars and so-called restaurants in town. There are fifty-five such places here." Apparently, he did not exaggerate, for the city directory of 1872 listed forty-nine saloons.

On the positive side, attendance at church every Sunday and at chapel daily continued to be expected of all students in the Literary Department, but not of those in the two professional departments.

Obviously, these rules, which look rather strict in retrospect, did not maintain uniform good behavior. Organized sports recommended themselves as one means of venting these high spirits and combatting vandalism. Football games between classes continued for the next dozen years. The returning veterans had learned baseball in camp, and the campus took up the game as a consuming fad. Various teams were organized locally, and a University team played Jackson, Ann Arbor, and Detroit, running up a score against the latter of 70 to 17 in 1867. There was no thought of intercollegiate competition until 1882 since there were so many intramural and municipal teams to play.

The *Palladium* for 1866-67 listed besides the fraternities and debating societies six baseball clubs and one cricket club, in addition to several oddly named organizations whose purposes were social and probably were based on boarding house clientele.

An occasional tournament or field day gave attention to track and field competition among individual students. Interest in athletics was growing so fast that 250 students in the fall of 1868 signed a petition for a gymnasium. President Haven presented it to the Regents, who took no action until September 1869, when they referred the question to the

LOOKING SOUTHEAST IN 1870 ALONG THE "LONG WALK" OF THE DIAG

faculty for a recommendation. The latter tried to dignify the request with culture by suggesting the establishment of a department of hygiene and physical culture under a professor. That killed the gymnasium.

Literary production was slight, but offered some outlet to students. the *Palladium* was a directory; it grew thicker, acquired hard covers, and became a yearbook honoring the graduates. Since it was issued by fraternity men, the independents started a rival publication in 1865 called the *University Castalia* that lasted five years. Meanwhile, the sophomore class in 1867 started its own annual, concerned with its own activities. It was titled the *Oracle*. Neither the Law nor Medical students felt the need of such periodicals.

The first student newspaper, the *University Chronicle*, was a biweekly of eight pages begun in 1867. It confined itself to campus and state news and student problems. Every issue reviewed the programs of the five literary societies and was bluntly critical of the student speakers. It became the *Chronicle* in 1869 and increased in size. Fraternity men and independents shared in its editorial board. It did not hesitate to criticize the faculty, the legislature, or the Board of Regents—the younger generation vs. the older. Otherwise, the *Chronicle* complained of class hazing as juvenile and ridiculed the senior class for introducing canes in 1868. It was angered by the Regents' refusal to entertain petitions from students and advocated that alumni be given a voice in running the University. It commended President Haven for his statement to the legislature against appointment of a professor of homeopathy.

Consistency was not the *Chronicle's* chief virtue. It declared in 1868 that the University was not on a par academically with most Eastern universities and ought to admit it. It decried the University's apparent policy of hiring too many young assistant professors without tested reputations. It demanded that the Library be opened on Sunday, and then it castigated professors who gave out such long assignments that students had no time for sports or relaxation; the academic standard was too high. Only the "rebels," it bemoaned, got exercise by refusing to study on Sunday, by playing billiards, by making effigies in the night, by tearing up sidewalks, and by parading to the tune of "Happy is the maid who shall meet us." All this was fuel for the cry that the students needed a gymnasium.

The editors were also so sure of student maturity at Michigan that they objected to rules and coercion. The average age of freshmen was nineteen and a half. They complained that the Students' Lecture Association was bringing back the same old speakers and ignoring new and challenging figures. Indeed, the *Chronicle* of 1868-69 resembles nothing so much as the *Michigan Daily* of today.

The class of 1867 selected maize and blue as class colors, and they became the official colors of the University. In the fall of 1867 one of the incoming freshmen was a tall, gangling youth from northern New Hampshire. "The fact that I had used during my preparatory course text books of four University of Michigan professors was a controlling one when I came to select a university," he wrote later. "Many friends thought it strange that I should leave New England, with its opportunities for higher education, and enter a western university. I did so because I was impressed by the scholarly work of Professors Frieze, Boise, Olney, and Fasquelle, as evidenced by their publications, and by the liberal and democratic spirit of the University, as indicated in its catalogue and announcements. Moreover, the University . . . was even then one of the large universities of the country." The young man's name was Harry Burns Hutchins, and in 1909 he became president of the University.

In the spring of 1869 the Regents raised the president's salary to $3000 plus a house. Professors were paid $2000, and assistant professors $1300. Law and Medical professors received only $1300 because of outside practice. The librarian was given $2000, and janitors $500. Also with their new state aid, the Board decided to erect a picket fence around the campus.

The faculty of professorial rank was organized as early as 1859 as the University Senate, over which the president presided. The Senate could make recommendations to the Regents, but ordinarily the deans of the two professional departments and the president acting as dean of the Literary Department met with Regental committees about budgets, appointments, and equipment. The Senate gave its attention in Haven's time to "literary and social exercises." Members met for a social evening and listened to a learned paper on some topic by one of the professors. Usually, they invited their wives. A local blue-stocking commented sardonically on one of these Senate socials: "The first was given by Dr. Haven, and he read the paper—his subject was 'The Origin of Public Opinion'. . . . I heard, however, that in the discussion which followed . . . poor Herbert Spencer was severely handled by Prof. Chapin and Ex-Prof. [Librarian] Ten Brook—the former of whom had not read Herbert Spencer, and the latter of whom could not understand him if he should read him a dozen times. Meantime the ladies sit by and say nothing, till their husbands have disposed of the literary part of the performance, when they come in on the small talk." The Senate also took care of ceremonial occasions, such as Commencement, and participated in funerals of faculty members.

In the spring of 1869 President Haven filled the pulpit of a Unitarian Church in Detroit for several Sundays, admittedly a bold step for a Methodist minister. Several newspapers and church papers professed to be shocked and wondered what kind of religious instruction the students must receive under such an administration. The *Chronicle* defended him, but Haven was disgusted. "It is not a godless education that they fear," he remarked, "but a Christian education not communicated through the forms and channels over which they preside." He visited Northwestern University, a new Methodist institution, in June and was offered the presidency. On his return to Michigan's Commencement and a Regents' meeting, he resigned, saying nothing about the other offer. The Board was surprised, but accepted his action.

Oddly enough, the Methodist *Zion's Herald*, of which he had formerly been editor, crowed that Haven's resignation "is a practical confession by one of the most experienced and successful of college presidents, of the weakness and ultimate dissolution of state and secular colleges." It was nothing of the sort, even though Haven felt he had accomplished little and had been subjected to unfair criticism. The University had achieved solid establishment and enjoyed an enormous reputation. The Library had grown to 26,000 volumes and pamphlets, although several smaller universities in the East held many more books. The University Museum contained more than 93,000 specimens: 37,000 geological, 34,200 botanical, and 22,400 zoological. More importantly, Haven had won state support on a continuing basis. He left a shining record.

4. *Henry Simmons Frieze, president pro tem.*

In August 1869, before Haven departed, the Board elected Professor Henry S. Frieze as president *pro tem.* He had been on campus

HENRY SIMMONS FRIEZE

for fifteen years, was devoted to the University, and was warmly regarded by everyone. Despite the loss of six children from illnesses, he remained a gentle, unembittered, dedicated teacher. If he lacked executive energy, he was still an able administrator for a holding operation. The interim was not expected to be long. Apparently the Board of Regents considered first the Reverend Dr. Martin B. Anderson, president of the University of Rochester, for president. Several Michigan faculty members urged him to accept if the appointment was proffered. He must have declined and no offer was made. In the fall of the year the presidency was offered to Professor Julius H. Seelye of Amherst College, who declined, and then to James B. Angell, president of the University of Vermont, where he had been only three years. He was certainly not tempted by the salary. The Regents then approached Haven about returning, but he refused. Informally, the office was tendered to Frieze, but he declined also. He was impressed by Angell, whom he had known at Brown, and thought he could still be obtained. The Regents renewed their efforts in that direction.

While the quest for a president prolonged itself to two years, Acting President Frieze was quietly pursuing three objectives on campus. One was set in motion by the Regents, in which he fully concurred; the other two were his own innovations, with their approval. The first resulted from a resolution introduced by Regent Willard at the Board meeting in January 1870. It simply stated that the University was open to any person who "possesses the requisite literary and moral qualifications." It was adopted after discussion by a vote of six to two. The door was now opened to women. The step was not as audacious as might appear, because two colleges, and four state universities to the west of Michigan, had already admitted women students. The reluctant Medical Department insisted it would have to offer separate lectures, but such segregation lasted only one year.

Frieze was delighted, even though part of the faculty was not. Almost immediately Miss Madelon Stockwell of Kalamazoo presented herself for the second semester, and such was her preparation that she was admitted to the sophomore class. The men students gave her a hard time. They were not so much impolite as they were studiously unaware of her. She was a determined woman or she would have been frozen out. In the fall of 1870 she gained the support of thirty-three other women, two in Law, eighteen in Medicine, and thirteen in the Literary Department. In March 1871 one woman graduated in law and one in medicine. In June two more received the degree of pharmaceutical chemist. Miss Stockwell graduated in 1872 and started a Michigan tradition by marrying a classmate. She became prominent in the cultural life of Kalamazoo and left money to Albion College for a library. She was given an honorary degree in 1912 by Michigan. A dormitory on campus also perpetuates her name.

It was Frieze's idea, similar to Tappan's concept, that if the University was to be the capstone of a state system of education as envisioned by Woodward and Pierce, it should be geared in with the high schools. The University should help upgrade the high schools and then accept their graduates as freshmen without entrance examinations. Implementing this integrated educational system was a minor revolution. First, he won the approval of the faculty, for faculty committees must visit the high schools to accredit them, and then of high-school principals. Frieze believed that such visiting committees could criticize teachers and courses, raise scholastic standards, and provide a goal for local achievement. Graduates of accredited high schools could look forward to automatic admission to the University, which in turn would receive a better-prepared freshman class and could better achieve the status of a true university.

Since the program was experimental and undertaken only by Frieze's faith in it, a few faculty members continued to grumble about it with dire prognostications. It did not go before the Regents, except as a report, because it was an internal matter of admissions. The public relations value, however, was incalculable. High schools sought University accreditation and then boasted of it. Communities whose high schools failed of University approval could not ignore it; they had to try to raise standards, even by raising school taxes. Other state universities watched Michigan take the lead in a policy that they would have to follow if it was successful. And it was. The Detroit, Ann Arbor, Flint, Jackson, Kalamazoo, and Adrian high schools were accredited first, followed by Pontiac, Coldwater, Grand Rapids, and Ypsilanti. For several years the University kept statistics on students admitted without examination from accredited high schools, and those admitted from other high schools after examination. The percentage of failure was larger in the latter group!

As a third project Frieze boldly took up Haven's struggle for a chapel or auditorium where all the students could be brought together. In March 1870 he told the Regents that the University "has no roof under which to assemble her various Departments. She has a family of a thousand children without a shelter." Six months later he reverted to the need for a big new building, now adding the argument that without adequate space for men students, how was room to be found for entering women? Since the legislature had urged the admission of women, Frieze encouraged the Regents to ask for buildings necessary to make its request effective. There was something to his logic. The Regents submitted a request for a building fund of $75,000 in January 1871, and to their surprise the legislature voted the appropriation.

It was ingeniously decided to erect a building between Mason Hall and South College and connecting to them, so that the old buildings would become the north and south wings of a central structure 350 feet long facing west on State Street. Architects were invited to submit plans, and the design of E. S. Jenison, "68*e*, of Chicago, was chosen. The Renaissance-style building rose as high as its "wings" and was surmounted by a dome sixty feet higher, with a base diameter of thirty feet. Inside were offices for faculty members and the president, eleven new classrooms, a chapel seating 550 and an auditorium holding 3000—1700 on the main floor and 1300 in the elliptical balcony. Ultimately, it cost $105,500, and the legislature provided an additional $25,000.

UNIVERSITY HALL

The name University Hall was given to the building when the cornerstone was laid on Commencement day, June 28, 1871. The student *Chronicle* regretted that so imposing a structure had to be built of brick and stuccoed, "but the amount of capital and the style of the old buildings left no choice." Various "sidewalk superintendents" were sure that the structure would never bear the weight of the dome, until Professor Wood calculated the stresses and reassured the public. Twenty-five years later, however, the dome was removed, mainly because it leaked, and a much smaller one, made of iron, was set on the hall, much to the disappointment of alumni.

Another distinction of Frieze's administration was a sudden accretion to the University Library. A collection of almost 10,000 books, periodicals, and pamphlets, chiefly on political economy, and assembled by Professor C. H. Rau of Heidelberg University, was bought and donated by Philo Parsons of Detroit. (Yale bid for it too late.) This 35 percent expansion of the Library boosted University holdings to 38,000 items by

1871, plus another 2000 volumes in the Law Library. Moreover, the Library was being cataloged on hand-written cards, the only library besides Harvard's being ordered in this modern manner.

From Frieze's annual report in 1870 it is learned that the average age of the freshman class had dropped to nineteen years. Students in the Literary Department, he added, were spending about $1400 on their education, at the rate of $350 a year. This figure contrasted with costs at Yale that amounted to $946 a year. For the year 1870-71 the University budget passed $100,000 for the first time.

With the appointment of a new President in February 1871, Acting President Frieze prepared to relinquish his responsibilities. His two years at the helm had been unusually successful, with important achievements: the admission of women, the inspection of high schools, and the erection of University Hall. The appearance of an alumni catalogue in the summer of 1871 revealed that the University of Michigan had granted 2900 degrees, and Frieze declared that all these men were making contributions to the building of the West.

The Regents were not unmindful of Frieze's exemplary services. They gave him leave to go to Europe the following year and raised his salary to $2500. In 1875 he became the first dean of the Literary Department, but his twin loves of teaching Latin and making music occupied his time for many more years.

It was unfortunate that Frieze's pleasant interim administration had to end on a note that was sour to the students. On the morning of May 23, 1871, forty-seven sophomores and fourteen freshmen "bolted" their classes to watch Van Amburgh's Circus come into town. The faculty met the following day, obtained the names of all the offenders, and on May 25 suspended the boys from the University until the fall term. They would lose their semester's credits. The juniors and seniors petitioned the faculty for leniency. The *Chronicle* deplored the faculty action, declaring that students had never been informed that bolting was a cause for suspension. It drew an absurd analogy to the method used by Philip II of Spain to quiet the Netherlanders—putting whole populations to death. With somewhat better logic it pointed out that "the number [suspended] is large enough to spoil a class and injure the University, but too large to be a disgrace or punishment."

The rankling penalty stood, but with the advent of a new president and the return of most of the suspended, enrollment mounted by 10 percent in the fall. The Board of Regents succeeded in hiring President Angell of Vermont at a salary of $4500 ($1500 more than Haven had been paid) plus his expenses of moving to Ann Arbor. His final stipulation was installation of a water closet in the President's House, the first in Ann Arbor. He was to assume his position on August 1.

VIEW FROM STATE STREET AND NORTH UNIVERSITY IN THE EARLY 1870s

CHAPTER FIVE

ANGELL AND THE PERSONAL PRESIDENCY

JAMES BURRILL ANGELL, a native of Rhode Island and a graduate of Brown University, was forty-two years old when he became president of the University. He had been professor of modern languages and literature at his alma mater until 1860, when he resigned to become editor of the *Providence Gazette*. His editorials vigorously supported the Union and President Lincoln. In 1866 he was called to the presidency of the University of Vermont.

JAMES B. ANGELL

Familiar with educational problems, at home in the world of journalism and politics, deeply cultured himself, and possessed of a persuasive eloquence, he embarked in 1871 on an executive career at Michigan that continued for thirty-eight years—the longest term any president has yet served. Such was his success that he is always ranked with his greatest contemporaries: President Eliot of Harvard (1869-1909), President White of Cornell (1867-85), President Gilman of Johns Hopkins (1875-1902), and President McCosh of Princeton (1868-88). In addition, he achieved significant recognition in diplomacy from three United States Presidents.

1. Old and new problems in the 1870s

If the completion of University Hall remedied the old complaint of painfully inadequate classrooms (but not the crowded Library), President Angell faced another old problem of equal severity: the small number of faculty members and their low salaries. At $2000 professors were paid two-thirds of what Yale paid, one-half of what Harvard paid, and reputedly one-third of Columbia salaries. At the same time, other universities were encouraged to raid the Michigan faculty.

The other side of the coin was that classes were entirely too large for the highest benefit to students. Over 1100 students were taught by thirty-three faculty members, while Harvard had 1316 students and a faculty of about 105. Both contrasted with one of the admired German universities, Marburg, which had sixty-two professors for 430 students. Harvard's income for 1870-71 was over $300,000, while the University of Michigan made do on $104,000. Raising fees was no answer, because it contradicted the philosophy on which the University functioned. With the federal land grants nearly all sold, Uncle Sam's cupboard was almost bare. Private philanthropy from wealthy alumni was an optimistically unreal hope. President Angell turned, therefore, to an assiduous cultivation of the state legislature, while, out of desperation, he operated with a deficit.

When two new Regents took their seats on the Board in January 1872, the Board was now half Michigan alumni: Dr. Charles Rynd '59, Claudius B. Grant '59, Jonas H. McGowan '61, and Hiram A. Burt '62. They agreed that salaries would have to be raised. Angell argued that it was better to raise assistant professors to $1800 a year and hold them than to endure a succession of temporary instructors at a lower salary. This meant that professors had to be upped to $2500. The result was a deficit of $13,000 in June 1873.

Holding the line elsewhere, the Regents refused Dean Sager's recommendation that the medical course be lengthened from two terms of six months each to two terms of nine months each. It would have cost an additional $3000, which the Board simply did not have. Northwestern University, having absorbed the Chicago Medical College, offered a medical course running for three years. Harvard Medical School, at the prodding of President Eliot, was changing from one year's instruction to three and suffering a decline in enrollment.

The state legislature granted the University $13,000 to cover its deficit, but realized deficits would recur if nothing more was done. Angell achieved a real victory by persuading the legislature to remove the $15,000 ceiling on the annual mill-tax revenue. Consequently, the ratio of one-twentieth of a mill from the property tax yielded $31,000 in 1874. Even so, the increase did little more than cover increased expenses for faculty and for maintenance of University Hall. The victory was impressive, neverthe-less, because payment of the mill-tax revenue ended legislative wrangles about the amount to be appropriated. Additional sums for buildings were still requested, and the legislature still attached conditions to such grants. The legal independence of the Board of Regents, freeing them from such conditions, was not confirmed by the state Supreme Court until 1896.

This type of financial support became the not-so-secret explanation of the University's increasing excellence. The mill tax, boosted to six-tenths of a mill ultimately, remained on the statute book until the Depres-sion persuaded the legislature of 1935 to abolish the state property tax and substitute for it a state sales tax. As a result the University had to turn to the legislature biennially for an appropriation, but by then the constitutional independence of the University was well established.

President Angell was told in 1873 that the existing mill tax could not be raised, but that it would yield more money in 1876 when a new assessment of property was scheduled. The Regents reluctantly increased the annual "dues" for students from $10 to $15, starting in the fall of 1874. For out-of-state students the change was from $10 to $20. This would raise about $9000 extra.

Still the University grew by special acts of the legislature. The homeopathic lobby would neither give up nor settle for another location. Once more, in 1873, the Regents, rather than attach a homeopathic physician to the Medical Department, agreed to take charge of an independent school of homeopathy and connect it with the University whenever the state legislature should provide salaries for its professors. Since this answer was not a definite refusal, the next move was up to the legislature. Early in 1875 it appropriated $6000 for two homeopathic professors. In June the president of the State Homeopathic Society appeared before the Regents and recommended two men for these positions, and they were appointed. Dr. Samuel A. Jones, Homeopathic Medical College of Pennsylvania '61, was to teach materia medica and therapeutics. He soon became dean. Dr. John C. Morgan, from the faculty of the Hahnemann College of Philadelphia, was to teach the theory and practice of medicine. Neither man stayed long.

Regent Dr. Rynd worked out an agreement with the Medical Department whereby students entering the new Homeopathic College would take other courses in the Medical Department. President Angell had grown anxious to end the perennial homeopathic controversy because it was an obstruction to every other legislative appropriation sought by the University. The separate but equal formula appeased the members of the Medical Department and the homeopathic lobby. The Homeopathic College began with twenty-four students and eventually achieved an enrollment of 125. Oddly enough, the state's homeopathic physicians quarreled among themselves and never supported the new college they had demanded. Courses and departments duplicating those in the regular medical school were created until the legislature complained. Enrollment steadily declined in the twentieth century, and the college was closed in 1922 by merger with the Medical School.

In a generous mood the same 1875 legislature also provided $3000 for a Dental Department (quickly called a College), and the Michigan Dental Association made recommendations for the first appointments. The two professors, who were to have outside private practice, were Dr. Jonathan Taft of Cincinnati, dean of the Ohio College of Dental Surgery and former president of the American Dental Association, to be dean and teach dental medicine and surgery, and Dr. John A. Watling, Ohio College D.S. '60, to teach clinical and mechanical dentistry. Both men were important to the profession in the state and served until 1903. There was no dental college west of Ohio and Michigan, and the only other one connected with a university was at Harvard. The new school opened with twenty students in a curriculum of two years of six months each and grew steadily.

President Angell had opposed the college on the ground that dentistry was not an intellectual discipline but a mechanical trade. But Harvard and Michigan so advanced knowledge of tooth decay and tooth care that the science became an American contribution far above the level of European knowledge. By the 1880's, wealthy and royal Europeans began coming to the United States for dental work.

In a third appropriation act the legislature provided $8000 annually for two years for a School of Mines at the University, although the money was not to be available until May 1876. Mining engineering had been offered since 1865, but now it was to be amplified into a separate school. Unfortunately, the appropriation was not renewed, and after four years the school collapsed. A course in architecture provided for 1876-77 was taught by William L. B. Jenney of Chicago, whose later work helped make the skyscraper possible and gave him a national reputation.

Finally, this legislative session appropriated $8000 toward a new hospital for the Medical Department, provided that the city of Ann Arbor would raise another $4000. The city responded, and two pavilions 30 by 114 feet were erected, extending from the rear of the original faculty house hospital. The new facility provided sixty beds, but as a teaching hospital it closed during the summers. The Homeopathic College shared in the use of this hospital until 1879, when the legislature converted another faculty residence on North University into a homeopathic hospital.

PAVILION HOSPITAL

All these special appropriations had the effect of increasing operating expenses without raising the general appropriation. The reassessment of property in 1876 was the only hope for University solvency.

Mention should be made of a few faculty changes in the 1870's. DeVolson Wood, the "father" of the College of Engineering, resigned in 1872 to go to the Stevens Institute of Technology in Hoboken, New Jersey. He was succeeded by Charles E. Greene, a graduate of both Harvard and Massachusetts Institute of Technology and a practicing professional engineer. He re-

1881 ENGINEERING BUILDING

mained at Michigan thirty-one years. Along with Greene, Joseph B. Davis, '68, was appointed assistant professor of civil engineering. He organized in 1874 the University camp (now Camp Davis) for field work in surveying, the first of its kind in the country. Charles S. Denison, Vermont '71, was named instructor and developed the Department of Engineering Drawing. He held his position until his death in 1913. A bachelor, he centered his whole life in his students. This triumvirate made engineering a separate college in 1895 and insured its high standing. Along with Wood they are commemorated by bronze tablets, formerly in the Denison Arch of West Engineering Building and now on the Engineering Campus on North Campus.

Professor Alexander Winchell resigned in 1873, after twenty years, to become chancellor of Syracuse University. Professor Charles I. Walker, one of the three original professors of the Law Department, took health leave in 1874 and then resigned. He was to return later for two intervals of teaching. The venerable and much beloved Professor George P. Williams retired in 1875 at age seventy-three. He had inaugurated collegiate instruction at the University in 1841. Alumni raised a fund in his honor, part of which was paid to him until his death in 1881 (there were no pensions), and the balance used for an endowed chair named for him. Dr. Abram Sager, dean of the Medical faculty, resigned in 1875. He had been appointed in 1842 and transferred to the Medical Department when it opened in 1850. Dr. A.B. Palmer succeeded him as dean. Dr. Victor C. Vaughan, one of the first two students to earn Michigan PhD's in 1876, was hired as lecturer in medical chemistry in 1878.

Professor James C. Watson, director of the observatory, resigned in 1879 to go to the University of Wisconsin, where he died the next year. His departure was due in part to his being the principal stockholder in a new Ann Arbor newspaper, which earned him editorial attack from the proprietor of the *Ann Arbor Courier.*

A discrepancy in fees paid to the Chemical Laboratory, discovered in 1875, ballooned into a scandal that split the Board of Regents, the town, and the state legislature. An examination of the laboratory accounts from 1869 through 1875 revealed that Assistant Professor Preston Rose, '62m, apparently had received from students more money for supplies and chemicals than he had turned over to his superior, Professor Douglas. After the first review of the accounts, Rose paid over $831, but later insisted that the rest of the loss had been in fact remitted to Douglas. The Regents listened to a long defense from Rose on December 21, 1875, then suspended him. At the same time they recommended a new system of bookkeeping for the Chemical Laboratory. Rose requested a speedy trial.

Unfortunately, the controversy soon became public knowledge. The Douglas-Rose affair was the most serious crisis weathered by President Angell during his long administration. Further investigation raised the defalcation to $6984, and Douglas was charged with withholding $1174. Rose was dismissed, and a motion to fire Douglas was almost passed.

Rice Beal, of the *Ann Arbor Courier,* and Professor B. F. Cocker came to Rose's defense—all three men being active Methodists. Douglas was an Episcopalian, and the town began to divide along denominational lines. Beal made sure that the controversy got into state politics in an election year. He also began attacking Angell much as the *Detroit Free Press* had once attacked Tappan. When the new legislature convened in January 1877, a joint committee was appointed to make a thorough investigation of the University's trouble. For two months the committee held hearings and in its report charged only $497 to Rose and $4477 to Douglas. Accordingly, the Regents dismissed Douglas.

Then the Board sued Rose and Douglas to collect. All parties met and agreed there was a deficit of $5671; the court was to fix the relative responsibility of the two defendants. The trial, begun in July 1877, produced a verdict which contradicted the report of the legislature's joint committee: Rose was held liable for $4624, and Douglas for $1047. The Detroit papers and two in Ann Arbor approved the decision, but not Mr. Beal.

Two new Regents took their seats on the Board in January 1878. They and two others were "Rose men," calling themselves the "People's Regents." The other four favored Douglas. Neither side could carry a motion, and debate was long and bitter. Former Regent McGowan, now a representative in Congress, wrote to Angell from Washington and advised him to leave the University if another offer came to him. "It's a glorious day for fools and demagogues," he added.

A new factor helped resolve the situation. Joseph B. Steere, '68, '70*l*, with a consuming interest in natural science, started on a leisurely trip around the world in 1870 with financial backing from Beal. He intended to send back to the University any interesting specimens he found, and in 1872 did send from South America an immense number of butterflies, bird skins, tropical woods, insects, fish, shells, fossils, and rocks. He also contributed regular travel letters to Beal's newspaper. His journey continued to the East Indies and China. By 1874 the quantity of specimens exceeded 15,000 items. Thousands more were received at the University in 1875. At Singapore Steere received a cable that he was granted an honorary PhD, the first ever given by Michigan. On his return in 1876, he was appointed assistant professor of paleontology.

As Beal was surety for Rose's immense debt, he would not be quiet. In June 1878 he was able to persuade the Regents to buy a half interest in the Beal-Steere collection for the University Museum at the price of their claim against Rose. The other half interest was a gift. Still, the Rose partisans were not satisfied. At a February 1879 meeting of the Regents with the legislature's joint committee on the University, from which two pro-Douglas Regents were absent, a resolution was passed that upon request of the joint committee the Board would appoint Rose assistant professor of chemistry again. It was adopted by a vote of four to two. The decision was greeted locally by a bonfire, cannon firing, and a parade led by a band to Rose's house. Rose taught only two more years and retired.

There remained Douglas. Because the University owed him money for laboratory and traveling expenses, which equaled his debt to the University, the two sums cancelled each other. But Douglas sued for relief from the verdict against him, and the tired Regents decided not to contest it. He had to carry his case to the state Supreme Court, which in January 1881 found in his favor. No one now could say what the truth was. The Board paid the award to end the six-year controversy, but never reappointed Douglas. He remained in Ann Arbor and was active in the local gas company. The University had refrained from collecting $4624 from Rose and Beal in return for a museum collection, paid out $3650 to Douglas and the court, and spent more than $8000 on attorneys, accountants, and handwriting experts. Worse, the Regents were forced to yield an appallingly large share of time to the business for six years. President Angell finally escaped the denouement in 1881, as will be related. Three of the "People's Regents" were gone by that year, and Mr. Beal died in 1883. Yet the effects of the controversy were still felt in Ann Arbor as late as 1940.

2. Class traditions, sports, and studies

President Angell quickly demonstrated that he had a way with young people. Hazing, class fights, vandalism, and frequent disorders were the accepted conduct of students on his arrival. Angell personally conducted chapel every day that he was on campus, and within the first three days reduced the students to respectful attention. He did it with a cherubic smile and an appeal to their sense of fair play. In 1872 he made chapel voluntary, and by the absence of the uninterested the others gained more.

Dancing, though not a frequent social activity, was nonetheless the top exhibition of sophistication. The senior class of 1868 (the same that had introduced canes) had sponsored a Senior Hop on the night before Thanksgiving and the annual dance was repeated by the senior class for two years. Then in 1872 the junior class sponsored the event, and the "J-Hop" remained the biggest party of the year until 1960 after which it was given up for lack of interest by a generation that preferred to sit and listen to folk music. The dance was first held in a local hotel, then in Hangsterfer's Hall, later in Waterman Gymnasium, and finally in the Intramural Sports Building. Eventually two orchestras of national reputation were hired to provide continuous dance music. Breakfasts at fraternity houses followed.

Hazing was more difficult to control, as it took place outside class hours and frequently at night. In April 1874, three sophomores and three freshmen were suspended for fighting, and their classmates objected violently. A group of eighty-one students filed a petition asserting that they were as guilty as the six who were punished. Angell moved decisively; to their consternation all eighty-one were suspended for the rest of the semester. It was an instructive lesson, although the incident was attended by wide publicity around the state.

Angell never pursued order just for the sake of order. In 1875 he wrote: "It is one of the conditions of work like ours that the petty mischief of some reckless students or a triumph in some athletic game will be paraded through the newspapers with more noise than the results of twelve months' manly and undemonstrative study of twelve hundred students."

Student behavior at this time was a national problem, and President Eliot of Harvard had warned parents and public, and especially the churches: "What is technically called a quiet term cannot be accepted as the acme of university success.... The criteria of success or failure in a high place of learning are not the boyish escapades of an insignificant minority nor the exceptional cases of ruinous vice. Each year must be judged by the added opportunities of instruction, by the prevailing enthusiasm in learning, and by the gathered wealth of culture and character."

About four hundred students attended Forepaugh's Circus— "three times the largest show on earth"—on May 25, 1876. A few of them carried tin horns. In anticipation of trouble the ring master brought in fifty roustabouts who had been deputized and carried tent stakes. Further, it was learned later that ropes had been attached to the bleacher supports so that they could be collapsed in case of student disorder—and probably at the cost of considerable injury. The students kept quiet, but later that night some of the pharmacy boys procured acid and threw it noiselessly on the tent; other rowdies sawed spokes on wagon wheels and lifted planking on two bridges on the road to Ypsilanti. Forepaugh declared damages of $2000 in Ann Arbor and a loss of $2500 by failure to reach Ypsilanti next day in time for a matinee performance.

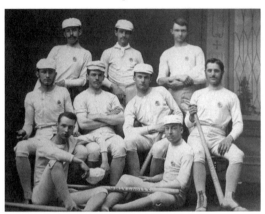

BASEBALL TEAM, c. 1875

Organized athletics began to drain off some of this pressure for physical activity. The University Athletic Club, formed in 1874, was concerned with track events. It supervised the annual field days held on the local fair grounds. Baseball and football continued to be interclass games until 1878. An attempt to challenge another university to a football game in 1873 did not succeed. When Michigan students invited Cornell to select a team for a game on neutral ground in Cleveland, President White replied to President Angell: "I will not permit thirty men to travel four hundred miles merely to agitate a bag of wind."

Michigan chose an all-University team that played against Racine College in Chicago on May 30, 1878. Michigan won 7 to 2. After this initiation into intercollegiate contests both the football and baseball teams began to play other colleges. Michigan's football team (11 regulars and 2 substitutes) invaded the East in 1881 and lost to Harvard, Yale, and Princeton. In the same year the baseball team played Wisconsin, Northwestern, and Racine. These teams were coached and managed by students. Fulltime coaches, faculty supervision, and organization of a Western Conference of scheduled games between teams of several universities were still a decade away—as was the building of a gymnasium and a field for athletics off the campus. Tennis was introduced about 1883.

In addition to seniors, who were now selecting most of their courses, limited elections were permitted juniors and sophomores. Harvard and Cornell were also allowing electives after the freshman year. The elective principle struck deeper than mere accommodation of the student. It subtly

LADIES CREW, UNIVERSITY BOAT, 1878

changed the emphasis from the subject matter of a course to the method or process of learning. If the latter was the significant aspect of education, then the subject could be a matter of the student's taste and choice.

The second request of the Medical Department to extend its two six-month terms to two of nine months was granted by the Regents, to begin in the fall of 1877. The Homeopathic Medical College was also affected and became unique in requiring nine-month terms. The Law Department lengthened its terms to nine months in 1882, followed by the Dental College two years later. Meanwhile, starting in 1880, the Medical departments increased their course of study to three years.

The pharmacy course was organized as a separate school in December 1876, with Dr. Prescott as dean. With a solid curriculum and able professors, the school grew in enrollment and reputation. In 1883 President Angell asserted that it stood at the head of all pharmacy schools in the country.

Music was introduced to the curriculum of the Literary Department in 1880 by the appointment of Calvin B. Cady, Oberlin '72, as instructor. He was allowed to give lessons to private pupils on the side. Eventually, as his private school grew, University students were given credit for lessons in practical music. In the same year Dean Frieze founded the University Musical Society, made up largely of faculty members, to sponsor concerts in Ann Arbor. It soon assumed direction of Mr. Cady's music school.

In 1881 a School of Political Science was started, with Professor C. K. Adams as dean. It was an upper division program for juniors and seniors from the Literary Department, of which it remained an anomalous part. The University believed that such a school would improve civil service appointments in the field of government (the National Civil Service Reform League was founded the same year, and the Pendleton Act of 1883 established the Civil Service Commission). It would also, hopefully, sharpen the political judgment of the students. It included even a course in forestry, the first in the United States, by Professor Volney Spalding, '73. But in 1885 Adams resigned to succeed his old mentor; Andrew D. White, as president of Cornell University. He was succeeded in turn by Thomas M. Cooley, formerly of the Law Department, who had given one course in the political science curriculum. But after Cooley left in 1887 to become first chairman of the Interstate Commerce Commission, the School of

Political Science expired, and courses in government reverted to the Literary Department.

In order to accommodate graduates of high schools which provided no courses in the classics, the Literary Department instituted in 1877 an English curriculum that required work in English, French, and German languages and literatures. Since it did not require Greek or Latin, the degree given was bachelor of letters. This was the fourth baccalaureate degree now offered by the University.

Then the required four years of study for the bachelor's degree was altered to 120 semester hours. Since fifteen hours of classes a week per semester, and thirty hours a year were the usual student load, the change might seem to mean nothing, but it did allow a bright student who wanted to carry more than fifteen hours to graduate in three and a half years. Further, students over twenty-one years of age and not seeking a degree were admitted to study what they pleased. In 1882 the so-called "University system" was adopted, by which after two years of undergraduate work the student entered upon a special program concentrated in three fields of his choice. At the end of two or three more years the student submitted to a comprehensive examination. Students who showed exceptional brilliance and wrote a thesis could attain a master's degree without getting a bachelor's degree. This was a bold step in educational discrimination, characteristic of Michigan, and it appealed to students. The opportunity to "major" in special areas of interest seemed to them a tremendous hole in the wall of generally prescribed education, yet it prevented the random sampling of elementary courses throughout their four years—the unhappy fate of Harvard's uncontrolled free elections.

One other innovation took place at Commencement in 1878. Up to this time the faculty had selected about ten seniors to deliver orations or poems on this occasion. This year, however, owing to the lengthening of the terms of the Medical departments, the medics and lits would graduate together. Since the medics had no tradition of student speakers, and the lits were beginning to feel that Commencement orations smacked of high-school ceremonies, the administration quietly changed the program and provided an outside speaker for the combined Commencement.

3. Growth and Angell's mission to China

In view of all the progressive and expansive measures taken, it seemed unappreciative, to say the least, for the Regents to slash salaries in 1878. But the country was experiencing a depression, and the state was reducing all expenditures. Professors were cut from $2500 to $2200, and assistants from $1800 to $1600. President Angell was reduced from $4500 to $3750. More lamentable was the fact that these salaries were not restored for ten years.

Despite this economy, a new fourth professorship of law, named for former President Tappan, was established in 1879. The Law Department could do this because its preponderance of out-of-state students paying higher fees supplied the department with more income than expense. The position was filled by the elderly Alpheus Felch, Bowdoin '27, former governor, U.S. senator, and regent. Another new position was created the same year in the Literary Department: a professor of the science and art of teaching, the first of its kind in the country. William H. Payne, superintendent of schools at Adrian and known for his writings on education, was appointed to it.

A subdued Alexander Winchell, having given up as chancellor of Syracuse University, returned to become professor of geology. A special Museum Building was erected at a cost of $40,000, and all the specimens of biology, geology, mineralogy, and archeology were soon moved into it, leaving more space in Mason Hall for classrooms. Unfortunately, the Museum was poorly built and soon required strengthening and then repairs. Then, in 1881 the University at last obtained an appropriation of $100,000, later augmented, for a badly needed library building.

Early in 1880 President Angell escaped part of this belt tightening by being offered the appointment of minister to China by President Hayes. He was to negotiate a new treaty with the Chinese government to deal with the immigration of Chinese laborers, which raised concerns about competition for jobs. They concentrated in cities and competed at lower wages for jobs with native laborers. Angell was to be assisted by two commissioners: one an experienced diplomat, the other adamant in representing the California anti-Chinese attitude. Secretary of State Evarts had no special advice for Angell beyond the warning that if the Chinese refused to negotiate, the United States would have to legislate.

The Regents were flattered by the offer to Angell and felt that they had a substitute at hand in Dean Frieze. After gathering enormous food supplies, the Angell family left Ann Arbor early in June 1880, expecting to be gone for a year but actually not returning until February 1882. Angell's Chinese mission was successful in that he persuaded that government to agree that the United States might regulate, limit, or even suspend the number of Chinese laborers admitted, but might not absolutely prohibit them. This agreement was accepted by the Senate, although later legislation went beyond treaty limits and completely prohibited immigration of Chinese laborers. Angell also secured for Protestants the privileges granted to Roman Catholics in China. On top of all this he could not help but advertise the University of Michigan among the Chinese.

During Angell's absence the University availed itself of a law passed by Congress allowing military officers to give military instruction in colleges. It applied to the secretary of the Navy for the appointment of a naval engineer to teach in the engineering program. The Navy Department assigned Mortimer E. Cooley, a graduate of Annapolis, to teach mechanical engineering, including steam engineering and naval architecture. A remarkable teacher and administrator, he soon resigned from the Navy and eventually became dean of the College of Engineering. Coincident with his arrival, Moses Coit Tyler resigned in 1881 to go to Cornell, where larger Eastern libraries were closer for his study of early American literature. Having published two volumes of a pioneer study of colonial literature, he now wanted to work on the literature of the Revolutionary period. Isaac N. Demmon, '68, MA '71, was promoted to replace him as professor of English, a position he held until 1920.

Angell was welcomed home in the winter of 1882 with a student escort from the railroad station to his house and a faculty and civic reception in the evening. In his absence the Douglas-Rose affair had finally been ended, and three of the Regents who had been most contentious about it were off the Board. One of the new faces belonged to James Shearer, Detroit and Bay City contractor, who had built the state capitols in both Montgomery, Alabama, and Lansing. He brought to the expanding campus considerable interest and expert knowledge in construction. Taking seats in January 1882 were two other distinguished citizens: Austin Blair, Union '39, of Jackson, governor of Michigan 1860-64 and member of Congress 1866-72; and James F. Joy, Dartmouth '33, Harvard '36*l*, president of the Michigan Central Railroad. The three continuing Regents were the Reverend George Duffield, Jr., Yale '37; Samuel S. Walker, '61, a banker in St. Johns and member of the state legislature; and Byron Cutcheon, '61, of Manistee, who had compiled a brilliant record in the Civil War, rising to the rank of brigadier general and winning the Congressional Medal of Honor. He had then returned to the University and taken a law degree. With this Board, feuding and division among the Regents ceased.

The Board still operated by committees: one each for the principal instructional units (Literary, Law, Medicine and Dentistry, Pharmacy) and one each for finance, the Library, the Museum and Observatory, and buildings and grounds. Three Regents and the president formed an executive committee. Questions of policy and appointments relating to any one of the departments reached the Board from the committee concerned or was referred to the committee in charge for a recommendation. In this setup very little business came to the attention of the Board directly from the president. He was still more of an administrator than an executive. An added danger lay in the fact that three of the schools had committee members who were also on the finance committee, which made up the budget and to whom the University treasurer reported. Nevertheless, the system functioned because University operations were still relatively small and simple, and because Angell was a supremely adroit and agreeable presiding officer. Real achievements occurred in the 1880's.

4. *The beginning of the Golden Era*

After several delays in construction the new Library was occupied in December 1883. Built of stone and having twin towers, it was located at the center of the campus. One of the towers contained a clock having a peal of five bells presented by Andrew D. White of Cornell, E. C. Hegeler of La Salle, Ill., and J. J. Hagerman of Milwaukee. The Library easily accommodated the 55,000 books and pamphlets, leaving the 4500 law books in the vacated—at last—Law Building. The dedication speaker was Justin Winsor, historian and famed librarian of Harvard. The new library promptly received one distinguished gift: James McMillan of Detroit purchased the Shakespeare collection of E.H. Thomson of Flint and gave it to the

UNIVERSITY LIBRARY, 1883, TYPICAL OF THE RED-BRICK CAMPUS

University, along with enough money to double the size of the collection to 2600 volumes. Later, he made further additions to it. In 1885 C. H. Buhl of Detroit doubled the size of the Law Library by donating his own collection of 5000 volumes and a fund of $10,000 for additions. Still, the University of Michigan had small libraries compared to several Eastern colleges.

Michigan joined a group of a dozen colleges that were supporting the American School of Classical Studies in Athens. The financial contribution of $2000 annually was supplied by Detroit friends. Two years later, in 1885, Professor M. L. D'Ooge was given a year's leave to serve as director of the American School. In a tribute to President Angell, the Chinese government presented to the University the exhibition of textiles, porcelains, and industrial products which it had had on display at the New Orleans Exhibition. The materials were added to the Museum. Then, Henry C. Lewis of Coldwater died and left his huge art collection of 450 paintings and 35 statues. Although many of the pictures were recent copies of old masters, the quantity and quality suggested to Angell that a school of fine arts was in order. The idea rose again the next year when Randolph Rogers, the noted sculptor, sent a collection of seventy models and casts of his statues.

A group of professors joined some teachers in the secondary schools of Ann Arbor and Ypsilanti to found the Michigan Schoolmasters' Club in 1886. It brought together two classes of teachers for discussion of their common professional problems. As the club membership grew, it developed more influence in the state than any other educational organization. Sometimes it published its proceedings and papers, and sometimes it didn't. John Dewey was one of its founders, and the Michigan Schoolmasters' Club flourished into the 1960s with as many as 3000 members meeting annually in Ann Arbor.

Enrollment had been declining ever since 1872 and in 1876-77 was down to 1109. But in the following year it rebounded and continued to rise for the next three years. The total of students reached 1534 in 1880, leveled off for a couple of years, and then climbed steadily. The attendance of women in proportion to men increased. The 100 mark was passed in 1875, the 200 in 1885, and 300 in 1888; the percentage change was from 9 to 16 percent of the whole student body. With a touch of just pride, President Angell noted in 1882 that six members of the Wellesley College faculty, including the president (Alice Freeman), were Michigan alumnae. A dozen years of educating young women with young men had exploded all the old shibboleths against the experiment.

Sororities began to develop in 1879 with the appearance of a chapter of Kappa Alpha Theta on campus. Sororities were new everywhere, and Michigan's men students ridiculed them as an attempt to imitate fraternities. Of course they were; no one denied the charge. The need was as respectable for the one sex as for the other. As the number of women students increased, so did the sororities. Gamma Phi Beta was established in 1882, and Delta Gamma in 1885. Two more professional fraternities appeared in 1885: Nu Sigma Nu for medical students, and Delta Sigma Delta for dental students.

In 1886 the University was charging out-of-state students in the Literary Department $55 the first year, and $30 each subsequent year; in the professional schools $60 the first year, and $35 thereafter. Certain critics thought they should be charged more, but Angell pointed out that existing fees were higher than those of any other university in the West. Private colleges in the East charged more, but also offered many more scholarships. Other critics thought that because the University charged such high fees it was becoming a place for the rich and aristocratic only. Angell thereupon polled 1406 students about their parents: 502 were farmers, 171 retail and wholesale merchants, 93 lawyers, 83 physicians, 54 mechanics, 52 manufacturers, 51 clergymen, 41 lumbermen and builders, 33 real estate and insurance agents, 28 bankers, and 26 teachers.

The boisterousness of the students of 1871-76 seemed to be declining. Angell commented in 1889 that cases of bad conduct requiring discipline had grown rare. The University had raised its academic standards and was also making the learning process more interesting. An impressive percentage of those attaining a bachelor's degree was going on to professional schools. Partly indicative of the mood of the times was the prosperity of the Student Christian Association. Among its members, its alumni, and the John S. Newberry family, $40,000 was raised to erect Newberry Hall, across the street from University Hall. The Student Christian Association published a monthly bulletin, a students' handbook, ran a student employment agency and room listing, and sponsored lectures, besides conducting Bible study and prayer meetings.

SAMOVAR CLUB MEETING FOR A DISCUSSION OF RUSSIAN LITERATURE

In 1886 Angell expressed for a second time his hope that the University would accept only upperclassmen and graduate students. "If the day should ever come when we could leave to the [high] school or the smaller colleges the work now done here in the first two years of the course, and could bend our energies entirely to the work of the last two years and to professional instruction, we should rejoice." But he was too much of a realist to believe that the high schools could give the first two years of college work or that the private colleges would willingly part with their students after two years.

Some distinguished faculty appointments were made. When Henry Carter Adams, PhD Hopkins '78, was forced to leave Cornell because the powerful Henry Sage did not like his criticism of American railroads, Angell welcomed him in 1887, to teach economics, a field in which he became preeminent. Another Hopkins PhD named John Dewey was appointed instructor in philosophy in 1884. He remained ten years and became a full professor before departing for the University of Chicago and ultimately Columbia University. Henry Wade Rogers, '74*l*, appointed professor of law in 1882, soon became dean, but resigned in 1890 to become president of Northwestern University. Harry B. Hutchins, '71, who had been an instructor in history, was recalled from law practice in 1884 to be professor of law. Thomas C. Trueblood, a recognized speaker who was conducting a school of oratory in Kansas City, was named lecturer in elocution in 1885, and gave the first credit-bearing course in speech offered by any university. Six years later the first department of speech in any university was organized. Under him the whole field of intercollegiate debating was developed. His career lasted until 1926.

Three other noted teachers all began in 1887. Andrew McLaughlin, '82, '85*l*, became an instructor in history and took over the work in American history of C.K. Adams. He also married a daughter of President Angell. G. Carl Huber, '87*m*, began his brilliant career of teaching anatomy that led him eventually to the deanship of the Graduate School. Similarly, Dr. Frederick G. Novy, with three degrees from the University, began as an instructor in hygiene before earning international fame as a bacteriologist. He outlived all his contemporaries, dying in 1957 at the age of ninety-two. Fred Newton Scott, '84, PhD '89, inevitably dubbed "Fig Newton," began teaching English in 1889 and developed the Department of Rhetoric, which gained renown for its help to aspiring authors.

There were losses, too. Besides Moses Coit Tyler, James V. Campbell resigned as law professor in 1885, having served since the department opened in 1859. Edward Olney, the mathematician, died early in 1887. When Payne resigned as professor of teaching in 1888 to become president of the University of Nashville, Burke A. Hinsdale, former president of Hiram College, succeeded him. Two years later the state legislature gave the Literary Department faculty the right to issue teachers' certificates. In December 1889 the incomparable Professor Frieze died, mourned by students, alumni, colleagues, townsmen, and especially by President Angell. His kind would not be seen again. After Cornell University made C.K. Adams president in 1885, he lured Professor Hutchins away to be dean of the new Cornell Law School. When Dr. Ford resigned as dean of the Medical Department in 1890, Dr. Victor C. Vaughan, '78*m*, was named to succeed him.

Angell took another short leave in the latter part of 1887. He was asked by the secretary of state to serve with him on the Fishery Commission to adjust with the British commissioners the rights of United States fishermen off the banks of Newfoundland, Nova Scotia, and New Brunswick. The final treaty was rejected in 1888 by the Republican Senate elected with President Benjamin Harrison, but an interim arrangement for licensing U. S. fishing vessels continued without a treaty.

An increase in the equalized value of property in the state caused the one-twentieth of a mill tax to yield more than it had done. The faculty cuts were restored in 1888, and President Angell's salary was raised to $5000 (only $500 more than he had received sixteen years earlier). A new laboratory was built that year for hygiene and physics; in it Dr. Vaughan began serving the state Board of Health in diagnostic and research work. The Chemistry Laboratory was also again enlarged. The legislature answered the old cry for a decent hospital by appropriating $50,000 if the city of Ann Arbor would contribute $25,000. Once more the local citizens promptly agreed, and two buildings were erected on Catherine Street, one for the homeopaths and one for the regular medics. The state had to add $25,000 in 1891 to complete them.

As if to crown these years of endeavor, enrollment increased to 2153 in the year 1889-90, and once again the University of Michigan emerged as the largest university in the country, edging out Harvard. It retained this position of primacy for the next two years, as the number of students rose to 2420 and 2692. Then Harvard once more overtook Michigan and grew at a faster rate.

It is significant to pause and ask why Michigan was the biggest university in the nation—certainly not because of low standards and the ease of acquiring a degree. In his first annual report (1872) President Angell wrote: "I have never seen a better average of class work than I find here." He was paying tribute to the reputation of the faculty as good teachers with high goals. There were a number of professors who not only knew their subjects but inspired their students to find excitement in the gruelling business of learning. A few, like "Punky" Williams in mathematics and physics, Henry S. Frieze in Latin, Denison in engineering, Cooley in law, and Angell himself, were much beloved by their students. Others, like Olney in mathematics, Tyler and Demmon in English, Adams in history, and Drs. Ford and Vaughan in medicine, were enormously respected. Whatever research and writing they did, they were first of all gifted teachers.

In addition, as has been mentioned, several of the faculty produced high-school and college textbooks that were widely used: Frieze in Latin, Watson in astronomy, Thomas in German, Prescott, Douglas, and Vaughan in chemistry, Olney in algebra and geometry, Payne in education, Jones in Greek and Latin, and Cooley in constitutional law. The publicity value of these texts in advertising the University cannot be overrated. Michigan was an institution that thousands of young people had heard of and even felt some acquaintance with at the very time they were considering entrance to a university.

Upon inquiry and comparison, they would also find that the University was reasonably inexpensive. Fees were a little higher than at other Western universities, but cheaper than at Eastern institutions. Board and room were probably about the same as at neighboring universities. Clothes requirements were modest.

The several avenues to a degree undoubtedly attracted students. Small colleges could not offer such diverse programs. Students who wanted to avoid the classics, or avoid the sciences, or pursue a profession, or generally select their courses could all be accommodated.

Bigness itself tended to promote bigness. Everyone seemingly wanted to go where the most went. Michigan had now a relatively large body of alumni scattered through the Midwest who served as carriers of the Michigan virus. And bigness made possible certain extracurricular benefits that small colleges could not support—lectures by noted persons, concerts and plays, a variety of sports, a student weekly newspaper, nine fraternities and five sororities in 1890 plus three professional fraternities.

Finally, word spread widely that at Michigan there was a spirit of democracy and tolerance in the student body that was inviting. Westerners may have secretly feared an aristocratic attitude in the East. Other prospective students disliked the chapel requirements and other prohibitions at denominational colleges. At Michigan the rules were few, there were no dormitories, many students held part-time jobs, and there was much cameraderie. Ann Arbor was hospitable and not a city. In short, students had fun.

LAUNCH ON THE HURON

Harper's Weekly ran a short article on the University in July 1887: "The most striking feature of the University is the broad and liberal spirit in which it does its work. Students are allowed the widest freedom consistent with sound scholarship in pursuing the studies of their choice; they are held to no minute police regulations, but are treated as persons with high and definite aims from which they are not easily to be diverted. No religious tests are imposed, but devotional exercises are held at stated times, which no one is compelled to attend against his choice, though all are welcome. Women are admitted to all departments on equal terms with men; the doors of the University are open to all applicants who are properly qualified, from whatever part of the world they may come."

It began to be clear that the older private colleges were losing their assumed right to speak for higher education, to set its standards, or to enjoy the best financial support. Leadership was passing to the state universities of the upper Midwest, of which Michigan was the acknowledged model. President Angell argued that education was a necessity, not a luxury for the wealthy, which must be made available to all who could qualify. He saw the state university as combining some of the practical and popular aspects of the land-grant colleges* with the high learning of the private colleges, and as the only institution capable of developing and supporting graduate instruction. Therefore, he was gratified by the spread of state universities generally. Almost every state outside the Eastern seaboard now had one. "They have all frequently and gratefully testified to the helpful influence of this University upon their life," he wrote. "They have in a large degree followed our methods. In their success and in their great promise we can heartily rejoice. From their increasing strength we also draw strength."

President Angell ended his first twenty years at the University in a satisfied frame of mind. He took the occasion of his annual report for 1890 to mark some peaks and contrasts. The University thus far had awarded degrees to more than 10,700 persons, of whom only about 1000 were no longer living. Enrollment had grown from 1110 in 1871 to 2420 in the current year. Of that latter figure, 1170 students were from Michigan and 445 were women. The ratio of Michigan students had barely changed: from 46 percent to 48 percent. The faculty had grown from thirty-six to ninety-two residents and eleven nonresidents, thereby reducing the ratio of students to professors. The budget had quadrupled, from $100,000 to $400,000. University Hall, the Museum, the Library, three laboratories, and two hospitals had been added to the campus, and some of the older buildings had been enlarged. Even so, Angell felt that the change in the range and methods of instruction had been more striking and important. One statistic will have to do here: fifty-seven courses of instruction were offered in 1871 and 378 twenty years later. The average age of freshmen remained at nineteen, and all classes were much better behaved.

Moreover, President Angell felt sure he knew the purpose of university education and how it should be achieved. No part of the curricula was mysterious to him. Educated as a humanist, he was also familiar with law and comprehended enough science to understand its methods and findings. He could readily communicate with all the professors in their

---

* The recent "land grant colleges" were those colleges offering courses in agriculture, mechanics, and home economics which were given federal grants of land to sell by the Morrill Act of 1862. In Michigan this benefit went to the Michigan Agricultural College in East Lansing and emphasized that technical and vocational training had become a legitimate function of higher education in the eyes of Congress.

disciplines and know what they were doing. He moved easily from the world of scholarship to the world of politics or business and back again. His Christian faith was broad and deep; he was the whole man.

CAMPUS AS IT APPEARED IN THE EARLY 1880s

CHAPTER SIX

ANGELL
THE GOLDEN YEARS

RESPLENDENT AS HIS RECORD WAS, 1891 is perhaps a watershed in the Presidentcy of James Burrill Angell. The University would soon change from the institution that he had fostered and knew so intimately. Its continued growth would force internal and external changes. For years he had no secretary and answered all letters himself in long-hand. He personally enrolled all the students in the Literary Department. He was still a teaching president in the fields of international law and the history of treaties. He conducted all chapel ser-

JAMES B. ANGELL

vices and always gave the baccalaureate address to the graduating seniors. At this point in time President Angell knew all of his 103 faculty, because he had had a hand in appointing all but seven veterans. Further, he knew hundreds of the students, and all of them knew him. All of these conditions changed by the time he retired. Mere growth alone would require a corporate organization, with a nonteaching administration of divided responsibilities, accompanied by loss of intimacy among a larger faculty and between students and faculty and administration. Internal communication would suffer.

Before he retired so much was being asked of university education that its goals and methods were under debate, and no president could follow the research of his increasingly fragmented faculty in their special-izations. The traditional "departments" were reorganized as "colleges" under deans with growing autonomy. Similar courses of study were grouped into subject departments under chairmen. Meanwhile, the responsibilities of the president in educational statesmanship had so multiplied that interpreting aims, raising money, and determining budgets constituted more than a full-time job. In the next half century the proliferation of knowledge, the depth of research, the increase in the number of colleges on campus, the growth of enrollment, and the conflicting demands of society for specialization in education dated the universal man like Angell and left him behind, just as the old concept of the faculty as a community of scholars was true only in the literal sense of place. The university president had to specialize, too, and his specialty was educational administration.

1. State and national leadership at the end of the century

Michigan unquestionably attained the status of a national university by the time Angell entered his third decade as University president. During his first term, President Cleveland had appointed Angell a member of the Fishery Commission, and Cooley chairman of the Interstate Commerce Commission, where he was joined by Henry Carter Adams as chief statistician. In addition, Don Dickinson, '67*l*, a Detroit lawyer, was named Postmaster General. He actually shook up his department and reformed it for better service. Other Michigan alumni were appointed to diplomatic posts, to the federal bench, and as customs collectors. Cleveland was defeated for reelection in 1888, but in February 1892 he addressed the students of the University on Washington's birthday. The reception his lecture obtained in the newspapers persuaded him to run again, and he was elected to a second term in 1892.

Don Dickinson was now national chairman of the Democratic party, and President Cleveland's private secretary was Henry T. Thurber, '74. In his second term Cleveland made J. S. Morton, '54*a*, secretary of agriculture and kept Edwin Willets, '55, president of Michigan Agricultural College, as assistant secretary. He appointed Edwin F. Uhl, '62, assistant secretary of state, later sending him to Germany as ambassador. He named T. Lawrence Maxwell, '74, as solicitor general, William F. Quimby, '58, as minister to The Netherlands, and Alfred Noble, '70, as a member of the Nicaraguan Canal Board. As Cleveland later confessed: "When I was in office and needed help I usually turned to the University of Michigan." Besides executive appointees, forty-seven Michigan alumni served in the four Congresses of Cleveland's two administrations, several in more than one session. They represented fifteen states besides Michigan.

Late in 1895 President Cleveland called on Angell a second time. He asked him to serve as chairman of a Deep Waterways Commission to meet with three Canadians to study the feasibility of canals which would make possible the passage of ocean ships into the upper Great Lakes. Canada had already built the Welland Canal around Niagara Falls, but it was not very deep. While lake shippers and big shipowners wanted an outlet to the ocean, the railroads fought it. Canals around the St. Lawrence rapids would favor some towns and ruin others. After much study and hearing of testimony, the joint commission reported to Congress and Parliament. These reports prompted further studies, the years passed, two wars and a

Depression intervened, and finally the St. Lawrence Seaway was begun in 1954 and completed in 1959.

President Angell's diplomatic talents were called upon a third time at the end of the decade. President McKinley, along with other heads of state, was shocked by the recent Turkish massacre of thousands of Armenians, many of whose relatives and friends fled to other countries and raised cries of anguish. Several U. S. mission schools were damaged. President McKinley appointed the sixty-eight-year-old Angell as minister to Turkey, and he left right after Commencement in 1897. The Regents named Dean Hutchins of the Law Department acting president, a decision that disappointed Dean D'Ooge of the Literary Department and caused him to resign his administrative office. Accordingly, Professor Richard Hudson of the History Department was made dean.

Angell's task in Constantinople was to seek redress for destruction of the U. S. schools. Although he met the Sultan promptly, he soon discovered that the despotic government would not admit any liability. Angell began a "persistent nagging" while the Turks procrastinated. The Sultan counted on the United States being preoccupied with its quarrel with Spain over Cuba, and it was. Angell utilized his vacation period to visit the Holy Land. Upon his return the diplomatic stalemate continued, and Angell departed in disappointment in August 1898. The only tangible benefit was a gift of 168 books to the University Library from the Turkish government.

Acting President Hutchins proved to be a good administrator. He diverted some business that customarily came across the president's desk and he systematized other procedures. The Spanish-American War enlisted 125 students, and nine of them lost their lives. In addition, Drs. Vaughan and De Nancrède served in the Medical Corps, and Professor Cooley was chief engineer on the U.S.S. "Yosemite," a cruiser manned by Naval Reserves from Michigan.

In his 1899 report President Angell took occasion to remind the state of services it received directly from the University. Dr. Vaughan's Hygienic Laboratory was testing water supplies and suspected foods for any town at nominal fees. The danger of typhoid fever was disappearing. The Engineering Department offered a course in naval architecture to help shipbuilders in the state. The Chemistry Laboratory was serving such Michigan industries as alkali plants, clay products, cement mills, and sugar beet refineries. The University Hospital, now open the year around, treated 1800 patients annually, the Homeopathic Hospital another 1200, while the Dental Clinic reached 8000. Angell now proposed courses to train men for business, banking, and international trade. His presentation of the University as an institution for state service as well as an educational plant appealed to the legislature, and up went the mill tax from one-sixth to one-fourth of a mill. He had also shown a new side of the University to the citizens of Michigan. Out of the "service" aspect also came extension courses.

Back on the campus things were happening, too. With ninety-five graduate students enrolled in 1890, it was time to organize a Graduate School, but only a department, supervised by an Administrative Council of faculty members, was established within the Literary College. Books and apparatus were needed as well as faculty specialists. Angell warned the Regents that it would be more expensive than other departments and that fellowships would be needed to attract graduate students. These two aspects of graduate education remain just as true today: it costs more to teach aspirants for masters' and doctors' degrees and to attract the most promising ones financial aid must be offered. The new department did not prosper for several years, and enrollment did not grow, but the University was turning a corner toward increased emphasis on research.

In 1891 the Regents had authorized the Medical Department to establish a training school for nurses, limited to eight. Thus, the School of Nursing Education began, and every year the class increased in size and the training period lengthened. The school came under the supervision at first of the University Hospital director. The Medical Department itself announced in 1892 that it would offer a four-year curriculum, the first in the nation to do so, although other schools soon followed.

The first summer school "under University auspices" was held in 1894. What this meant was that the professors were paid from the fees

NURSING CLASS OF 1900

collected from the eighty-eight students registered; the school had to be self-supporting. After it grew to 263 students in 1899, the Regents took responsibility for the summer session as a regular University function. In 1894 the *Michigan Alumnus* was started, at first under private ownership. Only Yale had such a publication. It was purchased four years later by the Alumni Association as the organ of this group, signaling the unification of the several departmental alumni societies into one association.

Ann Arbor enjoyed its first May music festival in 1894 with three concerts in two days. It became an annual event, from that day to this. The festival was increased to six concerts over four days in 1919. The two railroads ran special trains into Ann Arbor for the event. It was the idea of

Albert A. Stanley, appointed professor of music in 1888 and director of the Choral Union. The May Festival was a climax to a series of professional concerts presented throughout the year.

At the close of the World Columbian Exposition in Chicago the University was given two murals by Gari Melchers, "The Arts of War" and "The Arts of Peace." They now grace the ends of the reference room in the Hatcher Library. The University then purchased the Exposition's organ for University Hall and named it for Professor Frieze as a memorial. It was later moved to Hill Auditorium.

A Michigan Academy of Science, soon enlarged to include Arts and Letters, was started by University scientists in 1894. Membership included like-minded professors in other Michigan colleges.

Faculty salaries, long below the Eastern levels, took a step upward: professors were to start at $2500, move to $2700 after five years, and $3000 after ten years. In January 1893 the Regents asked the legislature to double the mill tax from one-twentieth of a mill to one-tenth of a mill, and for a special appropriation of $266,000 for buildings, repairs, and equipment. They lost the latter, but instead the legislature raised the tax to one-sixth of a mill. Accordingly, the Board contracted for a small classroom building that was named Tappan Hall.

The homeopathic quarrel erupted again in 1894 when the American Institute of Homeopathy requested the resignation of Dean Obetz. He was accused of proposing consolidation of the two medical schools at Michigan. Quickly the homeopathic faculty joined in the Institute's charge against the dean. Even if the charge were true, it hardly smacked of treason to the Board of Regents, which itself had talked of consolidation. The Board investigated the accusation against Obetz and found it untrue. Then Regent Herman Kiefer, a distinguished physician from Detroit, drafted an extended reply to the Institute that peeled off their collective hides. He accused the homeopathic profession of trying to ruin the college and declared that the pertinent question for them to consider was how long the legislature would go on supporting it amid such fault finding.

After the smoke faded Dean Obetz, his reputation cleared, resigned. The Regents promptly fired the rest of the homeopathic faculty. Then the profession persuaded the 1895 legislature to enact a law requiring the Regents to move the Homeopathic Medical College to Detroit. Although this had once been the devout wish of the Board of Regents, they now objected. Suit was brought to compel compliance with the law, and in a notable decision, 1896, the Michigan Supreme Court declared in plain, emphatic words that (1) the Regents and the legislature derive their powers from the same supreme authority, the constitution, and therefore neither can encroach on the other, and (2) the powers of the Board are defined in the constitution, whereas those of every other corporation provided for in the constitution are said to be such as the legislature shall give. Further, the power of "general supervision of the University" given to the Regents in the constitution is sufficient for their authority and excludes any subsequent directions for running the University from the legislature. This decision was delivered with great satisfaction by Justice Claudius B. Grant, '59, a former regent. It has not prevented later legislatures from attempting to issue directives to the University, but it has blocked their success.

The Regents' earlier acceptance of the Homeopathic Medical College had brought not peace but further legislative effort to dictate. Then the Board's stubborn refusal to go along with legislative directives, committee recommendations, lobbyists' pressures, or the advice of well-intentioned friends who could see no harm in accommodating insistent demands brought to a victorious end a forty-year struggle to preserve the constitutional autonomy of the Board. Faculty and students of the twentieth century have been the beneficiaries of the Regents' courageous stand, for the University emerged free to develop as the Board and faculty alone judged best. The same guarantee was repeated in the constitutions of 1908 and 1963.

Dr. W. B. Hinsdale, Cleveland Homeopathic Medical College '87, was appointed new dean of the Medical College in 1895, and he recruited a new faculty that inaugurated an era of peace in that school. Enrollment did not keep pace, however, since homeopathy as a theory of medicine steadily lost ground.

Engineering was organized as a separate department or college in 1895, with Professor Greene as dean. It had its own building in one of the old professor's houses, next to President Angell's. The University now had seven divisions or schools, and the annual budget passed $500,000.

Degrees were getting tougher to earn in law and dentistry, as a third year of instruction was required in 1897 and 1899, respectively. Library resources mounted until an enlargement of the stacks was made in 1899 to accommodate the 105,000 volumes; 28,000 volumes more were in the medical and law libraries. Regrettably, the increase was not owing to a steady and aggressive buying policy, but came largely from two bequests: the books of George S. Morris of the Philosophy Department, and those of Edward L. Walker of the Romance Languages Department. An innovation was the segregation of books to be read in conjunction with certain courses, or "reserve books," a practice that continues today. Somewhat reluctantly Librarian Davis let students take certain few books out of the building on loan in 1897. This radical experiment in circulation soon became standard practice.

One interesting development of the time was a fellowship in chemistry, given in 1895 by Parke-Davis Company of Detroit, which has continued the annual grant ever since and increased it to two fellowships. Similarly, Frederick Stearns Company gave a fellowship in pharmacy which continued until the company was sold.

Michigan's first large bequest came at this time. Dr. Elizabeth Bates of Port Chester, N.Y., died and left an estate that amounted to more than $100,000 to the University for a Bates Professorship of the Diseases of Women and Children. Dr. Bates was not an alumna; she was mo-

EMBRYOLOGY CLASS, 1893

tivated because Michigan was the first university to open its medical school to women.

Several distinguished appointments to the faculty were made at this time. Four instructors were appointed who were to gain fame as teachers and research authors: Max Winkler in German, Henry Sanders in Latin, Louis A. Strauss in English, and Dr. A. S. Warthin in pathology. Robert M. Wenley, Glasgow '95 PhD, arrived in 1896 as professor of philosophy and began a career of teaching and *bons mots* that rendered him immortal among his students. With him came Herbert C. Sadler, Glasgow '93, to be assistant professor of naval architecture and, eventually, to become dean of the Engineering College. Dr. Eliza Mosher, '75*m*, was called from practice to serve as professor of hygiene and first dean of women, now that there were 647 women students enrolled. Although she stayed only six years she made a deep impression. Victor H. Lane, '78*l*, resigned a judgeship in 1897 to become professor of law and earn the affection of his colleagues and many students. Appointments were few at this period because of the panic of 1893-94.

It was in 1899 that Charles H. Cooley, PhD '94, instructor in political economy, became assistant professor of sociology and inaugurated that discipline at Michigan. Where other sociologists had been somewhat superficial in their approach to this subject, Cooley (the son of Thomas M. Cooley) investigated society in depth, and his three books on social organization became classics that are still in print.

The Regents, working with a committee of the deans, prepared a program in conjunction with Commencement, 1896, to celebrate Angell's twenty-fifth anniversary as president. Numerous congratulations and good wishes poured in on him. He was a national figure in and out of education circles. Perhaps he prized most of all a warm letter from Alice Freeman Palmer, now retired from Wellesley, telling him how much he had meant to her for so long as mentor, colleague, and friend.

In spite of this almost universal adulation, there were murmurs among a few younger faculty members. They felt that the older members were not interested in research (they refused to count textbooks as examples), and that President Angell did not adequately recognize deep scholarship. Of course, he had had the prescience to hire them, but . . . . The broad fields of knowledge formerly encompassed by one professor, such as natural science, were being subdivided into specializations; research went deeper but was narrower in scope, and communication among faculty would grow accordingly more difficult. Undoubtedly, in this complaint there was the familiar impatience of younger scholars toward older ones.

In 1900 the Research Club was founded "to unite those members of the academic staff who are actively engaged in research and to originate and support such measures as are calculated to foster and advance research in the University"—in brief, to bring those who did research to the attention of the administration. This date is as close as any for marking a new dimension of the University: the responsibility for seeking newer knowledge in addition to the task of disseminating it. In one sense it was a coming of age, a new growth in the evolution of the University. The new responsibility did not diminish the old, but supplemented it. The University was now setting out to earn a new reputation as a research center. It would grow with the new century.

2. Athletics at the turn of the century

Athletics and physical education leaped to life in 1891. Joshua W. Waterman of Detroit offered $20,000 toward a gymnasium as a challenge for a like amount. Faculty and students were galvanized to action and by April had raised another $20,000. Plans were drawn for a gym, but the cost of construction was estimated at $60,000. The Regents decided to go ahead anyway, although construction proceeded slowly.

In the fall of 1891 the Athletic Association hired as part-time football coach one Mike Murphy, trainer at the Detroit Athletic Club, because the team played so badly. He was superseded by Frank Crawford, Yale '91, a former football player who was attending Michigan's Law School. Peter Conway, a National League pitcher at Pittsburgh, was hired to coach baseball. Track and tennis were the other major sports. (The first intercollegiate track meet was held in 1893, and Michigan won enough of the events to take the title. It won again five years later.) Hockey was popular in Canada, but not here, and basketball had just been invented. The Student Athletic Association, under its Board of Directors, managed all teams and games. The athletic program moved along satisfactorily for a couple of years, until it was discovered that two members of a University team were "subfreshmen"—evidently professionals recruited to bolster a weak team.

This incident prompted the University Senate, with concurrence of the Athletic Association, to create a Board in Control of Athletics of nine members: five professors and four students. The Senate could prescribe regulations. The Board was to determine eligibility of players, approve the hiring of coaches and trainers, arrange intercollegiate meets, and investigate charges of misconduct of players. In January 1894 the student Athletic Association dissolved and turned over its fund of $6000 to the Regents. Stands for spectators were erected at Regents Field.

Waterman Gymnasium was finally finished and equipped in the summer of 1894. Voluntary classes were organized, as no credit was granted for gym work. The students crowded the place, it being a novelty, long sought. Gym classes were made compulsory for freshmen in 1898 as a health measure, after it was discovered that students who needed exercise the most usually avoided it. Meanwhile, through a gift from Regent Levi Barbour, "65*l*, of Detroit a gymnasium for women was erected in 1896 and named for the donor.

In 1895 the presidents of seven midwestern universities met in Chicago to discuss means of controlling intercollegiate athletics, already succumbing to feverish efforts "to win." They devised a conference of faculty representatives, one from each participating institution, which met in 1896. Professor Albert H. Pattengill of Michigan's Board in Control

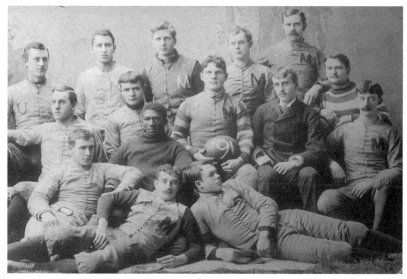

1890-91 FOOTBALL TEAM

joined with professors from Wisconsin, Minnesota, Illinois, Northwestern, Chicago, and Purdue to draw up some rules that would be observed by all the universities in this Western Conference. Thus, faculty regulation began, and the tempo of intercollegiate athletics increased. Indiana and Iowa were admitted to the Western Conference, and the phrase "Big 9" was heard.

Not everything went smoothly. In the spring of 1896 on the eve of a baseball game to decide the Conference championship, three Michigan players were found to have hired themselves out for a professional game, contrary to the new rule. They were immediately dropped from the team, and Michigan lost the game.

The Michigan Board in Control hired a manager of athletics in 1898 named Charles M. Baird, '95. That fall's football team won all its games, including the final one narrowly after a spectacular long run by a substitute player. The sensational play inspired a senior music student, Louis Elbel, to write "The Victors," Michigan's enduring and nationally known college song. It aroused a school spirit of almost visible strength. As a march it was played more frequently than the dignified and somber "The Yellow and the Blue," which had appeared in 1889 from the pen of Charles M. Gayley, '78, a professor of English, set to music from Balfe's "Pirates Chorus." The arrangement of "The Victors" for the Michigan band is unsurpassed, and no other band plays it with the same gusto. It is impossible to judge its musical merit because to Michigan students and alumni it is filled with delectable overtones.

Michigan compiled an impressive football record in the late 1890's, winning the Western Conference championship in 1898. In 1901 Baird brought to Michigan the highly successful coach at Stanford University. His name was Fielding H. Yost, West Virginia University Law School '97, but he loved football and boys who liked to play it. His first season in Ann Arbor was spectacular: his team went through a ten-game schedule undefeated. Not only that, the opponents never scored at all, while Michigan piled up a total of 550 points.

National excitement promoted a postseason game with Stanford. It was to be played on New Year's Day, 1902, in Pasadena at the invitation of the promoters of something called a Tournament of Roses. The Board in Control of Athletics did not have enough money to let Yost take more than fifteen boys west: the eleven regulars and four substitutes. They arrived in time for one practice after four days on the train. On New Year's afternoon the temperature stood at 85°. The change in drinking water had left the Michigan squad feeling queasy. The field was, of all things, dusty. The game was to be played in thirty-five-minute halves, and Stanford paraded forty husky players. At the end of the half the score was 37 to 0. Michigan had simply marched over and through and around the Stanford team, substitutes and all. The Stanford coach was willing to quit, but after a rest the game was resumed. By the middle of the second half, the score was 49 to 0, and the Stanford coach waved his boys off the field. The game was never finished.

Western Conference rules soon prohibited postseason games. Michigan did not go back to the Rose Bowl until New Year's Day 1948, when Coach "Fritz" Crisler found the University of Southern California the opponent. The score? Again 49 to 0, Michigan.

The football season of 1902 left Michigan undefeated, and the opponents making only twelve points altogether. It was the same story in 1903 and 1904. At the end of the Minnesota game in 1903, someone purloined Michigan's water jug, and it ended up in the Minnesota trophy room. Michigan did not meet Minnesota again until 1909 when, after winning the game, Michigan carried home in triumph "the little brown jug." It has been the trophy of the two universities ever since.

In the last game of the 1905 season, Chicago beat Michigan 2 to 0. But such a record over five years elevated Michigan football players to campus gods. Visibly and undeniably, they were "The Victors." Their appearance was imitated by the lesser mortals on campus: turtleneck sweaters or suit jackets with padded shoulders, and "chrysanthemum" mops of hair useful as skull padding.

Yost was ingenious at devising deceptive plays for his so-called "point-a-minute" teams. He drilled his boys without let-up and earned the nickname of "Hurry-Up" Yost. He wrote a book called *Football for Player and Spectator.* He encouraged the band to participate in home games. Football was the great fall sport. Dexter M. Ferry, wealthy seedsman of Detroit, bought seventeen acres adjoining Regents Field on South State Street and gave it to the University to enlarge the athletic grounds. The whole area was renamed Ferry Field.

In track events the coaching was done by Keene Fitzpatrick. Michigan won the Big 9 meet in 1901 and for four straight years.

The situation of athletics again required President Angell's attention after the 1905 football season. Across the nation eighteen players had died, and President Roosevelt threatened to abolish the game by executive order. The old plagues of overemphasis, unnecessary roughness, and professionalism recurred. Angell called a special meeting of the Western Conference faculty representatives in Chicago in January 1906. Professor Pattengill submitted Angell's suggestions for a drastic revision of athletic control. In the meeting the most radical positions were taken by Michigan, Chicago, and Wisconsin. The latter two even wanted to abolish football for two years to cool the fever.

After deliberation the Conference called for changes in the rules of football to remove brutality. If a satisfactory game could he provided, then certain restrictions on participation were proposed: (1) no student could play until he had been in residence a year (an effective blockade against recruiting professionals or star players at other universities), and he could not play for more than three years, (2) no more than five intercollegiate games should be scheduled each season, (3) no more training tables, (4) players must be doing satisfactory academic work in a full course of studies, (5) no coaching except by regularly appointed staff whose salaries should not be more than other faculty members of the same rank received, (6) no preliminary practice sessions before college opened, (7) admission fees to students should not be more than fifty cents, and (8) expenses of games should be reduced and any surplus should be devoted to university improvements.

These recommendations produced an uproar when made public. Students at Michigan greeted them with a "storm of indignation," largely out of fear that Yost would be dropped. They were also dismayed to learn for the first time that President Angell's recommendations underlay the conference reforms. The faculty Senate approved the recommendations with two exceptions: the University had a four-year contract with Yost, who was not a regular faculty member, and the prohibition of more than three years' eligibility should not affect current players. The Senate went on to resolve that all paid coaches should be abolished at all universities after existing contracts expired.

The Conference representatives met again in March and would not accept Michigan's reservation which would allow juniors who had already played three years of football to play during their senior year. They did endorse the idea that paid coaches be dismissed as their contracts expired. Unfortunately for Michigan, Professor Pattengill died suddenly after this meeting. His place was taken by Professor Victor H. Lane of the Law Department, who was also president of the Alumni Association.

The 1906 season was played under new rules that introduced the forward pass, opened up the game, and reduced injuries. The game was more interesting to watch. When Lane attended the postseason Conference meeting, he transmitted the wishes of Michigan's Board in Control of Athletics to eliminate the retroactive eligibility clause, to increase the schedule from five to seven games, and to establish a uniform date for opening practice. Chicago, Indiana, Iowa, and Illinois voted with Michigan for these changes, but the necessary two-thirds vote failed on the first two proposals.

The rejection aroused both students and some alumni of Michigan. Several prominent players, naturally, including the new captain, were juniors who had already played three years of football. They would not be eligible for the 1907 season. The same conditions affected other sports. Of course, this rule applied to the other universities too, but somehow

Michigan seemed to feel discriminated against. The immediate disadvantage obstructed the long view, and student leaders with ardent alumni who should have known better began to agitate for Michigan's withdrawl from the Western Conference. They naively believed that the other members would go on playing Michigan.

The Regents refused to take action, but informally recommended withdrawal to the Board in Control. That body declined to take such a responsibility and referred the matter to the faculty Senate. The Senate resented the fact that the Regents had voiced an opinion at all and passed a resolution expressing "the hope that the Regents will deem it wise to leave the regulation of student athletics with the Senate or its representatives" and "hereby expresses its confidence in the judgment of the Board in Control of Athletics."

Nevertheless, Regent Fletcher, whose son was one of the student leaders advocating withdrawal, introduced at the next Board meeting a resolution for withdrawal. It was defeated only by a tie vote. Two weeks later the Board voted against withdrawal, but declared that the University would obey Conference rules only in Conference games, not in games with universities outside the Conference. This effort to play by two sets of eligibility rules did not meet favor with the other Conference members, and spring baseball games were canceled.

In October 1907 the Regents acted foolishly and autocratically. They abolished the faculty Board in Control of Athletics, created a new Board whose personnel and duties were specified, and then declared the new Board responsible to the faculty! This manipulation was another violation of Western Conference regulations. The new Board consisted of four professors, two students, and one alumnus. At the end of January 1908 Michigan was dropped from the Western Conference—and rightly so.

The results were predestined. In scheduling games Michigan had to look to the East and South. Teams in those regions had rarely been in the same class with Michigan; why should they now schedule a game which would mean almost certain defeat? After Minnesota played Michigan, the Western Conference prohibited members from matches with the Maize and Blue. Only Ohio State, not yet in the Conference, was available as an opponent in this region. The whole athletic program dropped off noticeably, and attendance diminished. Alumni in the Middle West began to complain because they never had an opportunity to see the Michigan team. New classes of students wondered why their predecessors had been so shortsighted. Only the new Board in Control remained adamant and complained bitterly because the Western Conference boycotted Michigan.

3. The University enters a new Century

The University entered the new century with an enrollment of 3303, 54 percent from Michigan. Women were 20 percent of the total, but they were almost half of the enrollment in the Literary Department. After much argument, the Literary faculty reduced the several baccalaureate degrees to one: the bachelor of arts, effective in 1901. The classicists argued that an A.B. degree had always meant a proficiency in Greek and Latin and should continue to do so; the granting of an A.B. to students who had never studied the "dead" languages was a victory for the advocates of modern languages and literatures. It was the culmination of the movement started by President Tappan. Michigan was not alone in this decision, but was following a widespread trend. However, the bachelor of science degree was soon restored for those students majoring in science and mathematics.

Only freshman English remained a required course; students were allowed to elect other courses from three of ten prescribed fields. As a result, enrollment in Greek, Latin, and mathematics declined, while history and German gained.

The Law Building enlarged again to accommodate a thousand students, a figure never achieved. In 1902 the department launched a monthly magazine called the *Michigan Law Journal,* at the suggestion of a student. Gustavus A. Ohlinger, '02*l.* It became the faculty-student edited *Michigan Law Review.* Perhaps the more exciting development in law teaching was the institution of a "practice court," in which students argued cases under faculty "judges " and gained practical experience in pleading and procedure. All seniors had to take the course.

The Medical Department continued to earn fame. When John D. Rockefeller established ten fellowships for advanced medical research, he gave two of them to Michigan's faculty members.

The Mosely Commission from Great Britain inspected the University in 1903 and gave an enthusiastic report on what it termed "the oldest and most famous of the State universities." Perhaps their comment was no exaggeration, for in the same year Angell pointed out that for the first time the University had students from every state in the Union and from all territories except Alaska. As was customary, the largest number of out-of-state students came from Illinois, Ohio, Indiana, New York, and Pennsylvania.

After twelve years as professor of education ("the science and art of teaching"), Burke A. Hinsdale died in 1900. He was succeeded by the man he had succeeded—by the return of William H. Payne from his less congenial post as chancellor of the University of Nashville. Dr. Taft was relieved of his duties as dean of the Dentistry Department in June 1903, shortly before his death. He was eighty-three years old and had opened the school as dean in 1875. Mrs. Myra Jordan followed Dr. Mosher as dean of women in 1902. Harrison M. Randall, '93, PhD '02, was made instructor in physics in 1901, beginning a long and distinguished career that lasted till 1941, after which a physics laboratory was named for him.

Claude H. Van Tyne, '96, PhD Pennsylvania '00, came to Michigan in 1903 as assistant professor of history. Regent William L. Clements of Bay City, who was collecting source books on American history, began to turn to him increasingly for advice on the colonial era. Henry M. Bates, '90, Northwestern '92*l*, was appointed professor of law in 1903. In the same year a graduate student from Iowa was appointed assistant in zoology at $150. He was interested particularly in snakes and was working on a doctor's degree, which he won in 1906. His name was Alexander Grant Ruthven, and in twenty-six years he would assume the presidency of the University.

Also in 1903 instruction in forestry was resumed with the appointment of Filibert Roth, '90, as professor. While a student he had been employed as janitor of the Museum, then worked for the U. S. Department of Agriculture, and later had taught at Cornell. The state of Michigan was also interested in improving and preserving its remaining woodlands and in reforestation "if it proves practicable." Professor Roth demonstrated that reforestation was not only practicable but desirable, and when given a state appointment as forestry warden in 1904 he started a tree planting program. Five years later the federal government set aside two national forest preserves. Regent Arthur Hill of Saginaw was inspired to give an eighty-acre tract, called the Saginaw Forest, on the west side of Ann Arbor to the University. Out of the combined interest and facilities grew the School of Natural Resources.

At the urging of several life insurance companies Michigan offered the first courses in actuarial science in 1902 under Professor James W. Glover of the Mathematics Department. No other university gave such courses. Glover taught the "theory of annuities and insurance" and the "mathematics of insurance and statistics," which insurance company officers were sent here to study.

A Pasteur Institute was established in the Medical Department to treat victims of mad dogs, another service to the state; no longer did Michigan residents have to travel to Chicago or New York to receive treatment. In the first six months, twenty-three bitten persons were aided. A bequest from Mrs. A. B. Palmer added a ward to University Hospital for the care of children, as a memorial to her husband. A psychopathic ward was also under construction through a special appropriation of the legislature. The new stone Medical Building was completed in 1903 next door to the old one.

The large West Engineering Building was also well along in 1903 at the corner of South University and East University, with a distinctive

NEW (WEST) ENGINEERING BUILDING

archway over the Diagonal walk that emerged at this point. In addition, it contained a naval-testing tank, the first one in any university and the only one outside the Washington Naval Yard.

In connection with all this building, the names of A. B. Pond, '80, and his brother I. K. Pond, '79, eminent Chicago architects, recur. Former Ann Arbor boys, they were known as "Abie" and "Ikey." The talents of Albert Kahn of Detroit were also beginning to be used.

The period of 1890 to 1910 was one of slow growth in the University Library, when it should have been rapid in order to meet the expanding curriculum and rising enrollment. To accommodate more students the Library was rearranged internally so as to increase its seating capacity by 50 percent. Librarian Davis reported that although the Library was not as large as several other universities boasted, he was convinced that its use surpassed others. "The characteristic of the Ann Arbor student is the reading habit," he asserted. Davis retired in 1905 after twenty-eight years as librarian and was succeeded by Theodore W. Koch, brought from the Library of Congress. Davis had seen the University collections reach 200,000 volumes.

In the climate of rising interest in research, Professor Francis W. Kelsey of the Latin Department urged the Regents in 1900 to sponsor publication of a series of works to be written by certain professors. The Regents referred the matter to a committee. Hearing nothing further, Kelsey persuaded the University Senate in 1902 to consider the matter of establishing a series of University studies. Later in the year the Senate agreed that it was expedient for the University to issue volumes from time to time when worthy manuscripts were available, and that Professor Kelsey had such a manuscript. Nothing was said about where the money was to come from, but that problem was solved by donations.

The first volume in what was called *University of Michigan Studies*,

Humanistic Series, was authorized in 1903 and appeared the next year. The specific work was Professor Henry A. Sanders' *Roman Historical Sources and Institutions*. The Regents appropriated $500 to publish a second volume in 1906. A university press was thus launched uncertainly. Later on a History and Political Science Series, a Scientific Series, and a Language and Literature Series were added.

The Engineering Department suffered the loss of Dean Greene by death late in 1903. To fill his place as second dean, the Regents turned to Professor Mortimer E. Cooley, an urbane, witty mechanical engineer and naval officer. He held the position until his retirement in 1928. Similarly, the Pharmacy Department lost Dean Prescott early in 1905; he had held the title since the school was established in 1876. He was succeeded by Professor Julius O. Schlotterbeck, '87*p*, PhD Bern '96.

In 1904 the Michigan Federation of Women's Clubs gave $3000 as first payment on a fund to be called the Lucinda Hinsdale Stone Loan and Scholarship Fund. How many students needed help? President Angell provided a revealing statistic for the year 1906-7 when he found that 1200 of the 4300 students were earning part or all of their expenses.

Professor William J. Hussey '89*e*, was made director of the Observatory in 1904 and began work to enlarge it. A new 37-inch telescope was ordered. William H. Hobbs, PhD Hopkins '88, was appointed professor of geology in 1906, starting a long career here as teacher and Arctic explorer. Professor Arthur Fairbanks resigned as professor of Greek to become director of the Boston Museum of Fine Arts, and Professor Campbell Bonner, PhD Harvard '00, was named to succeed him.

Dr. and Mrs. Walter H. Nichols gave the University thirty acres of land on the east side of town in 1906 to be developed as a botanical garden. It adjoined twenty-three acres purchased by the city for a park. It was agreed that no fence would separate them, and so began the University Arboretum which many couples remember fondly. The Arboretum was also to serve instruction in landscape design. It was no coincidence that the Regents decided at the same time to resume a curriculum in architecture, it having once been offered in 1876. Instruction was attached to the Engineering School. Professor Emil Lorch, A.M. Harvard '03, was appointed the first chairman and professor.

4. Campus life at the end of the Angell Era

The King and Franklin Circus, playing Ann Arbor in May 1892 attracted about three hundred students who tried to "rush" the evening performance. The ensuing fight was a stand-off with the roustabouts and canvasmen. The audience fled; policemen, firemen, and President Angell were called; and fire hoses were turned on the fighters. A sideshow tent was burned. The students retired happy, feeling they had vindicated Michigan "honor" after being "attacked" merely because they had exercised a traditional "right" to rush a gate. The police could not follow such logic and arrested several students; Angell appeared in court to offer bail for them. Money was collected to pay damages, and no more circuses visited Ann Arbor for years.

Teddy Roosevelt, military hero and governor of New York, spoke in Ann Arbor in 1899 on the responsibilities of individuals in a democracy. Energetic, flamboyant, and personable, he aroused the students over opportunities to express themselves. Later appeared Carrie Nation, with upraised hatchet, warning the students of perilous temptations, the worst of which was liquor. She spoke in the open air at the corner of State and North University. As was her custom she called for a bottle of beer in order to smash it by way of vivid emphasis. Dutifully, a solemn student carried forward a bottle and handed it up to her. With one blow of her ubiquitous hatchet, she broke it. Then Carrie retreated, and her audience scattered. The bottle had been filled with hydrogen disulphide—the "rotten egg" compound familiar to all beginning chemistry students. In between these two representative Americans appeared a young British journalist early in 1901 showing lantern slides of South Africa and the Boer War. An interesting fellow with a slight lisp, his name was Winston Churchill.

After 1892 and the King and Franklin Circus trouble Angell rarely commented on student behavior in his annual reports. Fall hazing of freshmen and class rushes went on in spite of faculty disapproval. There was kidnapping of class officers and forced haircuts. A Student Council in 1905 tried to regulate this rowdyism by arranging interclass games on a day in late October which would signal the end of that year's hazing. The games included a tug of war across the Huron River, push ball, and climbing a greased flag pole.

When the senior lits decided to wear their caps and gowns for the first time to chapel in May (1894), followed by a parade called "Swing-out," the law seniors declined to participate. They went on to deride Swing-out by holding a burlesque parade, once in their nightshirts. Dean Hutchins' appeals for dignity made no impression. Finally, in 1907 after a dozen years of disorderliness, the senior laws voted to wear caps and gowns and participate in Swing-out. The rebellion was over, with no more reason than when it began.

Lit-Law rivalry, often tested in class football, went out of bounds in November 1900. After the junior lits beat the senior laws in football, some group late that night painted the front of the new Law Building red—almost the color of Dean Hutchins' face when he beheld the vandalism. Appeals were made for information on the culprits, but nobody would talk. The junior class wrote to the Regents disclaiming any responsibility. The perpetrators never were discovered. As the paint readily penetrated the soft sandstone, it never could be completely removed.

Two hangouts for students downtown gained fame at this time. Foremost was Joe Parker's saloon at 204 South Main Street, between

FROSH-SOPH GAMES, 1907

Washington and Liberty. Later, Parker bought the Catalpa Inn at the corner of Fourth and Ann Streets. He was careful to keep out freshmen, as the upperclassmen demanded, but was not always successful in excluding other students under twenty-one. His back room was filled with tables on which students carved their initials, class numerals, emblems, and even football scores. When Joe's was full, the overflow washed down the street to the Oriental Bar, in the block across from the courthouse. A song, written in 1913, perpetuates and probably exaggerates the importance of both places:

> *I want to go back to Michigan*
> *To dear Ann Arbor town;*
> *Back to Joe's and the Orient,*
> *Back to some of the money I spent . . . .*

At the same time more campus activities developed to absorb the time of students. From 1891 to 1909 was the period not only of intercollegiate athletic growth, but of the proliferation of sororities and fraternities, the Michigan Union movement, the establishment of various honor societies, the rise of student publications, and the organization of music and dramatics. University life became all-encompassing. There was hardly time for deviltry or lawlessness.

The student newspaper became a daily of four pages in 1890. The first editors were independents, or antifraternity men, elected annually by the subscribers, who formed the membership of the Independent Association. Organized and independent men had cooperated for years in editing the *Chronicle* until in 1889 the nonfraternity editors resigned and formed a new association to publish the *U. of M. Daily*. Its success killed the *Chronicle* in 1891 and gradually fraternity men were allowed on the staff of the *Daily*. It took courage to launch a daily, but by publishing University news with a heavy emphasis on athletics it won wide acceptance. It also achieved delivery before breakfast, and the University began to use it for general announcements. Steadily, the *Daily* increased its column length until by the turn of the century it was the largest student newspaper in the country.

Some faculty members were disturbed by the paper's complete independence and its critical tone toward professors and the University. In 1903 the publishing Association sold the *Daily* to the University Senate, which had created a Board in Control of Student Publications consisting of four professors and three students. If censorship was hoped for or feared, the Board under the leadership of Professor Fred N. Scott made clear that it had no such intention. It selected the senior editors and set the boundaries of taste, but within the broad permissible area the student editors were free to exercise responsibility; otherwise, student readers would lose faith in the *Daily* if they felt it were managed by the faculty.

1890 also marked the birth of the *Inlander*, the first successful literary magazine. It published many short works of merit before expiring in 1907, to be revived in the 1920's. The *Inlander* was followed in 1909 by a new literary magazine called *Gargoyle*, which soon devoted itself to campus humor. With great variation in quality, as talent appeared and disappeared, and occasional lapses in publication, *Gargoyle* is still appearing.

The *Michigan Technic* began as an annual of the Engineering School in 1887 and grew slowly into a semiannual, a quarterly, and finally a monthly. The chief yearbook of the University was the *Michiganensianian*, which has appeared every year since 1897. It succeeded two rival annuals published in the middle of the school year by fraternity and nonfraternity groups. The *Michiganensian* passed under the Board in Control in 1906, and its pattern of senior pictures, organization group pictures, athletic scenes, etc., early became set.

These publications, and other short-lived ones, appealed to many student writers, who put in unmeasured hours on their staffs. By and large they were the largest outlet for extracurricular activity outside of athletics. Third in appeal were musical organizations.

The Men's Glee Club, after several sporadic appearances, was revived in 1884 and has continued without a break. When Professor Stanley became director in 1890, the club acquired professional polish and a national reputation. Long concert tours were arranged with alumni groups in various cities. Far in the future lay European trips and recordings. The Women's Glee Club, organized in 1902, gained distinction under the direction of Professor Nora Crane Hunt, who conducted for nearly thirty years. The group grew from seventeen to seventy members and eventually gave concerts in other Michigan cities.

Student bands sprang up informally whenever a group of enthusiastic instrumentalists got together. A volunteer group appeared at football games in the 1880's. The first genuine University Band seems to have been organized in 1896, under a student director. It began playing regularly at the football games in 1897 and numbered thirty men. The Athletic

Association raised money for uniforms, and the Band even played for Athletic Association dances in Waterman Gymnasium. A bandstand was erected on campus in 1909 for spring concerts. The next year the Regents gave money to the Band on condition it furnish the music required during Commencement week.

Dramatics formed another outlet for activity. Student plays were not unknown before 1896, but by the organization of the Comedy Club that year a regular program of plays was insured annually by a continuing and rather exclusive group based on competitive tryouts. The Club enjoyed a great success until the Depression lowered its curtain. A somewhat similar venture involving both dramatics and music was the growth of the Junior Women's Play, first offered in 1904, into an annual production of a student-written revue with an all-women cast.

A variety of honor societies was organized in the first decade of this century to recognize excellence in attainment in several fields of activity. Michigamua (1901) was for senior men holding leading positions in athletics, publica-

J-HOP COMMITTEE

tions, student government, the Michigan Union, interfraternity council, or scholastic societies. Each spring they selected the juniors who would succeed them and offered a public initiation in Indian style. Sigma Xi, a national society formed to further scientific research, organized a Michigan chapter in 1903, which was open to both men and women. The Barrister's Society (1904), a senior honorary society for the Law School, became largely social in activity. The Vulcans (1904), an honorary society for engineers, emphasized scholarship and activity. Mortar Board (1906), a national honorary society for women, was organized by senior women at Michigan, Cornell, Ohio State, and Swarthmore. Sphinx (1906), a society for junior men, emphasized activities. Tau Beta Pi, a national engineering society, organized a chapter at Michigan in 1906. Membership in Triangle (1907), an engineering society for juniors, was based on extracurricular activities. Alpha Omega Alpha, a national medical society, founded a chapter at Michigan in 1907. Druids (1909), a senior honorary society for men of the Literary College, was based on services to the University.

Phi Beta Kappa, the best known national honorary society, did not have a Michigan chapter until 1907 because Michigan did not have a marking or grading system beyond "passed," "not passed," or "conditioned." Mortar Board helped petition the faculty to establish a chapter. Membership was based on the scholarship and character of senior men and women. Some sort of grading had to be instituted to identify the best students, and gradually the marking system of A to E was accepted. Although the lack of a marking system prevented a scramble for grades as such, it also was felt to engender a satisfaction with minimum work because nothing more was recognized.

It was Michigamua which initiated action at the end of 1903 to form a Union to bring together all the men students, increase their acquaintance with one another, and provide a center for various activities—social, athletic, and educational. It is worth noting that the most aristocratic of the honorary societies worked hardest for the most democratic of campus organizations. As early as 1892 *The Daily* was complaining that there was no way for Michigan students to get acquainted outside of fraternities and church groups. The passage of another decade intensified the problem as enrollment increased. Michigamuan Edward F. Parker, '04, is credited with the idea for a Michigan Union and was responsible for arousing student and faculty enthusiasm. The name bore no reference to a labor organization, but was taken from the student organizations at English universities. Professor Henry M. Bates of the Law Department drew up articles of association, and a board of directors was chosen. Parker was elected secretary. Alumni, faculty, and Regents were invited to participate.

The Michigan Union was an early unifying force and coordinating agency in the student body. Class elections were held under its auspices, a student council was set up, and the Union established a fund to buy an oil portrait of President Angell. A clubhouse or headquarters building was projected, for which there was no precedent on any other campus. The board of directors wanted a place for meals and snacks, for reading and talking, for organization and committee meetings, for billiards and games, for swimming and bowling, for dancing and assemblies, and for overnight guests. The idea aroused the enthusiasm of both students and alumni. A large and expensive building would be necessary, but no one was daunted by the cost. It is difficult to recall today, when the Michigan Union hardly attracts a second glance, what a challenging and exciting prospect its realization was. It was an extremely healthy enterprise for the campus.

When a campaign for building funds opened, the alumni were still raising money for a memorial building, and for a while the two projects tended to be confused. But the alumni tapered off their campaign after 1907 and ceased three years later. Meanwhile, in 1907 the Union campaign had raised enough money to purchase the house of Thomas M. Cooley on

State Street and remodel it for a clubhouse. Then each Union member was charged dues of $2.50 a year to maintain it. Membership, which was voluntary, began to rise. Since women students had parlors in Barbour Gym, they were felt to have a social headquarters. The Union committee sponsored a carnival and two minstrel shows and appealed to alumni for contributions.

In 1908 the Michigan Union sponsored the first of the famous Michigan Union Operas—musical comedies, actually, with book and music written by students, produced by students, and acted (including the female roles) by men students. They traveled widely during the Christmas vacation period. Up to 1927 the successive annual operas earned $125,000 for the Union after paying all expenses. More than that, these operas were responsible for some of Michigan's best-loved and most popular songs—songs which are no longer remembered as opera numbers but are associated with the University at large.

Angell reported in 1907 that the past year had been quiet. "The silly and sometimes dangerous amusement of 'haircutting' was omitted, and the friendly contests of the two lower classes in the trials of strength and cunning were carried on under supervision of upperclassmen and under regulations. This prevented serious bodily injuries and bad blood. For these reforms we are largely indebted to the organization known as the Student Council, composed of men elected by the body of students to secure the wise management of their affairs. I take pleasure in testifying to the great good sense and the excellent spirit with which they have carried on their work."

Then came the Star Theater riot of 1908. Located on East Washington Street, close to Main Street, this entertainment house offered moving pictures and vaudeville. One night in March student patrons persisted in heckling performers and whistling after the manager warned them to be quiet. A group was ejected by force. The manager announced that his theater was for townspeople and he did not care for student patronage. On the following Monday night, March 16, almost a thousand students gathered in front of the theater and began throwing eggs and vegetables at it. Then they hurled bricks from a building site across the street, and finally invaded the theater and tore out the seats. The fire department was called, President Angell and Dean Hutchins were called, and eighteen students were jailed. Charges were dropped after the student body contributed over $1000 for the damage done. President Angell never mentioned the incident in his next report.

The University was well into its Golden Age—or so it seems in retrospect. The two decades before World War I seem to have generated the most intense University spirit (reflected for decades in the class reunions) and the great joy in being college students in blissful suspension between home protection and adult responsibilities. For a four-year period they could be frenzied athletic fans, earnest fraternity members, extravagant dressers, admirers of honorary societies, singers of sentimental college ballads, chanters of college yells, and devotees of class activities. It may have been an innocent and unsophisticated era (they didn't think so, of course) that was finally shattered by the ugliness of the

STUDENT ROOMS IN THE 1890s

World War, but the classes reveled in their comparative freedom and thoroughly enjoyed their ivy retreat from hustling reality. Alumni from that period all seemed a bit different from later graduates, or at least succeeded in convincing their juniors that college life in the early years possessed an ineluctable charm that was somehow lost after the war.

J-HOP, 1911

5. *Closing years of the Angell era*

The minutes of the Board of Regents record an exhausting succession of minor decisions as to other University business in the first decade of this century, much of it relating to building: awarding contracts of all kinds, buying coal, purchasing various kinds of equipment, approving trivial additions to the budget, making hospital regulations, considering locks on some doors, receiving gifts and acknowledging them, and on and on. Obviously more top-level administrators were needed to handle many of these matters routinely according to prescribed procedures, if the Regents were ever to find time to sit back and discuss changing educational philosophy or view the University as a whole rather than as an agglomeration of small moving parts. But they were long committed to a three-man administration of president, secretary, and treasurer who needed approval from working committees of the Regents.

Members of the Board almost panicked in January 1905 when President Angell resigned, having turned seventy-six. Mrs. Angell had died two years earlier, and the twentieth century was bearing down on his mid-Victorian outlook. In virtual instantaneous unanimity, the Regents refused to accept his letter and offered instead to hire more help for him. From long habits of responsibility Angell could not delegate his duties easily, and the committee setup of the Regents precluded independent action. The Regents did not see the implications of a University enrollment that in 1890 had doubled over the 1870 figure, tripled in 1895, and would quadruple it in 1906.

The Board now contained several men who were closing out long and active terms. Dr. Herman Kiefer of Detroit, German-born and educated, finished thirteen years of service in 1902 during which time he had been a pillar of strength to both medical schools and applied great wisdom to their problems. Roger W. Butterfield, Princeton '66, Michigan '68*l*, was a Grand Rapids attorney and furniture company president, who ended sixteen years on the Board in 1904. Levi Barbour, '65*l*, whose gift for a women's gymnasium has already been noted, ended twelve years of service in 1908. Later he would build a dormitory and set up scholarships for Asian women. Henry S. Dean, Ann Arbor business man, was a Civil War veteran who had been colonel of the 22nd Michigan Infantry. He spent fourteen years on the Board after 1894 and was seventy-eight when he retired. Frank W. Fletcher, already mentioned, from Alpena, served from 1894 to 1910.

Two new faces in 1907 and 1909 belonged to men who would set new records of tenure. Walter H. Sawyer, '84*m*, of Hillsdale, succeeded to Dr. Kiefer's responsibility as guardian of the medical schools. He served twenty-four years, to the end of 1930. Junius E. Beal, Ann Arbor editor, succeeded Dean as the local regent and remained for four terms, or thirty-two years, until the end of 1939.

By 1907, as mentioned above, the alumni had raised $132,000 for a memorial building dedicated to former students who had served in the Civil War and in the Spanish-American War. This sum was still short of the goal, so the Regents added $50,000 in order that ground could be broken. Besides serving as headquarters for the Alumni Association, the new building would house the University art collection, which was taking up needed space in the Library. The Regents felt expansive, perhaps because the legislature had raised the mill tax from one-fourth to one-third of a mill. Alumni Memorial Hall, as it was finally named, was dedicated in 1910

The University Senate had taken a needed step in 1905 regarding the finances of student organizations. Charges and rumors of private profiteering had circulated around campus for too long. The Senate ordered all student organizations to submit their financial records for audit and continuous supervision. The Senate also changed the University calender. Thanksgiving and Christmas recesses were shortened, registration was delayed a week in the fall, and Commencement was postponed a week in June. It also created a Senate Council, made up of the president, the Literary Department dean and two professors, and one professor from each of the other departments. The Council was to consider questions to be laid before the whole Senate or before the Board of Regents.

Under the impetus of the Progressive movement, the voters of Michigan called for a convention to write a new state constitution. It met from October 1907 to February 1908, and in contrast to the 1850 convention was dominated by Republicans, not of Progressive persuasion. Professor John A. Fairlie of the Political Science Department was a delegate and introduced the system of home rule for cities. Hoped for provisions to permit women to vote and to institute the right of popular initiative and referendum to make laws or repeal them did not materialize. Much of the document was a revision of the old constitution and its amendments. The article dealing with the University was unchanged except to give the Board of Regents exclusive control of all University funds—the old land interest funds, legislative appropriations, student fees, gifts, bequests, etc. The Michigan Agricultural College was also given constitutional status, like the University.

The Angell administration began to break up. Harrison Soule, treasurer since 1882, resigned in 1908. Within a few months, James H. Wade, secretary for twenty-five years, followed Soule into retirement. He was succeeded by Shirley W. Smith, '97, who held the position until his retirement in 1945. The faculty financial outlook was suddenly brightened in 1908 when Andrew Carnegie extended his pension fund to include state universities. His philanthropy permitted the University to recommend for pensions those retiring professors who had taught for twenty-five years or those who had become disabled. Widows of veteran professors were also eligible to receive pensions. The plan became contributory on the part of the University and faculty as an insurance program and made possible a definite retirement age.

In January 1909 President Angell observed his eightieth birthday anniversary. Although still vigorous and mentally alert, he was feeling the physical burden of higher enrollment and proliferation of faculty. More strongly than ever, he believed the University should be consigned to younger hands. He may well have felt that he had earned relief. At the Regents' meeting in February he again submitted his resignation, to take effect in June. His intention to do so must have been known to a few Regents, because Regent Knappen promptly submitted a long and complimentary resolution accepting the resignation and designating Angell president emeritus with a continuing salary, or pension, of $4000 and permission to remain in the President's House. Angell was touched and grateful, and the parting was amicable and warm. He had completed thirty-eight years as president, a longer term than anyone else has filled. He had outlasted all his presidential colleagues except Eliot of Harvard, who, five years younger, held on one more year.

Angell possessed an almost charismatic charm for Regents, state legislators, Michigan citizens, faculty members, and students alike. Fortunately, this persuasiveness was coupled with great wisdom in educational matters, if not great originality. His greatest impact was on the students. Inevitably, the University prospered and achieved considerable renown under his steady guidance. It had also grown too large to carry the impress of a person. He was almost the last of the great educators whose campus kingdoms reflected the man; he would be impossible to follow in the father image because the nature of the job was changing. His successor inevitably must adjust to presiding over a group of enclaves governed by deans, and his principal responsibility would be to see that they moved in harmony, each strengthening the others and all benefiting a diverse student body. It would be a lonely post, for the Regents would be continually absorbed in meeting demands for more buildings, increased funds, and larger faculties.

ANGELL AND HUTCHINS

CAMPUS IN 1908, WITH THE FUTURE ALUMNI MEMORIAL HALL INCLUDED

CHAPTER SEVEN

HUTCHINS
AND WORLD WAR I

THE SEARCH FOR A SUCCESSOR to President Angell was an important responsibility, as the Regents well knew. Their initial reaction was to find another man with a name nationally recognized. Dean Hutchins was sent East to sound out first the governor of New York, Charles Evans Hughes, a Columbia-trained lawyer who had taught under Hutchins at Cornell Law School. Governor Hughes was flattered, but said that after his term he should go back to his law practice rather than venture into a field that was new to

HARRY B. HUTCHINS

him. There was no intimation, of course, that he would be a candidate for President of the United States, or a secretary of state, or a distinguished chief justice of the United States Supreme Court.

The summer of 1909 began without a likely candidate, and the executive committee of the Board of Regents in early August named Dean Hutchins as acting president for one year. During this period of grace the Regents approached Woodrow Wilson, president of Princeton University, but he was under pressure to run for governor of New Jersey. They also considered David Jayne Hill, former president of the University of Rochester and who was then ambassador to Germany, but he would not give up his diplomatic post. In June 1910 the Board concluded to make Hutchins president for a term of three years. Regent Chase Osborn held a stormy interview with Hutchins before their good sense and good humor prevailed. Hutchins was now sixty-three, and he agreed to accept the position for a term of five years. At the end of that time the Regents implored him to continue, and he stayed at the helm another five years, until 1920.

1. The prewar years

Michigan's enrollment of 1910-11 of 5339 made it the third ranking university in size, surpassed by Columbia and Chicago. Harvard was fourth. Three years later Michigan's registration of 5620 was not as heavy a gain as that of others; it was now exceeded by Columbia, California, Chicago, and Harvard.

The Hutchins decade saw the United States enter a great World War, more upsetting to the campus than the Civil War. His achievements in education, therefore, came before 1917 and should be considered apart from the military derangement of normal activities. If he had any special educational philosophy beyond faith in the University, he did not enunciate it. Where it should have appeared, of course, was in his annual reports, but he wrote none during his ten years. The fact that the Regents' *Proceedings* show no call for a report suggests that not rendering an annual report may have been a precondition of his accepting the presidency.

Hutchins was fortunate in the caliber of Regents with whom he worked. Although they were not educators, they were devoted to the University, reasonable in their attitudes and arguments, and judicious in apportioning and spending the monies made available to them. They trusted one another, were free of pettiness, and had no feuds. All but two were alumni.

Regent Walter Sawyer, a physician, continued, giving much time to the Medical and Dental schools. Regent Osborn resigned in 1911 to run for governor and was succeeded by Lucius L. Hubbard of Houghton, a scholar. He was a graduate of Harvard and held a PhD from the University of Bonn as well as a law degree from Boston University. A noted geologist, he was another collector of rare books, some of which were given to the University Library. Gentle and kindly by nature, he knew the pleasures and discipline of learning. He undertook to codify all the bylaws passed by the Board since its inception.

Regents Beal, Clements, and Leland were graduates of the University in the class of 1882. Beal has been mentioned; he was dependable and stood resolute after he had made up his mind. He was a lover of books and a student of forestry and conservation. Since he lived in Ann Arbor, he was readily available to the president and usually served on the executive committee. Clements of Bay City was an industrialist of great taste and scholarly leanings; he was building up a remarkable collection of rare books on early America, an interest left from a course taken under Moses Coit Tyler. He was also a talented executive, who soon took charge of campus building and saw to it that construction was sound, serviceable, and economic. Frank B. Leland of Detroit was a banker, an able man on the finance committee.

Benjamin S. Hanchett of Grand Rapids was a self-made man who never finished high school. President of the street railway company, he became very much interested in engineering research at the University for the benefit of Michigan manufacturers. He also supported a health service for students. For his good judgment he quickly earned the respect of his colleagues. Victor M. Gore, '82*l*, was a successful Benton Harbor lawyer who came on to the Board in 1914. A clear-thinking speaker, he had served in the constitutional convention of 1907. Harry C. Bulkley, '92, '95*l*, a Detroit attorney, was a tireless worker for the University, courteous but forceful. His refusal to accept another term in 1918 brought about the election of James O. Murfin, '95, '96*l*, another Detroit lawyer and loyal alumnus. He gave much time to problems of bequests and student welfare. His was the only new face on the Board until 1924.

If there was any fear that Hutchins would favor the Law Department, it was quickly dispelled. The Board of Regents promptly named Professor Henry M. Bates dean of the Law School, a post he held until his retirement in 1939. He became a national leader in legal education. Bates wanted first of all to require two years of college work before admission to the Law School. He led his faculty to general adoption of the "case book" method of instruction.

Hutchins was favorable to enlarging the scope of the University. Thus, a course in journalism was provided in 1910 which was a revival of Professor F. N. Scott's course in "rapid writing" of 1890 (the first course in newspaper writing in the country). It led to the Department of Journalism in 1929. An Extension Service was launched, aimed first at informing alumni and then at educating adults generally. It started in Detroit and spread to other nearby cities. Professor William D. Henderson of the Physics Department was made director in 1912 and supervised its steady expansion.

In conjunction with the Extension Service, Professor Trueblood organized a Michigan High School Debating League in 1915. The annual elimination contest on a given topic ended with the two best debating teams meeting in final argument at the University.

The Department of Fine Arts was established in 1911 with the appointment of Professor Herbert R. Cross. The Department of Political Science was reestablished in 1910 by separation of the courses in government from the History Department. Dr. Jesse Reeves from Dartmouth was brought to head it and remained in that position until his retirement in 1937.

Hutchins began pushing in 1911 for a real Graduate School separate from the Literary Department. He wanted it to be "tough" even if it attracted only a handful of students. Karl E. Guthe, professor of physics, was appointed the first dean in June 1912. His untimely death in 1915 led to his replacement by Professor Alfred H. Lloyd of the Philosophy Department. The new school grew steadily, especially with the help of $3000 in graduate fellowships provided by the Regents. A master's degree in public health was offered by the Medical Department in 1911, pointing toward establishment of a separate School of Public Health in 1939.

At the same time Hutchins resisted several petitions of alumnae to establish a department of home economics and a request of 1915 to introduce a course in optometry. Oddly enough, however, a course in the summer session of 1913, which was continued for several years, offered training in embalming.

Several striking appointments to the faculty were made in these early years of Hutchins' administration. Besides those professors already mentioned, U. B. Phillips from Tulane University was appointed professor of history in 1911. His courses on the antebellum South and the Civil War became noted in the next two decades. The effort to find someone to teach ancient history was rewarded by appointment of A. E. R. Boak from Harvard as instructor in 1914. Leroy Waterman of Chicago was appointed professor of Semitics in 1914; he wrote much, directed excavations in the Near East, and contributed to the Revised Standard Version of the Bible. A byproduct was his sensible rearrangement and beautiful new translation of the *Song of Solomon*, not accepted by the RSV, but published by the University Press.

In the Department of Engineering, both Lewis E. Gram and Henry E. Riggs were appointed professors of civil engineering in 1912. Riggs began testing highway materials and developed a program of close association with the State Highway Department. In the Medical Department, Dr. Udo J. Wile was named professor of dermatology and syphilology in 1912 and earned distinction for having established the first university hospital clinic for training physicians in these fields. His pioneering work in diagnosis and treatment gave him international recognition.

Among the young men brought into faculty ranks were Joseph R. Hayden, PhD '15, as instructor in political science, who ultimately succeeded Reeves as chairman and also served as vice-governor of the Philippines under Governor Frank Murphy. David Friday, '08, began his career as instructor in economics in 1911, rising to president of the Michigan Agricultural College in 1921. Roy W. Cowden, '08, was made instructor in rhetoric in 1909, and became director of the Avery and Jule Hopwood Awards in creative writing as well as a perceptive and beloved critic of student writing. DeWitt H. Parker appointed instructor in philosophy in 1910, became a noted class lecturer and wrote extensively in the field of aesthetics. In the tradition of Morris, Dewey, and Wenley, Parker was a Hegelian idealist, the philosophy dominant in this country. J. B. Edmondson, later dean of the School of Education, in 1914 undertook the position of inspector of high schools. Similarly, Wells Bennett, who became dean of the College of Architecture, began in 1912 as an instructor in drawing and descriptive geometry. Frank E. Robbins appeared in 1914 as instructor in Greek and lived to serve three presidents as administrative assistant, to manage the University Press, to write delightful doggerel, and to edit the *Quarterly Review.*

In the Medical School Paul De Kruif, PhD '16, taught bacteriology from 1914 to 1920, with time out for war service, before taking up his pen to become famous as the author of *Microbe Hunters, Hunger Fighters,* and *Men Against Death.* Dr. Max Peet, '10*m*, joined the Surgery Department in 1916 and before his death in 1949 became a noted neurological surgeon and famous teacher. He was the first to develop the technique of cutting the sympathetic nerve above the diaphragm to relieve high blood pressure. Dr. Albert C. Furstenberg, '15*m*, was added to the Department of Otorhinolaryngology in 1917 and later became dean of the Medical School.

When the Museum was separated from the Department of Zoology in 1913 and Professor Alexander G. Ruthven was named director, he introduced a conservationist's attitude toward museum materials. Heretofore they had been treated as warehouse supplies which could be utilized by students and used up. Ruthven encouraged demonstration without destruction. Also, while discouraging gifts to the Museum which must be kept on permanent display, he inaugurated a coterie of honorary curators among private collectors so as to encourage future gifts.

Salaries at Michigan remained low: for the regular two-semester year, Michigan paid instructors $1000 to $1400, assistant professors $1600 to $1800, junior or associate professors $2000 to $2200, and professors $2500 to $4000, depending on length of service and distinction. Deans received $5000 or more. The scale at several other universities ran much higher.

Medical professors were allowed to carry on some private practice to augment their incomes. Law professors had been allowed to practice since they were not full-time appointments; during Dean Hutchins' time their appointments were made full time. Engineering professors did outside consulting work with approval of the Regents. Professional men, then, held an advantage over Literary Department faculty. At the clerical level salaries were also meager, as evidenced by the resignation of 25 percent of these workers during the last half of 1916, when both the high cost of living and the wages offered by war factories took them off the University payroll.

Early in 1917 the forty-three married instructors in the Literary Department petitioned the Regents for a raise in salary. They declared that a married couple in Ann Arbor could not maintain a reasonable standard of living on less than $1200 a year, while a family of three needed $1353, and four required $1448. Twenty-seven of the forty-three instructors were receiving less than these minimums. The petition was referred to the budget committee of the Board, but nothing was done until after the war. The Regents were business and professional men used to paying employees only what the market required. The five dollars a day to which Henry Ford had raised his employees in 1914 invited comparison with instructors' salaries; although the auto company workers were subject to seasonal layoffs which limited their annual income, when they worked they earned $130 a month as against the instructor's $100 to $ 140 a month (for ten months).

In 1914 the faculty recommended a new nomenclature for the divisions of the University. Those which granted first degrees to students were to be called colleges; those which gave professional degrees were to be termed schools. Departments were to be subdivisions of colleges and schools which taught a given subject in several courses. Thus, it was proper to speak of the College of Literature, Science and the Arts (the Literary College), the College of Engineering and Architecture, the Medical School, the Law School, the Department of English and the Department of Philosophy. The Regents adopted the new terminology in January 1915.

Academic standards were raised to improve the quality of the degrees granted. The present marking system of letter grades from A to E was adopted in 1912 to go into effect in June. It was felt that some incentive for better work must be offered through recognition of degrees of proficiency, beyond the generic term "passed." The student *Daily* welcomed the change with enthusiasm. Furthermore, honor points were attached to each grade: an A was worth 3 points, a B was 2, a C was 1, a D was 0, and E was minus 1. Since a total of 120 hours of credit was required for graduation (the usual rate was fifteen hours a semester, or thirty a year), an additional requirement was added of 135 honor points. What this meant, in brief, was that a student must earn better than a C average, which would yield only 120 honor points, in order to graduate. This commendable elevation of scholastic standing was unfortunately lowered in 1916 to 120 honor points at the request of the Literary College faculty. At the same time in the Commencement program graduates "with distinction" or "with high distinction" were noted.

The Law School, lagging behind other law schools, made two years of college work a prerequisite for entrance in 1915. The Dental School decided to require a year of college work before entrance in 1916.

Despite the war, a conference of organizations interested in good government met in 1917 and decided to set up an office for research which Professor Robert Crane of the Political Science Department obtained for the University in January 1918. It became the Bureau of Government for political and social research on state and municipal affairs. The results were published for the benefit of local and state governments, and a large governmental library was created. The Political Science Department began offering a master's degree in municipal administration under Crane in 1917 for the purpose of training professional workers for careers in city, county, and state government. The whole program, soundly based, became of immense value to the state of Michigan.

Hutchins was keenly aware of crowded buildings. The new Dental

School Building was dedicated in May 1909, giving that school a respectable home. Six months later the new Chemistry and Pharmacy Building was finished. It was built with a tan brick, selected by Regent Fletcher, that matched nothing else on campus. Pharmacy had a home, and the frequently enlarged Chemical Laboratory was replaced by a four-story building with 635 laboratory tables and other equipment. The long-awaited Alumni Memorial Hall was dedicated in 1910; it relieved the Library of its art collection, provided headquarters for the Alumni Association, and classrooms for the new Fine Arts Department; the basement served as a faculty club. Other departments of the Literary College under pressure of rising enrollment were badly in need of space. The auditorium in University Hall no longer seated half the student body. Any further expansion, however, was also dependent on a new and larger heating and lighting plant.

The first of the new buildings under Hutchins came easily. Regent Arthur Hill, who died much lamented in 1910 left $200,000 to the University for an auditorium. A site on North University Street was bought and cleared, and an auditorium containing two balconies and seating 4300 for musical and oratorical events was planned by architect Albert Kahn. It went up grandly and by the time seats were installed, the Frieze Me-

HILL AUDITORIUM

morial Organ moved there, and the dedication held in June 1913, the Regents had spent $282,000. Its acoustical success followed from carefully planned engineering features. Still in use today, Hill Auditorium has become an indispensable gathering place, where student and nonstudent audiences have enjoyed famous lecturers, renowned symphonies, the best soloists, choruses, dance groups, and even some theatrical ventures. Freshmen were welcomed there, and convocations to honor outstanding students held in it. Commencements were conducted there for a dozen years.

Regent Clements had major direction of this building, as he did in locating and constructing the new heating plant in the hollow between Washington and Huron streets. This indispensable addition of 1915, like the laying of water mains for fire protection, did nothing for faculty or students directly. The next big project, also handed to Clements, was erection of a science building to house six growing departments: botany, zoology, psychology, mineralogy, forestry, and geology.

A wealthy man as well as an eminent business executive, Clements took President Hutchins, Secretary Smith, Mr. Kahn, and representatives of the six departments on a railway tour of Eastern campuses to inspect science buildings. Mr. Smith tells the story with awe and glee. Their local hosts were queried for criticisms of the buildings they inhabited, and all these were noted by Mr. Kahn. The six departments learned what they should have and what they should avoid. Back home, Mr. Kahn drew plans to accommodate the departments and to accord with what they had all learned. Windows were plentiful on three sides. Clements then conducted a display of the plans before all members of the six departments for discussion. Each department was assigned a vertical section from the basement to the top fourth floor. After all had expressed approval of their quarters, he whipped out a paper from his pocket.

"Fine! That's what this paper says. If there is no objection, will you all sign it."

Clements had learned, too, from the trip, and he wanted no changing of minds and no future complaints. He then announced that John F. Shepard, professor of psychology, would represent all the departments in communicating with the contractor and that none of the rest of them should even speak to the contractor. The building went up without a hitch, and the scientists were so well pleased that they gave a luncheon for Clements, the other Regents, the president, and the contractor. The Natural Science building, across from Hill Auditorium, opened in 1915. It cost $375,000.

The same year saw completion of two women's dormitories, the first of their kind at Michigan, both of them gifts. The children of Mrs. Helen Handy Newberry of Detroit gave $75,000 to the Student Christian Association for a women's residence to be built next to Newberry Hall. When the stucco dormitory was finished, the Student Christian Association turned it over to the University. It held seventy-nine women and is still in use as Helen Newberry Residence.

As for the other dormitory, President Hutchins first met William W. Cook, '82*l*, in 1911 at New York. Cook was attorney for the Postal Telegraph and Cable Company and the author of three legal works. He also invested in Cuban sugar and street railways. After a few meetings with Hutchins, Cook offered to build and furnish a handsome dormitory for women. Martha Cook, named for the donor's mother, was built on South University and Tappan, almost across from the President's House, and housed 125 upperclass women in suites. They also had two richly furnished parlors and a long terrace and lawn for use in spring. It cost $260,000.

In conference with the city of Ann Arbor, the University had agreed to staff and operate a contagious disease hospital if the city would raise $25,000 for a building. The city voted the money, and the new hospital opened in 1914. A whole new University Hospital was then discussed by the Regents. It was to be large enough to serve the Medical School adequately as a teaching hospital. The Board submitted a request to the state legislature at the end of 1916 for more than a million dollars, payable over six years. The legislature granted the money in April 1917, just as the country entered the war, and the project was postponed.

Meanwhile, a University YMCA building was planned through private donations. It was erected on State Street in 1916, half the cost of $125,000 being contributed by John D. Rockefeller. It was named Lane Hall for Professor Lane of the Law School, who had been active in promoting it.

The University Library soon began to find its space inadequate. Joseph Labadie, Detroit newspaperman of French and Indian extraction, gave his unusual collection of socialist and anarchist books, periodicals, handbills, and manuscripts to the University in 1911, and the Regents had the courage to accept it without a murmur. It has steadily been enlarged over the years until it comprises an extraordinary collection of the literature of dissent in America. Dean C. Worcester, '89, who left the Zoology Department in 1899 to go to the Philippines and remained there to become secretary of the interior and then superintendent of public instruction, accumulated a collection of books, documents, and photographs on the Islands which he presented to the University in 1914.

Librarian Koch went to Germany in the spring of 1914 to a meeting of the German Library Association and to install the American Library Association's exhibit at the Leipzig Book Fair. A year later Koch was dismissed with a year's salary. The two book collectors on the Board of Regents, Clements and Hubbard, had found him deficient as a bookman. William Warner Bishop from the Library of Congress was appointed librarian. He began planning with Albert Kahn the proposed rebuilding of the University Library. Sketches were approved in December 1915. The towers and existing reading rooms were to be torn down, and a new building wrapped around the old book stacks. The Regents obtained $350,000 from the legislature for the project and later $265,000 more.

2. Alumni and students

Apart from his concern for the University's growth and the quality of its faculty, Hutchins took a decided interest in the alumni, a hitherto neglected appendage. Angell was always proud of the alumni and regarded them as one measure of the University's success, but he viewed them individually and outside the University sphere. Hutchins wanted to reclaim them by organization, to persuade them to maintain a continuing

interest in the welfare of their University, to advertise it in their communities so as to attract the best new students, and to contribute financially
toward University development. Once a Michigan man, always a Michigan
man. He considered the great body of alumni an untapped source of funds,
such as private colleges had regularly exploited. In ten years of close
attention to the alumni he saw 141 clubs organized, and he developed in
them a sense of permanently belonging to the institution that had opened
their minds and trained them vocationally. In Wilfred Shaw, '04, who had
been elected general secretary of the Alumni Association, he found an
enthusiastic ally.

ALUMNI MEMORIAL HALL

After completion
of Alumni Memorial
Hall, a cause to which
the alumni could rally
was the movement for
a new building for the
Michigan Union. The
Cooley house was al-
ways considered tem-
porary quarters. The
Regents not only ap-
proved of a fund raising
campaign, but allowed
President Hutchins to spend as much time as he thought necessary to aid
the campaign. It is difficult now to recall how exciting and challenging was
the idea of a special center for all male student activities. It was the
democratic answer to fraternities; it was the solution to getting acquainted
amid rising enrollment; it would solve the problem of unsatisfactory
boarding houses, keep students out of saloons, remove dances from the
gymnasiums, be a splendid guest house for parents and visitors, provide a
place to study, and contain billiard tables and a swimming pool—the
prospects were well nigh intoxicating. There was no such building on any
campus in the country.

Hutchins kept the ball of enthusiasm rolling, and money began
flowing in. Ground was broken in June 1916, but war interrupted construction. The unfinished building was used as a barracks for 800 men and mess
hall for 4000 during 1918. After $1,150,000 had been spent, the almost
completed building was deeded to the University in 1920; the swimming
pool and library were finished later at a cost of $61,500. It was a red brick
building of four stories and a basement, with a front tower rising seven
stories.

The president's interest in the student body was genuine, even
though it was paternal. In his search for funds through gifts, he had the

students much in mind. When he assumed office there were only fourteen funds available to students as scholarships or loans. A decade later there were forty-seven such funds, and the University was committed to the course of making more and more student assistance available.

When a student health service was proposed by a Union committee in 1912, Hutchins pushed it along. A vacant house was taken over, money was found for a doctor and nurses, a dispensary was added, and in 1913 the University Health Service opened. In the first year 4200 students, men and women, made 18,250 office calls, and 1400 of them were referred to the hospitals. The commonest complaints were respiratory troubles and tonsilitis, but the cases of tuberculosis uncovered (fifty-nine in 1916) were revealing. Venereal diseases were not unknown either. Dr. H. H. Cummings was the first director, followed in 1917 by Dr. Warren E. Forsythe, who remained until 1955.

Drinking among students remained a problem from the University's point of view. In two letters of 1910 President Hutchins said frankly that "the saloon problem here is one of the most difficult problems with which the University authorities have to deal." Although he thought there was much less drinking in Ann Arbor by students now than there had been, "there is altogether too much." In the fall of 1916, when a state prohibition amendment was up for adoption, William Jennings Bryan spoke for the "drys" and drew an audience of 5000 in Weinberg's Coliseum on South Fifth Avenue, and the second night Billy Sunday aroused to salvation pitch an audience of 8000. A straw poll among students showed a vote of 2879 to 429 for prohibition.

The political temper of the students is somewhat revealed in two straw polls taken in 1912 and 1916. The first was participated in by only 2204 students. Wilson won 994 votes to Roosevelt's 972, and Taft's 173. While the majority were Republican in general, most of them were of Bull Moose inclination rather than party regulars. They were still Republican in 1916, although narrowly so. They favored Hughes over Wilson 1708 to 1605, contrary to national preference.

The Michigan Union Opera in these years steadily improved. The operas were always funny, especially the feminine-clad huskies, and the music was lively and tuneful. Some memorable songs from them belong in any anthology of the best Michigan music. "College Days" by Donald A. Kahn '10, and Earl V. Moore '12, came from *Koanzaland*, 1909. The "Bum Army" is from the *The Crimson Chest*, 1910, and "The Friar's Song" was heard in *Contrarie Mary*, 1913. "Men of the Maize and Blue" was written by W. A. P. John '16, and A. J. Gornetzky, '19*l*, for *Très Rouge*, 1916. Chase Baromeo, leading man in *Très Rouge*, became a basso for the Metropolitan Opera Company and later professor of voice in the School of Music. *Contrarie Mary* was the first opera to be played outside Ann Arbor,

PLAYBILL, MICHIGAN UNION
OPERA

when the alumni in Chicago arranged to have it staged there; after that there was always an opera trip during Christmas vacation.

In October 1911, Earl Moore met J. Fred Lawton, '11, on the street in Detroit and declared that Michigan needed a new marching song.

"All right, let's write one," Lawton responded typically.

They immediately took a street car to Lawton's home. On the way Lawton thought of the lines:

Varsity, we're for you,
Here for you,
To cheer for you—
We have no fear for you. . . .

Writing these down at the house, Moore began to set them to music. The chorus was completed, and then the verse was written. It was all done that afternoon and dedicated to Coach Yost. Three days later it was introduced at a prefootball pep rally in University Hall, Lawton conducting and Moore playing the organ. The students loved it. The song was a smash hit from that day to this. In 1961 in the Michigan stadium, Lawton led thousands in singing the famous song while Dean Moore conducted the University Band in a triumphal fiftieth anniversary celebration. First and last it is a football song, a rousing march, with easily remembered words. It soon rivaled "The Victors" and the two are equal favorites. Earl Moore, who wrote music for four operas, remained on campus to become dean of the School of Music.

For all his activity Hutchins was not much at ease with students face to face as Angell was. Rowdiness irritated him, and malicious destruction infuriated him. He liked earnest and respectful students and would help them patiently, but ill manners were met with austerity. He possessed tremendous dignity; like Tappan he looked the part of a university president. Students did not easily and automatically flock to him, and more's the pity, for behind his somewhat forbidding reserve he had a Yankee's dry humor and an attractive Christian character. He regarded the faculty as a "community of scholars" and considered dignity as their hallmark. It was his way of life.

On April 1, 1916, President Angell died quietly at his residence. Unknown personally to any of the current classes of students, he was yet revered for his long and illustrious tenure as president. When the funeral coach carrying his body rolled down State Street and up North University, it passed between two solid lines of silent students paying a last tribute.

To support the gymnasiums and to bolster the finances of the Athletic Association, the Regents in 1912 authorized a five-dollar athletic fee to be charged each student. It did not dispel the growing dissatisfaction with Michigan's lonely position outside the Western Conference. The faculty was vexed over its loss of authority over the Board in Control of Athletics, and in 1913 the Senate suggested to the Regents that the time was ripe for a change in policy. The Regents were miffed at the idea and spoke of the "dignity" of the University, which could not submit to any action by an outside group. When students urged a return to the Conference, the Regents resolved that it "deems undesirable the continual agitation on the subject on the campus."

But stubbornness is a virtue only in the face of injustice. In 1915 the Regents allowed the Senate to choose the majority members of the Board in Control. Professor Ralph Aigler of the Law School became chairman of the Board, a position he occupied with devotion until 1942. With great tact and adroitness he began some exploratory talks with Conference officials. Finally, in 1917 the Board in Control recommended to the Regents that the Board be allowed to report directly to the University Senate, as the Western Conference required. The Regents readily complied. As soon as the return of faculty control was made known to the Conference, Michigan was invited to resume its seat, to take effect in November 1917. As Ohio State had joined the Conference, there were now ten universities in the group—the Big Ten.

The "flirtation with foolishness" was at an end. The Regents voided its earlier assertion of power, the alumni realized their mistake, and the students (although not the same ones) learned, perhaps, that they could be wrong in matters of University policy. Michigan has not always agreed with Conference decisions since that date, but it has considered the wiser policy to remain in the Conference and try to achieve reforms rather than to secede.

Athletic Director Charles Baird had resigned in 1909 and was succeeded by his assistant, Phillip G. Bartelme, who remained until 1921. He brought in a college graduate and professional baseball player named Branch Rickey in 1909 to coach baseball. During the four years he was here, Rickey also earned a law degree. In his second year, early in the season when the team practiced in Waterman Gymnasium, Rickey's attention was called to a freshman who was batting the ball against the walls of the gym with alarming velocity and regularity. Somewhat fearful of the pounding the building was taking, he called the young man over and learned that his name was George Sisler. In the next three years Sisler earned stardom on the diamond and upon graduation from the Engineering College in 1915 he was signed by the St. Louis Browns, of whom Rickey had just become manager. Track Coach Fitzpatrick left in 1911 and was succeeded by the fondly admired Steve Farrell, who coached track teams from 1913 to 1930. After Michigan returned to the Big Ten, Farrell's teams won six outdoor championships, and four indoor.

3. The war in Europe

The war in Europe, coming on a summer's day in 1914, was a numbing shock to Ann Arbor and the University. The numerous families of German descent in the town held a sentimental affection for "the old country," even though they or their fathers or grandfathers had eagerly left it because of limited economic opportunities, rigid social classes, or required military service. They still admired German culture for its splendid educational system, its literature and music, its thoroughness and efficiency in manufacturing, its Christmas and Easter festivities. The local faculty shared this admiration, for the University of Michigan had been modeled on the German university. The Medical School looked to Berlin and Vienna for advanced research, and the Department of German Language and Literature taught a quarter of the students enrolled in the Literary and Engineering colleges. Now, suddenly, Germany on the march became a ruthless machine, casually indifferent to the guaranteed neutrality of Belgium, cruel in submarine warfare, and submissive to a kaiser and military hierarchy that flouted the moral order of the time. Within a few weeks Germany began to lose American respect and never recovered it.

American sympathy flowed at once to the side of the Allies. Almost nobody favored the Germans. The division was between those who wanted to help the Allies actively, or at least strengthen the defenses of the United States, and those who advocated a strict neutrality. Ultimately, since staying out of the war favored the Germans, the neutralists were accused of being "pro-German."

Petitions from various faculty members, from students, and from alumni groups poured in on the Board of Regents in the fall of 1914 advocating military drill for the students. The petitions were tabled, but in February 1915 the Board authorized a committee of four Regents and the president to consider the question of military instruction. The faculty was asked to submit a plan, but the recommendation of the Senate was not forthcoming until November 1915. The Senate suggested compulsory military training, three hours a week, for all freshmen and sophomores, starting in the fall of 1916. It should be elective for upperclass men. The instructor should be an army officer assigned by the War Department. This modest proposal was finally approved by the Regents in February 1916, but they refused to make the training compulsory for anybody.

President Hutchins could not be stampeded, and he perceived at the outset that the University's unique function was to furnish trained leadership for the nation. To make the University simply another military camp for privates was in his view a gross misuse of its potentials, and he resisted it. Officers were certainly going to be needed in quantity, experts in particular for a modern war whose weapons were applications of physical chemical, mathematical, and engineering principles. More than a hundred students had volunteered for training in January 1916 under Professors C. E. Wilson (retired from the Michigan National Guard) and Peter Okkelberg. The number increased to several hundred in May, and they were urged to attend summer camp at Plattsburg, N.Y., or Fort Sheridan, Ill., and earn three hours credit in the College of Engineering.

The War Department proposed that a Reserve Officers Training Corps be established at all universities (besides those already existing at land grant colleges under the Morrill Act), with practical drill to be given at summer camps. The University acceded to this proposal in March 1916 and asked for an ROTC commander to be assigned here. The students were ready to organize ROTC units at once, but the Board of Regents refused permission before an officer should arrive to take charge.

If the sequence of events seems leisurely, it was. President Wilson had urged neutrality of thought and action. He was reelected in 1916 chiefly on the slogan of having "kept us out of war," narrowly winning over Charles Evans Hughes. Nevertheless, American sympathies swung behind the Allied Powers with more warmth every passing month. There were American relief organizations to help the victims of German aggression, and there was a preparedness movement to "defend" the United States—certainly not against the Allies if they were victorious. A straw poll among the faculty in 1915 showed eighty-three favored military training for the students, and fifty-five did not. A similar poll among the men students showed 1040 for and 932 against. The opponents argued that technical military courses were proper for the University to offer, but not drill, which could be done better in four to six weeks at summer camp.

Preparedness-minded faculty members had organized a local chapter of the National Security League in October 1915 under the chairmanship of Professor Hobbs. It included Deans Vaughan, Cooley, and Bates. By his activity Hobbs earned a place on the executive committee of the national organization. The League aimed at securing legislation for universal military training and the building up of arms. It was enthusiastically supported by shipbuilders and munitions makers.

Hobbs complained that only pacifists were heard locally in lectures, and he wanted the other side presented. He called President Wilson an isolationist and Secretary of War Baker a pacifist. He obtained use of Hill Auditorium for three lectures on national preparedness in early 1916—provided, said the Regents, "that speakers upon the subject preserve an

*PATRIOTIC PROGRAM, HILL
AUDITORIUM, JULY 31, 1914*

attitude of strict neutrality in regard to the present European situation and avoid all references that imply an intent on the part of any particular nation or nations to attack the United States." The most enthusiastically received speaker was Major General Leonard Wood, who had already antagonized President Wilson by urging military preparedness to resist Germany. Hobbs so admired Wood that he wrote a biography of him when Wood was seeking the Republican presidential nomination in 1920.

Two naval militia units were organized in November 1916, each numbering about fifty-five students. Under reserve officers O. M. McNeil and Joseph R. Hayden of the faculty, they trained throughout the winter and spring and in May moved to the Great Lakes Training station. They were the first naval militia formed in any university, but they were broken up to help train other naval units. Several of the men served with the naval railway batteries in France and Lieutenant Hayden fired the last big cannon in the war, at exactly 11:00 A.M. on November 11, 1918.

1916 slipped away while Congress debated a defense act and the War Department fashioned a strict curriculum for campus use. The gist of it was that the government would provide arms, equipment, and uniforms for all ROTC units, which would study theoretical courses in military science and learn practical drill at summer camps. The Board of Regents agreed to this plan in November and daily expected an officer assigned to Ann Arbor. Then early in 1917 the government changed its mind and asked the universities to drill the students also on campus. The Regents agreed in March.

Meanwhile, an Intercollegiate Intelligence Bureau was set up in Washington to index the special talents of various faculty and alumni which might be of service to the government. The Regents joined this Bureau and appropriated $2500 for a director to begin a Michigan index. On March 29 a student poll showed 3369 favored compulsory military training and only 632 did not. The Regents refused to take this expression seriously because they were sure that the number of volunteers would tax all the available facilities.

The United States declared war on April 7, 1917. Major Charles W. Castle, an invalided officer, arrived in May to be commandant of cadets and was duly appointed professor of military science—one hundred years after Judge Woodward had recommended the subject. Although a West Point graduate he was less than an inspiring leader and spent most of his time examining students for officers' training camps. By the middle of June he had approved 315. A thousand other students volunteered for service, with 500 to enlist and 500 to do farm work during the summer.

When the call came for two ambulance units that spring, so many students responded that three sections were organized and sent to Allentown, Pa., in June for intensive training. One section, number 591, sailed for France in the summer and was attached to the French Army for almost two years, winning a unit citation. Students who left the University in the middle or latter part of the semester were given credit in their courses for that semester.

The policy of granting leaves to faculty had always involved an obligation on the part of the professor to pay for a substitute out of his salary. The advent of war changed this requirement. The University offered to continue paying professors the difference between their military pay and their faculty salary and also to pay a temporary replacement.

In the summer of 1917 an American University Union for Europe was organized so that American college students and alumni in France might find a headquarters. Michigan alumni subscribed $11,000 for the University's participation in the Union, and in August the Board of Regents sent Assistant Professor Charles Vibbert, '04, of the Philosophy Department, who could speak French readily, to Paris as director of the Michigan Bureau of the Union. He ministered to all college men from the state of Michigan and was especially effective with French officials. Near the end of the year Warren J. Vinton, '11, joined him as a volunteer assistant, and Assistant Professor Philip Bursley of the French Department was added to the staff in 1918.

Defenses of Germany and complaints against British blockade of Germany were heard in various quarters of Ann Arbor before the United States entry into the war. Then the reasonable changed their minds once we were committed to support the Allies, the prudent stubborn shut their mouths (although their previous statements rose to haunt them), and only a handful exposed themselves to the critical contempt of their neighbors.

The first draft of local men was the occasion for a farewell meeting at Hill Auditorium on September 4, 1917. President Hutchins spoke, and so did city officials. Responding for the draftees was Fred B. Wahr, instructor in the suspect German Department and member of an old Ann Arbor German family. He left no doubt where he stood: "In justice to our great cause and to ourselves who are now called into service, in justice to those of this community who have gone before us . . . we demand that those seditious and treasonable utterances which now and then find their way about in our community be silenced, and that those making such statements, whether they be laborers, tradesmen, professional men, teachers in our public schools or in our University, whoever they may be—we demand that they be treated with the contempt which they deserve. You are either for us or against us." His words hit hard and had influence.

ROTC UNITS MARCHING

Enrollment declined in September 1917 by 1500—from 7517 in the fall of 1916 to 6057. In the following months over 400 students withdrew to enter military training. As soon as the new ROTC was activated, 1800 men students signed up—the largest unit in any university. Such a large group could be drilled daily only by volunteer help from faculty members. At the same time the College of Engineering offered seven courses in military science. In addition, Assistant Professor Joseph Bursley, '99e, had started a six-week course in the summer of 1917 in the handling of military stores and ordnance in the Quartermaster's Department. It was repeated every six weeks, enrolling 800 altogether, until April 1918, when it became so obvious a need that the Army took it over and moved such instruction to a camp.

Students over twenty-one in the College of Engineering formed the Engineering Enlisted Reserve Corps in January 1917. They were deferred to complete their degree work. Similarly, in the fall a Medical Enlisted Reserve Corps and a Dental Corps were formed, which included almost every student in the two schools.

There had been so much indecision among the students over whether to continue their education that President Hutchins asked the advice of General Wood. He replied on April 23, 1917: "I should advise the student body not to enlist until the plans of the government are definitely known. Enlistment now means enlistment in the militia or the regular army. College men should make every effort to serve as officers . . . . The best thing to do at present is to go on with the college work, especially where the university has a military instructor as yours has."

Therefore, the president had no hesitation when he addressed the first convocation in October 1917 in saying: "The student who remains in the University awaiting the call from the government is just as patriotic as the one who enters the service immediately." Other university presidents were saying the same thing.

But new turbulence occurred before the end of the month by the War Department's replacing Major Castle with Lieutenant George C. Mullen, retired. The ROTC job was too much for one man, and Lieutenant Losey J. Williams, retired, was assigned here in December. In February 1918 two retired sergeants appeared, but Williams and Mullen were transferred in May. The War Department was sadly inept in directing the program it had started.

Meanwhile, war bonds and war stamps were being sold on campus. The University invested heavily, and students bought the incredible sum of $650,000 worth in the five bond drives. President Angell's

COACH YOST BUYING WAR BONDS

house was made headquarters for the Red Cross, and coeds dropped in regularly to roll surgical dressings. Alumni Memorial Hall was turned into a hostess house for families and friends who came to visit student and later nonstudent trainees. In the dormitories and fraternities, meatless, wheatless, and sweetless days were observed each week to conserve those foods.

Professor Hobbs was only partially satisfied by the ROTC establishment. He still urged compulsory military training for all men students, and he kept a watchful eye on his colleagues for any dereliction that smacked of pro-Germanism as he conceived it. He complained of talk by Assistant Professor Carl E. Eggert of the German Department. The Regents at their October 1917 meeting called in both Hobbs and Eggert for a confrontation. The Board agreed with Hobbs and dismissed Eggert, although paying his salary through December. Later, the American Association of University Professors asked for a copy of the record of the case, but the Regents tabled the request. At the same time the president of the National Security League asked the University to cooperate with the League. Exactly what he meant was not clear until a second letter came in February 1918: the League wanted an official inquiry made into the loyalty of all professors and University officers. The Regents quickly tabled this also.

A Red Cross field service unit was organized among the students by Thomas McAllister, '18, in early 1918, financed largely by alumni. It left in the spring for France. Another naval auxiliary unit was organized by Luther Beach, '18e, and went to Cleveland in the spring for training in transport service.

RED CROSS PARADE

In the spring of 1918 the problem of the German Department intruded on the Regents again. The alumni of Grand Rapids petitioned them to remove the study of German from the curriculum, as had been done in the public schools of Grand Rapids, but this kind of demagoguery did not appeal to the Board. However, enrollment in all German courses had declined from about 1300 to 150, and the department was left overstaffed when the Regents were facing increased costs. Professor Ewald Boucke, a German national, feeling uncomfortable and under suspicion by his colleagues, asked for a leave of absence for the duration of the war; it was granted "indefinitely." He discovered what that meant when he asked for reinstatement in 1919 and was turned down. Bitterly, he returned to Germany and taught at Heidelberg University until his death. The Regents also notified two instructors and two assistant professors—men without tenure—that they would not be reappointed after the current year. One resigned promptly; the others finished out the year. Whether any of them were considered pro-German is uncertain, least of all Assistant Professor Warren Florer, who had served as first president of the local chapter of the Sons of the American Revolution when it was organized in 1914. Their departure left only four men in the German Department, one of whom was shifted to teach French.

Two German citizens on the faculty were stoutly defended. In response to public questioning Dean Cooley vouched for Assistant Professor A. F. Greiner, and Dean Hinsdale vouched for Dr. Willy C. R. Voight (who died early in 1919).

Other universities faced the same problems. The University of Wisconsin, located in a heavily German state, saw the number of students studying German decline more than 40 percent. The teaching staff had to be reduced accordingly, and one professor was dismissed for indiscreet talk. The Regents revoked an honorary degree granted the German ambassador in 1910. The university was also under fire because it would not denounce Senator La Follette's war position, yet it reputedly sent more faculty into the armed forces than any other university. The assistant secretary of agriculture spoke to the University cadets and complained publicly later that they were unresponsive to his patriotic talk. The president, faculty, regents, and students all resented it. Then in April 1918,

Professor Robert M. McElroy of Princeton addressed the students on behalf of the National Security League. Afterward, he gave a newspaper interview in New York and declared that the Wisconsin students showed little interest in what he said. His report created a furor. President Van Hise pointed out that student cadets had marched two and a half miles in the rain to sit in a cold pavilion to hear McElroy, who turned out to be a poor speaker who could not hold his audience. Students burned McElroy and the kaiser in effigy.

Ohio State University went through much the same experience. The number of students taking German declined from 2300 in 1915 to 150 in 1918, while enrollment in Romance languages tripled. Consequently, the faculty teaching German had to be reduced. Two instructors enlisted, two others served in civilian agencies, and three were dropped in 1917 because their sentiments came under suspicion. Two of the latter were German nationals. Location in a city and in a state noted for its German settlers seemed to prevent any campus hysteria. German plays and German music continued to be offered, and the same chaos resulted from military training imposed on academic training as occurred at Michigan.

At the request of the War Department The University of Michigan agreed in April 1918 to train noncollege draftees as gunsmiths, machinists, motor mechanics, blacksmiths, telephone repairmen, and even carpenters. They were to come in batches and remain for two months. It was a real problem to house the men and to round up contract instructors for them, but the Engineering College supervised the program and Professor Henry H. Higbee directed the work. Captain Ralph H. Durkee represented the Army as commandant. By the end of November some 2200 men had received this technical training here. They were also given lectures on war aims and offered academic courses at night. On December 1, 1918, the War Department abruptly cancelled the whole program, although the special instructors were under contract to June 1919. The department brushed them off with the word that an "adjustment" of contracts would have to wait. The instructors appealed to the Regents, who paid them an extra month's wages.

On top of the ROTC, the mechanics' training, and the volunteer units, the campus soon felt the impact of the War Department's next program for colleges. A Students Army Training Corps (SATC) was conceived in early 1918 in which college students could be learning and training at the same time, pending transfer to officers' training camps, to noncommissioned officers' training camps, or to specialized and regular training camps. All of them received pay as privates and were furnished uniforms and arms. The objective had some merit, although it utilized only in part the University's potential for officer candidates. The programs for mixed study and drill were largely incompatible, and administrative prob-

CONSTRUCTION OF THE S.A.T.C. MESS HALL BY THE UNION, SEPTEMBER 1918

lems were not resolved before the Armistice permitted the quick dropping of the whole snarled idea— but not before the Michigan SATC emerged as the biggest in the whole country.

The mechanic trainees were incorporated into the SATC as Section B. Section A, the college students, entered on their training program in September 1918, and Major Durkee was given command of them also. Dean Cooley was made Seventh District educational director at Chicago. 2150 students were enrolled, plus 1000 in Section B, plus 600 in the SATC, a total of 3750 on campus in the government program. To accommodate the students along with the mechanics, the unfinsihed Michigan Union was taken over as a barracks and mess hall. Another temporary mess hall for 1900 was quickly erected next to the Union. Waterman Gym was utilized as a barracks, and thirty-five fraternity houses were occupied. Classes, drill, and study time were apportioned by the military, but not with regularity. Academic classes suffered from the outset. Rarely did a professor see one-third of his class for two periods in succession. New faces appeared by transfer as old faces were removed. Two miles of trenches were dug in the slopes east of the Observatory. Afternoon drill cut into attendance of laboratory sections. KP or other military assignments had priority over classes. Major Durkee was sensible enough, but much of the trouble stemmed from the Army's use of newly commissioned officers who thought they were appointed to fight the faculty. Some needed military equipment was slow in coming. Certain improvised courses were unsatisfactory because of the divergent backgrounds of the students. Even Professor Hobbs was disgusted by the SATC.

On top of these conflicts, in early October came the country's worst epidemic of influenza, which although it lasted only a few weeks reduced disorder to chaos. The disease spread rapidly because the men were crowded together and almost continually tired out. More than 1200 fell ill. The Union was made into a hospital, and Newberry Hall was taken over as an infirmary. Ann Arbor housewives organized to care for patients in their homes and even fitted up a rented house as an extra hospital. All University and city physicians made the rounds with medicines. But the virulent epidemic cost the lives of fifty-seven in the SATC, two nurses, and fifty-eight local citizens before it subsided.

By contrast stood the SNTC, the Students' Navy Training Corps, a volunteer group limited to 600 and commanded by Rear Admiral Robert M. Barry, with Lieutenant A. E. R. Boak as executive officer. Half the group were by design engineering students. Because of its smaller size and the academic minds of its officers, this organization proceeded on its educational course successfully. Only one of the trainees died of influenza.

Two weeks after the Armistice the SATC and SNTC were disbanded, to the immense relief of everyone. Even the War and Navy departments learned that this was a misuse of university potentials.

Altogether, more than 12,600 students and alumni served in the Army and Navy. About 38 percent, 4761, were officers, which is not surprising considering their educational qualifications. 234 men and 97 officers are known to have died or been killed. Of the faculty, 166 were in service. Besides the men already mentioned, Dean Vaughan was a colonel on the staff of the Surgeon General. Dr. Walter R. Parker was a lieutenant colonel in the Medical Corps, and Dr. Udo Wile was a major in charge of the first American hospital in England. Dean Bates and Professor Reeves were in the Judge Advocate General's Department. Peter Field of the College of Engineering was in charge of tests for the Ordnance Department, and Moses Gomberg of the Chemistry Department investigated poisonous gases for the same department; both were majors. Lieutenant Colonel Alfred H. White was in charge of building government nitrate plants; Lieutenant Colonel William C. Hoad supervised sanitation at training camps; Colonel Alfred H. Lovell commanded a regiment of engineers; Lieutenant Colonel Walter T. Fishleigh had charge of designing and purchasing ambulances. All four men were from the College of Engineering. Major Gordon Stoner of the Law School worked with Fishleigh.

Professor Herbert Sadler designed ships for the Emergency Fleet Corporation. Professor David Friday of the Economics Department was statistical adviser to the Treasury Department. Professor James W. Glover of the Mathematics Department was a member of the War Risk Board. Librarians Bishop and Goodrich worked on military libraries, the latter going to France for a year and the former being in charge of SATC library service. Professor H. R. Cross of the Fine Arts Department served with the Red Cross in Italy. Professor Claude Van Tyne of the History Department lectured for three months throughout the East for the National Security League.

One result of the disrupting, frustrating SATC experience was that in December 1918 the faculty Senate voted against continuance of any military training. Nevertheless, a small unit of the ROTC was reconstituted in the fall of 1919 in the College of Engineering, which agreed to accept twelve hours credit of military science toward graduation. Gradually, the unit grew larger, but on a voluntary basis entirely.

4. Postwar recovery

After the war the University quickly reverted to normal functioning. Faculty in service began to return, although not all of them. A few remained in government service and a few others found highly paid positions in industry. The higher cost of living was increasing dissatisfaction; fifty faculty members petitioned the Regents for a general increase in salaries, and the Board recognized the need and replied that it was hoping to obtain more state money. One step it did take was to join the Teachers' Insurance and Annuity Association as set up by the Carnegie Foundation. A contribution of 5 percent of salary by the University and a similar contribution by each faculty member insured a pension at retirement.

For the year 1919-20 the new salary ranges were set at $1300 to $2100 for instructors, $2200 to $2600 for assistant professors, $2700 to $3000 for associate professors, and $3200 to $6250 (in the Law School) for professors. Deans were paid from $6250 to $7500. This small step upward was only a stopgap; in the second semester new minimums were established of $1500 for instructors, $2500 for assistant professors, $3500 for associate professors, and $4000 for professors. Deans' salaries began at $7500. Harvard, however, was paying minimums of $1600 for instructors, $3500 for assistant professors, $5000 for associate professors, and $6000 for professors.

President Hutchins had borne a heavy and distasteful burden during the war, and he offered his resignation in March 1919, hoping a successor would be named by summer. The Regents approached James Rowland Angell, son of Michigan's old president and now dean at the University of Chicago. He was willing, but attached several conditions to his acceptance which the Regents did not approve. Negotiations were amicably broken off, and Angell became president of Yale in 1921. The Board asked Hutchins to continue until June 1920, and he acquiesced.

Returning students pushed enrollment in September 1919 to 8560, taxing not only all the available housing, but all the available classrooms. Yet only thirty turned out for football, and the *Daily* was as distraught as

Coach Yost. About 40 percent of the students worked part-time to pay their expenses. They found the Union building nearly finished. The men who envisioned it felt amply rewarded. Undoubtedly, the prohibition of the sale of liquors and beer in January 1920 enhanced the position of the Union as a healthy hangout for students. Joe Parker's, the Orient, and other saloons were forced to close.

In the spring of 1920 a straw poll of 4171 students and faculty showed that 1485 of the 3503 Republican votes cast hoped to see Herbert Hoover nominated for President—and so did 424 of the 668 Democratic votes! The Republican students named General Leonard Wood a weak second choice, and Senator Warren G. Harding was fifth choice.

Another poll of the students asked their views on the United States joining the League of Nations. An Intercollegiate Treaty Referendum was sought on 700 campuses and four choices were offered: 1, to join without reservation; 2, not to join at all; 3, to join with Senator Lodge's reservations; 4, to join with compromise reservations between those advocated by Lodge and those by the Democratic party. Only 2780 students and 169 faculty participated, although a week of lively discussion preceded the poll. Out of this number, proposition 4 received 1116 votes, proposition 3 received 774 votes, and proposition 1 got 714 votes. Only 345 favored not joining the League at all, a position now agitated by Professor Hobbs. In each of these straw polls the person or proposition favored by the fewest students turned out to be the choice of the country. Nationally, the Intercollegiate Treaty Referendum revealed that Michigan was pretty much in line with thirty-two other universities and colleges: they favored proposition 4, then 1, 3, and 2 in descending order.

As a state institution the University was interested in serving Michigan industry, much as Michigan Agricultural College served Michigan farmers. Regent Hanchett and a regental committee met with a committee of the Michigan Manufacturers' Association and by January 1920 had worked out a plan. The Board agreed to set up the Department of Engineering Research in the College of Engineering, appoint a director, and support the overhead and miscellaneous expenses. This department would undertake research projects for specific industries which would bear the costs of those experiments under contract arrangement. The Regents retained the right to make public the results of the research. Professors who were involved part-time in the research would be paid extra by industry, and graduate students (for whom the whole program opened exciting possibilities for learning relevant and up-to-date problems of industry) would be used through fellowships from industry. To help supervise the department, the Regents asked that a committee of industrialists be appointed, and one hundred leaders were named. They operated through an executive committee of seventeen. Professor A. E. White was appointed the first director and remained until his retirement in 1952. Out of this beginning grew not only a mutually advantageous research program, but an even larger program of government research in matters of health, water resources, wildlife, military weapons, and space exploration.

Museum expeditions were resumed after the War. Bryant Walker again proposed to pay for another expedition into Colombia under Professor Ruthven. He also contributed something toward an expedition to Venezuela initiated by E. B. Williamson of Bluffton, Indiana, an entomologist. Another exciting prospect was Regent Clements' offer to the Board to give his collection of source books on early America and build a suitable building for them on campus. The Regents in turn agreed to maintain the new building, pay a staff, and provide modestly for future acquisitions. Francis W. Kelsey began a two years' leave in 1919 to travel around the Mediterranean in search of ancient pottery and papyri.

EXPEDITION TO THE MIDDLE EAST IN 1919

In December 1919 the Board of Regents found their president, and to get him they had to offer $18,500. He was Marion LeRoy Burton, president of the University of Minnesota. A graduate of Carleton College in 1900, he obtained a divinity scholarship to Yale and stayed on to earn a doctor of philosophy degree. He had been president of Smith College for seven years before going to Minnesota in 1917. To redecorate and remodel the vacant President's House for the Burtons, the Board was generous, even lavish, adding a sleeping porch and porte cochere.

CAMPUS VIEWED FROM THE SOUTH IN THE EARLY 1920s

CHAPTER EIGHT

THE BURTON BOOM

WHEN MARION LEROY BURTON arrived in Ann Arbor in the summer of 1920, he was not yet forty-six years old. A tall, redhaired man of commanding presence, he had the gift of making other people like him immediately. He was a noted and persuasive speaker with a voice that never ceased to enthrall the students and the legislature. Like Angell and Hutchins he was a faithful Congregationalist; he had also been a minister. Most important of all, perhaps, he possessed an unusual talent for organization. The Board of Regents had hired

MARION L. BURTON

a driver, and with unsuspected meekness they succumbed to being driven. They could not forget that this man had raised ten million dollars for Minnesota, and perhaps his magic touch would bring forth money here.

President Hutchins and Secretary Smith were alike in their background of New England frugality and humor. Not only did they work harmoniously together, but they abhorred waste and could make dollars perform beyond the dreams of spendthrifts. But in the postwar world the University stood in need of additional buildings, more faculty, and higher salaries. It must spend boldly rather than conserve expediently, because one subtle result of the war was to make more young people prize a college education. And if the University was to expand and grow, a willingness on the part of the state to spend must be aroused. A new vision and a different talent were required, and Burton had them.

His tenure was, tragically, so short—less than five years—that his accomplishments are better discussed topically rather than chronologically. First of all, he brought to his position a refreshing attitude of not being afraid of growth or great size. Further, he resumed writing and publishing an annual report. It was several times longer and more discursive than any report by Angell; with subtlety he was educating both Regents and faculty about what the University of Michigan should be and could be. His reports still make exciting reading forty-five years later.

"A state university," he wrote in his first annual report, "must accept happily the conclusion that it is destined to be large. If its state grows and prospers it will naturally reflect those conditions. Consequently, we are liable to continue to grow as the population of Michigan increases and as the high schools increase the number of their graduates. . . . The uncritical mind simply assumes that a small institution *ipso facto* does excellent work and that a large university must maintain mediocre educational standards. I insist that excellence does not inhere in size."

The size of the state university is thrust upon it, he pointed out the next year, but large size has certain advantages over small size. "In the large institution, it is entirely possible, to the advantage of every student, to separate each course into sections, where each student can be kept at work at his best, rather than drag them all down to the level of mediocrity . . . . Large numbers of students now ensure wide educational experimentation."

1. Plans for a larger university

The postwar bulge in enrollment saw the 8560 students in the fall of 1919 increase in the fall of 1920 to 9610, taper off in 1921 with an increase to only 9800 students and a similar rise to 10,000 in 1922 and to 10,500 in 1923. Enrollment stayed the same in 1924. Significant for the future was the doubling of Graduate School enrollment. In the same period the teaching faculty was increased from 444 in 1919 to 652 in 1924.

The most visible achievements of the Burton regime were new buildings, although this chapter will make clear that they were equaled by organizational and academic accomplishments. The Board of Regents knew at the end of the war that a decided effort must be made not only to finish the new University Hospital but also to provide several other buildings. A special committee was appointed to make a survey before Burton arrived. He energized it in his first few months on campus so that by January 1921 the Regents were able to demonstrate that $19,000,000 needed to be spent. However, the Board formulated a budget request to the state legislature of $8,700,000 for buildings in the next biennium, and an increase in the mill tax from three-eighths to five-eights for operations. Burton invited the legislative committees to visit the campus and showed them the needs. At the end of the session the University was voted $4,800,000 for construction and a tax revenue of six-tenths of a mill, which in view of increased property valuation virtually doubled the University's income to $3,000,000. The Regents allocated the capital funds as follows:

East Medical Building (plus $225,000 for land)	$900,000
Literary Building [Angell Hall]	$800,000
East Engineering Building (plus $175,000 for land)	$750,000
Model high school (plus $125,000 for land)	$525,000
New physics laboratory	$400,000
University Hospital continuation	$600,000
Addition to Dental Building	$200,000
Additional land	$100,000

These estimates included equipment. The sums for land purchases indicated that the University was spreading outside its original forty acres and faced the unpleasant necessity of buying up surrounding houses and possibly closing streets.

The building program was to be in direct charge of a Committee of Five: Regent Clements, President Burton, Secretary Smith, Architect Kahn, and Professor John Shepard who had supervised the erection of the Natural Science Building. Work on the Hospital, the addition to the Dental School, and construction of the model high school and East Engineering Building were started first. Meanwhile, a Ferry Field clubhouse was begun by the Board in Control of Athletics out of its own income from games, and a huge "field house," named for Yost (who coined the phrase), was planned for football practice in bad weather and for basketball games. Then Regent Clements began the building that was to hold his Americana library, both gifts.

The William L. Clements Library opened in 1923. It was devoted to source materials—books, manuscripts, maps, and newspapers—relating to early American history from Columbus' discovery to the end of the War of 1812. Mr. Clements

WILLIAM L. CLEMENTS LIBRARY

found a librarian in Dr. Randolph G. Adams, a historian with a deep appreciation of book collecting. Under him the library earned a national and international reputation while it grew in holdings.

During the next meeting of the legislature early in 1923, Burton entertained the whole body in Ann Arbor. The University was given $3,800,000 to continue its building program, most of it going toward completion of the Hospital. The buildings started in 1921 were finished, and work had begun on the new physics laboratory and a big classroom building for the Literary College. The heating plant had to be enlarged again. Two gifts of buildings improved the campus immensely. William W. Cook, who had built the Martha Cook dormitory, offered to build a Lawyers Club, a dormitory for 150 law students and a dining hall that would seat 300. Obviously, further building would be forthcoming—more dormitory space, a classroom building, and a law library. This impressive quadrangle in Tudor Gothic architecture began to take shape in 1923-24 in the block bound by South University, State, Monroe, and Tappan streets. Senator James Couzens of Detroit contributed $600,000 for a nurses' dormitory across the street from the Hospital and near the Observatory.

WILLIAM W. COOK LAW QUAD UNDER CONSTRUCTION

By the fall of 1924 President Burton was preparing another request to the legislature, this time for a new museum, an administration building, a new observatory, a building for architecture, and the necessary land for them. He also sought to have the ceiling of $3,000,000 on the mill tax removed. Due to his fatal illness beginning at the end of October, he was unable to present this request in Lansing. In the emergency the Board of Regents appointed President Emeritus Hutchins (now seventy-seven years old), Secretary Smith, and Regents Clements, Beal, and Stone to assume this responsibility. On February 18, 1925, President Burton died.

The legislature respected the University message and sadly missed the president's steady hand, but at the end of the session provided only $1,800,000 for a museum and the architecture building, and the land requisite for them. It did not remove the ceiling on the mill tax, but raised it to $3,700,000. The momentum of Burton's building program then expired with two splendid structures long needed. The Architecture Building, on Tappan Street next to Martha Cook, relieved congestion in the Engineering College and hastened the independence of the College of Architecture. The old Museum, overcrowded and unsafe for exhibits, was turned ironically into a classroom building for Romance languages and served another thirty years before being demolished. The new Museums Building allowed the various museums adequate space conducive to instruction and proved to be a tremendous attraction to public-school students all over Michigan.

Forgotten now is the string of decisions incident to this huge building program. The labor necessary in buying land or locating buildings on their sites, in initiating and approving plans, in letting contracts and supervising construction, in selecting equipment and arranging heating tunnels were time consuming and energy draining on all members of the Committee of Five. The model high school was named University High School, and the enormous classroom building that ran in front of University Hall and was joined to it at its rear was named in honor of James B. Angell.

Mrs. Thomas H. Simpson of Detroit in 1924 offered the Regents a building for medical research in memory of her husband—the Thomas Henry Simpson Memorial Institute, for investigative work in anemia. She provided $150,000 for a building, if the University would furnish a site and maintain the building, and $250,000 for endowment.

Ironically, just before the Institute was opened the liver diet for anemia was discovered. This was a therapeutic breakthrough, but not a cure, and the cause and prevention of the disease remained unknown. The Institute worked on the concentration and purification of liver extract and discovered a second treatment through prepared hog stomach called Ventriculin. The active principle in both extracts was found to be vitamin B_{12}. During World War II the Institute concentrated on blood and blood substitutes for the treatment of shock. Then leukemia became its chief concern. Support, in addition to University funds, came from federal health agencies and foundations. The first director, Dr. Cyrus C. Sturgis, served until his retirement in 1956.

Burton was under no illusions about the significance of new buildings, and he warned others. "When the University of Michigan succumbs to megalomania her vitality will begin to diminish. All of our statements about brick and mortar, all of our descriptions of the expansion of the campus and the development of shops and laboratories are of value just in proportion as they bear, not upon the means, but upon the ends of a true institution of higher learning. My sole concern is that Michigan shall meet the real tests of a university. What are these tests? The traditional answers deal with research and teaching." But Burton believed new emphasis must be placed on other considerations. The first test he advanced was "accuracy."

"A new world situation is developing and in that new world America's part will depend largely upon her ability to manifest new standards of thoroughness and accuracy. We have been a race of pioneers. We have simply done the best we could under all the circumstances. No longer is that enough; world leadership demands higher standards of work in every field, while our vice is superficiality.... Our institutions of higher learning will have a right to command support if gradually they can help in developing a generation of citizens who have learned to work with thoroughness and patience and to think with cogency and accuracy."

His second test was that "the American university must stimulate and arouse its students." This can only be brought about by inspiring teaching. "Education is not a process in which a youngster sits still while an oldster tries to tell him something. A student gets into the process of becoming educated when something inside his own head goes to work."

Finally, he said, "the university of today must reckon with the present.... We should not and could not teach these young citizens what they should think about the problems of the nation or the world. But we can make them feel at home in discussions dealing with those subjects.... Each one must be equipped with a magnificently sharpened tool by means of which he can cut his way through the rudely shaken and twisted social and economic order of the day."

To achieve these educational goals, President Burton started reshaping internal operations by straightening out and broadening the chain of command. The committee structure of the Board of Regents seemed antiquated to him, as indeed it was, and he reformed it. Instead of committees devoted to particular colleges and units, he persuaded the Regents to concern themselves with broad policies affecting the University as a whole. Hence they formed themselves into committees on the budget, on salaries, educational policies, promotion of research, student welfare, libraries, and buildings and grounds. The executive committee remained, chiefly to approve routine business, such as resignations, appointments, and promotions, which did not affect the budget and should not take up the time of the Board as a whole.

The change also meant that the deans, lacking regental committees to run to, must report their needs and plans to the president. To help meet the increasing work of the president, Burton had insisted on having an assistant. Dr. Frank E. Robbins was appointed to the post in 1921. To strengthen his administrative relationships, Burton met weekly with the deans and directors (of hospitals, library, and museums), where policies could be discussed and ideas developed for submission to the Regents.

Suggestions began to flow upward and burst out in showers. The Deans' Conference emphasized that educational policy is primarily in the hands of faculty administrators. The faculty as a whole might speak to the president through its Senate.

Each teaching department was encouraged to elect an executive committee to conduct departmental business along with the chairman. Also, each dean was assisted by a college executive committee elected by that faculty. This representative structure encouraged expressions of individual judgments. The faculty was made to feel more important by general meetings called by Burton to keep them informed of administrative thoughts and developments and to answer questions. The unnecessary mystery of administration began to evaporate as the faculty saw doors opening for introduction of new courses, new departments, new schools. Promotions were publicized. Sabbatical leaves were instituted, so that faculty who had taught for six years might have the seventh off at half-pay, or a semester at full pay.

The higher salary scale of February 1920 was made largely on faith, and the increased income could do no more than sustain it while additional faculty was hired to meet the swelling student body. But in 1921 Burton was able to raise the lowest and highest salaries, and in 1925 it was possible to state new minimums: instructors $2000, assistant professors $3000, associate professors $4000, and professors $5000. The qualifications of the four grades of teachers were defined and published. An esprit de corps made itself felt as morale soared. Burton was building a faculty team.

Burton also revived a custom dropped by President Angell in 1899 and devoted part of his annual reports to pointing with pride to what the University did for the state besides educating some of its youth and supplying communities with needed professional men. He mentioned the University Hospital, the Extension Service, the Highway Laboratory, the Dental Clinic, Engineering Research, public health lectures, Conservation Department investigations, and the high-school inspections.

During his administration the Alumni Association staff in Ann Arbor was increased by a field secretary and an associate editor. The latter was needed because the *Michigan Alumnus* became a weekly, and talk arose of starting a University quarterly. As field secretary T. Hawley Tapping, '16*l*, began his annual tours around the country to visit local alumni clubs, rekindle their enthusiasm, and demonstrate that they were not forgotten by their alma mater. His remarkable memory for names and his indomitable cheerfulness were powerful assets in a career that continued until his retirement in 1958. In 1923 Professor Lane retired from the presidency of the Alumni Association after twenty-two years in office. An Alumni Fund was created as an ongoing project for which contributions were always welcome.

Mrs. Burton repeated what she had done at the University of Minnesota. In 1921 she called together some wives of faculty members and proposed forming a Faculty Women's Club to be divided into sections according to interests: play reading, art, music, cooking, book reviews, interior decorating, needlecraft, child study, bridge, gardening, sports, square dancing, and a special section for newcomers. It has flourished ever since.

2. Changes in research, teaching, and curriculum

Opportunities for research were enlarged. Not simply were sabbatical leaves encouraging, but an appeal was made for funds that might be allotted for research. Meanwhile, the Regents began to make grants. The amount of money available to the Graduate School to publish the results of research was boosted, and an editor of scholarly publications appointed— Dr. Eugene S. McCartney, of Northwestern University. The Engineering Research Department, after most modest beginnings, attracted projects costing industry $57,000 in 1923-24.

Research materials on campus were increased. The Clements collection of early Americana was the most conspicuous example, but Librarian Bishop spent the fall of 1921 in Europe buying thousands of desired titles. He also arranged for the purchase of the library of the late Henry Vignaud, longtime secretary of the American embassy in Paris, a collection rich in books and atlases relating to the discovery and exploration of America. The material was divided between the Clements Library and the University Library, with Mr. Clements paying a good share of the cost. In addition, 139 legal documents dated in the first half of the first century A.D. were obtained in Egypt and bought jointly by John W. Anderson, '90/ and the Regents. Another group of forty-three Greek papyri relating to the Bible was presented to the University. These additions raised to about 6000 the pieces of papyri owned by the University, dating from the third century B.C. to the eighth century A.D. Then in 1923 Horace H. Rackham of Detroit provided $50,000 a year for three years for excavations in the Near East and Africa. Under the direction of Kelsey, Boak, and others excavations were undertaken at various sites, including Karanis, ancient Carthage, and ancient Antioch in Asia Minor.

Scientific expeditions flourished in these years. A zoological trek up the Amazon in 1921 was paid for by E. B. Williamson of Bluffton, Indiana. Professor Hobbs made an extensive trip through the North and South Pacific islands in 1921-22 studying volcanoes, on $5000 given by former Regent Osborn. An archaeological expedition to the Philippines started in September 1922 under Carl E. Guthe, who was appointed to the newly created Museum of Anthropology staff. Its cost of $30,000 was underwritten by an anonymous donor, and former Professor Dean Worcester, who had initiated the project, was on hand to greet the party and lend his yacht. Robert P. Lamont, Chicago alumnus, presented to the University a 27-inch refracting telescope (the fourth largest in the country) to be set up in South Africa to map the southern skies. Professor William J. Hussey left in 1923 to select the proper location. The Lamont-Hussey Observatory, as it is known today, is near Bloemfontein.

OBSERVATORY, SOUTH AFRICA

The new vitality and surge of the University quickly found expression in a broadened scope of teaching. A separate School of Education was created on July 1, 1921, with Professor Allen S. Whitney as dean. It trained upperclassmen to become teachers and granted a bachelor of arts or a bachelor of science degree in education. Teachers in the state had long agitated for this development at the University, even though there were four teacher-training normal colleges in Michigan. The Department of Hygiene and Public Health was established under Dr. John Sundwall, who was also to teach in the Medical School and have charge of the gymnasiums and a program of intramural sports. The Department of Intercollegiate Athletics was organized, responsible for coaching teams and for courses in training coaches in the new School of Education. Fielding Yost was made director, to be paid from physical education fees and to be a member of the Board in Control of Athletics.

A Detroit group asked the Regents to train social workers. A curriculum was prepared and Professor Arthur E. Wood was made director. From this beginning grew the School of Social Work in 1951. Newspaper editors of the state, whom President Burton cultivated assiduously, formed a University Press Club to meet annually on the campus. They urged a separate department of journalism, but as a first step journalism was added to the Department of Rhetoric and a curriculum set up. The journalism faculty gave attention also to the quality of high-school publications in the state. In 1921 it invited the student editors and their sponsoring teachers to confer in Ann Arbor, and out of this meeting the Michigan Interscholastic Press Association was formed. The separate Department of Journalism emerged in 1929.

A program for dental hygiene was arranged in the Dental College.

Next came the Department of Biological Chemistry in the Medical School, with Dr. Howard B. Lewis from the University of Illinois in charge. The College of Engineering created the separate Department of Geodesy and Surveying, and the Department of Geography was established in the Literary College.

Henry Carter Adams, chairman of the Economics Department, retired in 1921 and was replaced by Edmund E. Day. Three years later Day divided the department and following the lead of other universities created a School of Business Administration. Three years of college work were required for entrance, which only a very few other schools demanded. The College of Architecture broadened its curriculum by offering a bachelor's degree in design for students interested in decoration. Only three other schools offered such training.

A momentous change came in 1922. The state legislature in 1921 passed a resolution advising the University to consolidate its two medical schools for reasons of economy and then removed the ancient provision in all its appropriation bills that specifically mentioned providing for the Homeopathic Medical College. The Regents were not averse to closing the failing college. However, a public hearing was held at which the homeopathic profession and Dean Hinsdale vigorously assailed the proposal from the legislature, which had previously so favored the profession. But financial facts could not be argued away, and on June 30, 1922, the Homeopathic College ceased to exist. Provision was made in the regular Medical School for two courses in homeopathy to be offered for those students who wanted such instruction. The small faculty was largely absorbed, and since Dean Hinsdale had already resigned for age there was no difficulty there. As a matter of fact, he was appointed to the Museum of Anthropology to pursue his hobby of Indian archeology, which he did for another twenty-two years!

ROBERT FROST

One of Burton's innovations was a Fellowship in Creative Art, at a salary that would attract poets or painters to the campus for a year. They would not teach, but pursue work and make themselves available to talk informally with groups of students or with individuals. It was to be teaching by exposure to a creative mind at work. To finance the fellowship, Burton obtained a gift of $5000 from former Regent and Governor Chase Osborn. The first appointment, for the year 1921-22, was Robert Frost. His attraction to students and his friendly wisdom made his stay in Ann Arbor a great success, so much so that he was invited to remain another year, financed by another donor. For the year 1923-24, Robert Bridges, poet laureate of Great Britain, settled in Ann Arbor but because of ill health could stay only three months. President Burton also increased the number of free lectures during the academic year by outside scholars.

Dean Vaughan retired from the Medical School in June 1921 and was replaced by Dr. Hugh Cabot, new head of the Surgery Department. He attempted to solve the problem of holding high-priced physicians as professors, not by letting them carry on a private practice, which aroused the jealousy of their colleagues who could not practice, but by paying them two salaries: one from the Medical School for teaching and one from the University Hospital for clinical work as a demonstration to students. The Regents approved of this double-salary arrangement. The new chairman of surgery was Dr. Frederick A. Coller, whose surgical techniques and teaching ability became famous. He performed the first thoracoplasty (collapse of the lung for tuberculosis) in the state in 1927.

Dean Myra Jordan retired in 1922 and was succeeded by Jean Hamilton. Dr. C. G. Parnall, director of the University Hospital and one of its planners, resigned in 1924 and was succeeded by Dr. Harley A. Haynes. Filibert Roth retired in 1923 as professor of forestry and so did Frederick C. Newcombe as professor of botany. Edward D. Campbell, '86, died in 1925 after long service as director of the Chemical Laboratory, an administration the more remarkable because he had lost his eyesight in a laboratory explosion. He was succeeded by Professor Moses Gomberg, who isolated the first free radicals in solution.

New men were coming in, however. Besides those already mentioned, in 1921 O. J. Campbell became professor of English and began his popular course in modern drama; in 1922 Louis I. Bredvold started to develop his reputation in eighteenth-century literature and later became chairman of the English Department. Everett S. Brown and Thomas H. Reed were appointed professors of political science; Charles P. Gordy and Orlan W. Boston, '14*e*, MSE '17, joined the Engineering College faculty. John S. Worley, a railroad executive, was made professor of transportation engineering in 1923 and began what became an extraordinary library of transportation. In 1924 E. Blythe Stason joined the Law School faculty, and Clarence S. Yoakum joined the new School of Business Administration. Dr. Margaret Bell was added to the University Health Service and taught women's physical education. Palmer Christian was appointed University organist to succeed Earl Moore, who was made professor of music. Dr. James D. Bruce became director of internal medicine at University Hospital in 1925.

On the Board of Regents, Ralph Stone, '92*l*, a founder of the *Michigan Daily*, an attorney, and president of the Detroit Trust Company, was elected to succeed Frank Leland.

3. Academic standards and student life

Mortar and men certainly improved the University, but Burton was also concerned with raising its academic standards, making a degree from Michigan a badge of increasing distinction. He raised the requirement for admission of high-school graduates, and right away the number of University students on probation decreased. Librarian Bishop reported an enormous increase in use of the library, as Burton emphasized thoroughness and excellence. Grades D and E carried no honor points, and 120 were required for graduation; Burton persuaded the faculty to make grade E carry a negative 1, so that it would have to be offset by a B (two points) in order to maintain a one-point or C average. Things were getting tougher for the poor student. Then three professional schools turned the screws: to enter Law School, three years of college work in certain fields, or preferably a bachelor's degree, were now required; the Dental School demanded two years of college work; and the Medical School, in an effort to check rising enrollment, simply demanded higher grades in college work for entrance.

To provide for the more gifted students Burton encouraged honors courses in English and history that entailed heavier assignments, asking that recitation sections of large lecture courses be graded by ability so that more could be expected of the brighter sections. He inaugurated an Honors Convocation in Hill Auditorium each spring to pay public recognition to scholarship holders and students elected to honorary societies or who otherwise excelled intellectually.

Burton was intent on battling mediocre standards of values and performance with which students were infected before they came to the University. Children base their sense of values on what their elders have worshipped, he said, and right now business achievement is the magnetic fact in American life. Furthermore, among students it was considered bad form to be a "highbrow." This attitude fostered a disposition inimical to scholastic attainment. Student leadership in athletics or activities was the measure of success, the status symbol. While this might be commendable, Burton conceded, he insisted that the University did not exist for such students. It was not going to cater to them, but to those who came for intellectual development.

The University itself, he diagnosed, suffered from two anti-intellectual diseases. The first was brought on by the decline of the universal classical curriculum and the rise of free elections. Students became "adept in scattering and smattering," with the result that there was a lack of unity in the intellectual appeal of the University. Then major and minor courses were demanded "in the hope of regaining some of the unity and depth of the older curriculum." The danger of excessive departmentalization was that "students have imagined that the universe, in some mysterious way, is actually departmentalized." Methods must be devised, Burton warned the faculty, to correct "this rather baffling but fundamental mistake. Knowledge is one and it is inviting. Intellectualists must even forget that intellectualism needs defense. Today it has too much of the outward look and not enough of the inward thrust. The real intellectualist is not proud of his knowledge. The first mark of a real scholar is intellectual modesty. Some of us forget that just here the mind proves its winsomeness. Students will want to be intellectual when scholars are intrinsically real—that is to say, when they seem to be citizens of a universe rather than of one of its provinces."

This was the voice of a neo-Angell protesting against specialization. The consequence of it at the student level was, Burton perceived, the lack of a common background of knowledge for comradeship. The only thing they had in common to talk about was, of all things, athletics. Burton did not have a quick remedy; all he could do was throw out suggestions to the faculty. General and comprehensive final examinations for seniors or required courses in contemporary civilization might help. Opportunities for student conversations with faculty members outside of class and with men of affairs brought to the campus perhaps would be stimulating. He urged the faculty to try to make learning exciting.

Burton addressed the students, too, for learning was a two-sided experience. "Learning does not come in a hurry. She cannot be won by force. She is a jealous god and does not bestow her blessings upon those who run after false idols. She does not sit all day in the market place or worry about quick returns. She has rarely received the plaudits of the crowds. Learning has a quiet and simple beauty all her own which deepens with the years. And this is the habitation of learning! Our jazz bands, our saxophone orchestras, our whirling giddy parties, our 'busts,' our proms, our hops, our moving pictures, our schedules which make way for 'second shows,' our joy rides, all these and many other things gather into a noisy rushing rabble and banish learning. They may have, they do have, their proper place but just now they occupy an unduly large place in student interest. The emphasis is false."

DIAG IN THE MID 1920s

Despite his insistence on high performance in the pursuit of learning, Burton was remarkably tolerant of the excesses in student behavior. He possessed a saving sense of humor, and he needed it. For this was the age of the "flapper"—the coed with bobbed hair, painted face, a falling waist line approaching a rising hem line, and rolled stockings. Her escort was little improvement on nature either. He favored sideburns, pomaded hair, a felt hat of improbable convolutions, bellbottom trousers, and "loud" socks. He wore a coonskin coat and unbuckled galoshes in winter, and a yellow slicker, prolifically inscribed, in rainy weather. Both male and female could and did dance interminably, and the strenuous "Charleston" was in favor; otherwise a roadster seemed to be required for movement.

The ukulele and the saxophone replaced the mandolin as part of the mating call. Radio broadcasting began in 1920 and spread like the flu, but movies were the great entertainment. Of course, a vast number of students still dressed sedately, danced occasionally, and walked almost everywhere, but the era tended to be characterized then and later by its extreme types. There were all-campus dances, to student jazz orchestras, every Friday and Saturday night at the Union ballroom and at the Armory. In addition, an average of eight to ten fraternities and sororities were holding dance parties on the same evenings. Big class dances, besides the venerable J Hop, were the Freshman Frolic, the Sophomore Prom, the Senior Reception, the Military Ball, and the Architects' Ball—all part of the rites of spring. Waring's Pennsylvanians, a new orchestra of college students, played for the J Hop in 1922.

These were the years that fraternities boomed. Local clubs and fraternities were quickly formed and after a year of satisfactory existence usually sought na-tional affiliation. By the end of 1924, Michigan had sixty national and local social fraternities, twenty-one profes-sional fraternities, and twenty-two so-rorities. They claimed about 32 percent of the men students, and about 22 percent of the women students.

GLEE CLUB IN THE 1920s

Football games aroused frenzied enthusiasm. Michigan won the Big Ten championship in 1922 and again in 1923. From these teams Henry

Vick, Jack Blott, Paul Goebel, and Edliff Slaughter were named All-Americans. Harry Kipke, '24, developed a deadly toe for punting and won another All-American berth. He was retained as an assistant coach and soon became head coach. Another distinction came when track star De Hart Hubbard won the Olympic broad jump title at Paris in 1924.

Burton flattered the students and relieved his office of burdensome detail by creating a deanship charged with the affairs of students, distinct from the role played by the familiar Dean of Women's office. Professor Joseph Bursley was appointed to the new office and remained until his retirement in 1947. He interpreted his role to be a friend to students rather than a policeman. To reinforce this role, a Student Advisory Committee was created to consult with Dean Bursley on complaints and to make recommendations.

Aside from disciplinary problems, which were handled by faculty committees in the various colleges or were referred to a University Disciplinary Committee of faculty members, the greatest problems presented by the students to the dean were finding part-time jobs, locating decent rooms in private homes, counseling students academically, and securing loans of money. In brief, jobs could not be found for all students needing and wanting them, especially for women. As for housing, Dean Bursley became convinced by 1924 that some supervision of rooming houses was both desirable and necessary to obtain essential cleanliness, ventilation, and fire protection and that housing conditions for men would never be what they should be "until we have University-owned dormitories," at the very least for freshmen.

These were also the years in which "Doc" Lovell and Railroad Jack flourished. They may be coupled only in that both were born in 1863 and sometimes engaged in debate. Thomas Lovell was an Englishman, a cobbler by trade, who migrated to Canada in 1907. By 1910 he was running a shoe repair shop in Ann Arbor and lecturing to students on every conceivable subject, although not always coherently. The *Daily* found him good copy and posed him in various athletic uniforms. Lovell began publishing his poetry in 1915 and also printed two forgettable songs: "Goodbye Sweetheart," and "As I Stood and Looked at Her up in the Tree." He was dubbed Michigan's poet laureate. Even more, students purloined or fabricated official letterheads of organizations on which they gave him honorary memberships and degrees. Within a few years he had accumulated more than a dozen distinctions: besides being a PhD and DD, he was given the degree of LLD (Doctor of Love Letters) and TNT (Thinks New Thoughts). One of the students' favorites, and his, was the rank of lieutenant colonel of archery. In March 1922 the *Daily* solemnly reported that the prince of Lapland had conferred on him the degree of SOS (Society of Scribes), carrying with it a permanent seat in the League of Nations. At times Lovell seemed to know that the students were making fun of him, but at other times he took it all seriously, especially when they presented Hill Auditorium to him. He usually addressed the students on campus, at the corner of North University and State Street, frequently disputing Darwin's theory of evolution. Encouraged by students after President Burton's death, he applied to the Board of Regents for the position of president. He was a most cheerful and kindly man, and faculty, townspeople, and students were genuinely fond of him. He died in 1930 at the county hospital, ending two decades as a Michigan fixture.

Railroad Jack was of a different stripe. Born Harry Cooper in Wisconsin, he entered Rush Medical School and then quit to practice journalism. While he was a staff writer for a railroad magazine, he took the pen name of Railroad Jack. He was an incessant reader of history with a remarkable memory and became a minor publisher in Chicago and a friend of Eugene Field. In 1895 he took to the open road, usually riding freight cars. He made a livelihood by appearing on various midwestern campuses advertising himself as the "World's Champion History Expert." His performance was to ask students to call out various dates, and he would recite what had happened in those years. Then he took up a collection. If his income were thin, he would wash dishes in some fraternity for board or carve members' names on a plank plaque until he rode the rails again. He was arrogant, agnostic, defiant, and loved the sound of his own voice. He enjoyed replying to Doc Lovell's lectures, and of course the students relished bringing them together. He was also a living lesson to students that accumulation of mere factual knowledge did not make an educated man and was as pathetic a figure, in a way, as Doc Lovell.

Railroad Jack was found dead from exposure in Coldwater in 1933. To everyone's surprise, Father Carey, University pastor in Ann Arbor, claimed his body and buried it in the local Catholic cemetery. They had been longtime friends, though Jack was not a convert.

The dean of women reported that the 1827 coeds, exclusive of nurses and graduates, were housed as follows: 314 in sororities, 327 in dormitories, 402 at home or with friends, and 784 in league houses. There were 102 league houses, inspected and approved, with four to twenty women. Thrown together by chance, the women in the league houses often had little in common and were not always congenial. The dean tried to have them organize and accept collective responsibility. In 1921 Mrs. Burton first opened the President's House for three freshman teas by way of welcoming the new women and helping them get acquainted. The one activity that united all the women was raising money for a Woman's League building, similar to the Union, and it involved a series of annual events— plays, bazaars, flower shows, rummage sales, the Junior Girls' Play, the Senior Women's Play, etc. By June 1924, $440,000 had been raised by students and alumnae.

Further, to show consideration for the student body President Burton had the University buy space in the *Michigan Daily* for a "Daily Official Bulletin" containing announcements and news for students. The readers felt they knew what was going on in the University that was of immediate concern to them. Handsome and a spellbinding speaker, Burton won the

admiration of the students and resumed the tradition of delivering the baccalaureate address each June. The student who found the size of the University awesome was reassured by him: Here at Michigan, he said, is "a richly di-

JUNIOR GIRLS PLAY

versified and versatile community. A student may find as friends just those persons who will prove most stimulating to him. The modern college student must live in a large world. He must be able to go into a huge modern city and feel at home. He needs orientation and the capacity to deal with large groups without losing his sense of mastery or of personal significance. It is just here that the man who has the necessary capacities and potentialities will acquire much by being part of a large institution. It prepares for life." Burton also advocated an office to advise students on vocations and to help them find the kind of job they wanted.

Hazing raised its ugly head again in the spring of 1922 when two freshmen who considered certain freshman customs silly refused to conform. Freshmen themselves objected that these two classmates would not wear their green pots or toques. The Underclass Conduct Committee threatened both, and the freshman class voted to "ostracize" them and threatened to ask for their expulsion. Both students relented for awhile, but after again omitting his toque, one was abducted and his hair clipped. The fathers of both supported the independence of their sons, accused the Student Council of complicity, and the administration of laxness.

President Burton thought the incidents were ballooned out of proportion to their importance. Nevertheless, he appointed a faculty committee to investigate. "Conformity to student customs," the committee warned, "cannot be made a prerequisite to the enjoyment by any student of the privileges of the University." Burton added that student self-government was an effort to substitute reason for force, and if the students

FROSH HAZING

continued to use force they were only attacking their own government. If force prevailed, then student government would be voided.

Late that fall, when the football team returned victorious from its last game, students celebrated by rushing two movie theaters and damaging both places. Student leaders took up a collection to pay for the vandalism. Part of the blame rested on the Student Council for permitting the *Daily* to publish that "free shows might be expected" on the team's return. Burton lowered the boom and asked the Senate to recommend that the Student Council reorganize itself in a way to serve more responsibly and effectively. Before the new Council got under way, a milder theater rush occurred on May 9, followed by Swing-out the next day in which several students appeared intoxicated. Burton recommended dismissal of such offenders when they could he identified, and the Regents authorized abolishing any student function if its conduct was injurious to the reputation of the University.

The new Student Council was reduced in size to nine elected members and three ex officio members (the editor of the *Daily*, the president of the Michigan Union, and a representative of athletic teams). Alfred B. Connable, Jr., '24, was elected the first president of the reorganized Student Council. He later became a regent. The Council was also empowered to make preliminary investigation of behavior cases referred by college faculty committees to the University Committee on Discipline. Since the latter employed no detectives or investigators to gather evidence, it relied on the Student Council to provide the facts in each case. Ten cases were heard by the University Committee in 1923-24: four students were expelled, seven were suspended for a semester, and three were placed on probation. No theater rushes occurred during the year, and Swing-out passed without incident. The absence of hazing was marked, but public drunkenness of students continued to be a vexing problem.

The next student problem beginning to bother the administration was the proliferation of student automobiles. The Conference of Deans urged a statement of University disapproval of cars, and the Regents agreed in June 1923 by asking the president to send a form letter to the parents of all students urging them to prohibit or limit the use of cars by their sons or daughters. But Dean Bursley sadly reported that the number of cars around campus increased in the fall of 1923. Evidently the University would have to make its own curb on cars.

One other activity aroused a curious reaction. The Michigan Union Opera's 1923 production, "Cotton Stockings" was the best one ever seen on campus for music, dancing, costuming, and scenery. During the Christmas vacation it played in five other Michigan cities and then embarked on the most ambitious tour of any opera. It played in Toledo, Cleveland, Buffalo, New York, Philadelphia, Washington, Pittsburgh, Cincinnati, and Chicago and took in more money than any other opera. Instead of being pleased by this professional success, several alumni groups complained that the performance was too polished, that the revue formula deprived it of its reflection of University life, that it was too obviously extravagant. (The Princeton Triangle Club struck the same chord of response to its best shows.) The University Senate joined in the criticism and advised the Union board of directors to reduce the cost of the next opera and make it more representative of student life. The board complied, and some alumni argued that there never was another opera in the same class with "Cotton Stockings," music and lyrics by Charles H. Sword, '24, and William C. Kratz, '24e, and book by Charles H. Sword. Lionel Ames, the leading "lady," went on to a stage career.

In June 1924 President Burton was called on to make the nominating speech in the National Republican Convention for Governor Calvin Coolidge of Massachusetts for President. His oratory was widely acclaimed, and another Michigan president achieved national visibility. Late in October he suffered a heart attack and was confined to bed. The angina prevented him from seeing anyone besides his family. He remained at home the rest of the fall and through Christmas while anxiety for his recovery grew. When the state legislature met in January 1925, it sent a resolution of sympathy and good wishes. On February 9 he died. His body lay in state in Alumni Memorial Hall, from which place it was taken to Forest Hills cemetery for burial.

The Regents' resolution of sorrow and respect rambled on but summed up the loss in one telling sentence: "Rare, indeed, is the man who can combine in such unusual degree his many superlative attributes of head and heart." Like Tappan, his passage from the scene stirs speculation on how much more the University could have benefited from a continuation of his driving administration. Not only had he more than doubled the University's annual income, but he had won $10,400,000 in appropriations for new buildings and gift buildings costing $2,400,000. Undoubtedly, had he lived he would have concentrated more of his attention on improving the quality and variety of education than he had been able to do.

Since he had not been able to obtain life insurance and had not been in academic work long enough for his widow to be eligible for a pension from the Carnegie Foundation, and his University contributory insurance was so far trivial, a memorial endowment fund of $106,000 was contributed by twenty-five friends of the University for Mrs. Burton, at the inspiration of Shirley Smith. A permanent memorial in the form of a carillon tower was suggested by the students, ultimately realized in 1936.

President Emeritus Hutchins signed the diplomas issued in February 1925, and after Burton's death Dean Alfred H. Lloyd of the Graduate School was appointed acting president. A committee of three Regents and three professors selected by the Senate Council—Regents Clements, Beal, and Sawyer and Professors Huber, Reeves, and Sadler—began to search for a successor.

CAMPUS, VIEWED FROM THE EAST, MID-1920s

CHAPTER NINE

PRESIDENT LITTLE EMBATTLED

APPROXIMATELY FORTY-FIVE suggestions for president were handed to the joint committee by faculty members in 1925. Less than ten survived the first scrutiny. The committee finally investigated thoroughly only a couple of individuals. It wanted a man young and in vigorous good health, a scholar with character fit for exercising leadership of young men and women, a proven administrator, and an able interpreter of university purposes to alumni and the public. This was a large order, but the committee believed it had found its man in Clarence Cook Little.

CLARENCE C. LITTLE

He was thirty-six years old and had been president of the University of Maine for three years. Before that time he had directed research at the Carnegie Institution's Station for Experimental Evolution on Long Island and had served as assistant dean at Harvard. During the war he had been a major in the Adjutant General's Department. He held three degrees from Harvard, the highest being a doctor of science in biology. The Board of Regents appointed him president at $15,000 a year, plus $2000 for living and entertainment, plus an unprecedented $5000 for research assistance— for he intended to continue his laboratory research into the nature and causes of cancer.

1. The University College

Little was the first of a small handful of new generation educators, including Robert M. Hutchins who came to the helm of the University of Chicago in 1929, and Robert G. Sproul who became president of the University of California in 1930. They had ideas which were opposed not by students or regents, but by the older generation of faculty members. Little favored the university ideal of faculty research, but clung to the New England collegiate ideal of a selected student body, character emphasis, small dormitories, and a common curriculum for the first two years.

Coupled with Dr. Little's genuine talents and abilities in education was a mischievous indifference to the views of persons or organizations outside the University. Rarely could he pass over in silence any evidence of ignorance, prejudice, or hostility. He took a sophomoric delight in needling those he didn't care for, consequently arousing their personal dislike for him and irritation with the University that employed him. In short, although he could be charming he was deficient in the patience and tact requisite in public relations; rather than cultivate them he turned ultimately to research work.

For instance, he spoke out boldly and repeatedly in favor of birth control—even from a pulpit—at a time when the subject was seldom mentioned in polite society. His view alienated many Roman Catholics. He once invited the members of the House and Senate finance committees to a football game, but omitted one member whom he did not like, thus ensuring a powerful University enemy in the legislature. Patriotic genealogical societies irritated him, and once upon receiving an invitation to join the America First Foundation, he embroidered his sharp refusal with the comment: "My chief detailed regret in looking over the literature is that Washington's Farewell Address and not yours was enclosed."

In dealing with the faculty his boldness was not shocking, but his decisiveness and impatience were discomfiting. Inevitably, the faculty contained a few veteran professors whose reputations (they felt) entitled them to be consulted and to participate in executive decisions. Burton knew how to handle them; Little was not willing to humor their egos. Thus, his chief innovation in educational philosophy ran into opposition that sought in part to rationalize offended dignity and preserve old jurisdictions.

The innovation that he proposed in his first year was to enroll all freshmen and sophomores in a separate University College under its own dean. The aim was to provide the students with some common knowledge in several fields of learning and to winnow out those who would be satisfied with two years of general courses. In such a college the underclassmen would become known personally to their instructors. The classes would be geared to their high-school preparation rather than to the demands of advanced courses. Freshmen would be held together as a group rather than divided among colleges. Upon completion of the two years, some students would be given a certificate and not encouraged to continue. The others, who wished to enter another college of the University at the junior level, would have to pass a comprehensive examination.

The Regents requested the University Senate to appoint a committee to study and report on the proposal. President Little was made chairman of the committee, which consisted of all the deans and sixteen professors. Getting a barrage of criticisms, the committee submitted a brief preliminary report recommending that the year 1927-28 be devoted to extended discussion of the plan.

The Senate committee met eight times, meeting last in February 1928, and rendered a generally favorable report, although recommending an executive committee of ten rather than a dean to head the new college, and not a separate faculty but one that was an integral part of existing departments. This report was submitted to the faculties of all colleges for further analysis. The Literary College and the College of Engineering and Architecture both found fault with the plan. Committees of those two faculties met with the Regents on April 25, 1928, and expanded on their objections.

The Literary College faculty charged that the University did not have enough money to support such a college (a question not within their purview) and listed other complaints: a separate student body making up the University College would affect adversely the unity and spirit of the Literary College (naturally); the two-year terminal students would not be worthy alumni (!); the University would be in effect establishing a Junior College on campus and such colleges were still new and questionable; the University must be guided by scholars, whereas the new college was in danger of being led by a committee "of mere educators" (!); and a faculty for underclass teaching would be hard to recruit. There was something to this last objection, for in each department a schism was likely to develop between those who taught upperclassmen and graduate students and those who were assigned to teach underclassmen. A separate faculty under its own dean might have forestalled this divisive situation. The Engineering College committee had further objections involving the demands of state-regulated professions and the frank desire of the College to supervise its students during their first two years.

The Board of Regents was not impressed by the negative attitude of the two colleges, and neither was President Little. His plan was actually reactionary in the sense that it would revive a collegiate ideal, while the Michigan faculty considered it radical because they had been so long committed to the university ideal. Little represented the New Humanism that was critical of free elections, the large impersonal lecture courses, the failure to emphasize character training, and the general atmosphere of scientific materialism. The Board of Regents voted to proceed with appointment of an executive committee to develop plans to open the University College in September 1929. In a sense, the gauntlet was flung down.

2. Faculty and campus

While this controversy was simmering, other educational changes

UNIVERSITY HOSPITAL (OLD MAIN)

took place. After considerable delay to secure needed funding for completion, the new University Hospital (Old Main), finally opened in 1926. The
Forestry Department was elevated to a School of Forestry and Conservation in 1927, with Dr. Samuel T. Dana, director of the U. S. Northeastern
Forest Experiment Station as dean. It has now developed into the School
of Natural Resources and Environment. The Department of Postgraduate
Medicine was organized under Dr. James Bruce to help practicing physicians brush up on new developments. This work has become one of the
most important services of the University to the state. Courses in library
science, heretofore offered only in the summer session, were expanded
into a regular department in 1926. Persons with baccalaureate degrees
were admitted and given a second bachelor's degree in library science.
This anomaly was removed in 1949, afterwhich graduates were awarded
master's degrees. Twenty year later, it became the School of Library
Sciences, which in 1987 was renamed the School of Information and
Library Studies.

The private School of Music was consolidated with the University in
February 1929 and although its president, Charles Sink, continued as
president of the University Musical Society, its director, Earl Moore,
served as a de facto dean. Journalism was made a separate department, with
Professor John L. Brumm as chairman. The separate departments of
English, mathematics, and modern languages in the College of Engineering were united with the same departments in the Literary College; then
the departments of English, rhetoric, and speech were combined into a
division because of their common substance.

A dean of administration was created in May 1927 as a kind of vice-president in charge of the budget. Dean Day was appointed to the position. He resigned in 1928 to head the division of social sciences of the Rockefeller Foundation, later going to Cornell as president, Michigan's third contribution to that position. Dr. Alexander G. Ruthven succeeded Day as dean of administration, and Professor Clare Griffin took his place as dean of the School of Business Administration. A registrar was appointed in 1925 to center all admissions in one office. Previously students were admitted by the deans of the respective colleges. Ira Smith was named the first registrar and continued until his retirement in 1955.

Retirement and death deprived the University of some of its great teachers and scholars. Dean Lloyd died in 1927 and was succeeded as head of the Graduate School by Dr. G. Carl Huber of the Medical School. Dean Mortimer E. Cooley retired in 1927 but remained a noble figure on campus for another seventeen years; he was succeeded by Professor Herbert C. Sadler. Professor Henry E. Riggs retired the next year from chairmanship of the Department of Civil Engineering. Dean Allen S. Whitney gave over the reins of the School of Education to Professor James B. Edmondson. Willard C. Olson, as director of research in child development, and George E. Carrothers, as inspector of high schools, were added to the School of Education faculty.

In the Law School Professors Horace L. Wilgus, who had taught corporation law since 1895, and Victor H. Lane, who had taught evidence and conflict of laws for thirty years, both retired; new appointees were Laylin K. James from the University of Pittsburgh, and Paul Leidy from private practice. Dr. Reuben Kahn, a research chemist, was appointed director of laboratories in the University Hospital and developed the famous Kahn test for detection of syphilis. Dr. Philip Jay, '23d, was brought back to the School of Dentistry from the University of Rochester to take charge of research in controlling dental caries.

Losses in the Literary College seemed especially severe. Professor William J. Hussey died in London in 1926 on his way to the Lamont-Hussey Observatory in South Africa to install the telescope given by Robert P. Lamont, '91, of Chicago, for viewing southern skies. Ralph H. Curtiss succeeded as chairman of the department and director of the Observatory. Professor Francis Kelsey died in 1927 while directing archaeological excavations in Egypt. Professor Robert M. Wenley of the Philosophy Department died early in 1929; he was succeeded as chairman by DeWitt H. Parker, another great teacher. Psychology was separated and made a department under Professor Walter B. Pillsbury; its course offerings were beginning to grow in popularity.

Charles H. Cooley, noted early sociologist and textbook writer, also died in early 1929; his chairmanship was taken over by R. D. McKenzie. Thomas C. Trueblood retired from the Speech Department and debate activity in 1926, and Fred Newton Scott from the Rhetoric Department the next year. Fred M. Taylor, professor of economics and author of the textbook *Principles of Economics*, standard since 1911, retired in 1929 after a Michigan career of thirty-seven years. Always interested in economic theory, his studies made him a sharp critic of socialism, and he had no faith that collectivism would work. Arthur G. Canfield, who had taught Romance languages since 1900, retired, as did Max Winkler, chairman of the German Department. He had resisted the "direct method" of instruction, adopted in many places, by which classes were conducted in German, with the resulting conversation being restricted to an elementary level. The department emphasized grammar in an effort to prepare students to read comprehensively in German literature, philosophy, and science; conversational ability was a secondary objective. It would take a second European war to reverse these goals in foreign language study.

Arthur W. Bromage and James K. Pollock, Jr., joined the Political Science Department. Dow Baxter, PhD '24, began a forty-year career in forestry in 1926. Leonard Watkins, PhD '26, started a notable teaching career in economics, and Kenneth Rowe joined the Rhetoric Department and soon began his famous playwriting course.

Other faculty members added to their reputations by foreign service. Professor Sanders was given a three years' leave in 1928 to head the School of Classical Studies, part of the American Academy in Rome. Professor Bonner was named a visiting professor at the American School at Athens, and Professor Waterman filled a similar appointment at the American School of Oriental Studies at Bagdad. He identified the site of ancient Seleucia on the Tigris River, and five years of excavation followed, supported by the Toledo Museum of Art. Librarian Bishop was asked to advise the Vatican on reorganization of its huge and rich library. Professor Reeves was named one of two U. S. representatives to a meeting of the Pan-American Commission of Jurists in Brazil. Professor Hobbs led two expeditions to Greenland to study meteorological conditions. Professor Van Tyne delivered the Sir George Watson Lectures on American history in England. The University's international reputation was widely recognized.

With the transfer to Michigan from Oxford University of hundreds of thousands of slips bearing quotations illustrating uses of words in Shakespeare's time, and a grant of $100,000 from the Rockefeller General Education Board, work on an Early Modern English dictionary (1475 to 1700) was begun under Professor Charles C. Fries. A Middle English dictionary (1100 to 1475) had been started at Stanford. Because it would be of great help to the later dictionary, it was transferred to Michigan in 1930, and work was concentrated on the earlier period first.

Support for research was growing. The University raised its funds available to faculty from $3000 to $30,000 in 1927. From private sources came a grant of $225,000 to President Little to underwrite his cancer research. The archaeological excavations in Egypt continued for several years. The General Education Board gave another $150,000 in 1928 for advanced humanistic research, while the Carnegie Corporation granted $100,000 to the Fine Arts Department for graduate instruction, although the emphasis remained on the history of art. Frederick W. Stevens, '87*l*, of Grand Rapids, who had lived in Peking, died in 1926 and left his collection of Chinese art—textiles, jewelry, porcelain, ivory, bronze, and paintings—to the University. Ground was broken for Mr. Cook's Legal Research Library which carried with it a fund to encourage investigations of interest to the legal profession. The Guggenheim Fund granted $78,000 to the College of Engineering to encourage instruction in aeronautics.

President Little succeeded in persuading the legislature in 1927 to remove the ceiling on the mill tax. As a result, the University's income jumped from $3,700,000 to $4,600,000; in 1929 it rose to $4,900,000. The Regents presented a building program for the biennium that led the legislature to grant $4,150,000, but the businessman Governor Fred Green cut back the amount to only $1,350,000. Left was only enough for land for the Michigan League, a model elementary school, and additions to the power plant.

From other funds building proceeded, however. Alumnae had raised $587,000 in cash and $1,000,000 in pledges toward a Woman's League building. Robert Lamont had donated $100,000 as a memorial to his friend, Mrs. Ethel Fountain Hussey, '91, first president of the League. Construction started in 1927, and the building opened in May 1929. If there was no swimming pool, as once hoped for, there was a splendid small theater made possible by a gift from Gordon Mendelssohn of Detroit in memory of his mother, L y d i a Mendelssohn.

LAYING THE CORNERSTONE FOR THE MICHIGAN LEAGUE

The Board in Control of Athletics issued bonds for construction of a large football stadium farther away from campus, a bowl that would hold 85,000 people and later enlarged to hold over 100,000. The bonds were

MICHIGAN STADIUM, 1929

redeemed from gate receipts, and in spite of the ensuing depression they were paid off before maturity. The new Michigan Stadium opened for the last game of the 1927 season. Receipts were such that the Board was able to authorize a large Intramural Sports building on the edge of Ferry Field to encourage more participation in sports by men students. President

Little had been critical of an athletic program that engaged relatively so few students as University teams did. In addition, a small field house was erected for women on Palmer Field, between the campus and the Observatory.

MARCHING MEN OF MICHIGAN, 1927

The Regents purchased 120 acres at Jackson Hole, Wyoming, seventy-five miles south of Yellowstone Park, early in 1929 for a surveying camp for the Engineering College. Heretofore, surveying had been practiced to a limited extent at Camp Davis, Douglas Lake, which was then given over completely to the Biological Station. The Wyoming tract was then called Camp Davis. Engineering Research contracted for investigations that amounted to $234,000 in 1928-29. The year before the College of Engineering had started cooperative programs with industries by which students could earn up to ten hours credit by working a summer or semester in a factory.

To reach alumni and others, the University embarked on a regular radio broadcast through Detroit's WJR in 1925. Music by student groups, and talks by professors constituted the series. Waldo Abbot of the Rhetoric Department became program director. The second year the series went out over WWJ. Thereafter, the programs grew in depth and scope. A network of small state stations was developed for the broadcast of athletic events. Abbot wrote a textbook on educational broadcasting, and finally in 1947 the University secured a license and a station of its own, WUOM.

When President Hoover announced his first cabinet appointments in 1929, he included three Michigan alumni: Robert P. Lamont, '91, as secretary of commerce; James W. Good, '93, secretary of war; and Arthur M. Hyde, '99, secretary of agriculture.

3. The needs and activities of students

Little displayed a genuine concern for students. He spoke up boldly for dormitories in order to improve their living conditions. He advocated dormitories housing 350 to 450 students and two or three faculty members. Each such house would serve as a small residential college, a unit for intramural sports, and a center for social intimacy to foster lasting friendships. They would, he argued, combine the advantages of small college living with big university libraries and laboratories. He besought the alumni to provide units for men students, and the state to build women's units, and the University was eventually successful with the latter.

MOSHER-JORDAN UNDER CONSTRUCTION

Money for scholarships and loans was increased during his administration. Alfred J. Brosseau of New York gave $115,000 for these purposes, and Miss Mary S. Manelle gave $60,000 for Simon Mandelbaum scholarships. A Senate committee on vocational guidance was set up under Professor Yoakum in 1926 to test aptitude for certain occupations and professions so as to help steer students into proper vocations. It was later combined with the teacher placement service of the School of Education into the Bureau of Appointments and Occupational Information. T. Luther Purdom came from the University of Missouri to head it and remained until his retirement in 1956.

Little inaugurated Freshman Week in 1927 as an orientation period for new students before other students arrived. They were addressed by the president, given talks on how to study and use the Library, broken up into groups to get acquainted, given class placement tests, entertained at lawn parties by Dean and Mrs. Bursley, offered preprofessional counseling, and generally welcomed and inducted into university life. Little also invited high-school principals to visit Ann Arbor late in the fall and meet with their graduate freshmen. The latter talked about their high-school preparation, and the principals got reports on how these students were doing in the University.

For all his youth and modern outlook, President Little had some ideas about students that would not be heralded today as progressive. For one thing, he was not willing to make academic proficiency the sole criterion of admission to the University. He wanted some further information about the character of the applicants so as to judge whether they were actually worth educating, a jarring thought. "A real and lasting education cannot be obtained by an individual whose character and personality are not worth educating. 'To educate' means 'to lead out,' to cause the mind of a person to react in such a way as to send forth for further development mental processes that are constructive. This involves concentration, imagination, seriousness of purpose, industriousness, courage, and a number of other qualities of character.... It is very unlikely that a method can be devised which will give us entirely reliable information concerning a candidate before that candidate is admitted. We can, however, look forward to the detection of some who, by lack of maturity or other defects of character, are clearly unfitted for a college training...."

Further, Little did not think that the curriculum for men and women should be the same. He advocated a different group of studies for women, which would include physiology, general science, nursing hygiene, human behavior, and heredity and genetics. His reasoning was that most of the women would become homemakers and mothers, and he thought it foolish not to prepare them for these roles.

The Little years covered the climax of the jazz decade. The craze for dancing increased; every Friday and Saturday night there was dancing at the Union, and later at the League, and at Granger's Academy on East Huron Street. Each ballroom accommodated 400 couples, and the orchestras were not five-piece "combos," but bands of twelve to fourteen pieces playing sophisticated harmonic arrangements. Such orchestras were often made up of medical, dental, and law students who could play together for several years, and they were the elite among student wage earners. Graduate student Bob Carson conducted one such orchestra, and Don Loomis led the orchestra at the Union. Phil Diamond, later professor of German, played at Granger's.

There was dancing every night at the Hut and the Den, two restaurants at either end of the Diagonal, and at Drake's Sandwich Shop on North University. There were ten or a dozen fraternity and sorority dances each weekend. In late spring and all summer there were dances at Whitmore Lake. If you couldn't dance, it seemed, you were literally or figuratively crippled.

The three movie theaters near campus—the Majestic on Maynard Street, the Michigan on East Liberty, and the Arcade on North University—were jammed with long waiting lines on Friday, Saturday, and Sunday nights. Two other movie houses were located on Main Street. Sound and "talking pictures" were introduced in 1928. Most of the students had radios in their rooms, and every fraternity house owned a phonograph.

There were frequent causes for student celebration, for the unbelievable football years continued. In 1925 and 1926 Michigan won the Big Ten championship. These were the seasons of such All-American

WOMEN'S GYMNASTICS, 1926

stars as Bennie Oosterbaan (for three years), Robert Brown, Harry Hawkins, Ben Friedman, and Otto Pommerening. Edward George won the Olympic heavyweight wrestling championship at Amsterdam in 1928. In 1926, 1927 and 1929 the Michigan basketball team won the Big Ten title. Matt Mann's swimming team began its domination of Western Conference meets. "Hail to the Victors—The Champions of the West" was not a hope or boast, but simply a statement of fact.

Even the University debating team, coached by Professor R. D. T. Hollister, went to England in 1926 and won four out of five debates with British university teams. The members were Ephraim Gomberg, '27, William King, '27*l*, and Gerald White, '27, '29*l*.

John Held Jr. cartooned the jazz set, and *College Humor* was its scripture, although the more sophisticated humor of *The New Yorker* was beginning to be preferred. *Gargoyle* steadily diminished its two line jokes and tried to write satirically of campus happenings and personages. Its art editor, Maurice Lichtenstein, '29, became a noted cartoonist as "Lichty."

It was a time of prosperity for the *Michigan Daily*. It published eight pages regularly and a Sunday literary supplement. Space advertising was plentiful. Circulation ranged from about 4100 to 4500 copies during the decade.

Despite all laws and regulations, hip flasks were the mark of sophistication, and liquor was widely regarded as the sovereign remedy for keeping warm at a football game. A related "thing to do" was to take one's date to a Detroit speakeasy. Fraternity dances were frequently aromatic with spirits. "It" meant sex appeal, and Clara Bow personified it in the movies.

Such behavior did not have President Little's approval. He was tolerant, but not to the point of indifference. At a mass meeting of organized students in December 1925 he laid down the law against liquor in fraternity houses, even that brought in by alumni, who should have known better. The houses must regulate their conduct if they expected to stay on campus. In another meeting with "Greeks" in January 1926, he continued his warning on liquor and discussed fraternity scholarship and deferred rushing. As there was no improvement in behavior at fraternity dances after football games in 1926, they were prohibited in the fall of 1927. The fraternities then promised faithfully to restrict attendance to members only and to police against drinking, so after-game dances were permitted again in the fall of 1928. But the dean's office found too many violations of rules which no outside agent could enforce and recommended suspension of such parties. Swing-out in May 1928 also revealed a disgusting spectacle of drunkenness in public, but the situation was corrected in 1929.

Dean Bursley also had to warn fraternities, and especially honorary societies, against rough initiation practices, such as physical abuse, the taking or destruction of property, noise or actions that disturbed the neighborhood, and work requirements that interfered with studying. Sphinx was suspended for a year for its carelessly rough initiation. He found the Interfraternity Council too self-centered or indifferent to be of any value in regulating fraternity affairs. The dean's office also began examining fraternity scholarship standings in 1926 and issued warnings to those houses averaging below seventy. If they did not pull themselves up the following year, they were subject to probation which eliminated pledging and social activities.

President Little viewed the automobile as another disturbance in student life, affecting "scholarship, industry, and morals." He recommended reducing the number of cars in 1926, and in 1927 advised the Regents to ban them altogether. This was done, except as the dean of students might allow exceptions. For the year 1927-28 about 700 permits were issued: 221 to Ann Arbor residents, 204 to married students, 123 to students needing cars in their jobs, 69 commuters, etc. Forty violators, who thought the University couldn't mean what it said, had to be disciplined: fifteen were put on probation, twelve suspended, and one expelled. In the

ALTERNATIVE TO THE AUTO BAN, 1927

following year, sixty-five students were disciplined. For those with or without the ever-present auto, roller skates began to appear.

In March 1929, after the basketball team had won the Conference title, students rushed the Michigan Theater, even though the manager had provided a free film at Hill Auditorium. Local police used tear gas to disperse the mob and arrested six men. $800 worth of damage was done, for which the *Daily* apologized on behalf of the students. The University suspended three of the mob leaders for a year and placed three others on probation. An attempt to raise money for the damage petered out.

League houses continued to be unsatisfactory residences for women. Of the seventy-nine operating in 1926-27, twenty-two were considered good, twenty-nine fair, and twenty-eight unsatisfactory. Fifty-four of them had inadequate parlors for entertaining. When the University announced in 1929 that it would build a large dormitory for women, local landladies protested and refused to do anything further to improve their houses.

Women's Adviser Alice Lloyd also found herself caught between opposing factions on the racial problem. A league house was available to African-American women at some distance from the campus; otherwise, the women were relegated to the homes of local African-Americans, which the dean found inadequate. Therefore, a University-owned house close to campus was fitted up for African-American women, with the enthusiastic approval of the women and of the president of the Michigan Association of Colored Women. However, during the summer of 1929 some African-American groups protested against what they saw as segregation, and the plan had to be abandoned. The situation was somewhat remedied when Mosher-Jordan Hall opened in 1930, and later a better league house for

African-American women was provided. However, true inter-racial housing was still decades away, for both women and men.

Church attendance by students was diminishing. Church-sponsored programs for students that were oriented around church commitment and Bible study suffered; programs that provided means for students to become acquainted and enjoy games, suppers, discussions, and dances were preferred. President Little observed in 1926 that "students as a whole appear to have arrived at a point of sufficient honesty to admit that a religion to which they must come through authority and fear is not true and lasting. They desire a simple unostentatious form of faith devoid of formalism and of most ritualism. They realize the imperfections of humanity, including themselves, and they have ceased to consider these imperfections to a large degree as anything except human and natural . . . . They are, I believe, ready to serve, to help, to live active useful energetic lives, believing that in so doing they are 'giving their goods to feed the poor' in a very real and spiritual sense. For this reason deputation teams visiting small rural communities and conducting services and social evenings have been popular . . . . Because many of them are trying to understand and to learn to love the general principles of Christianity one finds that discussion in small congenial groups is alive and vigorous . . . . The holding of nonsectarian Sunday morning services in Hill Auditorium started in the spring of 1926 and has proven interesting and valuable. They were attended by an average of 2500."

Despite his success with the students, the approval of the Regents, and the progress of his own research, Little felt some chill from the faculty over his main proposal in educational policy, the University College. His domestic life was coming apart, and at the meeting of the Board in January 1929 he submitted his resignation to take effect in June. The Regents were dismayed and sought to make him change his mind. The *Daily*, which had previously criticized him, was quick to praise him. His decision, just as the state legislature began its biennial session, left others to push the University budget. Little suggested to the Board that the plan for a University College be held in abeyance until the views of his successor were known. He left Ann Arbor in June and became director of Jackson Memorial Laboratory (named for Roscoe B. Jackson, '00, of Detroit) at Bar Harbor, Maine, until his retirement in 1956. He was also a director of the American Cancer Society, and his experimentation contributed invaluably to the study of the dread disease.

The dean of administration was the closest office to a vice-president, and Dr. Ruthven was asked to carry on in the interim. Once more the same Regents, with one new member, were faced for the third time in a decade with the responsibility of finding a new president.

CAMPUS, 1930

CHAPTER TEN

RUTHVEN
AND THE DEPRESSION

ALEXANDER G. RUTHVEN WAS well known to the Regents from his position as President Little's right hand and for the way he defended the University budget request before the legislature. After some perfunctory consideration of other candidates, the Board offered Dr. Ruthven the presidency at its postponed September 1929 meeting. He accepted.

Ruthven had been on campus since 1903 first as a graduate student, then up the ladder to professor of zoology and museum director. In the

ALEXANDER G. RUTHVEN

latter capacity he had discharged administrative responsibilities while cultivating numerous alumni and nonalumni donors. His year as dean of administration had familiarized him with the needs and problems of the several schools and colleges. He was forty-seven years old, and he had developed ideas about how a large university should operate.

1. Growth of the corporate university

Ruthven introduced a definite corporate type of organization in the structure of the University. Writing of universities in general, he said in his first annual report that "the present administrative plan is essentially militaristic ... in general, one in which there is a continuous line of authority from the board of trustees, through the president and other officers, to the department heads and individual faculty members, all problems being routed along much the same course, and most of the executives having too little authority and responsibility .... It is clearly absurd to expect that the members of the board of trustees are or can be familiar with the details of the institutions, that the sole business of the faculty is to teach and investigate, and that the president can efficiently be a kind of headmaster or superintendent capable of directly supervising the financial affairs, instruction, the alumni activities, and the public relations of his institution and still find time to study educational problems and even to explain to society in general what it should do to be saved."

He regarded the Regents as "guardians of a public trust, [who] function as custodians of the property and income of the University and, as the governing body, give final approval to educational policies and staff appointments." He viewed the president as "chairman of the faculties," as moderator and budget director responsible to both Regents and faculty, as initiator of policies, as coordinator of the interests, problems, and policies of the several units, as interpreter to the faculty of the Board of Regents, and as chief personnel officer in developing the staff. Many of these duties were to be delegated to vice-presidents, deans, directors, and a registrar. Secretary Shirley Smith was therefore made vice-president for business and finance; Clarence Yoakum was made vice-president in charge of educational investigations, to study educational methods and serve on the Faculty Personnel Committee. Two years later Dr. James D. Bruce was named vice-president in charge of University relations, mainly with other institutions and groups. Professor Lewis Gram was made director of Plant Extension—that is, all new building and allocation of space. In 1933 Professor Henry C. Anderson was made director of student-alumni relations, at the vice-presidential level. In 1937 Professor E. Blythe Stason was named provost, a kind of executive vice-president.

Ruthven regarded deans as chairmen of their faculties and administrative heads of their schools or colleges. As a group they served as an advisory committee to the president on academic affairs—the Conference of Deans. The faculties, Ruthven believed, should be required to determine educational policies for their units, have a voice in appointments and promotions in their departments, and make recommendations for deanships. He made sure that executive committees were appointed to advise each dean.

These views stimulated the faculty to assume a larger role in determining the character of the University. At the same time Ruthven undertook to regulate the various titles held by assistants and instructors, and to ask the Regents to provide an adequate pension for 162 faculty members caught between new rules of the Carnegie Corporation and its subsidiary, the Teachers' Insurance and Annuity Association, in which these professors had participated but briefly. Then he moved on to inaugurate a survey of nonacademic positions so as to equalize the pay of similar jobs.

Under President Ruthven, the University entered into a closer relationship with its alumni and assumed greater responsibility for their activity. The Alumni Association had always been an independent and self-supporting organization, with offices in Alumni Memorial Hall. Wilfred Shaw, '04 had been secretary and editor of its periodical since 1904. He had organized the alumni by twelve geographical districts, each of which elected a director of the general Association. In 1927 President Elmer J. Ottaway, '94, instituted the Ten-Year Program by which each district or each club undertook to raise money (over a ten year period) to satisfy some specific need of the University. Another part of the program, started with President Little, led to establishment of an Alumni University, an extension program tailored to appeal to alumni. Little's resignation delayed realization of this aspect, but a University Bureau of Alumni Relations was created in 1929 with Shaw as director. He was succeeded as secretary of the Alumni Association by T. Hawley Tapping, '16*l*, who had been serving as field secretary.

The Bureau began publishing two or three bulletins a year about the University which were sent to all alumni. Then in 1930 it sponsored the first Alumni University, which ran for a week immediately following Commencement. It consisted of a variety of lectures by University professors that "updated" alumni in science, current events, educational concepts, social problems, etc., or broadened them in art, music, contemporary drama, and literature. An average of 100 alumni attended until World War II forced abandonment of the series. In 1934 Shaw began publishing a *Quarterly Review* magazine which went out to subscribers of the *Michigan Alumnus*. As a talented etcher as well as editor, Shaw was able to illustrate the articles he accepted. He also conceived and started the monumental *University of Michigan: An Encyclopedic Survey*, a remarkably detailed account of all activities and units of the University which ran to four volumes and was not completed until after his death.

Ruthven set the tone of University participation in alumni affairs by declaring in 1932 that a student "enrolls in the University for life and for better or worse he will always remain an integral part of the institution." Two years later the Alumni Association was broke and in debt. The University had to rescue it and assign certain limited revenues to its support. The executive committee of the Board of Directors was reorganized to include four faculty members and to exercise fiscal control of the Association. It was a mutually advantageous move. By the end of the decade, the alumni were organized into some 195 local clubs, and more than $22,000,000 had been given to the University by alumni.

President Ruthven also felt that a high administrative officer should have general supervision of both alumni and student activity. In November 1933 he created the office of Director of Student-Alumni Relations and named Professor Henry C. Anderson of the College of Engineering to this sensitive post. Ruthven called it "a major administrative position of the rank of vice-president, and will be advisory and supervisory in its functions." It was. Anderson found that much of the difficulty in dealing with students was a lack of frankness and a misunderstanding of fundamental issues involved. He was able to unite the two overlapping women's organizations in the Michigan League Council, while the business management of the Michigan League Building was placed under the management of the dormitories. He asked the University Committee on Student Affairs to make a study of all committees dealing with student affairs and revise them. It did so. Anderson advocated a simpler supervision, not additional rules and regulations already resented. He believed that "the student would in time realize that, after all, the University asks only that a man, while on the campus, behave as a gentleman and a scholar." His death late in 1939 was a severe loss; he was succeeded by Professor Carl G. Brandt.

Finally, Ruthven stated his belief that extension service for adult education was a legitimate function of the University. Therefore, extension instructors should maintain the academic standards of their departments in credit-bearing courses. At the same time, noncredit courses were permissible. Extension work should be self-supporting, he added. All these moves and intentions represented not merely a scientific mind at work, but a shrewd administrative grasp of a highly complex organism.

As for the University College plan left dangling by Little's resignation, although Ruthven had supported it without regarding it as a panacea for the ills of higher education, he was not going to force it upon a reluctant faculty. He considered the issue dead unless faculty opinion should revive it. Meanwhile, he saw other reforms needed in undergraduate education, and this was one of the objectives of the vice-president for educational investigations. The next year the Literary College divided the evaluation of undergraduate work: students must complete sixty hours of work with at least a C grade average before they could be admitted to junior standing and candidacy for a degree, and in the last two years they were required to concentrate in a field of study.

The winds of change began to disperse the fine fellowship of veteran regents who had acted together for years. Late in 1929 Benjamin Hanchett's failing health forced his resignation after service since 1911, and Governor Green appointed Mrs. Esther Marsh Cram, '98, of Flint, a former teacher, as the first woman regent. She quieted apprehension among her masculine colleagues by firmly announcing at the first meeting: "Gentlemen, I expect to be a woman regent, not a women's regent."

In January 1930 Victor Gore, who had served since 1914 and had not run for reelection, was succeeded by R. Perry Shorts, '06*l*, of Saginaw. The next year Dr. Walter H. Sawyer died, after serving twenty-three years and devoting himself to the Medical School. Governor Brucker appointed Dr. Richard R. Smith, '92*m*, Grand Rapids surgeon, to finish out his term.

Then at the beginning of 1933, the venerable scholarly Lucius Hubbard resigned, and Governor Comstock named Edmund D. Shields,

'96*l*, Lansing attorney and Democratic national committeeman, to complete his term. Elections brought the defeat of Republicans Murfin and Clements. The latter had served twenty-four years and besides the gift of his magnificent library had earlier served as building planner and adviser. Their successors in January 1934 were Franklin M. Cook, '84, Hillsdale banker and former trustee of Hillsdale College, and Charles F. Hemans, Detroit lawyer and amateur horticulturalist, who had attended the University just before the war. But in a quick reprise, Regent Shorts resigned and Democratic Governor Comstock reappointed Republican Murfin for the remaining half term.

President Ruthven now suggested to the Regents the abolition of two committees and the realignment of two others. As a result the Regents formed themselves into six committees: executive, finance, plant and equipment, educational policies, student and alumni relations, and public relations.

In 1936 David Crowley, '05*l*, state attorney general from Detroit, displaced Regent Shields by election; but two years later Shields came back and with him John D. Lynch, '12*l*, Detroit lawyer and president of the National Conference of Legal Fraternities. They unseated Murfin and Dr. Smith. Then at the end of 1939 Junius Beal of Ann Arbor closed out thirty-two years as regent, the longest period anyone has ever served. A rock of stability, he had always put the University first in his affections and decisions. Ralph Stone also retired after sixteen years of service. Two later alumni were elected and took their chairs in January 1940: J. Joseph Herbert, '17*l*, Manistique attorney, and Harry Kipke, '24, the former football coach. The average age of the Regents declined abruptly.

At the end of the decade there was no regent whose service antedated Ruthven's presidency. It was a whole new team. The eldest in service was Cram, and there was no one who had worked with Hutchins, or Burton, or Little. Ruthven himself was the veteran.

The University Senate realized it was getting too large to function properly. In 1930 there were seventy-five administrative officers, of whom twenty-six taught, and 833 other instructors. A smaller representative body called the University Council was formed consisting of the deans and major administrative officers (twenty-two members), and thirty four elected members from various faculties. They were able to meet monthly or more often and convey faculty views to the administration, or discuss changes of regulations entirely within faculty purview.

2. Depression and private response

Hardly had Ruthven been in office a month before the stock market crash of 1929 set off what was called a temporary financial crisis. The University barely felt the shock. Its budget for two years had been determined by the legislature in the spring when prosperity seemed assured. But the panic did not subside; it deepened into a general economic depression. Trade contracted, employees lost jobs, businesses failed, more workers were let out, savings were used up, taxes could not be paid or mortgage payments met, and state and local relief funds were doled out. University enrollment remained virtually the same in 1929-30 and 1930-31 at a little more than 10,100. Then a decline set in, and 1933-34 was the year of lowest enrollment—8713. The following year attendance bounced back and moved steadily upward until it reached 13,000 in 1939-40, the last "normal" year before the war.

The legislature of early 1931 met amid growing want. Local relief measures were proving inadequate, and property taxes were a burden. In some states the whole idea of state support for universities was attacked. In Lansing there was talk of limiting or repealing the mill tax, but in the end the University received its due allotment of $4,921,000 for each year of the biennium. Plant expansion slowed down, of course, and the University undertook a study to economize in its operations.

Then in 1932 the legislature met in special session and reduced all appropriations by 15 percent, or $738,000 in the case of the University. The assessed valuation of property was lowered, so it was clear that the mill tax was going to yield less revenue. The University had to institute salary cuts of 6, 8, and 10 percent for 1932-33 and to leave unfilled positions vacant. In February 1933 all of Michigan's banks closed, and many did not reopen. It was the beginning of the nationwide "bank holiday." Savings and checking accounts in banks that could not reopen were frozen until assets could be liquidated.

The University faced a second belt tightening when the 1933 legislature further reduced its appropriation. As a result sixty-six teaching positions and twenty-nine nonteaching—a total of ninety-five positions—were eliminated, and 122 employees had their time reduced. The rest of the faculty and staff then took a second salary cut as follows: 8 percent on the first $2000 above $1500; 12 percent on the second $2000; 15 percent on the third $2000; and 20 percent on any portion above $7500. Thus, a professor earning $7500 found his salary cut to $6800; while an instructor at $1800 was only down to $1776. As salary reductions bottomed out, the University faced the problem of trying to enlarge the faculty sufficiently to keep up with rising enrollment; it never caught up or restored pay cuts before the country was plunged into war. The legislature of 1939 gave the University $4,475,000, which was $200,000 less than it was receiving, and $450,000 less than it had obtained eight years before. Student fees were raised slightly.

The prolonged financial Depression brought out the genius of President Ruthven. He proved to be a magnificent rear guard fighter, fending off legislative bills and other ill-considered proposals that would have crippled the University. When the legislature abolished the state property tax, thereby wiping out the mill tax, and substituted a sales tax, he persuaded the 1935 legislature to pass an act specifying that "from the general fund of the state a sum equal to .73 of a mill on each dollar of assessed valuation of the taxable property of the state" be appropriated for the University of Michigan. Thus the mill tax principle was preserved, a great Ruthven victory. In all the controversies that swirled around him, he smoked a cigarette, remained calm and courageous, and exercised good judgment and perspicacity. It was a good augury for the war years to come.

Although the rate of building greatly diminished after the expansive 1920's, visible changes on the campus continued. The University Elementary School Building was opened in 1929, followed in the next two years by the Legal Research Library and the John P. Cook dormitory, which was added to the Lawyers Club. William W. Cook, whose munificence made possible the Law Quadrangle, died in 1930 and bequeathed to the University his estate of $15,000,000. Part of the money was used for a classroom building, Hutchins Hall, completed in 1933 and named for President Harry B. Hutchins, and part for a Legal Research Institute within the Law School.

As great a change as any in the appearance of the campus was the installation in 1930 of fifty-one lamp posts around the forty acres, affording much-needed illumination of sidewalks. Hitherto, only the porch and front door lights of buildings ringed the glow emanating from the General Library windows.

In 1930 the observatory got 200 acres near Portage Lake, fifteen miles northwest of Ann Arbor, as the site for new telescopes. Since completion of the University Hospital and the growth of Ann Arbor industry, the old Observatory's usefulness had been reduced by lights and smoke. The new hilltop, hopefully called Peach Mountain, was in a rural area, and a radio telescope was planned for it. Then an observatory erected at Lake Angelus, Oakland County, by three friends, Francis and Robert McMath and Judge Henry Hulbert, was presented to the University in 1931. The three donors, who had been named honorary curators of astronomy two years earlier, were interested in making celestial motion pictures. They continued to improve such equipment and earn the praise of professional astronomers. The new facility was named the McMath-Hulbert Observatory. A grant of $20,000 from the Rackham fund, another from the McGregor Fund, and private contributions made it possible in 1935 to build a solar tower telescope. It brought certain suspected phenomena into clear view and disproved a theory about light-pressure advanced in England. The desire to replace the ten and one-half-inch telescope with a twenty-four inch reflecting telescope was realized in 1939, and for simultaneous recording a second tower and telescope were built by another grant from the McGregor Fund. Robert McMath designed all the instruments and buildings. The new equipment made possible concurrent observations of space motion and of the energy in solar activity and to demonstrate them pictorially.

CARILLON BELLS ARRIVING AT BURTON TOWER

In 1935 Charles M. Baird, '95, former athletic director now in business in Kansas City, offered to give the University a set of carillon bells to be cast in England. There would be fifty-three bells ranging four and one-half octaves, from a twelve-pound bell to a Bourdon bell of more than twelve tons. The University of Michigan Club of Ann Arbor undertook to raise money for a campanile or tower as a memorial to President Burton. The Regents and the city of Ann Arbor offered help, and Mr. Baird added a great clock to his gift of bells. The University Musical Society contributed $60,000. A site was selected at the rear of Hill Auditorium where the tower would stand between that building and a proposed new School of Music. A great stone tower 212 feet high was erected, forty-one feet square at the base. The bells were hung in the fall of 1936 and ever since then the Baird Carillon has taken its place as a landmark and civic asset. The hour is struck on the great Bourdon bell, and chimes are rung on the quarter hours. Regular concerts are also played by the carillonneur. Later, Mr. Baird gave a fountain on the mall opposite Burton Tower in memory of Professor Thomas M. Cooley. It is the work of Carl Milles.

In 1935 also, the trustees of the Horace H. Rackham and Mary A. Rackham Fund of Detroit gave the University $6,500,000 of which $2,500,000 was for a building for graduate studies and $4,000,000 for endowment in support of scholarly investigations. In addition, Rackham's widow, Mary A. Rackham, gave $1,000,000 for research in the field of human adjustment. The Institute of Human Adjustment was established in 1937 with Clark Tibbitts as director.

The Rackham gift was the largest received after the Cook bequest, and it came when annual giving to the University had dwindled in the Depression to $100,000. Promptly, the Graduate School was renamed the Horace H. Rackham School of Graduate Studies, and plans were made for a new building at the end of the mall opposite the General Library.

Completed in 1938, it provided offices for the School, two auditoriums, an art gallery, and various lounges for studies, conferences, and seminars, as well as private research offices.

BURTON TOWER AND RACKHAM

Ruthven reversed the University policy since 1852 and urged the Regents to accept responsibility for housing some of the men as well as women students. Taking advantage of federal funds offered to create jobs, the Regents embarked on a program of building more and more dormitories on a self-liquidating basis. The government provided about 45 percent of the cost, and receipts from board and room eventually paid off the remaining cost of University bonds. A series of houses and quadrangles began to rise, despite complaints of Ann Arbor landladies and the fears of fraternities. Housing had grown unsatisfactory for all groups—for the 300 foreign students, for the thirty-five African-American students enrolled, and for many of the thousands of the other students. The University had picked up Fletcher Hall in 1933 for taxes and refurbished it for fifty-eight men students.

The Michigan Union launched a building program by adding a wing for dormitory use in 1936. It held 114 men and was named Allen-Rumsey House, for the two founders of Ann Arbor. The Regents guaranteed the bonds that were issued. It was the first dormitory since the opening of Mosher-Jordan Hall for 442 women in 1930. Then the Regents in quick succession started a group of seven houses for men, with four dining rooms; connected to Allen-Rumsey, they formed West Quadrangle holding 932 students. The University of Michigan Club of Chicago pledged itself to contribute toward one house, and it was named Chicago House. The Board authorized the building of Victor Vaughan House near the University Hospital for 150 medical students, and a hospital dormitory for ninety interns. All three structures were finished in 1939. Madelon Stockwell Hall (named for the first coed) was started next to Mosher-Jordan and opened in February 1940 for 400 women. At the same time a beginning was made on East Quadrangle, with houses and dining rooms for 400 men; these units were not finished until 1941.

WEST QUAD, P.W.A. PROJECT #1559-F

A new Health Service Building was also constructed in 1939-40 with a PWA grant and a bond issue. Then the W. K. Kellogg Foundation provided the University with its share of the cost, after the PWA contributed 45 percent, of an addition to the Dental School called the W. K. Kellogg Institute of Graduate and Postgraduate Dentistry.

A University of Michigan Press was formally organized—more accurately, recognized—in 1930, because for more than twenty-five years scholarly books had been published under University auspices and at University expense. But now a manager was appointed to supervise all such publications in the person of Frank E. Robbins, assistant to the president. A classical scholar with considerable taste in typographical design and technical knowledge of printing, he with an advisory committee and very limited funds began publishing selected manuscripts of faculty members. The responsibility formerly exercised by the Graduate School was transferred to this committee. The marketing of Press books left much to be desired, but the University productions maintained a high standard of meticulous scholarship.

The work in architecture was separated from the College of Engineering in 1931 and made part of a new Division of Fine Arts, which included the Department of Landscape Design and the Department of Fine Arts, and the play production work in the Speech Department. The College of Architecture already had its own building, completed in 1928.

The Earhart Foundation, a local philanthropic fund, provided in 1935 for a chair in industrial relations and a Bureau of Industrial Research, both in the School of Business Administration. The purpose was to promote an understanding of industrial relations by teaching, acquisition of current literature, and research. John W. Riegel was made director of the Bureau. A curriculum in social work, started in 1921, led to the establishment of the Institute of Public and Social Administration in 1935. It was to correlate political science training in public administration with the social work program and make possible a master's degree. It was criticized in some academic circles as being outside the field of customary intellectual interests, but Professor Arthur E. Wood argued that "the needs of our democratic civilization are many, not the least of which is the existence of a body of trained personnel in the various fields of public service. The Depression has served, as nothing else could, to throw into strong relief the multifarious social problems which must be dealt with sympathetically and expertly if even greater chaos is not to ensue."

In 1928 Avery Hopwood, '05, a highly successful playwright, had died and left a bequest to the University to encourage student writing. The rest of his estate went to his mother, who died shortly and added largely to his original bequest. Hopwood had worked his way through the University and had written more than two dozen farces of such genre as *Up in Mabel's Room, Getting Gertie's Garter*, and *Ladies Night in a Turkish Bath*. In 1930 the University announced the Avery and Jule Hopwood Awards on the income from nearly $500,000. It is the richest of college writing contests. Hopwood's wish was to encourage "the new, the unusual, and the radical." The awards were first made in 1931 and continued annually. Perhaps the most noted prize winners have been novelists Betty Smith, special student '31, and Mildred Walker, MA '32 ; playwright Arthur Miller, '38 ; and poet John Ciardi, MA '39.

A reform-minded governor demonstrated how a university can serve its state. In 1935 Governor Frank Fitzgerald appointed a civil service commission with Professor James K. Pollock of the Political Science Department as chairman. Out of his studies he drafted a model civil service act. It was submitted to the legislature in 1937, when Frank Murphy occupied the governor's chair, and he pushed it through the legislature, with the concession of blanketing in office the existing Democratic appointees. As a statute it was always subject to change by any legislature. In 1938 Gov. Fitzgerald swept back into office without patronage to bestow. His untimely death in March 1939 brought an elderly bumbling lieutenant governor into power whose vaunted piety was soon equaled by his political weakness. A Republican legislature passed a "ripper" bill in 1939 and Governor Dickinson signed it, removing two-thirds of the state offices from civil service.

Professor Pollock promptly organized a citizens' movement called the Merit System Association. It procured more than 200,000 signatures to require placing on the 1940 ballot an amendment to incorporate civil service in the state constitution. Both political parties fought the constitutional amendment, but the Merit System Association, quarterbacked by Pollock, carried the day and ensured Michigan a real civil service system. Twenty-three years later, when a constitutional convention was called, Professor Pollock ran for delegate and was elected, primarily to make sure that civil service was retained in the new constitution. It was. Further, the Political Science Department had given a splendid demonstration to students of how political reform and upgrading of government could be achieved in the arena of practical politics.

With the approach of 1937 and the centennial of the University in Ann Arbor, the Regents created a Bureau of University Archives to take custody of old University records. Professor Lewis G. Vander Velde of the History Department was named director. He began collecting correspondence of past regents and professors and soon gathered up any material on the history of education in Michigan. Quarters were obtained in the new Rackham Building, and the staff grew. Since no other institution or society was actively collecting in the state, the renamed Michigan Historical Collections solicited source materials on Michigan generally, developing a rich collection in which graduate students could do research.

The legislature of 1937 created a Neuropsychiatric Institute, made it a department of the Medical School, and agreed to support it. A separate building was required, and it was built behind the University Hospital in 1939. A Michigan Children's Institute, created by the same legislature, was placed under the Board of Regents as a clinic for inquiring into the causes of child delinquency and for prescribing for the treatment of such neglected and defective children. Professor Lowell J. Carr of the Sociology Department was appointed halftime director.

3. Intellectual transitions

As in earlier periods the 1930's were a decade in which big faculty names disappeared and big names appeared. One disagreeable task faced President Ruthven immediately. There was discord and dissatisfaction in the Medical School faculty, and it had become evident that the dean was casual and careless in budget making. Reluctantly, the president obtained permission from the Regents to relieve Dr. Cabot of the deanship in February 1930. The Medical School was placed under an executive committee with Dr. Novy as chairman. In 1932 Dr. Novy's title was changed to dean.

John Effinger, the dean of the Literary College since 1915, died in 1933 and was succeeded by Edward H. Kraus, who had been dean of the College of Pharmacy and director of the Summer Session. Dean G. Carl Huber of the Graduate School died in 1934, and his duties were given to Vice-President Yoakum. The following year Dean Novy had to retire for age, and there passed from the Medical School a pupil of Pasteur and Koch and a distinguished bacteriologist. He was succeeded by Dr. A. C. Furstenberg, head of the Department of Otolaryngology and highly regarded for his surgical techniques and his research. In 1938 Herbert Sadler stepped down from the deanship of the College of Engineering to continue as a professor, and Emil Lorch retired as head of the School of Architecture and Design. The former was succeeded by Professor Henry C. Anderson, the latter by Wells I. Bennett. Dr. Russell W. Bunting, DDS '08, was made dean of the School of Dentistry in 1937 after two years as acting dean and twenty-five years in research on dental caries. In 1939 Dean Henry M. Bates of the Law School retired after twenty-nine years in the office and was succeeded by Professor E. Blythe Stason. Bates had resolved the debate over whether law should be taught as a vocation or as a means of social control in favor of the latter. The School of Music was separated in 1910 from the jurisdiction of the University Musical Society, and Director Earl V. Moore was continued as dean. The Society continued in charge of the Choral Union, the May Festival, and other public concerts.

Claude H. Van Tyne, chairman of the History Department, died in 1930, a few weeks before his book, *The War of Independence*, recieved the Pulitzer Prize in history. He had helped to shape the Clements Library and had taught American history for twenty-six years. He was succeeded by Verner W. Crane from the University of Pennsylvania.

O. J. Campbell and Howard Mumford Jones resigned from the English Department in 1936 to go to Columbia and Harvard respectively. Campbell's famous course in contemporary drama filled the largest classroom in Angell Hall; moreover, it was one of very few courses that attracted auditors (students not enrolled for credit). Jones, a productive scholar who had come in 1930, had conducted a seminar in American literature that was lively and popular. Then the beloved Louis A. Strauss, who taught the Victorian novelists and poets, died in 1938; he had been teaching forty-five years and had been chairman of the department for sixteen years. He had introduced the English honors course in 1924 for particularly bright students. He had also served as chairman of the Senate Committee on Student Affairs and of the Board in Control of Student Publications, where he won the acclaim of students and faculty alike.

Science, too, had its losses. Lawrence M. Gould, second in command of the first Byrd Antarctic Expedition, resigned from the Geology Department in 1930 to go to Carleton College, of which he later became president. Two years later the vigorous and fearless William H. Hobbs reached retirement age. In the same year James W. Glover resigned as chairman of the Mathematics Department to take a federal office. He was on leave two years after 1930 as president of the Teachers Insurance and Annuity Association. He had also presided over the merger of the mathematics departments of the Engineering and Literary colleges in 1928. The *Annals of Mathematical Science* as founded here in 1930 and edited here till 1938, when it moved to Princeton. Moses Gomberg retired in 1936 from the Chemistry Department after forty-two years of teaching.

In physics Michigan was recognized the world over for its work in spectroscopy of the infrared. Ernest F. Barker's development of a ruling machine to make gratings for measuring wave lengths was a significant instrument. Ralph Sawyer was also investigating visible and ultraviolet radiation. But more fame came with the addition of a cyclotron and million-volt transformer, built in 1936, which made possible the production of a great variety of radioactive atoms not occurring in nature. David M. Dennison was working in molecular mechanics, and H. Richard Crane offered the first course in nuclear physics in 1939. What focused much international attention on Michigan was the series of Summer Symposia on Theoretical Physics, while Randall was chairman. Modestly begun in 1923 with two special lecturers, it developed into several courses appealing to graduate students and distinguished guests. Such men as Enrico Fermi, who was here five summers in the 1930's, Niels Bohr, P. P. Ewald, and J. Robert Oppenheimer participated.

The peppery classical scholar, Henry Sanders, retired in 1939 after forty-one years on the faculty. His great industry had resulted in publication of many Biblical texts under the canons of highest scholarship. But Latin as a discipline was slipping in this decade: fewer students entered with high-school Latin, so the department was obliged to give more elementary courses and fewer advanced courses, although the graduate courses attracted superior students from all over the country.

When Jesse S. Reeves retired in 1937, he had given international standing to an always distinguished Political Science Department. He was succeeded as chairman by Joseph Hayden, whose interest in the Philippines had led to his appointment as vice-governor from 1933 to 1936 under Governor Frank Murphy, '14*l*. In 1940 John W. Anderson, '90*l*, gave $200,000 to endow a James O. Murfin professorship of political science.

In the first half of 1940 four more distinguished professors died; Bruce Donaldson, chairman of the Fine Arts Department; Hugo Thieme, chairman of the Romance Languages Department and forty-two years a faculty member; Arthur Lyon Cross, professor of English history for forty-one years and author of an eminently readable textbook; and Roderick McKenzie, chairman of the Sociology Department.

The School of Forestry and Conservation was strengthened in 1930 by the gift of $200,000 from Charles L. Pack to establish the George Willis Pack fund for use in forest management. One result was the appointment of Willett F. Ramsdell as Pack professor of forest management. The fund was subsequently enlarged. In the Law School, Joseph Drake retired in 1930, and Edwin C. Goddard in 1935; John E. Tracy and Marvin Niehuss were added to the faculty. In the School of Music, Albert Lockwood died in 1933 after heading the piano department for thirty-three years, and Arthur Hackett came as voice professor and director of the Men's Glee Club. Dr. Theophile Raphael was added to the Health Service in 1930 as its first psychiatrist.

The Literary College was strengthened by the addition of Warner G. Rice to the English Department in 1929. He became director of the University Library for a decade and then chairman of the English Department. William Haber, PhD '27, joined the Economics Department in 1936 from his position as state director of the National Youth Administration. He rose to the deanship of the college. William Randolph Taylor was added to the Botany Department in 1930 and began his intensive study of algae.

In the first years of the decade the Medical School suffered losses. Dr. Warthin retired, Dr. Canfield was killed in an auto accident, and Dr. Peterson retired from the Bates professorship of diseases of women and children. Dr. A. M. Barrett, one of the country s leading psychiatrists, died in 1936. He had organized the first university hospital and clinic for treatment of mental diseases in America. After forty-four years on the faculty, thirty-three as head of the Department of Pediatrics, Dr. David M. Cowie died in 1940. New men had to be found. Dr. Norman Miller, '20*m*, succeeded Dr. Peterson, and Dr. Raymond W. Waggoner, '24*m*, took the place of Dr. Barrett. Dr. Carl Weller, '13*m*, was promoted to Dr. Warthin's position as chairman of the Pathology Department. Bradley M. Patten from the Rockefeller Foundation had succeeded Dean Huber as professor of anatomy. Dr. Fred J. Hodges of Wisconsin was appointed professor of roentgenology, and Dr. Bruce Fralick, '27*m*, of the University of Chicago was made assistant professor of ophthalmology.

The Surgery Department was enlarged by the return of Dr. Carl Badgley, '19*m*, from Henry Ford Hospital, as professor of orthopedic surgery, and by Dr. Reed Nesbit, as assistant professor of genitourinary surgery. The thoracic surgery section had so developed under Dr. John Alexander that in 1931 Dr. Cameron Haight was added. In 1932 he did the first pneumonectomy (removal of a lung) in the Western Hemisphere and the second in the world. He also performed the first successful direct repair of esophageal atresia in 1941. Dr. Alexander resected the first aneurysm of the thoracic aorta in 1943. Other surgeons at Michigan attracted national attention for their techniques.

4. The death of "Joe College"

In February 1931 five fraternities were raided by local police, liquor was found, and seventy-nine students were arrested, including the football captain and two *Daily* editors. At first the students blamed Dean Bursley for the raids, as if there were something unfair about them, but learned later that the information came from campus bootleggers recently arrested. The five houses were closed, and 184 students evicted. Charges against the seventy-nine were dropped.

Certain collegiate customs fell by the wayside in the Depression. The Union Opera was given up for awhile, after a loss of money in 1929. The frosh-soph class games and the hazing of freshmen played out in the 1930's. The wearing of green frosh pots disappeared in 1932, and Swing-out was abolished two years later. Class Day exercises were not held after 1933; no one cared about being elected class poet or class orator. "Joe College" was dead.

Yet in the late spring of 1933 a handful of students bought or rented roller skates and began using them one evening on the campus sidewalks. Next night they were joined by other skaters. Within a week hundreds of students were on roller skates, and the whirr of their wheels on the Diagonal penetrated the General Library. The pasttime was encouraged by the city's having resurfaced several streets, making it possible to skate all over the east side of town. As quickly as it caught on, the fad subsided in the face of approaching exams.

Although the Michigan football team held the Big Ten title 1930-33, it fell on years of defeat and rising criticism afterward. In 1938 the Board in Control appointed Herbert O. Crisler head football coach and assistant director of athletics. Harry Kipke and Franklin Cappon resigned. Tom Harmon, '41, Ed Frutig, '41, and Forest Evashevski, '41, starred on Crisler's early teams, the first two winning All American berths. Kipke ran for the Board of Regents in 1939 and was elected. Some people immediately construed this step as motivated by revenge. It was not, and President Ruthven testified that Kipke was a very able but disinterested regent; his reelection would have been welcomed by the administration had he not moved from the state.

Michigan had been noted as a dressy campus: men always wore neckties and usually suit jackets to class; women appeared at 8:00 A.M. classes in hose and heels *and* hats *and* gloves. But the deepening Depression no longer permitted such dressing. Young men enrolled who owned one suit, or perhaps none, and they wore sweaters and trousers to class and finally neckties disappeared. The change in the womens' attire was much slower and more gradual and did not become marked until after the war.

As always, the dissatisfied and rebellious who were articulate gravitated toward the *Michigan Daily* to find suitable outlet. But there they faced competition from other "try-outs" who merely wanted to become good reporters, and the training then in vogue weeded out all but the most competent and industrious by the end of their first year. Accordingly, radicals resorted to writing public letters to the *Daily*. The Board in Control had laid down in 1929 certain standards of fairness and taste and had designated the senior editors as an editorial board four of whom must approve all editorials. A given editorial might not represent the view of more than those four students, but at least it did not reflect a solitary opinion. The *Daily* still aimed at complete campus coverage with some state, national, and international news. It archly regarded the *Detroit Free Press* as its competitor because it was the only other morning paper distributed in the Ann Arbor community.

DAILY STAFF IN THE LATE 1930s

In 1931 the *Daily* was managed at the top by three seniors who amied to continue in journalism as a career and did so with distinction. Managing Editor Richard L. Tobin went on the *New York Herald Tribune* for years and then became managing editor of the *Saturday Review*. Editorial Director Beach Conger went to the *New York Herald Tribune* also and after a period as foreign correspondent became Sunday news editor; he then moved to the *Reader's Digest*. News Editor David Nichol became foreign correspondent for the *Chicago Daily News*. Even City Editor Carl Forsythe, who went on to Law School, later specialized in litigation relating to newspapers. These young men started off the year with a bang: attacking the American Legion national convention in Detroit for its public drunkenness (no Detroit paper would mention it seriously) and for beating up some University pacifists who demonstrated in Detroit; campaigning against local taxi drivers who were gouging their fares, until the city council passed an ordinance requiring meters; and uncovering the charge that a recently resigned foreman of the Buildings and Grounds Department had been hiring men on the basis of their buying lots in a real estate development he was making.

All this was too much for the administration. Vice-President Smith so far forgot his famed sense of humor as to cancel the 917 faculty subscriptions for which the University paid the *Daily* $3600, and Tobin was suspended. The Board in Control met and reminded Smith that faculty subscriptions had been provided by the Regents and could not be stopped except by them. Accordingly, they were continued. Then the regular Regents' meeting occurred the day after Tobin's suspension, and he was promptly reinstated. This flurry subsided as quickly as it blew up, and few heard of the incident. The *Daily's* vigorous policy inspired a story in *Time* magazine. Thirty-odd years later Tobin recalled the episode and wryly remarked: "I sometimes shudder when I think how one-sided the editorials were, but we hit some exposed nerves."

The following year Dean Bursley remarked that the Student Council was undertaking to change its composition and bylaws. It was his opinion that such changes would never strengthen student government, because the basic trouble was that the majority of the students were not interested in any form of student government, regarding it perhaps as a hangover from high school. At the same time, student attitudes were changing. If students of the 1920's seemed intent on having a good time as carefree collegians, those of the 1930's were made more serious and questioning by the Depression. The sophisticated and liberal student of the 1930's prided themselves on being "socially conscious."

President Ruthven's very real concern for the students became evident from the beginning of his administration. Philosophically, he believed that the University should offer more than intellectual training; an education should include the character training and social orientation that colleges emphasized. He never subscribed to the perennial student dictum that they were mature persons when they enrolled, but rather that they needed and deserved guidance. If this were paternalism, so be it.

For one thing, he was worried about the growing gulf between teachers and students, in and out of the classroom, under the pressure of increasing size. In 1929-30 there were 833 teachers for 10,200 students; ten years later after two cutbacks in faculty and some new hiring the ratio was 773 teachers for 13,000 students. To meet this situation academic counseling was extended to upperclassmen in 1934. In his own orbit he and Mrs. Ruthven instituted in early 1930 a succession of student teas at the President's House so that he could meet and talk with hundreds of undergraduates every year.

He was concerned also about the religious development of adolescents. Each of the major church denominations maintained a center and a special program on weekends for University students. An assistant minister or campus pastor gave most or all of his time to counseling students, yet Ruthven felt that the University itself should evince more religious interest. In the fall of 1933 he appointed the Reverend Edward W. Blakeman as counselor in religious education, with offices in Lane Hall. Blakeman, a former Methodist pastor who had taken up work with students, had for the preceding two years been director of the Wesley Foundation at Michigan. "His office is open daily," the bulletin of *General Information* said, "and any student is welcome. The Counselor has an advisory faculty committee and enjoys close association with the campus rabbi, the campus priest, and the student pastors provided by the Protestant churches . . . . The strain produced by University work and the inescapable questions which inquiry brings to the fore are met frankly. In the spirit of religion and for the purpose of nobler living, students are helped toward a solution."

Late in 1936 the Student Christian Association gave to the Regents its two properties: Newberry and Lane halls, which the Association could no longer maintain. The latter was continued as a center for University religious study and activities. Newberry was partly used for classes, but gradually changed into a museum of classical archeology named for Professor Francis W. Kelsey. A year later the Regents established a Student Religious Association open to all students interested in religious activity. It was placed under a joint faculty student Board of Governors, and Dr. Blakeman was made director.

Ruthven recognized the financial plight of students during the Depression. The Board of Regents tried to help with more scholarships: fifty for nominees of the alumni clubs, ten for graduate students, and five for Native Americans. Student loans increased from 885 in 1929-30 totalling $110,000 (a jump of 33 percent over the previous, pre-crash year) to 2600 loans of $147,300 in 1935-36. A gift of $100,000 from Mr. and .Mrs. Rackham increased the amount available for loans. A textbook lending library was started in the fall of 1937 under the supervision of Professor Erich A. Walter. It lasted about eight years.

The Federal Emergency Relief Administration (FERA) granted funds to employ students in February 1934. This agency was succeeded by the National Youth Administration (NYA) in 1935, making possible the employment of more than 1800 students with federal funds and continuing until after war began. There were hundreds of other students, of course, who held board and room jobs and other employment of their own getting. In 1934-35, for instance, 75 percent of the men and 25 percent of the women earned some or all of their expenses, while 19 percent of the men and 12 percent of the women were wholly self-supporting.

Foreign students were a particular charge on the conscience of the University. Once the principle of individual counselling was extended to all undergraduates, it was natural to give attention to foreign students. A faculty committee worked with them in 1932-33, then Professor J. Raleigh Nelson of the College of Engineering English Department volunteered to advise them. At first he helped them acquire greater facility in the English language, but soon he was hunting rooms for them and seeking contacts with American students and local residents so that the foreign visitors might gain some insight into our culture. Eventually, it became Mr. Nelson's full-time job, which he filled with distinction for many years. In 1935-36 the University had 288 foreign students from fifty eight countries, more than any other university except three on the east and west coasts. But Michigan had more Asian students than those three, owing to the impression made by President Angell as minister to China and to the attractions of the Barbour scholarships. An International Center was established in a new wing built on the Union in 1938. The number of foreign students grew to 1550 in 1962.

Fraternities and sororities suffered a triple financial blow: the general decline in enrollment, a further decline in the percentage of students who could afford to join, and a new deferred rushing system aimed at keeping freshmen in supervised dorms rather than in fraternity houses. The new rule against pledging freshmen until the second semester and then not letting them live in houses until their sophomore year had a good effect on deportment in the houses, but it meant a year in which no initiation fees and fewer living fees were received. With a semester in which to look around, the freshmen were also more discriminating in the houses they joined. The critical year was 1932-33, when seven fraternities were forced to close their doors, and three more were in financial straits. Five others gave up their houses to take cheaper quarters on a rental basis. The dean of students invited the National Fraternity Secretaries Association to send a committee here. It found that of the forty-nine fraternities remaining, twenty-one were in questionable financial condition. Several recommendations toward regularizing financial practices and reporting monthly were instituted. To help matters the Committee on Student Affairs allowed freshmen pledges to live in the houses their second semester. As a means of economy, the several fraternity house managers formed a Fraternity Buyers Association in 1934 for the bulk purchase of food. It operated one year and then broke down for lack of cooperation. It was revived later as a financial necessity.

In spite of this dark situation, several new societies were recognized: Alpha Gamma Delta, a general sorority; Alpha Lambda for Chinese students; Delta Epsilon Pi for Greek students; Kappa Alpha Psi for African American students; and Zeta Pi Sigma for Polish women. These latter societies, along with Theta Phi Alpha, a Catholic sorority, were never considered discriminatory in an unpleasant way.

In August 1934 Dean Bursley submitted a report about student discipline in line with Director Anderson's views. The Regents referred it to their Committee on Student and Alumni Relations, and at the Board's September meeting Regent Murfin submitted a committee statement on students which was adopted as policy:

"Students should realize that their enrollment in the University carries with it obligations in regard to conduct, not only inside but also outside the classroom, and they are expected to conduct themselves so as to be a credit both to themselves and to the University. They are amenable to the laws governing the community as well as to the rules and orders of the University and University officials, and are expected to observe the standards of conduct approved by the University. Whenever a student organization fails to observe the principles of conduct above outlined, or conducts himself or itself in such a manner as to make it apparent that he or it is not a desirable member of the University, he or it shall be liable to disciplinary action." This forthright effort to inform students of the responsibility they shouldered upon enrollment appeared in the bulletin of *General Information* thereafter for as long as Ruthven was president.

5. *From isolationism and pacificism to World War II*

Aside from the financial hardships of the Depression, the decade was exciting and significant for students. There were all the New Deal agencies, the repeal of prohibition, kidnappings, the debate on neutrality and pacifism, teacher oaths, industrial unions and sit-down strikes, chain letters, and rabble rousers like William Randolph Hearst, Senator Huey Long, Father Coughlin, and Dr. Francis Townsend. Abroad the decade witnessed the rise of Hitler, diplomatic recognition of Soviet Russia, the Italo-Ethiopian War, the Spanish Civil War, the Chino-Japanese War, the Munich episode, and finally World War II. It was a wilderness for students to find their way through.

On campus, pacifism and neutrality were the consuming issues, reflecting national concerns. Agitation was first confined to objections to war movies, baiting the American Legion, and complaining against the ROTC, which being voluntary at Michigan did not make a good adversary. The Depression-born National Student League petitioned the Committee on Student Affairs for recognition in May 1933 and received it, but within two weeks was in trouble for not following regulations governing extracurricular organizations. The next year there appeared the League Against War and Militarism. In 1935 another group asked for recognition: the Student League for Industrial Democracy, calling itself a socialist organization. Its complaint was that the National Student League was made up of communists who were trying to capture other groups, and the socialists wanted separate recognition. It was granted. There would be a succession of such radical organizations with changing names and overlapping memberships. In relation to the size of the student body they were minute in membership, but their stands on various questions indicated the ideas swirling around and over the heads of most of the students.

Senator Gerald P. Nye of North Dakota was conducting an investigation of munitions makers in 1934 in which he exposed their activities and influence. He felt that they were largely responsible for our entry into World War I, an attitude of disillusionment fostered also by the failure of several of our allies to repay their loans and by disappointment in the power of the League of Nations. Nye wanted to limit the President's power in foreign affairs by increasing Congress' power based upon a determined neutrality policy. This was not the neutrality President Wilson had tried to maintain in 1914-17 in order to act as arbitrator and bring the belligerents to the peace table, but a neutrality of isolationism. Nye seemed unaware of how much such a policy appealed to the rising dictators of Europe, and he was naive in thinking that we could remain unaffected by a major war in Europe. But his oversimplification of the issues made a strong appeal to college students. Their isolationism was a reactionary hope, rather than a helpful modern policy, just as their stand for disarmament and pacifism was no discouragement of the war-minded abroad. Shucking off the responsibilities of power in a quarreling world did not seem to them an escape from reality. The same attitude would crop up again thirty years later.

Early in October 1934 Senator Nye was invited to speak by the Michigan Union. He called for the elimination of profits by munitions makers and a double tax on high incomes during the war. He believed that if the profits could be taken out of war, it could be avoided. He characterized the business of national defense as a "vicious racket" and declared that "preparedness for war leads to war." Roger Baldwin, president of the American Civil Liberties Union, spoke the same week and said that the United States must choose between left and right— communism or fascism. The *Daily*, with more maturity than the speaker, termed his choice nonsense and prophesied that democracy would still stand after the Depression was over. At this time the *Daily* was not sympathetic with pacifists because it felt they did not work to eliminate causes of war but simply railed against it. It also ridiculed a local meeting of communists on the steps of the county courthouse. If such a meeting appears unbelievable today, it is matched by a public address by Professor Lowell J. Carr urging all professors to join an American Federation of Labor union.

WILLIS WARD

Also in October 1934 Michigan played Georgia Tech in football. Willis Ward, a first string player usually, was a African American. A rumor swept over the campus that Georgia Tech had requested Coach Kipke not to let Ward play. Lending credence to the rumor was the refusal of both Kipke and Yost to say anything. The night before the game a student rally was held to advocate keeping Ward in the game; it was rudely interrupted by professed "friends of Ward" who asserted that he would only be injured by vengeful Georgia Tech players! Michigan won the game, 9 to 2, but Ward did not even appear on the bench in uniform. The *Daily* remained silent editorially until after the game, then urged the Board in Control of Athletics not to schedule any more games with Southern universities.

In February 1935 the *Literary Digest* announced the results of its "college peace poll." Michigan's vote was typical of other universities: the students voted 1819 to 1432 in favor of the United States joining the League of Nations; 2818 to 403 against bearing arms if the United States should invade another country; 3027 to 271 in favor of the federal government curtailing the munitions industry; and 2336 to 947 against the general proposition that increased armaments would insure us against being drawn into another war. Although only 3250 students out of 9850 in Ann Arbor voted, the poll probably measured the feelings of all.

In March 1935 the National Student League invited Evelyn John Strachey, an English Marxist visiting America, to speak at Hill Auditorium. Strachey's manager demanded $300 in advance. After some scrambling the NSL raised $100 and wired it, but the University Committee on Lecture Policy decided no University building could be used because the NSL obviously was not financially responsible enough. Strachey agreed to come on March 14, but two days before that date he was arrested in Chicago for false statements about himself on entering the country. He was released on bail, and the NSL rented Granger's ballroom. Because of all the newspaper publicity, about 1000 people turned out. After all this effort, Strachey's analysis of the Depression and comments on the European dictators were so preposterous as to defy discussion or criticism. Certain professors complained against the Lecture Committee for denying use of Hill Auditorium and raised the accusation of denying free speech. This was too much for Professor Ralph Aigler of the Law School. In a public letter he pointed out to his colleagues that the "right of free speech" by no means includes the "privilege to speak when and where one may desire."

Next the NSL announced a student protest against war for April 4, on which day students all over the country would walk out of their classes and hear a pacifistic appeal. Cooler heads intervened. A joint student-faculty committee assumed sponsorship of the antiwar rally, obtained use of Hill Auditorium, and engaged Professor Robert Morse Lovett of the University of Chicago to speak. With *Daily* support, this late afternoon lecture attracted about 1200, who heard Lovett denounce the ROTC, Hearst, and the Versailles treaty. Not to be upstaged, the NSL scheduled its rally on the campus at 11 A.M. About a thousand students congregated to see what would happen, and perhaps 450 took the "Oxford pledge" against serving in the armed forces at any time.

At the end of a fairly turbulent year, the *Michigan Daily* in May 1935 was given a "superior" rating and was among only five papers designated as "Pacemakers" in a contest of 214 college newspapers sponsored by the

CO-OP STUDENTS BEFORE THE WAR

Associated Collegiate Press. It scored 880 points out of a possible 1000 on news values, writing and editing, headlines and makeup, and special features.

After the semester closed in June, four students were asked not to return in the fall. President Ruthven told them by letter their actions had interfered with the work of the University and of other students. Those who objected were granted a conference with the president, but still were not readmitted. To clarify the administration's attitude, President Ruthven issued a warning that the work of the University was not to he interfered with, and "perversive activities" would not be tolerated. In his annual report, written in the fall of 1935, he enlarged on the powers of the University over its students:

"There is widely current in Michigan an erroneous belief that the University, being a state institution, is required to accept any graduate of the high schools who applies for admission. Somewhat akin to this thought is another to the effect that an enrolled student cannot be asked not to reregister at the beginning of any year if his scholastic standing is satisfactory. Finally, it has been the practice to place the principal emphasis on scholarship in judging qualifications for admission.

"Without any question the Regents have full power to prescribe the entrance requirements. In addition, they have the moral responsibility of not wasting State funds in attempts to educate those who in the best judgment of the officials are unfitted or unwilling to take full advantage of the opportunities provided by the State. If education is essentially character building and the University is designed to develop and not reform the individual, then are the University authorities both privileged and morally bound to use every known device to limit attendance to honest, sincere, and ambitious, as well as scholastically trained, young men and women . . . .

"As the recent rewritten qualifications for admission state: The University expects that those who enter shall have shown intellectual capacity, shall be able to apply themselves to their studies, and shall be able to work systematically. While definite evidence of intellectual capacity is indispensable, the University believes that, after such evidence is established, positive qualities of character and personality should operate as determining factors in admission . . . . Attendance at the University of Michigan is a privilege and not a right. In order to safeguard its ideals of scholarship, character, and personality the University reserves the right, and the student concedes to the University the right, to require withdrawal of any student at any time for any reason deemed sufficient to it."

The latter paragraph appeared in official bulletins thereafter during Ruthven's administration. He had no tolerance for students who came not for what the University had to offer, but for such other purposes as exhibitionism, drinking, and playing, or devotion to off campus controversies. He made it clear that he expected interviews, aptitude tests, and psychological examinations to be utilized, along with scholastic records, in selecting students.

Shortly before the University resumed in the fall of 1935, Congress passed a neutrality act prohibiting the selling or transporting of munitions to belligerents, later amended to include loans of money and travel on the ships of belligerents. Its great defect was that it deprived the State Department of power to distinguish between aggressors and defenders, but the isolationists were satisfied. Professor Preston Slosson of the History Department prophesied in a public letter that in the event of war in Europe the neutrality law would fail, but no one paid him any heed.

The *Daily* printed a special "Goodfellow Edition" in December to be sold by student leaders and faculty members, including President Ruthven. Proceeds were used for the benefit of needy students, townspeople, and hospital patients. This charitable gesture continued annually until the war.

Early in 1936 Scott Nearing, an avowed communist, lectured in the Natural Science Auditorium and repeated the warning that the world must choose between fascism and communism; individualism was a thing of the past. He declared that there was more freedom in Russia (this was the year Stalin's bloody purges began) than elsewhere under capitalism. Earlier, he spoke directly to the National Student League and their friends—a total of thirty—on how to work for the coming communist order. Again, the *Daily* refuted Nearing, but he was followed by Norman Thomas in Hill Auditorium who assured his audience that the United States was headed straight for war and fascism and could be saved only by substituting socialism for capitalism.

At the other extreme, in October 1936 the University's conference on education and research heard the New Deal denounced by visiting industrialists. An executive of Chrysler Corporation praised Hitler, whom he had met, for the industrial order in Germany. The *Daily* jumped him and published a sarcastic and indignant letter on the speech by Arthur Miller, '38, the incipient playwright. At this time the *Daily* also confessed to changing its mind about disarmament. The situation of the world, especially the civil war in Spain and Japanese aggression, caused it to support an increase in our armed forces if necessary to preserve peace and democracy against a fascist menace.

The *Daily* conducted a presidential straw poll among the faculty which showed 276 for Landon, 271 for Roosevelt, 33 for Thomas, and 10 for Browder. Regent Murfin said the latter ten should be dismissed if they could be identified.

"Friends of Spanish Democracy" began collecting money on campus in the spring of 1937 with *Daily* approval. Another liberal group was recognized in April as a chapter of the National American Student Union, but called the Progressive Club at first. It too collected money for Loyalist Spain, where four Michigan students were fighting. For the next two years visiting lecturers on Spain kept forecasting an ultimate victory by the Loyalists.

Arousing much more interest than any of these appeals was the first Michigras celebration, a fair and festival involving a parade of floats and fun booths in Yost Field House. Hundreds of students worked furiously on this event, and thousands attended. In the fall of 1937 there was a resurgence of collegiatism. After a football pep meeting, students marched on the Michigan Theater, doing damage to the place and injuring a policeman. Tear gas was used to disperse the mob of 2000, and three students were arrested, but not prosecuted. It was the first riot in nine years. The next adolescent upsurge came in 1939 with the live goldfish swallowers. The competition over who could gulp down the most was largely confined to the East and held little appeal at Michigan.

Depression or not, these were still the years of big class dances. Many of the name bands in the nation came to play for them, such as those of Paul Whiteman (with Mildred Bailey singing), George Olson, Ted Weems, Kay Kyser, Ben Bernie, Red Nichols, Herbie Kay (with Dorothy Lamour), Coon-Sanders, Fletcher Henderson, Wayne King, Jan Garber, Count Basie, Louis Armstrong, Tommy Dorsey, Duke Ellington, Benny Goodman, and Glenn Miller.

The Student Religious Association and the *Daily* conducted another peace poll, but drew only 1831 ballots. 961 students favored boycotting Japan, and 676 rebel Spain; 810 were against any boycott. As for our business interests in China, 789 would protect them by diplomatic protests only, and 587 would withdraw all protection. A large majority surprisingly voted against neutrality and would support the United States in war; only 360 were against such a stance.

Suddenly, in November 1937 *Daily* editorials appeared signed by the individual writers. A notice was printed in every issue that they were the opinions of the writers only. The Board in Control had decided that the *Daily* should not be so construed by outsiders as representing student opinion. The editorials now carried no more weight than letters to the editor. Shortly afterward the last attempt to carry on a humor column was given up; it ended a long tradition.

President Ruthven addressed the New York City alumni in February 1938 and assailed a growing notion that students should be indoctrinated with certain beliefs and have their thoughts curbed. He said universities tended to be too conservative anyway. The *Daily* was so enamored of the speech that it published the following excerpt under its masthead every day for the rest of the year: "It is important for society to avoid the neglect of adults, but positively dangerous for it to thwart the ambition of youth to reform the world. Only the schools which act on this belief are educational institutions in the best meaning of the term."

As President Roosevelt pressed for more armaments, a Michigan Anti-War Committee sponsored a meeting in April 1938 at which students were urged to make clear that they would not fight in a coming war. Professor Lovett of Chicago returned for a "Strike Against War" sponsored by forty campus organizations, but attracted an audience of only 600.

At this time the campus had forty general fraternities, seventeen sororities, and fifteen professional fraternities, the number remaining fairly constant for the next three years. The Depression had taken its toll, and the problem of a few fraternities getting large pledge classes and others getting only one or two pledges continued as unsolvable.

Before the Munich conference at the end of September 1938, an editorial in the *Daily* condemned appeasement. Another urged students to attend a rally on campus sponsored by the local chapter of the American Student Union and by others to "save" Czechoslovakia, with warning that appeasement of Hitler would only encourage Nazi aggression. Only about 250 attended, whereas that night after a football pep meeting at Hill Auditorium about 5000 students paraded through the streets, set bonfires, tried the Michigan Theater (which was locked up), and finally were driven to Ferry Field by fire hoses and police tear gas. The *Daily* was disgusted. After Chamberlain's settlement at Munich, Managing Editor Robert Mitchell, '39, expressed the hope that the sacrifice of Czechoslovakia had not been in vain, although he termed the easing of tension a "false peace" and warned that the war for democracy had yet to be won. He was clearer in his thinking than his successor a year later.

The American Student Union retreated from its neutrality stand and favored sending arms to Loyalist Spain. It still argued that the struggle for peace was a struggle against fascism, not communism. But it was getting difficult to be antifascist and pacifistic as well as isolationist and anxious to help Loyalist Spain. A Young Communists League now existed separate from the American Student Union and in succession to the National Student League.

In January 1939 Professor Pollock warned the students that Hitler would not remain appeased by Munich, but would move next against Poland. Bertrand Russell lectured on campus in February and in his hopeful pacifism declared that the Munich settlement might well lead to the downfall of Hitler from internal pressures.

With spring, two antiwar rallies were held. A group of 600 in front of the General Library heard pleas for the United States to cooperate against fascism with nations "who think as we do." The Michigan Anti-War Committee engaged UAW leader Leonard Woodcock of Detroit to speak. He railed against cooperating with Britain and France, those "sham defenders of democracy," and was sure that Hitler was working toward his own destruction, so the United States need aid only the alien peoples he was bringing under his rule. A student speaker demanded a cessation of bigger armaments and a vote on the question of declaring war.

Late in August 1939, as if he had been waiting for the University to recess, Hitler announced a nonaggression pact with Soviet Russia. It defied everything the campus liberals had been saying and brought together the two antagonists of the recently concluded Spanish civil war. Within a week Hitler invaded Poland without a declaration of war, and two weeks later Stalin joined him in partitioning the country. On September 3 Great Britain and France declared war on Germany. Russia turned on Finland. The dreaded war in Europe had begun at last. It was no mystery where Mussolini's sympathy lay; he was biding his time for a price.

When the University reopened in September, the *Daily* announced its stand in a front-page editorial signed by the managing editor and editorial director. It contained some interesting pronouncements: the United States must keep out of the European war; it is "nothing but a clash of rival imperialisms." Americans abhor Nazism and should try to restore democratic government in Germany, Austria, and Czechoslovakia, but that isn't what England and France are fighting for. The neutrality act should not be modified, as President Roosevelt proposed; instead, we should have complete non-intercourse with any of the belligerents, develop a self-contained economy, and forego the "five percent of our national income" derived from foreign trade.

Professor Slosson replied in the first of several letters he was to send to the *Daily* in the next two years in an effort to sharpen its thinking. He pointed out that an embargo on our foreign trade would be the greatest boon Hitler could ask for. He said it was inconsistent to condemn Chamberlain for indifference to Czechoslovakia and couple it with a declaration of indifference to England, France, and Poland. Isolationism, he said, only divided the world, rather than united it. Professor John P. Dawson of the Law School also replied to the editorial.

Two graduate students writing jointly—James Duesenberry and Robert Roosa, both to assume national stature in the Kennedy-Johnson administration—defended modification of the neutrality act to permit cash and carry purchases arguing that we should help the allies and could do so without being dragged into the war.

The *Daily* suddenly found itself keeping strange company with the American Legion, the Hearst newspapers, the *Chicago Tribune*, and the Young Communists League. The Legion *et al* were all for maintaining the neutrality act, as were Norman Thomas and Gerald Nye. So was the Young Communists League, but only because Russia was now on Hitler's side. The American Student Union also favored strict neutrality, on the ingenious premise that England and France had built up Nazi Germany to encourage German expansion eastward, but used Poland as an excuse to declare war when Germany discontinued her eastward drive by signing a nonaggression pact with Soviet Russia! Nothing was said about Finland.

In November the Bureau of Student Opinion took a poll on the question: should the United States intervene in the war if England and France appeared to be losing? 77 percent of the men and 63 percent of the women said no. H. V. Kaltenborn lectured at Hill Auditorium in December and urged that the United States keep out of the war. He was echoed by Major George Fielding Eliot, a later speaker.

Nevertheless, the neutrality act, as Professor Slosson had predicted in the event of war, was modified to permit cash and carry sales to the belligerents, which meant Britain and France only, and to grant a loan to beleaguered Finland. The *Daily* condemned Russia for bombing Finland, and the stubborn and surprisingly successful defenders earned the admiration of all.

During the Christmas vacation of 1939 the Michigan American Student Union sent ten delegates to the national convention, where a resolution condemning Russia for its attack on Finland was defeated, 322 to 49. The majority feared that passage of such a resolution would affect the country's neutrality! Two months later the local American Student Union denounced the Finnish Relief Drive on campus. The chapter then had a membership of about eighty, split in its views.

Senator Nye was invited back to another peace rally in April 1940. About 3000 students heard him. Buttons were offered for sale saying the "Yanks Are Not Coming," a sentiment the editorial director of the *Daily* approved. Predictably, Nye denounced all of President Roosevelt's war measures.

Events moved fast in May. The Young Communists League challenged Professor Slosson to take the negative in a debate on "The sovereignty of small countries is better secured by closer cooperation with the Soviet Union." There was no decision, but two days later Hitler invaded Holland, Belgium, and Luxembourg. Two months later his ally, Stalin, swept into the Baltic countries and "secured" them. Italy entered the war in June, just before France fell

In June 1940 President Ruthven sent letters to nine students denying them readmission in the fall. His action was supported by the Regents and was kept confidential so that the students could register elsewhere without difficulty. Seven of them did so. The other two, both graduate students, bounced back to Ann Arbor in September and demanded reinstatement or a public trial. They asserted that they had been dismissed without any reason given, but only because of their liberal opinions. Finally, in the middle of October, Ruthven issued a statement saying that the action had been taken because of the students' actions, "disruptive of good order in the University," not their affiliations. Each had been informed of the reasons, and each had been offered a conference with the president if desired. He had had conferences with the two complainants. "Their reasoning seemed to be that since they were avowed 'liberals,' their activities could not be questioned without infringing upon their 'academic freedom.' " Ruthven included a reminder that University students are "guests of that state, and even if they do not respect this hospitality they should not, in justice to the other students, be permitted to abuse it." Fortunately, there were only a very few "who interpret their civil rights to include license to do anything they want to do on the plea that they are 'liberals.' This is a perverted concept of civil rights."

A couple of professors from other universities fished in these troubled waters, with the result that a mock trial of the two students was held at Island Park on November 9. About 600 attended. Since no one appeared on behalf of the University, of course, the stunt fell somewhat flat. A *Daily* editorial by the city editor commended Ruthven for his liberal stands in the past and expressed faith in him. It regretted the "mystery" surrounding the expulsions and hoped it wasn't a reactionary turn.

The Men's Judiciary Council supported the University action. The American Student Union condemned it in a letter that went out of its way to impugn the motives and honesty of the Regents. For printing this letter, knowing that the Regents were not to be criticized personally in the *Daily*, two editors were suspended from the staff for a week by the Board in Control. The Men's Judiciary Council returned to the fray and referred to the faculty disciplinary committee charges against the American Student Union for defying University regulations. The committee questioned American Student Union officers and then suspended the organization indefinitely in December

The first national legislation directly to affect the students was the Burke-Wadsworth bill calling for compulsory military training of single men between the ages of twenty-one and thirty-six for one year. It was introduced, debated, and passed between June and September 1940. The local chapter of the American Student Union urged students to write to their congressmen in opposition to the bill. Similarly, twenty-seven members of the Fellowship of Reconciliation, a pacifistic group, appealed to Congress against the bill. Several editorials and a columnist of the *Summer Michigan Daily* expressed objection to the bill. In the fall of 1940 the managing editor of the *Daily* publicly thanked Senator Vandenberg for his steady opposition to conscription.

When the Burke-Wadsworth bill became law on September 17, it contained a blanket deferment for enrolled college students until the end of the academic year, or July 1, 1941. But students over twenty-one had to register for the draft, the same as all other young men, on October 16, and the Registrar's Office supervised the registration of the eligible University students and sent their cards to their respective local draft boards. Looking back on that troubled decade, it is clear that repudiation of the past and social protest were characteristic. Further, it is sad to contemplate how much pressure was brought to bear on students—pulling and hauling. The wonder is not that a few espoused impossible causes or positions, but that on occasion they could see so clearly. It is astonishing in retrospect how little faith there was among so-called intellectuals in the endurance of democracy or the recuperative power of capitalism. The situation was not helped by the floating prophets who drifted from campus to campus delivering gloomy lectures and from whom greater acuteness should have been expected. They united in one tiresome refrain: the United States must make a choice between communism and fascism. If a handful of students echoed them, it is no surprise. More remarkable is it that so many students ignored them or doubted them, and that the *Daily* had the wisdom to refute their diagnosis. Perhaps it is not too much to suggest that the faculty may have helped provide the students with enough critical insights to identify phony reformers.

With regard to the European war, the student body was probably less sure of itself than strident voices might suggest. The emotions of doubt about Munich, disdain for the Nazis, sympathy for the allies, and suspicion of Soviet Russia proved a better guide to reason than the warped and superficial arguments of the isolationists and pacifists, who could not discriminate. Lumping the belligerents together, they insisted on avoiding their quarrel out of fear of bloodshed or of loss of democracy here. Gradually, the students began to separate their dislike of war from the hard necessity of stopping brutal aggression first before paths to peace could be explored.

Having emerged from a decade of Depression and political turmoil, President Ruthven found himself faced with a fresh problem: managing a University in a world at war. But now he had a dozen years of experience behind him, he was more sure of himself and the faculty, and he had been through World War I. Michigan was fortunate to have him at the helm when military considerations gathered in avalanche.

CAMPUS AT THE BEGINNING OF WORLD WAR II

CHAPTER ELEVEN

THE UNIVERSITY AT WAR

IN THE YEAR PRECEDING Pearl Harbor, the University had adjusted itself to the growing emergency and had demonstrated that it was not a delicate instrument geared only to operation in a peaceful world. For two decades it had offered a Reserve Officers' Training Corps that annually enrolled about a thousand students in basic and advanced training and graduated about one hundred commissioned Army officers each year. The Civilian Pilot Training Program, sponsored jointly by the Civil Aeronautics Authority and the Uni-

ALEXANDER G. RUTHVEN

versity, had been teaching students to fly since the spring of 1939, utilizing the Ann Arbor Airport. When the Navy Department instituted reserve officers' training early in 1940, the University was among the twenty-seven institutions selected for trial work.

It was clear to the University administration that the draft deferment granted students was only a warning and a postponement of a blow that could cripple the University unless National Selective Service Headquarters modified its sweeping intentions. The months of grace permitted educators, army officers, and manpower directors to meet to evolve a more permanent policy for the proper utilization of college students in the defense program. President Ruthven had taken the position that "the greatest service which the universities can provide is the training of young men and women according to their aptitudes, for only in this way can the country be assured of a citizenry properly prepared for both peace and war." It took a year for the War and Navy departments to come around to this point of view.

1. The Univeristy's response to the War

At the first meeting of the Conference of Deans in the fall of 1940, a steering Committee on National Defense was proposed to consider all the problems of policy and personnel growing out of the draft and other national defense measures that might be taken. President Ruthven appointed Deans Hopkins (chairman), Edmondson, and Yoakum, and this committee then added a faculty advisory committee of eighteen professors which it could consult and to whom it could pass along relevant information. Dean Hopkins made several trips to Washington to learn what the Army and Navy intended to do with young men in general and to consult with them and congressional leaders on how the universities could contribute to the defense program and the building of a large military force. The American Council on Education assumed leadership in meeting with the deputy director of the Selective Service System (Brigadier General Lewis B. Hershey) and the Federal Security Administrator (Paul V. McNutt) during the winter of 1940-41. The Council urged continued deferment of college students on the ground that the Army and Navy would need a continuing flow of professionally and technically trained men. Michigan supported this argument.

National Selective Service Headquarters being charged with the duty of producing as many soldiers as possible, General Hershey would not at first admit the contention of the educators. He naively believed that enough professional and technically trained men already existed to satisfy the needs of the Army and Navy. He assumed that the educators were interested primarily in the survival of their institutions and questioned whether "the colleges can afford to be accused of demanding privileges which appear to be for the benefit of the individuals concerned." He asked whether the educational system was not flexible enough to operate within the terms of the Selective Service Act, training students until they were called up, then receiving them again after they were discharged.

The arguments of the universities soon received support, however, from the generals and admirals concerned with planning the personnel of our greatly expanding military forces. The estimates submitted by those experts underlined the statement of the educators that a continuous supply of technically and professionally trained young men must be provided. General Hershey quickly reversed himself, and the only remaining problem was to defer a sufficient number of college students to provide the needed technicians and officers. On March 7, 1941, he issued a directive to all state draft directors to permit the continued deferment of all college students "in training or preparation" for "any industry, business employment, agricultural pursuit, governmental service, or any other service or endeavor the maintenance of which is necessary for national health, safety, or interest." This was interpreted to include medical, dental, and pharmacy students, and also premedical and predental students. The Bureau of Labor Statistics of the Department of Labor then entered a special request to allow the deferment of all students preparing to enter certain professional fields where the supply of man power had been found to be at a dangerously low level. The first list of critical occupations included chemistry and several branches of engineering, and deferments were granted.

Two weeks later in an address before the University of Michigan Club of New York, President Ruthven asked that the University be allowed to assume responsibilities commensurate with its facilities for serving the nation. "Until the time arrives when mass training is essential to the national welfare, [Michigan] will continue to ask if there is not a better way to give basic military training to men at the college level than that which is now in prospect. She will suggest that it would be far wiser to work out a plan involving extensive use of summer encampments and stepped-up winter training in the ROTC programs, and will insist that cooperation between educational institutions and the military forces will produce better citizens both for peace and war, than an isolated year of instruction in military science. . . . The general position of the University will be that the safety of the nation in war as in peace requires that the schools as well as the industries be kept at peak production."

In February 1941 the College of Engineering and the Extension Service, in cooperation with the U.S. Office of Education, had begun offering twenty-seven technical courses in Detroit and Ann Arbor for workers in defense industries. This Engineering Defense Training Program was destined to continue throughout the war under the supervision of Professor Robert H. Sherlock. Similarly, the Department of Engineering Research was carrying on a number of research projects important to defense industries, with as little publicity as possible, in cooperation with the National Defense Research Committee.

The faculty was not silent on the crowding events of the year 1940-41. They were interviewed, gave lectures, and wrote public letters trying to give the students informational background for judging the occurrences in Europe as well as in Washington. 2214 faculty members signed a petition in February 1941 directed to Senators Vandenberg and Brown urging passage of the Lend-Lease Bill to aid the Allies. Reserve commissions were held by 125 faculty, but by June 1941 only fifteen had been called into military or government service. It must be recorded that the recommendations of the University's Committee on National Defense did not strike every faculty member with like force. Some believed the war in Europe would be ended before this country became involved; some objected to any change in University routine until and unless war came; some thought the committee was needlessly excited and overly pessimistic. Unlike 1917, however, no one had a good word for Nazi Germany.

Among the students a Campus Peace Council was formed in April 1941 and engaged Senator Burton K. Wheeler, '05*l*, of Montana to address a peace rally. As the new organization was denied recognition, however, by the Student Affairs Committee, Senator Wheeler's isolationist speech was sponsored by another group, the Michigan AntiWar Committee. It was delivered on May 5. Wheeler had been vigorously opposed to lend-lease.

Meanwhile, the Campus Peace Council engaged another speaker and held an antiwar rally, attended by 300 persons, at Felch Park on May 1. The Michigan Anti-War Committee also brought socialist Norman Thomas to the campus on May 28. He replayed his old tune, that the continuance of democracy in the United States depended upon our staying out of war. He was as isolationist as Senator Wheeler. But symptomatic of changing feeling was the formation in May of the American Student Defense League. It circulated a petition favoring convoys to deliver war goods to England and obtained 1100 signatures.

Incredibly, Hitler committed the colossal blunder of turning on Soviet Russia late in June. If the campus "pinks" were relieved not to have Stalin tied up with Hitler, they encountered a new problem in reversing their neutrality stand. With the greatest ease, however, they now demanded an end to neutrality and help for Russia.

When University classes resumed in September 1941, deferments based on occupational shortages continued in effect, although decisions were made in every case by local draft boards. National Selective Service Headquarters also permitted other students who might he called for induction during the last half of a semester to receive a postponement of induction until the end of the semester, so that they would not lose academic credit for work started and interrupted. On this basis the University was able to enroll 7521 men and 3760 women, a total of 11,281. This was a loss of good men students from the previous fall, but an increase of more than 100 women students.

The Engineering Defense Training Program was enlarged to an Engineering, Science, and Management Defense Training Program that utilized the Literary College and Business Administration School as well as extension courses. Enrollment grew.

The Student Defenders of Democracy, a new campus organization started in the fall of 1941, reflected a new grasp of the war issues. It circulated a petition at the end of October urging the repeal of the Neutrality Act, so much favored by the students when enacted, and obtained 1131 signatures of students and faculty members which were sent to Congress. It also sponsored an Armistice Day rally in Hill Auditorium with the slogan "Win the War—Win the Peace." The women students formed a University Women's Defense Committee early in October, which arranged credit and noncredit classes in nutrition, Red Cross work, and home nursing.

The Japanese surprise attack on Pearl Harbor, December 7, jolted everyone's thinking by abruptly altering the conditions on which action was discussed and by turning attention from Europe to the Pacific. It rendered obsolete and irrelevant most of the questions campuses had debated for four years, and it drove America into war united. The academic community could no longer talk about what ought to be done if—because the "if" had been fulfilled, from an unexpected direction.

In the first hasty confusion of a state of war, the Army on campus leaped to the suggestion that the University open its plant facilities for a training program to be conducted by military instructors. Had Michigan acquiesced, it would have abandoned its primary function and dismissed most of its faculty. The state would have been left after the war with a totally disabled institution, a casualty of war, and in President Ruthven's view a needless casualty. If the armed forces wanted only barracks, mess halls, and classrooms, then they could find better accommodations by requisitioning hotels.

The University administration persisted in the belief that it could perform a more effective military service. It had to offer an educational organization equipped and experienced for teaching and research. Let the armed forces designate the subjects they desired to have taught and send selected trainees to the campus who could learn, and the University would train them in their specialities. Neither the Army nor the Navy had crystallized its thinking on college programs beyond knowing that certain techniques and languages would be needed, and a year was required to work out the several academic programs.

During the year of indecision and conflicting proposals, Ruthven was subject to all kinds of pressures. Colonel William A. Ganoe, new ROTC commandant, was self-confident, aggressive with his views, and impatient. He even complained to certain regents about the lethargy of the University in a time of crisis—when the Army itself could not put together a specialized training program for the experts it must have. As many as three regents grew dissatisfied with the president, but they could gain no other adherents. For the *Michigan Technic* Colonel Ganoe wrote a scathing appraisal of collegiate health, complaining that colleges turned out too many "low-browed gladiators and high-browed enemies." He wanted men students to take ten hours a week of physical exercises.

The Committee on National Defense was replaced by a University War Board. The original three members—Hopkins, Yoakum, and Edmondson—were supplemented by Professors Gram, James of the Law School, and Heneman of the Political Science Department. The latter was made executive director, and Clark Tibbitts was named secretary. Professors William C. Hoad and A. E. R. Boak were soon added to the board. It initiated a schedule for a three-term year of continuous operation, additional funds being provided by the state legislature. It set up a clearing house of information for students, started a plant protection committee, and began a course in leadership of civilian protection work for townspeople. It asked H. O. Crisler, director of athletics, to formulate a plan for increased physical training of men, and he proposed four and a half hours a week in physical education. The board ordered an inventory of faculty specialities and of research facilities. It appointed a War Bond Committee to supervise bond sales.

By April 1942 the federal government had awarded thirty-one research contracts to the University, most of them classified. The State Department placed in the hands of the University, because of its experience in teaching English to Latin Americans, the training of instructors who could be sent to Latin America to teach English and the culture of the United States. In addition, selected graduates of law schools in Latin America were sent to Michigan for further study in InterAmerican law. Soon engineers, dentists, and physicians from Latin America were sent to Michigan by the State Department for graduate study.

On top of the Engineering, Science, and Management War Training program, the Engineering College was asked to begin in June a twelve-week course for ordnance inspectors. Nearly a thousand inspectors were trained in the twenty-two months this course lasted. An invita-

JUDGE ADVOCATE GENERAL'S SCHOOL, LAW QUAD

tion from the University was sent to the Judge Advocate General's Department of the Army to move its school from Washington to Ann Arbor. It was accepted, and the Lawyers Club was taken over in September 1942. Enrollment in the regular Law School plummeted from 720 to 71. Before the so-called "JAG School" closed in January 1946 it had graduated 2467 Army lawyers.

The Medical School and Hospital School of Nursing responded to a call early in 1942 to staff a military hospital. Twenty-four physicians and dentists, eleven nurses, and six technicians volunteered and were sent to camp in June. Lieutenant Colonel Walter G. Maddock, M.D., organized the unit and ultimately commanded it as the 298th General Hospital.

Nurse Margaret K. Shafer ultimately became a lieutenant colonel and chief nurse of the European Theater of Operations. The 298th sailed for Liverpool in October and operated a hospital near Bristol. It was joined by thirteen more physicians and six more

298TH HOSPITAL IN FRANCE AFTER D-DAY

nurses from the University in 1943. All the hospital personnel were moved to France in July 1944 after the invasion.

Among the students there was not much war-related activity in 1942 until the Student War Board of nine campus leaders was formed at the end of March. Robert Wallace, '42e, was chairman. Student groups were

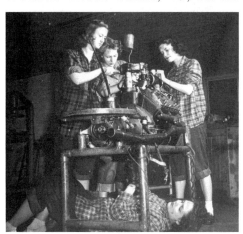

AUTO SHOP

encouraged to assist in civilian defense activities. In the fall of 1942 the Board created a Manpower Mobilization Corps under Marvin Borman, '44. More than a thousand men students signed up for war-related jobs. The corps sent out crews to pick apples, pull sugar beets, and husk corn. Other volunteers worked at the University Hospital. Teams worked on scrap metal drives, bond sales, and foreign relief. Two hundred coeds served as volunteer nurses' aides, while others made surgical dressings and bandages.

A committee of which Arthur Rude, '42, was chairman looked beyond the war and established a Student Bomber Scholarship. The intention was to raise $100,000, believed to be approximately the cost of a bombing plane, and invest it in war bonds. After the war ended, the bonds would be sold and the money used to assist veterans who returned to the University. The Student War Board approved the project, of course, but it was too ambitious. Only $25,000 was raised and invested.

By 1943 the Army and Navy knew what they wanted from the

universities. Professor Marvin L. Niehuss of the Law School had been appointed coordinator of emergency training to deal with all service contracts. The Army's Japanese Language School was opened here in January 1943 under the direction of Assistant Professor Joseph K. Yamagiwa, who had to procure instructors from the resettled Nisei. During a twelve months' course the students were taught to read, write, and speak Japanese for service as combat intelligence officers. The men lived in East Quadrangle. Two classes attended concurrently until the program ended at Christmas 1945.

In March the Army Air Force sent in a group of 330 men for meteorological training in a B curriculum running for six months. All the recruits had survived a C program and would proceed finally to an A curriculum. A sec-

DRILL ON SOUTH STATE STREET

ond group of 200 entered May 31, but after the two classes finished, the Air Force had no need for more. All instruction was given by faculty members under the supervision of Professor Sumner B. Myers.

The Army began sending various detachments for specialized training in April. They were to study engineering, medicine, or dentistry. Two large groups arrived in July to study special area and language programs. One group concentrated on the history, geography, government, and culture of Western Europe and one foreign language; the other studied the same aspects of Japan and Japanese. Professor A. E. R. Boak, who had been active in 1917-18, supervised the former group, and Professor Carl E. Guthe the latter. This program expired by October 1944. A similar program for officers who would administer occupied territory in Europe was taught in a Civil Affairs Training School here. Professors William C. Trow and Willett F. Ramsdell supervised this curriculum for three classes in succession. The second CAT School began in July 1944 for officers who would conduct military government in the Japanese Empire. Enrollment embraced as well a few Naval officers, several British and Canadian officers, and eighteen WAC's. Professor Ramsdell also directed this program, and Professor Yamagiwa had charge of the language instruction.

For the Navy, the University operated the Reserve Officers Naval Architecture School, moved here from Annapolis in June 1943. Eighty-one officers with engineering degrees were taught here for eight months concerning the construction and repair of naval vessels. The big Navy educational effort was the V-12 program, written for the Navy by Dean Ivan C. Crawford of the College of Engineering. Apprentice seamen were sent here, as well as to other universities, to get a college education prior to becoming officers. Most of them studied engineering, but a few were premedical and predental students. Along with the enlarged Naval ROTC, these 1300 sailors lived in West Quadrangle, which became the "ship." The Navy was more relaxed than the Army about its educational program. Sailors and marines could join fraternities and participate in athletics. They made varsity teams possible.

During the fall of 1943 the campus had more than 4000 men in uniform. In addition, there were 2500 civilian men, chiefly freshmen, and 4650 women. Most of the fraternities were taken over to accommodate soldiers and civilian students. The Extension Service through its Correspondence Study Department gave courses to approximately 4700 men and women in the Army and Navy, either directly or in cooperation with U. S. Armed Forces Institute. Harris Hall was made available for a USO headquarters.

In all, the Regents granted leaves to 223 faculty members for government service. Many others engaged in war-related research on campus, under the general direction of Professor Albert E. White. The total cost of this program was $6,600,000. Some of the achievements were notable.

One of the most deadly weapons of the war was the V-T Fuse, which three Michigan professors had a hand in perfecting. Called also the proximity fuse, it was a radio mechanism built into the nose of a shell which caused it to burst at a predetermined distance from its target. Because the explosion could be timed to occur where it would be most effective, shells equipped with the V-T Fuse were especially destructive. They blasted robot bombs over England, helped turn back the Germans during the Battle of the Bulge, and knocked Japanese suicide planes out of the sky before they reached their objectives.

Working in a Maryland laboratory, Professor Franklin L. Everett of the Engineering College helped design the Fuze and solve the problems involved in producing radio equipment small enough and sturdy enough for the purpose. Professors H. R. Crane and David Dennison of the Physics Department carried on experiments in a field near Ann Arbor to determine the most effective timing of the explosion, using miniature planes on a cable. Twenty-five other Michigan physicists aided them on this vital project.

Another spectacular product of wartime research was the "Tuba," a giant 125-ton device for jamming the radar equipment of enemy aircraft. This invention, which blinded the German nightfighter planes over England, was developed and perfected by scientists working under the direction of Professor William G. Dow of the Engineering College. Five of his assistants were also Michigan men. In November 1944 he went to England to supervise the installation of three "Tubas." Effectiveness of enemy radar equipment was reduced 75 percent by the use of these instruments.

Professor Werner E. Bachmann of the Chemistry Department made an invaluable contribution by developing a mass-production process for manufacturing RDX. This most powerful explosive known, before the invention of the atomic bomb, was produced only in small quantities and at great expense by the British during the early years of the war. In his laboratory Professor Bachmann solved the problem of quantity production. Adopted by the government, his process made possible the manufacture of sufficient RDX for use on all fronts. Depth bombs loaded with it destroyed German submarines built to withstand the shock of TNT.

The University had a share in the development of the atomic bomb. Professor James M. Cork of the Physics Department, and Professors George G. Brown, Clarence A. Siebert, and E. M. Baker of the Engineering College worked on various phases of the project. Similarly, two professors from the Physics Department, Samuel A. Goudsmit and George E. Uhlenbeck, and Professor Dean B. McLaughlin of the Astronomy Department contributed to the perfecting of radar devices.

The influenza vaccine used effectively by the Army was produced by Professor Thomas Francis, Jr., of the School of Public Health. The bombsight used in naval aviation was perfected by a group from the Lake Angelus Observatory led by Dr. Robert R. McMath. Professor Floyd E. Bartell of the Chemistry Department produced a fabric called Aerobond which, highly resistant to water and cold, was most useful for the apparel and equipment of soldiers and sailors. For these and other important scientific achievements, the University received citations from the Army and Navy, and many of the research men were awarded certificates in recognition of their services.

Altogether, the Navy sent more than 4000 enlisted men and officers to the University, the Army over 8000, and 12,350 civilian men and women were enrolled in the ESMWT courses. In addition, the Correspondence Study Department of the Extension Service provided instruction for nearly 4700 men and women in the services. The number of former students who served in the armed forces is believed to be something above 32,000. The known killed or died in service stood at 520. Most of their names were published in *Victory Reunion*, a memorial booklet printed for the 1946 Commencement of the University.

In 1943 the University created the office of war historian. His principal duty was to encourage alumni in the armed forces to collect and send back printed materials relating to the war. A veritable avalanche of books, leaflets, service newspapers, broadsides, posters, and other documents poured into his office from all the theaters of war. The University Library was enriched with more than 5000 books and thousands of newspapers and other items for future research work.

2. *Return to a peacetime university*

With the return of peace the University shook itself loose from wartime restrictions and objectives. The special classes melted away, and the scattered faculty members returned to campus. The calendar was changed back to two semesters. From Rackham money a Rackham Educational Memorial building had been erected in Detroit, half of which was for use by the University's Extension Service. In 1941 grants of $500,000 each from the Rockefeller Foundation and the W. K. Kellogg Foundation brought about the establishment of a separate School of Public Health. Half the grant was used for a building on Observatory Street next to the Simpson Memorial Institute.

In addition to all the visible changes on campus wrought by war conditions, other changes accompanied the inevitable march of time. Deaths and elections introduced new faces to the Board of Regents. In 1946 Harry Kipke and Joseph Herbert were the veteran members; the others were Alfred Connable, '25, Kalamazoo attorney; Ralph A. Hayward, '17*e*, industrialist of Parchment; Vera Baits, '15, of Grosse Pointe; Dr. Charles Kennedy, '13*m*, of Detroit; Otto Eckert, '12*e*, of Lansing; and Roscoe Bonisteel, Ann Arbor attorney. Five standing committees were formed: for finance, educational policy, University relations, property, and emergency. Kenneth M. Stevens, '16*l*, of Detroit replaced Kipke in January 1947.

President Ruthven had been invited by the British embassy in Washington to England late in 1943 to inspect and advise British schools. Although he did not think that their primary and secondary education was superior to our system, he returned full of admiration for England's elaborate outreach in adult education. As early as 1944 he warned the Regents that the University must begin planning for the postwar period. He anticipated continuation of universal military training, a huge enrollment of returning veterans and consequent housing problems, a bigger faculty, and a wider interest among Michigan citizens in extension courses. However, his administrative team began to break up.

Vice-President Bruce had retired, and Provost Stason and Vice-President Yoakum wished to give full time to their deanships. Vice-President Smith and Plant Director Gram were nearing retirement age. James P. Adams, vice-president of Brown University, was brought in to succeed Stason as provost and to be concerned with educational policies as

Yoakum was. Smith's double job was divided: Professor Robert P. Briggs of the School of Business Administration became vice-president for Business and Finance, and Herbert Watkins was named secretary of the University. Professor Marvin L. Niehuss, who had administered military contracts, was appointed vice-president for University Relations. Walter M. Roth, '26*e*, was named Plant superintendent to succeed Gram. Arthur L. Brandon was appointed director of information to handle public relations under Niehuss.

During the war several distinguished professors reached retirement age or died. Dr. Charles W. Edmunds, chairman of the Department of Materia Medica since 1907, died in 1941. Astronomer Heber D. Curtis died in 1942, and political scientist Joseph R. Hayden in 1943. Dean Yoakum died in 1945. Retirement claimed Librarian William Warner Bishop, physicist Harrison Randall, and Athletic Director Fielding Yost in 1941, Walter B. Pillsbury, who had built up the Psychology Department, retired in 1942. William C. Hoad, professor of civil engineering, and Edson R. Sunderland of the Law School taught their last classes in 1944, Leroy Waterman, chairman of the Department of Oriental Languages, retired in 1945. Dr. Harley Haynes retired as director of the University Hospital and was succeeded in 1945 by Dr. Albert C. Kerlikowski, '24*m*.

A few hundred discharged veterans enrolled in 1944, but the rush came in 1945-46. In the fall enrollment reached 12,000 and in February jumped another 2500. The 6350 veterans included were not only older than the civilian students, but one-third of them were married. A tremendous increase in the number of students eligible to drive cars was first apparent. Then crowded housing, spilling over into nearby towns, taxed all available facilities. In the dormitories single rooms were made doubles, and doubles were made triples. The Willow Run village of apartments and dormitories, built to accommodate workers in Ford's famed bomber plant, was leased by the University, and bus service started for the ten-mile run to campus. The village quarters contained 1300 married students, 1500 single men, and 200 coeds. As quickly as possible the University undertook the building of the Terrace Apartments near the Hospital for married students. But in September 1946, 19,000 students presented themselves for registration on campus, and a year later the resident enrollment reached 20,000, of whom 11,000 were veterans. They helped inflate Summer Session enrollment to between 10,000 and 11,000. Peak enrollment came in the fall of 1948, when 21,360 registered.

A Veterans Service Bureau was set up to help veterans obtain their benefits under the G.I. Bill of Rights passed by Congress. Similarly, a social program was started for the Willow Run residents, most of whom were veterans.

To meet the problem of mounting enrollment, a director of admissions was appointed early in 1947 distinct from the registrar. His task was to determine which applicants were qualified and to admit no more to each college than the total determined by the faculty of each unit. By rigorous screening the

VETERANS' HOUSING, NORTH OF CENTRAL CAMPUS

director of admissions also made sure that the students admitted could presumably pass the courses offered.

The Willow Run airport was acquired by the University on condition that it continue to be used as an airport and that the federal government could take it back on one day's notice. The buildings were useful to the Aeronautical Engineering Department as well as for engineering research projects. Rented out as a terminal for airlines flying into Detroit, the airport yielded some income. Eventually, the city of Detroit obtained an old army airport fifteen miles closer to Detroit, refitted it with federal aid, and enticed the airlines away from Willow Run.

The University moved out in several directions. The School of Nursing was made independent of the University Hospital and under its own dean, Rhoda Reddig, began granting bachelor of science degrees. A Great Lakes Research Institute was established under a faculty council to encourage scientific studies of the lakes, including the bottoms and shores. A Center for Japanese Studies was set up in the Rackham Graduate School with Professor Robert B. Hall as first director. The Institute of Public Administration was separated from the Institute of Public and Social Administration to promote instruction, research, and service in government fields requiring technical knowledge based on the social sciences. The Bureau of Government continued as a subdivision of it, and John W. Lederle was named director. Then a Survey Research Center was set up by a group of scholars from the U. S. Department of Agriculture who had perfected a technique of sampling public opinion by interviewing relatively few persons. The director was Rensis Likert, '26. The Center was supported by government agencies and industries who wished to know public attitudes toward certain developments or products.

One division of the Institute for Human Adjustment was earning a distinguished reputation: the Speech Clinic. Originally begun for research on speech difficulties and defects and the training of teachers in this field, it developed an invaluable clinical service for speech disorders under Professor Harlan Bloomer, PhD '35. As a result the Kresge Foundation provided funds in 1949 for purchase of a summer camp for afflicted boys, to enable them during their vacation period from school to mix freely with other boys having the same difficulties and to work intensively with special teachers.

BUSINESS ADMINISTRATION

Encouraged by the legislature, the Regents embarked on an $8,000,000 building program. Four housing units were added to East Quadrangle, and another women's dormitory was begun. A building to house the School of Business Administration was started, along with an Administration Build-ing next to the Union to house executive and business offices of the University, and a Food Service Building for storing and processing food for the several dormitories and hospitals. All were completed in 1948-49. A Women's Hospital was going up, as well as additions to the Chemistry Building and a south wing for the East Engineering Building. Then the complete destruction of Haven Hall (the old Law School) in 1950 by fire, set by a student arsonist, forced the University to take stock of old Mason Hall, South College, and the remnant of old University Hall that tied them together at the back of Angell Hall. These three venerable structures were razed, and two much larger buildings, called Mason and Haven halls, were put up and connected to Angell Hall.

The death of Dean Yoakum resulted in the promotion of Professor Ralph A. Sawyer of the Physics Department to head of the Rackham School of Graduate Studies. He had just returned from serving as civilian director of the underwater atomic bomb experiment in the South Seas. Dean Kraus of the Literary College was succeeded in 1946 by Professor Hayward Keniston of Romance languages. Joseph Bursley in 1947 gave up the post of dean of students, which he had held since its creation, and was suc-ceeded by Professor Erich A. Walter, MA '21, a counselor to students. The respected and widely admired Alice Lloyd, dean of women since 1930, died in 1950; she was succeeded by Deborah Bacon. The new women's dormitory was named for Miss Lloyd. Randolph G. Adams, director of the William L. Clements Library since its opening in 1923, died at the beginning of 1951.

Professor John S. Worley retired from the College of Engineering in 1946, leaving behind a remarkable collection of books, broadsides, printed reports, pictures, and documents relative to all forms of transportation. A born collector, he spent all his spare time gathering materials, and not until the General Library began cataloging it was the richness of his accumulation realized. Many new faculty appointments were necessary as replacements as well as to meet expanded enrollment. The number of teaching fellows was also increased. The postwar years saw such additions as Charles W. Joiner and Allan F. Smith to the Law School; John C. Kohl and Wilbur Nelson to the Engineering College; Allen P. Britton, Philip Duey, and Ross Finney to the School of Music; Paul W. McCracken and Wilbur K. Pierpont to the School of Business Administration; Stanley A. Cain to Forestry; Algo D. Henderson to Education; and Dr. Jonas E. Salk to Public Health. Gardner Ackley and Kenneth Boulding joined the Economics Department, Kenneth Pike was appointed to the Linguistics Department, and George H. Forsyth, Jr., became chairman of the Fine Arts Department. These are only a sampling of the distinguished or promising scholars brought here.

Provost Adams in his first annual report spoke out boldly on giving the students an affirmative faith in the fundamental values of our way of life. He said the University could not assume that young people acquired it by absorption. Religion, he felt, was worthy of intellectual inquiry and should be part of our educational program. Meanwhile, the Reverend Edward W. Blakeman resigned at the end of 1948 and was succeeded at Lane Hall by the Reverend DeWitt C. Baldwin who, with the campus pastors, started a Religion-in-Life Week with various penetrating lecturers.

3. The post-war student bulge

There was a noticeable difference in the student body of the postwar period from the prewar years. On retiring Dean Bursley testified that the current behavior of students was much improved over that of World War I veterans whom he had encountered on taking office. Because the new veterans were mature and many of them married, they were in a hurry to complete an education that had been interrupted by war. They were serious students and little interested in collegiate pranks of destructiveness or in student government. Professors found them a challenging, no-nonsense group to instruct, and later looked back fondly upon them.

Foreign students increased, too, rising to 760 in 1948. Fraternities were reactivated, and 1948 saw fifty-four general and twenty-two professional fraternities on campus, along with nineteen sororities.

This is not to say that "causes" did not flourish, as in the Depression. The rivalry and "cold war" with Soviet Russia heightened postwar tensions, especially after the Russians discovered atomic energy. Student Federalists were an organization favoring world government. There were the American Veterans Committee, the Interracial Association, and a student branch of the semipolitical Americans for Democratic Action. There was a Karl Marx Society and a Student League for Industrial Democracy (socialist). The students also solicited funds for Native American famine relief, World Student Service, Red Cross, heifers for Europe, besides such local philanthropies as Galens' drive for the young patients' Christmas at the University Hospital, and the University Fresh Air Camp for emotionally disturbed children. They even sponsored seven displaced students from Europe, paying their board and room while the University granted tuition scholarships. At the same time loans to students reached a high watermark of 5881 totaling $406,000, many of them to veterans whose G.I. benefits had been delayed.

A War Memorial Committee, composed of Regents, faculty, and students, came up in 1947 with the idea of exploration of the peaceful uses of atomic energy as a living memorial to the University war dead. Named the Phoenix Project, the plan called for raising $6,500,000, of which $2,000,000 was for a laboratory. Alumni, friends, and business corporations all were solicited. Students contributed generously.

Michigan's return to the Rose Bowl (as Western Conference champion) on January 1, 1948, excited the student body. Athletic Director Crisler coached this team, which defeated South-

ANNOUNCEMENT OF THE PHOENIX PROJECT

ern California 49 to 0, but he then bowed out and Assistant Coach Bennie Oosterbaan, '28, took over. His 1950 team again went to the Rose Bowl on New Year's day 1951 and won over California 14 to 6. The Buick Motor Division of General Motors sent the University Band to Pasadena on both occasions. Oosterbaan developed such other All-Americans as Pete Elliott, '49, Dick Rifenburg, '50, Al Wistert, '50, Allen Wahl, '51, Lowell Perry, '54, Art Walker, '55, Ron Kramer, '57 (twice), and Jim Pace, '58.

Before the national elections of 1948, political clubs of several hues mushroomed on campus: Young Democrats, Young Republicans, Young Progressives, Wallace Progressives, and Students for Douglas. Still the Regents would not allow University buildings to be used by speakers in support of political candidates unless the meetings were open only to members of the sponsoring organization. The plight of minority groups also impressed the students, and in May 1949 the joint faculty and student Committee on Student Affairs decided not "to recognize any organization which prohibits membership in the organization because of race, religion, or color."

This warning was presumed to apply to future organizations applying for recognition, but the next year the committee aimed its shaft at existing Greek-letter bodies and demanded that any "discriminatory clauses" in membership rules be removed by the fall of 1956. President Ruthven felt obliged to veto this recommendation, not because he approved of such clauses, but because he felt that fraternities and sororities as voluntary associations should not be penalized if the national organization refused to remove such clauses. His view prevailed for another dozen years. Out of 16,132 men on campus, only 3741—23 percent— belonged to fraternities.

Ruthven was pleased by the combination of the Men's Judiciary and Women's Judiciary into a Joint Judiciary Council with power to hear all cases of student discipline, except when immediate and confidential action was called for. The Council findings and recommended penalty were referred to the dean of students or dean of women, who was to notify the student concerned and deal with any objections. Having students judged by their peers broke the image of the faculty and administration as policemen. Apart from drinking in fraternities and dormitories there was little trouble with the postwar students.

Inflation and its effect on young people worried President Ruthven. In 1945 the Regents were obliged to raise the range of semester fees to $65-$140 for instate residents, and $160-$225 for out-of-state students. Soon this was not enough. In 1949 he declared that colleges and universities were in serious trouble. Back in 1932 the country spent one percent of its national income on higher education; now it spent less than 0.5 percent. Since in a democracy, he pointed out, it is essential that people be educated to rule themselves wisely, the colleges could not go on raising fees without diminishing the ratio of those who could afford to attend. In 1929 Michigan had asked students to provide about 20 percent of its operating cost; now it asked for 40 percent. "The simple fact is that the preparation of youth for citizenship in a developing democracy should be accepted as a public responsibility not only in the precollege years but also at the college level." To provide more and more scholarships was only a partial solution. Obtaining the ever-growing grants from the legislature was not easy, even though that body now met annually.

Provost Adams remarked on a change in the attitude of students: many no longer regarded themselves as merely beneficiaries of an educational opportunity, but thought of themselves as a constituent part of the University with an obligation to evaluate University policies and a desire even to participate in its management. Yet our postwar society, he said, is asking individuals to relinquish more of their freedoms of choice in the interests of social control. "What we need, then, is not the processes of coercion which are inherent in social controls, but an elevation of the moral plane on which the individual makes his own voluntary decisions. Of course, this is an age-old problem . . . ." One concession to students was to let them make an annual evaluation of the faculty in the Literary College. The results were of use to the professors concerned as to how well they were putting across the information they gave out.

Students were not the only group seeking a voice in managing the University. Before he retired in June 1951, Dean Keniston referred to the problem of keeping a proper balance between educational policy and public relations policy. "If we are to maintain our place of distinction and our role of leadership, we cannot allow the pressure of the uninformed to determine the decisions we make in matters that affect our educational program. We should soon lose our influence and our reputation if the legislature or the schools or the press were to dictate our policies and practices in such matters as admission requirements, graduation requirements, minimum standards, and the like."

As the veterans began to graduate, the Korean War started in mid-1950, and the specter of being called to active duty troubled many students. They grew restless and anxious. The annual congress of the National Student Association was held at the University at the end of August in 1950, and the delegates showed themselves to be serious and orderly.

In early 1951 a School of Social Work was organized to supersede the old Institute that had operated under the Rackham Graduate School. The new dean was Fidele Fauri, formerly director of the Michigan State Department of Social Welfare. The Medical School shouldered responsibility for turning out more physicians by enlarging the freshman class to 200. The Legal Research Center of the Law School provided service to the state government by submitting studies on laws governing subversiveness and sex offenders. These were fresh evidences of a desire to serve the people of Michigan.

By issuing bonds the University was able to start another huge dormitory for men, South Quadrangle, eight stories high. An addition was also put on Couzens Hall for women. But building in those postwar years illuminated a grave problem. Since the main campus was surrounded by houses and business blocks, the cost of obtaining land for expansion and demolishing the structures on it was growing prohibitive. The Regents came to a far-reaching decision. In a daring move in 1950 the Board purchased 300 acres north of the Huron River for a second campus. Divided areas were a disadvantage which could be somewhat reduced by moving certain schools and colleges and institutes to the North Campus and eventually building dormitories there. No other solution to the problem of land cost was as satisfactory.

With President Ruthven due to retire in 1951, the Board also began looking for a new president. Vice-President Briggs resigned to take a business position, and Wilbur K. Pierpont, who had become his assistant and controller, was named vice-president. Provost Adams resigned, and the position was left vacant for the next president to fill. As Ruthven bowed out, the faculty numbered 1289, the libraries on campus contained 2,000,000 volumes, and endowment funds invested were just shy of $30,000,000. Enrollment, not including summer session, had eased off to 21,000 of which 7700 were still veterans under the G.I. Bill.

Completing the second longest incumbency, President Ruthven had exercised the managerial function of his essentially lonely post with great competence and courage. He had neither dodged nor postponed decisions, whether they involved the legislature, faculty personnel, students, academic programs, or campus expansion. With a scientist's sense for order he created an administrative setup by which he could be fed information and policies could be executed. Even those who were disappointed by his decisions knew that they had not been arrived at capriciously or out of ignorance. Other university presidents held him in enormous respect.

CAMPUS, 1950

CHAPTER TWELVE

HATCHER AND THE COLD WAR YEARS

THE SEARCH BY THE BOARD of Regents for a new president soon focused on the Ohio State University, where the vice-president for faculty and curriculum, Harlan Hatcher, a former dean and professor of English, enjoyed a growing reputation for administrative skill. Shortly after his acceptance of the position in 1951, the Board of Trustees of Ohio State University sent to the Board of Regents a statement of their high regard for Dr. Hatcher and their regret at losing him, but

HARLAN H. HATCHER

concluding "in the common cause of teaching, research, and service the Ohio State University congratulates the University of Michigan upon the choice of its new President."

1. Building for a larger university

As he became familiar with operations, Hatcher undertook some administrative reorganization. He made Marvin Niehuss vice-president and dean of faculties, eliminating the vacant position of provost. Niehuss was made responsible in addition for seeing the University's appropriation request through the legislature, and Robert L. Williams was named assistant dean of faculties. Arthur L. Brandon inherited part of Niehuss' former duties and was made director of University relations. Upon the retirement of Frank E. Robbins as assistant to the president in 1953, Erich Walter was given the position. His old position as dean of students was elevated to a vice-presidency for student affairs, and Professor James A. Lewis, director of the Bureau of School Services, was appointed to it. Under him were placed the deans of men and of women, the Health Service, registrar, the International Center, Lane Hall, Bureau of Appointments, and Bureau of School Services. In 1957 William E. Stirton, vice-president of Wayne State University, was appointed to a new vice-presidency for liaison with industry, business, and professional groups. With

Wilbur K. Pierpont continuing as vice-president for business and finance, this was the new team that shaped the early years of Hatcher's regime.

The University presented to the state legislature a vivid picture of its needs and responsibilities. If it never received as much support as it asked for, it succeeded in only six years in doubling the state appropriation. From something less than $15 million for operations in 1951-52, the sum exceeded $30 million for 1957-58. In addition, a total of $26 million was appropriated in those same years for new buildings, repairs, and extension of the heating plant. All this was done while state government was divided between a Democratic governor, a Republican Senate, and a House that wavered between the two parties. It speaks well for the representatives of the people, especially when only a third of the state tax revenue was at the disposal of the legislature, the rest being already earmarked and committed.

As for enrollments, President Hatcher was allowed a brief breathing spell in which to prepare for the deluge. As the postwar bulge flattened out, enrollment declined, slipping to just under 17,000 in 1956-57. Then, as the steadily increasing freshman classes gave warning, the total began to rise. By 1956-57 enrollment stood at 22,180, a figure that surpassed the largest postwar total, and the only certainty was that it would inexorably rise. Fortunately, Hatcher was not afraid of numbers. He was not willing to concede that the quality of Michigan's education must deteriorate before this onslaught at the gates. Had it declined when enrollment went from 2000 to 4000, or 4000 to 8000, or 8000 to 16,000? If buildings and faculty could be provided to accommodate the qualified students, he was ready to guide and administer a giant university.

It was, admittedly, a race, but University growth kept pace in the early years. For instance, after a loss of faculty positions at the low point of enrollment, 66 more faculty members were added in 1953, 100 more in 1954, 71 in 1955, and 123 in 1956. However, the rub was that in 1957 20 percent of the faculty were teaching fellows, compared to 9 percent in 1939. The change resulted from the unpleasant fact that professors were scarce— not enough PhD's had been trained during and after the war to supply the accelerated demand from all colleges and universities affected by rising enrollments. Teaching fellows (who were candidates for doctors' degrees) were the only recourse, and their effectiveness depended partly on their natural ability and partly on the amount of supervision each teaching department could give them.

When supply does not equal demand, prices or wages go up. The University found it had to pay more to attract professors, as well as to keep those it had from going elsewhere. President Hatcher welcomed this sudden improvement in the economic status of the professor. He argued for a greater share in the economy for faculty members, although they continued to lag behind factory workers, for instance, in the degree of improvement of purchasing power. The University also sought to improve "fringe benefits": group life insurance at low group rates was offered the faculty; by federal act and a special state appropriation faculty members came under Social Security in 1955; physical examinations were provided by the Health Service. The Development Council began in 1956 an annual awards program of $1000 each to the five most distinguished professors, enlarged four years later to include awards of $500 to the most promising instructors or assistant professors.

In addition to state appropriations there were three other possible sources of funds: private gifts, the federal government, and student fees. Private contributions were suddenly munificent. The Phoenix Project— raising money for peaceful exploration of atomic energy— went over the top in 1953 at $7,300,000. This achievement was capped by the gift of $1,000,000 from the Ford Motor Company for the nuclear reactor itself. A laboratory was completed in 1955, and uranium was supplied at no charge by the U. S. Atomic Energy Commission. The bulk of the money was used to underwrite research projects in a variety of fields related to atomic power.

Next, the Flint Board of Education asked the University to establish a branch senior college in Flint to continue higher education for students who finished the junior college there. While the University considered this invitation and referred it to the state legislature, the Charles S. Mott

MOTT AND HATCHER OPENING THE FIRST BUILDING AT FLINT COLLEGE

Foundation of Flint promised a building for the college if the University would open there. The legislature provided an initial budget, and Dr. David M. French, former Rhodes scholar and Department of State foreign officer, was appointed dean in February 1956 to recruit a faculty. Flint College opened that fall to 174 juniors; it grew to 600 upperclassmen.

In December 1956 the Ford Motor Company presented to the University the former residence and grounds of Mr. and Mrs. Henry Ford, called Fairlane, in Dearborn and $6,500,000 so as to encourage establishment of a senior college operating in connection with business and industry. It would also provide opportunities for graduates of the Henry Ford Community College and elsewhere to obtain degrees. The Dearborn

Center, as it came to be known, was to arrange a program of engineering and business administration courses alternating with semesters of practical experience in factories and offices. Vice-President Stirton caught the vision of this coopera-tive program and was made director. Build-ings were erected with the company's gift of money, and the new branch opened in 1959.

The Kresge Foundation gave $3,000,000 for a new medical science re-search building in 1953 to adjoin the hospital. A wing for the Medical School Library was soon added by the Founda-tion.

PLAN FOR THE DEARBORN CAMPUS

Out of the experience gained from the Phoenix Project, the Univer-sity established a permanent Development Council to continue appeals to alumni and friends for funds. The Council consisted of fifteen to twenty-five members supervising a paid staff, of which Alan MacCarthy was appointed director. President Hatcher asked Dr. Ruthven to serve as consultant to the Council. Besides encouraging bequests and gifts, it developed a plan for annual alumni giving that brought in $110,000 in 1954, $510,000 in 1958, and $1,237,000 in 1964. Prospects were exciting.

Federal agencies, both military and civilian, were leaning on the universities for research work. Investigations undertaken by contract were paid for by federal funds. The University had experienced such work during the last war, and contract research continued. Scholarly investiga-tors were hired who did no teaching whatever. In 1951-52 the University accepted contracts amounting to $5,000,000; by 1957-58 government research accounted for more than $10,000,000. In 1962 Michigan had more contracts with the National Aeronautical and Space Administration than any other university.

As for student fees, the University was caught between the desire to make higher education as inexpensive to the student as possible, and the triple demands of rising costs, a legislative insistence that dormitories should be fully self-supporting (board, room, custodial, and administrative expenses), and a growing concept that the benefactors of a University education should pay for it. Although the latter philosophy was contradictory to the values of education in a democratic society, and never was carried to its conclusion, it required some recognition. The inevitable consequence was that board and room rates had to be raised in 1954 and again in 1956. Fees rose also.

In these various ways the University obtained money for expanding operations and new buildings to take care of more and more students. On the central campus the eight-story South Quadrangle for 1200 men was completed. An

OUTPATIENT BUILDING

Outpatient Building was added to the University Hospital Center, Couzens Hall for women was much enlarged, and a Women's Swimming Pool was built from sports revenues. A Student Activities Building and a small University Press building were constructed, and the old Ann Arbor High School and Public Library were acquired, remodeled, and enlarged as the Henry S. Frieze Building. Crowded conditions in the University Library were relieved by erection of a storage stack on North Campus and of an Undergraduate Library. An addition was made to the Legal Research Library. An auto parking structure, the first of several, was put up close to campus for faculty members and paid for by their annual parking fees.

COOLEY BUILDING AND PHOENIX LABORATORY

On the new North Campus the Mortimer E. Cooley Laboratory was the first building, followed by the Phoenix Memorial Laboratory next door, to which was attached a building for the Ford Nuclear Reactor. Looking to the day when the College of Engineering would shift locations, an Automotive Engineering Building and an Aeronautical Laboratory were constructed. A printing and binding plant was added to the growing complex. Several apartment units for married students and staff members were built at the north end of the new campus.

2. Trouble and growth during the early Cold War years

In the midst of the University's scramble for more money and faculty, a disturbing incident occurred. As part of the national "purge" of alleged communists from all walks of life under the political direction of Senator Joseph McCarthy, Congressman Kit Clardy of Michigan, a member of the House Subcommittee on Un-American Activities, decided to hold a one-man hearing in Michigan in May 1954. He notified the University that several faculty members would be questioned relative to their onetime communist connections. Procedures by the Regents relative to faculty dismissals had been set out in amended bylaws in 1953, based on suggestions received from the University Senate. Three faculty members and two students were called before Clardy, and all of them refused to answer some of his leading questions, citing the first or fifth amendments to the Constitution.

On May 10 the three faculty members—mathematics instructor Chandler Davis, Assistant Professor of Biology Clement Markert, both in the Literary College; and Associate Professor of Pharmacology Mark Nickerson in the Medical School—were suspended by President Hatcher "without prejudice and with pay." Committees selected by the Senate Advisory Committee were to study the cases and make recommendations for resolution of them. In Nickerson's case, the evidence was also weighed by the Medical School dean and executive committee. After several months of collecting detailed information and hearing testimony the various committees reported.

Opinion was united on Chandler Davis, who had based his case on the freedoms granted in the first Amendment and refused to discuss his politics even with his colleagues. If he was to be dismissed, he argued, it would have to be for inadequate performance as a teacher and scholar, not for his political beliefs. The Literary College Executive Committee recommended only censure, but the other committees voted dismissal. On Hatcher's recommendation, Chandler Davis was dismissed and eventually served time in prision for contempt, losing appeals all the way to the Supreme Courts. Markert cooperated fully with his colleagues and received their support, with the recommendation that he be censured. Hatcher followed this recommendation as well, and Markert stayed briefly at Michigan before going on to a distinguished career in biology at Johns Hopkins.

Nickerson's case presented more problems. He too cooperated with the university committees that interviewed him, and they therefore recommended that he be treated similarly to Markert–retained with a mild censure. However, the Medical School Dean and Executive Committee, at the vigorous urging of the head of Pharmacology, Maurice Seevers, reached a different conclusion regarding their colleague and recommended his dismissal. The president now had conflicting recommendations. He consulted with the Regents in August, and they concurred in his decision to dismiss Nickerson. This decision rankled some of the Senate members; they voted their disapproval of the penalty—meaning that the Senate supported its own committee against the Medical School's executive committee. The matter was eventually dropped but not quickly forgotten. Two years later the Regents revised slightly some definitions and procedural details in cases of dismissal or demotion, but no similar cases arose during the rest of Hatcher's administration.

In these years some distinguished appointments to the faculty were made. Charles E. Odegaard, secretary of the American Council of Learned Societies, was named dean of the Literary College in 1952. Richard G. Folsum of the University of California succeeded A.E. White as director of the Engineering Research Institute in 1953. Both men left in 1958 to assume the presidencies of other universities. Frederick H. Wagman of the Library of Congress was appointed director of the University Library and forwarded plans for the Undergraduate Library. Charles Sawyer, former dean of Yale's Fine Arts School, was made director of the Museum of Arts upon the retirement of Jean Paul Slusser. In addition, faculty of growing reputations came here, such as Marston Bates in zoology, a writer and original thinker; Stephen H. Spurr in silviculture, who was to become a dean; Waldo E. Sweet, who had some ideas about teaching Latin as a living language; A. Geoffrey Norman in botany, later a vice-president; Leland Stowe in journalism, a roving correspondent for *Reader's Digest;* and Merle Lawrence in the Medical School, who was beginning pioneer research on hearing and its disabilities.

In the mainstream of education the University was developing some exciting new programs. In 1955 at the instigation of the Medical School's Department of Psychiatry a group of scientists from the University of Chicago was recruited to establish a Mental Health Research Institute under Dr. James G. Miller as director. Scholars in related disciplines came together to do physiological work on the brains and nervous systems of animals and to investigate mental diseases, perception problems, and social aspects of mental health. The institute received a direct appropriation from the legislature, but most of its funds came from the U.S. Public Health Service and the National Science Foundation.

Educational television shows had started through Detroit's WWJ-TV in 1950. Three years later the Regents applied for an ultra high frequency channel and were awarded channel 26. But the failure during the next dozen years of manufacturers to offer sets capable of receiving more than twelve channels (until compelled to do so by law) and the absence of money to erect a broadcasting station resulted in loss of the channel. Meanwhile, a studio for making kinescope films and tapes was equipped in a former funeral home, and Michigan's educational television programs under Director Garnet Garrison, formerly of the National Broadcasting Company, began to win award after award for their absorbing intellectual content and their technical excellence. The films were furnished to television stations throughout Michigan as an educational service and to a growing network of educational stations in other states. They "advertised" the University in the widest and highest sense. Courses in television production were added to the Speech Department. Similarly, the high standards in radio programs developed under Waldo Abbot were continued after his retirement in 1957, when the radio work also came under Garrison's administration.

Three films of college life were made in 1952: *We'll Remember Michigan*, by the Audio-Visual Education Center, and two by RKO-Pathé which were seen by forty million people—*Here Comes the Band*, and *Songs of the Colleges* featuring the Michigan Glee Club.

With the retirement of Dr. Robbins, the University Press obtained its first full-time director, who launched a sales organization, royalty contracts, and a broader publication program. A degree in physical therapy was offered in the Literary College. The College of Pharmacy embarked on a five-year program for the degree it granted. The School of Business Administration began training federal internal revenue agents each semester and enlarged the number of short seminars offered to several kinds of businessmen. Katherine Anne Porter, the noted writer, served as visiting lecturer in English, 1953-54, in a revival of the artist in residence program. She was followed by Malcolm Cowley, poet and critic. Under Dean Odegaard the various museums were united with the related teaching departments, and the curators began to teach, too.

In 1952 the Institute of Public Administration entered into contract with the federal government to establish a similar institute at the University of the Philippines to train Filipinos for service in their own government. Certain Michigan professors taught at the University of the Philippines, and some nationals were brought here for graduate work. The cooperative program ran for four years and was regarded as one of the most successful technical assistance programs undertaken by the United States.

The University closed its Observatory in South Africa upon retirement of Director Richard A. Rossiter in 1953, bringing back the lens and optical equipment. The Astronomy Department turned to the development of a radio telescope on Peach Mountain near Portage Lake, in conjunction with the Office of Naval Research. The new installation was within a mile of the reflector telescope of 1948. It required a precision paraboloid antenna and three sweep-frequency receivers capable of detecting reception of solar signals in certain frequency ranges. A slow-speed movie camera was added.

An event that focused world attention on the University occurred on April 12, 1956. For more than a year Dr. Thomas Francis, Jr., of the School of Public Health, had been directing the poliomyelitis vaccine evaluation program at the request of the National Foundation for Infantile Paralysis.

HATCHER, FRANCIS, SALK, AND
BASIL O'CONNER

With help from the U.S. Bureau of the Census and the University's Survey Research Center, the testing of former Professor Dr. Jonas Salk's vaccine was carried on. Physicians, public officials and newsmen converged on Ann Arbor that spring day when word was flashed—"The vaccine works. It is safe, effective, and potent." The Television Center cooperated with stations and networks covering the announcement and later presented a one-hour closed circuit broadcast from its studio to 52,000 physicians assembled in cities across the country and in Canada. What the vaccine has meant is summarized in two figures: in 1955 there were almost 24,000 cases of polio in the United States; in 1965 there were 59.

At the instigation of the Michigan Press Association, the Regents agreed in 1954 to open their meetings, starting in September, to accredited news representatives, with the understanding that there would be closed executive sessions for consideration of property purchases, confidential personnel reports, and matters under security restriction. Whether or not the meetings were better reported, the newspapers were better satisfied.

In this period the University also found itself on the State Department's tour for foreign dignitaries. Most of them wished to visit Detroit's auto industry, and the next stop was the University. Following Queen Juliana's visit in 1952, five distinguished guests were entertained in the next three years Crown Prince Akihito of Japan, Emperor Haile Selassie of Ethiopia, Prime Minister U Nu of Burma, Prime Minister Pibulsonggram of Thailand, and Prime Minister Sukarno of Indonesia.

3. The student body in transition

President Hatcher may be said to have been subjected to something like a "rough initiation" from students his first year. He started conferences with student leaders shortly after his arrival, a means of direct confrontation of problems which the students felt to be important. This "honeymoon" lasted until spring. Then the Committee on Student Affairs for a second time adopted by a one-vote margin a motion to require fraternities to press their nationals for removal of discriminatory membership clauses. Like Ruthven, Hatcher felt obliged to veto this proposed action: "We believe that the process of education and personal and group convictions will move us forward faster and on a sounder basis, than the proposed methods of coercion." For this decision he was scored in a front-page editorial by the *Daily* senior editors and by the Student Legislature.

In a sense this was a climax to two earlier disturbances which had occurred in March 1952. The Young Progressives, a minuscule group more communistic than progressive, had been denied use of a University building for a lecture by a civil-rights advocate who had been militantly defiant at a House Un-American Activities Committee hearing in Detroit. In consequence he was invited to speak at what purported to be a "private dinner" at the Michigan Union. It turned out, however, that anyone could buy a ticket to the dinner, that it was booked under a fictitious name, and that newspaper reporters were invited. President Hatcher asked for a special investigation, and the Joint Judiciary Council recommended that five students be placed on probation. They were.

The second affair was much more notorious. On the first balmy spring evening, some of the men in West Quadrangle and South Quadrangle gathered to do something. It was not a mob, not a riot, but an outburst of "spring madness." In high spirits they moved across campus to the women's dormitories, invaded them through doors conveniently unbolted, and proceeded to ramble through the upper floors and emerge with pieces of feminine underwear. Thus occurred the first "panty raid" on any campus—another Michigan "first"! Police were on hand but made no arrests. Hundreds more students watched and cheered than actively participated. The newspapers and *Life* magazine played up the demonstration, and other universities and colleges suffered imitative panty raids. In some other year the episode might have passed with smiling tolerance or mild irritation, but in March 1952 the country was heavily engaged in military measures in Korea. "Why," rose the cry, "was such horseplay permitted when other young men were dying in Korea?"

The question was not easily answered or turned aside. Many of the participants undoubtedly had draft deferments. But it was impossible to suppress such occasional outbursts, and there were obvious practical difficulties in meting out punishments. Total loss and damages amounted to $188, which was promptly paid by the students. There was nothing to do but live out the gust of wrath. It is ironic that the episode occurred at the very time that certain faculty members and student leaders were lamenting "student apathy" and the Student Religious Association had uncovered a genuine student interest in more courses concerning religion.

The picture of student mores that spring would not be complete, however, without mentioning a contrasting incident, as difficult to explain, perhaps, as the panty raid. It concerned a woman named Wendy (actually Rosemary) Owen. She had entered the University in 1947 from Ann Arbor; her father, a professor in the Speech Department, had just died. She was one of those personalities who appear on campus once in a decade or two. It was not long before almost everyone knew Wendy Owen, or wished they knew her, or at least had heard of her. She joined Chi Omega sorority. Later, she was tapped for Wyvern, junior honorary society, and Mortarboard, senior honorary society. Meanwhile, she became secretary of the Gilbert and Sullivan Society, worked on the *Michigan Daily*, and became sales manager of *Gargoyle*. She majored in religion and ethics, and earning her degree in 1951 was a real triumph because she was ill from time to time, suffering from aplastic anemia. A month after she was graduated she died. Events of the summer frequently are forgotten in the bustle of the opening of the fall semester. But some students remembered, and young minds determined to transcend this defeat of a human spirit. A movement got under way involving every organization Wendy Owen had ever touched to raise a fund of $5000 for research on aplastic anemia in the Simpson Memorial Institute. The *Daily* contributed all proceeds from sale of its J-Hop extra in February 1952. The Michigras gave more than $1500 from its profits. A special issue of *Gargoyle* produced additional funds. Hundreds of students contributed individually. A total in excess of $5300 was turned over to Dr. Frank Bethell at Simpson. What is one to say about this— except that it remains one of the proud moments in the long history of the University.

After this first year of President Hatcher's administration, the students seemed to simmer down. The "Hell Week" of fraternity initiations was replaced by a "Help Week" at the recommendation of the Interfraternity Council. Pledges undertook work projects of benefit to the University and the community, and parties for underprivileged children were given by fraternities. A straw poll of students in the fall of 1952 showed them favoring Eisenhower over Stevenson for President, despite a *Daily* editorial endorsing Stevenson signed by the senior editors. The vote was 7837 (64 percent) for Eisenhower and 4041 (33 percent) for Stevenson. A poll

STUDENTS VOTING

conducted nationwide by the Associated Collegiate Press showed exactly the same percentage for Stevenson and 57 percent for Eisenhower.

The stopping of the warfare in Korea, and the use of certain men's houses in the quadrangles for women, with the consequent dining together, seemed to raise the tone of student relations. The Young Progressives, who chose not to obey the simplest University regulations, dissolved in December 1952, to everyone's relief. In 1953 and again in 1955 the Michigan Interfraternity Council won the trophy for the best fraternity organization on any campus in the United States and Canada. Students collected books and money for a Joseph R. Hayden Memorial Library at the University of the Philippines and in 1954 shipped 120,000 volumes and $7000 in cash! It was a tremendous boost to the university that was rising from the ashes of World War II, as well as a tribute to a professor who had served both countries.

In 1955 the Student Legislature and Student Affairs Committee were dissolved by student action, and a new Student Government Council was created to assist in formulating University policy affecting students. Under the first presidency of able Henry A. Berliner, '56, who was even invited to address the University Senate, the Council concerned itself with auto regulations, housing, student conduct, and those clubs and teams that represented the University in intercollegiate competition but were not responsible to any official body. In the same year the Fraternity Buyers Association was revived and found economies in cooperative purchases of food. The University through its food service for the dormitories afforded assistance.

Inasmuch as the auto patrol officers employed by the University lost their commissions as deputy sheriffs in 1954 and could no longer stop student cars by authority, the enforcement of driving regulations became fortuitous and irregular. The Student Government Council recommended letting all students over twenty-one drive. The Regents approved the measure in February 1956 for a two-year trial. Auto permits more than doubled that fall, and every car was registered at a fee of seven dollars. Traffic on the east side of town seemed to triple. The policy became permanent, and enforcement was carried out by city policemen supplied by a University contribution to the police department from the registration fees and from fines for violations.

The Student Religious Association was active in sponsoring a religious emphasis week each year by bringing in theologians and world commentators to arouse the student conscience. Vice-President Lewis believed that the University could better express its religious concern if the Coordinator of Religious Affairs at Lane Hall was brought into an administrative position in the rising Student Activities building. Accordingly, in 1956 an Office of Religious Affairs was created under the vice-president, and Dr. Baldwin moved into the new structure with the deans of men and women and other all-campus organizations. The office was to encourage the religious growth of students through the special campus pastors of various denominations and through recognition of religion in instructional programs as a valid area of intellectual Inquiry.

Increasing casualness of dress by students on all campuses now approached a kind of climax with the appearance of something called a "beatnik." The young men let their hair and beards grow and combed neither; young women similarly allowed their long hair to fall at will and shunned cosmetics. Both sexes favored jeans, old shirts worn with the tails out, and sweaters, and the scruffier their shoes the better. There was more than a suspicion among those with whom they mingled that an aversion to soap was part of this self-conscious and conforming drive toward nonconformity. The beatniks were in rebellion—against society in general and all that it stood for. The other students sensed in these exhibitionists a lack of commitment—except to sensation. For a few short years they were noticeable for obvious reasons, but then the small number of beatniks dwindled to a disheveled handful, to be replaced by a new generation of activist political dissenters.

STUDENTS IN THE LEAGUE

Perceptive comments on student conduct by Dean Bacon provided one perspective on the clutter of events. In 1956 she wrote: "The general student attitude is one of an urgency to hurry toward a future of the University which the students actually cannot picture, combined with a nostalgia for a past of the University which they personally never experienced. They are clearly discontented with, but not very accurately aware of, the only thing they have actually experienced—the immediate present. Insofar as I have read history and literature this remains par for the course over several millenia." Students, of course, saw things differently.

The opening of the Student Activities building not only gave space to the University offices dealing with students, but a home to the Student

Government Council, the Joint Judiciary Council, and other student services, and a visible proof that the University was concerned for students. This concern was emphasized again by construction of the air-conditioned Undergraduate library that stayed open till midnight, offered access to the shelves, permitted smoking, and provided 2400 badly needed chairs for those who came to study.

The Student Government Council started a health insurance plan for students and a student exchange program with the University of Berlin. It also undertook once more to require fraternities to press their national organizations to remove discriminatory membership clauses from their constitutions. Inasmuch as many other colleges and universities did not feel as strongly about this as Michigan did, the national organizations were not urgently impelled toward change. The Michigan chapters found themselves harassed on one side and ignored on the other.

Rising enrollment overtaxed the women's dormitories and forced the University to allow senior women to live in apartments, unsupervised. It was hoped that a new giant complex—Mary Markley Hall, to hold 1200 women—would relieve the situation, but female enrollment increased

faster and made it clear that the University could no longer expect to house all women students. Nor were there enough supervised league houses left. Philosophy had to give way to expediency.

MODEL FOR MARKLEY HALL

4. Adjustments during the Sputnik era

The steadily growing enrollment in all the state-supported universities and colleges in Michigan produced annual requests for ever larger appropriations. Nothing leveled off once the era of low birthrates late in the Depression was passed. Moreover, as a rising percentage of the increasing number of high-school graduates was entering college, the public and the legislature developed a hardening attitude against the constantly rising cost of higher education. Since every student cost the state something to educate, clamor rose to ask students to pay more of that cost. In the face of this stiffening resistance, President Hatcher could only point out the regrettable fact that the most vital and productive part of the state's spending was most vulnerable to economy.

The 1957 legislature advised and presumed that all state-supported institutions would increase student fees by 25 percent in the fall. The University acceded to this request, although it had just raised fees. The legislature then granted $30,000,000 for University operations in 1957-58. This was the year designated as an International Geophysical Year, when scientists in all countries would undertake special investigations in the fields of physics, geology, meteorology, astronomy, and geography and share their findings. Actually, the "Year" ran from July 1957 to December 1958. By way of participating the University was readying its new radio telescope, some of its physicists and engineers were experimenting with upper atmosphere rocket research, and its geologists undertook a study under Professor James Zumberge of the ice fields of Antarctica.

But almost at the outset of the Geophysical Year, the Russians launched a successful satellite that circled the earth in outer space—the "Sputnik" of October 1957 that shook the international community. Its destructive possibilities when combined with an atomic bomb were frightening. The United States was used to excelling in technical progress and was frankly mystified by the Russian achievment. It released some peculiar "fall out."

One answer to the public demand to know why the Russians were able to solve scientific problems that so far had eluded us seemed to be that our educational standards must be lax or low. Immediately, a parental cry went up to stiffen all school courses by giving the students more home work. Congress passed a National Defense Education Act in 1958 to encourage science and language instruction and to allow monetary grants to needy students. More students were urged to enter engineering, and they did; but interest and even will power were not enough to carry along those who did not possess the requisite type of mind. Undergraduate enrollment soon declined, although graduate students in engineering at Michigan increased.

The increase in study assignments struck the high schools first. Higher qualifications were then presented by applicants for University admission, and greater performance was expected from them afterward. A noticeable effect was less time for extracurricular activities. Campus organizations and publications encountered difficulty in attracting staff.

President Hatcher appointed a committee of scientists and engineers after Sputnik to make recommendations. The members' proposal in December 1957 was to establish an Institute of Science and Technology to serve as a center for scientific and technological instruction and research, to administer grants to research-minded students, to determine methods of increasing the effectiveness of scientific education, to cooperate with other educational institutions in the state, and to enlist the interest of business and industry as research might stimulate the economic development of the state. It was approved by the Regents.

An Honors Student program had started in September 1957 with selection of about 5 percent of the brightest freshmen to enter special small classes taught by senior professors. They were given tougher assignments, encouraged in their special interests, and urged to elect interdepartmental courses for the broadest liberal arts education. Professor Robert C. Angell, former chairman of the Sociology Department, directed the program. This attention to the more gifted has continued with annual invitations to the top freshmen, so that an elite group flowed through the University along with the main stream of students. It is a singular achievement of the Hatcher regime, demonstrating the flexibility of a large university to open its special advantages to the superior student.

At the same time two great reservoirs—or perhaps springs—were uncovered for students to dip into. One was the already mentioned Undergraduate Library, which besides being a great convenience to the student body stimulated a quiet expansion of teaching. An inviting arena for satisfaction of curiosity, it prompted the assignment of more background reading and aroused the student to look into related books standing on the open shelves beside the assigned books. The keys to knowledge suddenly jangled freely, and the habit of reading began to take hold. Circulation of books out of the Library began to soar. A million and a half readers used the Undergraduate Library—affectionately abbreviated to "UGLI" —the first year. The hallowed General Library became more the preserve of graduate students and faculty, with the stacks thrown open and more individual carrels provided.

STUDENTS IN THE "UGLI"

The other development was the tardy decision of the Regents to provide a purchasing fund for the Museum of Art so as to accelerate its growth and narrow the gap between its collections and those available at certain Eastern university galleries. Courses in the appreciation of art grew less dependent upon photographic slides.

There were other progressive steps. A Center for Research on Conflict Resolution was authorized by the Regents on recommendation of social scientists determined to address themselves to problems of peace and war. A building for the Mental Health Research Institute was started.

Frederick C. Matthaei, Detroit industrialist, gave 200 acres of his estate near Dixboro for a new and larger Botanical Gardens. A new School of Nursing building was finished and opened. The seventy-seven-year-old Romance Languages building, originally the proud museum, was razed. Foreign student enrollment reached 1427, and special attention and services were provided for these students through the International Center. The International Cooperative Administration (ICA) sponsored a program by Michigan to teach English as a foreign language in Southeast Asia. The University created a staff of fourteen under Professor Edward M. Anthony to show native teachers how to teach English in Thailand, Laos, and Viet Nam. The Television Center put together the most extensive kinescope network in the nation: twenty-nine stations which carried 1742 University made television programs to millions of viewers.

Presidents of the Big Ten universities plus the University of Chicago pioneered a program of working together by forming a Committee on Institutional Cooperation in 1958. These eleven universities enrolled more than 200,000 students and granted half of the nation's doctoral degrees in medicine and business, nearly two-thirds of those in pharmacy, one-third of those in engineering and the biological sciences, and 43 percent of those in agriculture. Some of them had facilities for graduate concentrations that others lacked, and it seemed sensible to them to permit students at any of the member universities to use the expensive assets wherever they were available. Traveling fellowships were offered, as well as dual enrollment. In addition, such programs as Far Eastern language institutes were rotated from one university to another each summer. The geography departments of all members have combined to sponsor research projects too big for any one university to undertake alone. The CIC has acted as agent for all to deal with requests to and from the federal government and has undertaken studies of its own region's economic growth.

It was in this same year of 1957-58 that one of the Eastern universities undertook an extensive study of academic standings, measured by the quality of graduate programs in twenty-four departments. In this ranking, twenty-one of Michigan's departments were rated as being among the first ten. Michigan was outranked only by California, Harvard, and Yale.

In the midst of these high accomplishments and energetic plans, the state legislature of 1958 found it necessary not merely to disappoint the University's request for larger appropriations, but actually to reduce the amount granted for 1958-59 over the current year by more than $900,000! Anticipated state income could not be stretched to cover the needs of all state institutions and services, Russian competition or not. Suddenly, the University was forced to eliminate or not fill ninety teaching positions and over one hundred staff jobs, to cease planning new buildings, and to close admissions in an effort (not successful) to halt any growth of enrollment. The Institute of Science and Technology, for instance, remained a paper hope.

Worse was yet to come. The state treasury did not receive enough tax revenues to be able to forward to Ann Arbor each month the appropriation that was granted. Amid unwelcome national publicity over the state's financial crisis, Vice-President Pierpont had to borrow money in 1959 to pay salaries and to delay payments to suppliers. Faculty members were discouraged about the future, although the Board of Regents resolutely declared that faculty salaries would have first call on the next increase of appropriations. All of Vice-President Niehuss' considerable skill was taxed in making the unpleasant decisions about appointments and programs.

The break came the next year with a 9.5 percent increase, most of which did go into salaries, plus $500,000 designated for the Institute of Science and Technology, but other needed building remained stalled for two more years. Only a third of the eliminated teaching positions could be filled for 1959-60, and again the reins on enrollment were pulled.

Meanwhile, in 1959 President Hatcher headed a special education mission to Soviet Russia, sponsored by the U. S. State Department and the Ford Foundation. He found that the USSR was putting 2.5 percent of its national budget into higher education exclusive of medical training, while the U.S. was putting slightly less than I percent into all higher education including medical. Further, 80 percent of Soviet university students received a stipend for attending and paid no tuition or fees. An amount equal to the budget of higher education was spent on research. Such was our challenge, Hatcher pointed out. The USSR, he said, had seen that we had achieved our position of world leadership through universal education to the limit of each person to learn. Hence they have copied us and intend to overtake us. Yet the state of Michigan was retrenching in educational developments.

If the state could not rise to the challenge, the University would do what it could with other financial aid. The Phoenix Project was coming to the end of its original funds and decided to raise another $2,000,000 to continue further work on the largest independent atomic research program in the world. James C. Zeder, '22, a vice-president of Chrysler Corporation, headed the drive. Indicative of what was being accomplished, the first direct conversion of nuclear energy into electric power was jointly reported in April 1959 by the University and the federal government's Los Alamos Scientific Laboratory. Professor Robert W. Pidd of the Physics Department played a leading role in the three years of experimenting in this effort.

The next year the Phoenix Project issued its first ten-year report, by Professor Henry J. Gomberg, director. It revealed that support was given to 189 research projects in the fields of medicine, chemistry, physics, mineralogy, archeology, engineering, and law. They ranged from the medical uses of radioactive iodine, a method of sterilizing bones by radiation before surgical transplants, the structure of cells, the production of radioactive isotopes, the nuclear emulsion scanner's tracking of atom particles, the radiocarbon dating of prehistoric artifacts and remains, a guidance system for BOMARC missiles, to the effect of radiation on petroleum cracking. Dean Stason directed an investigation of the legal rights of the United States Atomic Energy Act and opened the door to industrial uses of atomic power. Two law books on atomic energy were produced by Stason and two of his Law School colleagues. Most dramatic of all was Professor Donald Glaser's development of a liquid bubble chamber in which the paths of cosmic rays could be traced. He got the idea one night at the Pretzel Bell restaurant watching the effervescence of a glass of beer. Unable to secure federal funds for experimentation, he was given a Phoenix grant. Later, the federal authorities poured in money when they saw what he was accomplishing. For his success in making visible the paths of fast-moving particles through their ionizing action, Glaser won the American Physical Society prize and then the 1960 Nobel Prize in physics.

In reorganization of the Engineering Research Institute the name disappeared. It was supplanted by a University of Michigan Research Institute, created by the Regents, to support research activities in all units of the University and to serve as the overall supervisory agency to recommend policy and procedure to the administration. Later, it was called the Office of Research Administration, and Professor Robert E. Burroughs was named director.

Research projects in engineering sponsored by government and industry were transferred to the Willow Run Laboratories under Joseph A. Boyd; soon this unit became attached to the Institute of Science and Technology, and its staff of 270 gave work to 165 graduates and undergraduates. It developed a high resolution radar system which was called the most significant advancement in radar technique since World War II. The Ford Foundation gave over $1,000,000 to the College of Engineering for development of highspeed computers in engineering education.

WILLOW RUN RADAR EXPERIMENTS

Nuclear Engineering became a department of the college and immediately had the nation's largest enrollment of graduate students. With research activity going on all over the campus, and parts of it becoming highly structured, the Regents created a vice-presidency for research, and appointed Dean Ralph Sawyer of the Rackham Graduate School to the new position.

TAIWAN ALUMNI CLUB

The Literary College was similarly enlarging its scope. It started a program in Asian studies for undergraduates. The National Defense Education Administration provided money for three language training centers at the University, for Arabic, Russian, and Chinese/Japanese. The University joined with Princeton in an investigation of art treasures in the sixth-century Monastery of St. Catherine at Mt. Sinai. Professor George H. Forsyth, Jr., was field director. Visits to the monastery continued.

The revitalized University Press issued the first four volumes in a projected multi-volume *History of the Modern World*, and then began an eleven-volume critical edition of *The Complete Prose Works of Matthew Arnold*, edited by Professor Robert H. Super of the English Department. It also published the first Russian language edition in the United States of *Dr. Zhivago*, the novel by Boris Pasternak, as well as the first collected edition of his works. Parts of the *Middle English Dictionary* under the editorship of Hans Kurath continued to appear, and a line of paperback reprints was inaugurated.

Time produced its inevitable casualties, too. Six deanships fell vacant in 1958-59. Associate Dean Roger W. Heyns replaced Dean Odegaard in the College of Literature, Science, and the Arts. Dr. Furstenberg retired from the Medical School and was succeeded by Dr. William N. Hubbard, Jr., of New York University. Dean Stason of the Law School was followed by Professor Allan F. Smith of that faculty. Dean Henry F. Vaughan of the School of Public Health gave way to Dr. Myron E. Wegman, secretary-general of the Pan-American Sanitary Board of the World Health Organization. Dean Russell A. Stevenson retired from the School of Business Administration, and was replaced by Dr. Floyd A. Bond, an alumnus and director of the Business Education Division of the Committee for Economic Development. Dean Earl V. Moore finished forty-seven years with the School of Music and was succeeded by Assistant Dean James B. Wallace. 1953 also marked the passing of the University's first two classroom buildings, when University Hall, which included North and South College, was demolished.

DEMOLITION OF UNIVERSITY HALL

Membership of the Board of Regents altered, too. Alfred B. Connable, '25, finished two terms, or sixteen years, at the end of 1957, as did Vera B. Baits, '15, appointed in 1943 and then reelected. They were succeeded by Carl Brablec, AM '40, school superintendent of Roseville, and Irene Murphy of Birmingham. When Paul Adams, '36*l*, resigned at the same time to go on the Supreme Court bench, Governor Williams appointed Donald Thurber of Detroit to finish out his term. Roscoe O. Bonisteel of Ann Arbor and Leland I. Doan of Midland finished their terms at the end of 1959 and were succeeded by Frederick C. Matthaei and William K. McInnally, Jackson banker. The other members entering the new decade were Eugene Power, MBA '30, of Ann Arbor, Dr. Charles Kennedy of Detroit, and Otto Eckert of Lansing.

The University entered the 1960's strong in its diversity. It was committed to a broad program of teaching (always first), research, and public service.

CAMPUS IN THE LATE 1950s

CHAPTER THIRTEEN

THE 1960's
A DECADE OF CHANGE

PRESIDENT HATCHER'S STATURE as a university president took on national and international dimensions in the 1960's. He served as president of the Association of American Universities from 1963 to 1965, after previous terms as secretary and vice-president. In 1966 he was one of those selected by the State Department to attend the third United States-Japan Conference on Cultural and Educational Interchange, held in Tokyo. Shortly afterward he delivered the Paul Anthony Brick Lectures on Ethics at the University of Missouri.

HARLAN H. HATCHER

The University's annual budget, made up of state appropriations, research contracts, student fees, and gifts and grants, passed $100 million in 1960, fifty-two years after it reached $1,000,000 in 1908. During the first half of the twentieth century, state appropriations and student fees comprised the majority of the University's budget. Both sources had their limits. In the decades that followed, research contracts, foundation grants, and giving in general therefore played increasingly important roles in the life of the University.

1. Expansion of the University's research base

In the early part of the 1960's the state's appropriation for the University improved very slowly. After the year of budget reduction in 1958-59, the next grant brought a 9.5 percent increase for operations, and the following year 6 percent, but nothing for building to meet increased applications for enrollment. Then for 1961-62 the appropriation stayed virtually the same (increased by 0.5 percent), and Michigan slid to seventeenth place in salaries among universities, while the ratio of students to teachers was rising. But $2,700,000 was provided for the new Physics-Astronomy Building, an eleven-story structure on the central campus.

For the next two years the appropriation climbed slowly, running about $5,000,000 below University requests, but capital funds were made available for the Hospital renovation, additions to the heating plant, the new School of Music building on North Campus, and for starting a second unit of the fluids engineering building. Then Governor Romney appointed a "Blue Ribbon" Citizens Committee to study educational needs in the state and make a report. A subcommittee under former Congressman Alvin M. Bentley of Owosso issued a report at the end of 1963 recommending an appropriation of "not less than $135,000,000" for higher education generally. Startled by the report the legislature that met in January 1964 approached the minimum figure after deliberation.

As a result the University's appropriation was raised 15 percent to $44,000,000, with another $5,750,000 for building. The increase was continued for 1965-66 to $51,000,000 and $4,000,000 for new construction and remodeling. Nevertheless, as the latter sum was well below anticipated needs, the Board of Regents felt obliged to raise student fees again. This time, curiously, the legislature objected, although in 1960 and 1962 it had insisted that students be asked to pay higher fees. For the year 1966-67 the state granted $58,095,000, and the University's operating and research budget climbed to $186,570,000.

These improvements in income made possible additions to the faculty, higher enrollment, and intensive year-round operation, as will be noted. A cyclotron structure and a splendid building for the Institute of Science and Technology went up on North Campus. The handsome and immensely useful School of Music building, designed by Eero Saarinen, also erected there, contained offices, practice studios, classrooms, a library, and a recital auditorium, all in a beautiful setting of woods and pond. In 1964 the School gathered up its offices from twelve assorted locations besides its antiquated Maynard Street home and

SCHOOL OF MUSIC

settled into its new quarters. Now that North Campus had a whole school, the University added a commons, or student lounge and eating place. Beyond the School of Music two great dormitory complexes were started. Cooperative housing for women was added at the head of South University Avenue by the University, and at the Dearborn Campus the first housing for students was begun. Early in 1966 ground was broken for the biggest

NORTH CAMPUS IN THE LATE 1960s

undertaking of all: a new building for the School of Dentistry, on the site of the first one, that would cost $17,000,000.

Apart from this construction, funds raised privately or contributed by agencies of the federal government made possible a new pharmacy research laboratory, completed in 1960. A Kresge Hearing Research Institute Building was erected, where Dr. Merle Lawrence conducted experiments of profound interest to otorhinolaryngologists. The unit is for research on deafness, not treatment. Dr. and Mrs. Harry A. Towsley of Ann Arbor gave money for a building to be used by state physicians when they gather in conferences at the Medical Center. The Buhl family foundation in Detroit gave money for the Lawrence D. Buhl Center for Genetics Research, which resulted in a building at the Medical Center. Besides providing a building at Flint for the University's senior college, the Charles S. Mott

MEDICAL CAMPUS IN THE LATE 1950s

Foundation gave $6,500,000 for a Children's Hospital at the Medical Center.

Enlarging on the Transportation Institute established in 1952 with Professor John C. Kohl as director to conduct training courses and conferences for personnel in the transportation industry, an additional program was announced in 1965: a Highway Safety Research Institute to develop and coordinate studies of highway transportation and safety, which the University had begun in 1916. A laboratory building was constructed on North Campus with grants from the Ford Motor Company and the General Motors Corporation amounting to $4,000,000. Operating expenses for the first few years were underwritten by a $6,000,000 grant from the Automobile Manufacturers Association. The Chrysler Corporation gave $1,500,000 for a center for continuing engineering education. The Upjohn Company of Kalamazoo gave $1,000,000 for a clinical pharamacological center at the University, the first such research center in the nation, to train persons at the Medical Center in the techniques of modern drug evaluation. Calumet and Hecla, Inc., presented the University with a tract of land on Keweenaw peninsula as a launching site for its continuing research in space rocketry.

The growth of research activity made clear to President Hatcher— and he carried the word to Lansing and Washington—that the University was particularly suited to support the development of space industry in Michigan. The intellectual facilities, coupled with other advantages in the state, were the equal of space industry complexes being developed in Massachusetts and California. New corporations had been organized out of University research, and twelve of them were in the Ann Arbor region. Other older firms had been attracted here for research work. The University was carrying on some 220 research projects for industry besides all of its government contracts. These developments greatly expanded the University's research base in engineering and the physical sciences, relying heavily on Department of Defense contracts, and links to private industry.

The Law School, largely through its alumni, installed a closed-circut TV camera in the local circuit court early in 1962 so that students could watch actual proceedings. In a program similar to that which the Medical School carried on to update the state's physicians, the Law School's Center for Continuing Legal Education began in 1950 an annual Advocacy Institute to acquaint practicing attorneys of new legal rules and court decisions as well as new laws. In 1966 some 3000 lawyers and judges from all over the United States and Canada attended the Institute, and demonstration cases were played out and criticized in Hill Auditorium. Proceedings were put on tape by the University Television Center for wider use.

The Great Lakes Research Division, growing out of a unit of Rackham Graduate School started after the war, was placed under the Institute for Science and Technology in 1960 with Professor David Chandler as director. By 1963 it had acquired four ships ranging in length from 34 to 114 feet. The United States Public Health Service granted money for research on preservation of water quality in Lake Michigan. Another Great Lakes project involved boring a 600-foot hole in the bottom of Lake Superior to find out the nature sedimentation since the last glacier. Funds were provided also by the Office of Naval Research and the National Science Foundation.

The Aswan Dam project up the Nile in Egypt prompted the Dental School to undertake an excavation in the area that was to be flooded. Nubian burials dating back 4000 years were uncovered, and skulls were X-rayed to gather information on dental troubles to correlate them with the diet of the region. The project was supported by the School, by a Rackham grant, and by the National Institutes of Health.

With a grant from the National Science Foundation, the Lamont-Hussey Observatory in South Africa was reopened in 1963, since it had the largest telescope in the Southern Hemisphere. The United States Defense Department asked the Institute of Science and Technology to plan and build an astrophysical observatory on Mt. Haleakala, Hawaii, for tracking satellites and ballistic missiles and for astronomical studies. Three infrared telescopes were installed for the first extensive use of infrared measuring devices in tracking. Two federal laboratories were located on North Campus in 1965: one for the Bureau of Commercial Fisheries Research, the other to be built for Great Lakes Water Research. They made use of information gathered by the University's Great Lakes Research Division.

The Botanical Gardens were opened in their new location near Dixboro; they contain the third largest university herbarium in the Western Hemisphere. 463 adjoining acres were given by Regent Matthaei in 1961 for a golf course, faculty residences, classroom buildings, or whatever scholarly or recreational uses the University might prefer.

The Institute for Social Research moved into its own building in 1965. It had gained an international reputation for its investigations of consumer economics, political behavior, public health questions, youth and family life, and the behavior of groups and organizations. Support grew from governmental agencies, foundations, and private corporations. In 1965 the value of this contract research exceeded $3,000,000. The staff

INSTITUTE FOR SOCIAL RESEARCH

had grown to sixty-five research scientists under Rensis Likert, director, with 217 interviewers in the field, and 264 supporting personnel. In their first nineteen years of work the staff issued 1500 books, monographs, and journal articles. Similarly, the Mental Health Research Institute grew to forty-seven researchers and 150 associates under the direction of James G. Miller. It became the only place in the world of its size studying problems of the behavioral sciences.

The University's scholarly assets continued to grow. The Library passed the 2,500,000 mark in 1961, and reached 3,000,000 volumes early in 1966. With the other libraries on campus, the total reached 3,500,000 volumes. In one year alone the Michigan Historical Collections obtained the papers of former Governors G. Mennen Williams, John Swainson, Wilbur Brucker, and Frank Murphy, and of state Democratic chairman Neil Staebler. The growth was so remarkable that a separate building for all its materials on Michigan become a necessity. The Clements Library more than tripled its original holdings of source books on early American history and bought many manuscript collections out of private hands. The Law Library reached a total of 345,000 volumes.

Leading the way in a new national trend, the University established several new "Centers" in the 1960s. The Ford Foundation granted the University $3,500,000 in 1961 to be expended over five years for teaching and research on the non-Western world: the areas of Russia, China, South Asia, and the Near and Middle East. A second grant of $4,000,000 was made in 1966 to continue these programs and launch others. In 1962 the faculty recommended that a Center for Research on Teaching and Learning be established to investigate the learning process and evaluate various mechanical teaching aids. It was created and has advised faculty seeking ways of improving instruction.

The strength of the University's growing research base manifest itself in many ways. By the mid 1960s, eight faculty were members of the National Academy of Sciences: H. Richard Crane and David M. Dennison, physics; Robert C. Elderfield, chemistry; Thomas Francis, Jr., epidemiology; Berwin P. Kaufman, zoology; James V. Neel, human genetics; J. Lawrence Oncley, biological chemistry; and Raymond J. Wilder, mathematics. Dwight L. Dumond's book, *Antislavery: The Crusade for Freedom in America* (1961) was given the Anisfield-Wolf award for its contribution to racial understanding. William B. Willcox and Bradford Perkins won two of the three annual Columbia University Bancroft Prizes in history in 1965. In the spring of 1966 Leslie R. Bassett of the School of Music was awarded the Pultizer Prize in music for his composition "Variations for Orchestra." It was the first time a Pulitzer Prize had been given in music since 1963.

Other faculty members were active in government service. Similar to the group who served under President Cleveland, the Kennedy-Johnson administrations made use of several Michigan faculty. Wilbur J. Cohen of the School of Social Work was undersecretary and later secretary of Health, Education, and Welfare, with Dean Costen of WUOM as his deputy. In the same department John C. Kohl of the Engineering College served as director of the Office of Mass Transportation. Gardner Ackley, chairman of the Economics Department, became chairman of the President's Council of Economic Advisers. Stanley Cain of the School of Natural Resources was named assistant secretary of fish and wildlife in the Interior Department. Gerald F. Else of the Classics Department was appointed by the President to the National Council of the Humanities.

Alumni served, too. Jack Hood Vaughan, '43, former instructor in Spanish, was assistant secretary in the State Department before being named director of the Peace Corps. Jerome B. Wiesner, '37, PhD '50, was director of the new Office of Science and Technology to advise President Kennedy. Robert J. Roosa, '39, PhD "42, was under-secretary of the Treasury. Lynn M. Bartlett, "27, PhD '54, was deputy assistant secretary of defense for educational affairs. José Teodoro Moscoso, "32*ph*, was United States coordinator of Alliance for Progress among American Nations. Hobart Taylor, Jr., "43*l*, served on the President's Committee on Equal Employment Opportunity. Roger W. Wilkins, '53*l*, was named director of the federal Community Relations Service. James Duesenberry, '39, PhD '48, joined the President's Council of Economic Advisers. Fifteen alumni were members of the Senate and House of Representatives.

As rapidly as the University's research base grew in the 1960s, it was not allowed to overshadow the primary function of the University--teaching. On retiring in 1965 Vice-President of Research Sawyer summarized his view: "At every opportunity, this office has exerted influence to continue the integration of research with instruction. Our primary purpose is to pass on to new generations a cultural heritage which research is constantly expanding, testing, and scrutinizing . . . . No university, so far as I know, has been more successful than the University of Michigan in integrating its research program with its graduate teaching and training activity. As long as this is true I cannot be concerned about the size of our research program . . . ." Perhaps the best indication of the University's commitment to teaching was the spring 1966 report of the American Council on Education on the best teaching departments for graduate education among 106 major universities. The University of Michigan was rated first or second in all twenty-eight disciplines. In a general ranking it was placed after California, Harvard, and Stanford and in fourth position in company with Yale, Columbia, Princeton, Illinois, and the California Institute of Technology. Michigan's top categories were the humanities, social sciences, and biological sciences.

2. Administrative and constitutional change

The administration structure of the University changed very little in the 1960s. Marvin Niehuss was made executive vice-president, or right-hand man to the president. A vice-presidency for academic affairs was created in 1962, and Dean Roger Heyns was elevated to that position. He was responsible for all educational programs and for faculty appointments, promotions, and salaries. Upon his resignation in 1965 to become chancellor of the University of California, Berkeley, he was succeeded by Dean Allan F. Smith of the Law School.

With the retirement of Vice-President Ralph A. Sawyer, his dual position was split in two: Dean Stephen Spurr of the School of Natural Resources was moved to the Rackham Graduate School as dean, and Professor A. Geoffrey Norman, director of the Botanical Gardens, was promoted to vice-president for research. A new director of University Relations, Michael Radock, was made a vice-president. The vice-president for student affairs, James A. Lewis, resigned in 1964 to return to duties in the School of Education and was succeeded by Professor Richard L. Cutler of the Psychology Department. William Stirton remained as vice-president and director of the Dearborn campus, while Wilbur K. Pierpont continued as vice-president for business and finance, the only man besides Niehuss who antedated President Hatcher's appointment. In 1966 some of Pierpont's operational duties were assigned to Controller Gilbert Lee, Jr., who was named vice-president for business.

New deans appeared, too. Professor Stephen Attwood was made dean of the College of Engineering, only to die prematurely in 1965. He was succeeded by Professor Gordon Van Wylen, chairman of the Mechanical Engineering Department. Professor William Haber of the Economics Department became the dean of the Literary College. Professor William R. Mann succeeded Dr. Paul J. Jesserich as dean of the School of Dentistry in 1962. Reginald F. Malcolmson was brought from the Armour Institute of Technology to be dean of the College of Architecture and Design after Dean Youtz retired. Professor Francis A. Allen of the University of Chicago Law School was appointed dean of the Law School in 1966. Dr. Keith Arnold, director of the Forest Protection Division of the United States Forestry Service, was named dean of the School of Natural Resources.

Glenn Gosling, alumnus and former Rhodes scholar, was appointed director of the University Press in 1962, and Beverley J. Pooley, assistant professor of law, became law librarian in 1965, succeeding Hobart Coffey.

The faculty had grown so large that it accomplished little in the semiannual meetings of the Senate, and the committee structure was cumbersome. To reflect faculty views more efficiently and more quickly, the Senate reorganized itself in 1966 by electing a legislative Assembly of sixty-five members, representing all schools and colleges, to meet monthly.

In turn the Assembly selected a nine-man Senate Advisory Committee as its active executive committee; Dr. William E. Brown, Jr., of the Dental School was made chairman.

While the internal organization of the University changed little in the 1960s, there arose the possibility of significant change from the outside as the result of the rare but important conveyning of a State constitutional convention in 1963. Several faculty members played a major role in the '63 convention. Professor James K. Pollock of the Political Science Department was elected a delegate and contributed his deep knowledge of state government and civil service. Professor Charles W. Joiner of the Law School was co-director of research for the convention. His colleague, Professor William J. Pierce, served with the joint committee on constitutional implementation. Professors Daniel McHargue, Arthur Bromage, and John White of the Political Science Department were called in as consultants, as was Ferrel Heady of the Institute of Public Administration and Professor Paul Kauper of the Law School.

The new state constitution drawn up at the convention was accepted by the people and went into effect on January 1, 1964. It reaffirmed the autonomy of the Regents of the University of Michigan, which had been established in the constitution of 1850 and continued in the revised constitution of 1908. The new constitution also created a new State Board of Education, which was to appoint the state superintendent and have general supervision over all public education, "except as to institutions of higher education granting baccalaureate degrees." It was also to serve as "the general planning and coordinating body for all public education, including higher education, and shall advise the legislature as to the financial requirements in connection therewith." But the State Board's power was limited: "The power of the boards of institutions of higher education in this constitution to supervise their respective institutions and control and direct the expenditure of the institution's funds shall not be limited by this section."

Seemingly, that proviso was clear enough, but alarming developments soon appeared. In 1964 the legislature appropriated all moneys for planning and constructing university buildings to the state controller, with directions to that office to plan and let contracts. The attorney general ruled this act invalid, and that such appropriations should be released to the universities for expenditure. But the next year the legislature enacted a similar law authorizing the state controller to complete plans and specifications for all new educational buildings, and that if any part of the act were declared invalid the entire act would become void and the appropriations for such buildings be lost. Two universities refused to accept the provisions of this law.

Then a controversy developed over the powers of the State Board of

Education. It objected to enlargement of the Flint Senior College into a four-year college branch of the University, as requested by the Flint Board of Education. The legislature listened to the State Board's reasoning on this issue, but at the same time it also set up an authority empowered to create an osteopathic medical school without gaining consent of the State Board and in the face of the attorney general's opinion that the legislature was without power to establish such a school.

The attorney general went on to say that the State Board of Education had the power to determine the location of colleges and the addition of departments to existing colleges. Such power to authorize departments was a distinct invasion of the autonomy of the Board of Regents and of the governing boards of any of the state universities. The legislature next empowered the state Labor Mediation Board to designate unions as sole bargaining agents for various areas of public employment including the universities, although the latter were barred by state law from signing contracts with unions, and the unions were forbidden to strike. The attorney general ruled that this law was not in conflict with the constitutional power of the Regents to manage the University. The State's universities felt otherwise. Thus, the scene was set for a continuing and ongoing battle over the autonomy of the Regents.

While the debates were ongoing, changes took place in the members of the Board. The terms of two Regents expired at the end of 1961: Otto E. Eckert, '12, of Lansing, and Dr. Charles S. Kennedy, '13m, of Detroit. They were succeeded by Paul Goebel, '23, an All-American football player, of Grand Rapids, and Allan Sorenson, '48e, of Midland. William B. Cudlip, '26l, Detroit attorney, was elected to the Board in 1963. The death of Mr. McInally in 1964 and the resignation of Mr. Power in 1966 allowed Governor Romney to appoint to the Board Robert P. Briggs, MBA '28, former University vice-president and a utilities executive from Jackson, and Alvin M. Bentley, "40, MA '63, former congressman and delegate to the state constitutional convention from Owosso.

In April 1962 the Board decided to open its "formal meetings" to the public, in addition to press representatives, limited only by the capacity of the Regents' Room for seating. Requests for admission were to be made twenty-four hours in advance and tickets procured. Visitors could not speak, applaud, or otherwise interfere with the conduct of the meeting. The Regents hoped by this move to win greater support and understanding of the University's needs and problems. About forty interested persons attended the first open meeting, a number that has since varied considerably depending on the issues being addressed.

One internal issue that unquestionably came under the Board's control was the organization of the academic year. Pressure was growing to open the University for year-round operation. A calendar of three terms a year was approved by the faculty and sent to the Regents for approval, if additional funds could be found to support it. The Regents endorsed the idea and asked for detailed plans. Planning came under the supervision of Vice-President Heyns. The semesters had to be shortened slightly as did the period of final examinations. Since it was deemed desirable to finish the first term before the December break, the "fall" opening was pushed back into August. The second term began in January and ran through April, with only half a week of spring vacation and with the traditional June Commencement moved back to May 1. The third term was made flexible by being broken into two eight-week sessions. By this means school teachers and students from other colleges, who would not be free until the middle of June, could enter the second session of the third term, much like the old summer session. Michigan's own students could enroll for the full third term or attend either half. The calendar was remarkably like that in vogue before 1856, except that students in a hurry could compress the normal four years of work for a bachelor's degree into two years and eight months.

The state's appropriation in 1964 made possible the inauguration of the new schedule that fall. The third term in 1965 was larger than any summer session alone, and the faculty began to adjust. The students who applauded the new calendar had some second thoughts after experiencing the stepped-up pace. There was no vacation period in which to write term papers or to catch up in the event of earlier illness, spring sports were upset, final examination periods were compressed, and the favored jobs at summer resorts conflicted with registration before Labor Day. The terms were later shortened so that registration once again took place after Labor Day.

3. Civil Rights and the War in Vietnam

In the fall of 1960 the students were aroused by the presidential political campaign. A vociferous faction may have given the impression that Kennedy, while acceptable, was too conservative, while Nixon was hopelessly reactionary. A more moderate group was enthusiastic for Kennedy and greeted him on his post-midnight stop in Ann Arbor on October 14. He drove to the steps of the Michigan Union, where he defined the peace corps idea which had been strongly advocated locally by two graduate students, Alan and Guskin, leaders in Americans Committed to World Responsibility, a campus group promoting a student foreign service. The spot on the Union steps is now marked by a bronze seal and plaque as a memorial to the President.

Nevertheless, a straw poll among seven of the Big Ten universities showed Nixon the winner on every campus, including Michigan, suggesting that the majority of students were basically somewhat conservative. In

KENNEDY ON THE STEPS
OF THE UNION

1964, on the other hand, a straw poll of six of the Big Ten showed a preference of 12 to 7 for Johnson over Goldwater. Michigan did not take a poll.

After Kennedy's election, the Peace Corps became a reality, carrying a powerful appeal to the idealism of young people. Here was an opportunity to serve fellow humans with enriching ideas and technology, and with honor to oneself. Language and cultural training centers were set up at several universities. Michigan trained two groups to work in Thailand and another group to go to Iran, under the direction of Dean Harold Dorr. The training period helped the Peace Corps winnow the mature and dedicated from the merely enthusiastic. By the beginning of 1966, 332 Michigan alumni had served or were serving in the corps.

Some of the undergraduates focused on a domestic problem: the civil rights of African-Americans and their integration into American society. As demonstrations occurred in the South over the slowness of the states and municipalities to accept the clear consequences and implications of the United States Supreme Court decisions of 1954 and later, students took part in sympathetic and sometimes remote picketing, rallying, public letter writing, and bucket drives. Concern was manifest over the small number of African-American students in the University (under 200). Student Government Council made demands on fraternities that they prove their secret constitutions contained no "bias clauses." The *Daily* led the campaign, reducing its coverage of other eventsJohnson's Great Society Speech. It even ignored the Athletic Department's decision to charge students for football tickets in the fall of 1963.

The University's efforts to deal with the issues of the Civil Rights era began modestly in the early 1960s. In 1963 the University embarked on a mutual assistance program with Tuskegee Institute in Alabama, involving exchanges of faculty and students and joint research. It was an effort to exceed traditional integration here by actively aiding a venerable African-American college. In another direction the University discovered seventy African-American youths in Michigan whose potential for education seemed greater than their high-school performance. They were high-school graduates who were not expecting to attend any college. Under the University's Opportunity Awards program they were enrolled for 1964-65 and given both financial aid and tutorial assistance. At the end of their freshman year, twenty-two could not continue, but only fourteen of them for academic

reasons. The other forty-
seven moved into their second year. A new group of
sixty-three disadvantaged
youth was started in the fall
of 1965, and forty-nine were
eligible to continue in their
second year.

The assassination of
President Kennedy in No-
vember 1963 was a greater
shock to academic commu-

CIVIL RIGHTS MARCH

nities than to other places, perhaps because the faculty and students felt
they had lost an intellectual leader. A football game was canceled, and on
Monday, the day of the funeral, classes were dismissed so that students and
faculty could attend a memorial service in Hill Auditorium conducted by
President Hatcher, not unlike the similar service for Lincoln in April 1865
conducted by President Haven. President Kennedy had been invited to
deliver the Commencement address the following May, and he had
expressed definite interest, although he had been unable to commit
himself. The invitation was later renewed to President Johnson, who
accepted in April. He appeared at the Michigan Stadium by helicopter on
May 22, 1964, and spoke on the characteristics of "The Great Society,"
which he summoned all to help create. School children from around the
state and thousands of Michigan citizens nearly filled the stadium for this
signal visit.

JOHNSON'S GREAT SOCIETY SPEECH

By 1965, the fo-
cus of student interest
and activism was be-
ginning to change. Af-
ter about seventy stu-
dents participated in
the march on Selma,
Alabama, in March
1965, the racial issue
was eclipsed by con-
cern over the warfare
in Vietnam, inspired by
the faculty demonstra-
tion. The new topic
required more wire
news from Washington and Asia, and the *Daily* columns achieved a better
balance. At the end of the year the *Daily* received an award from the

Overseas Press Club of America for the college daily having the best national and international coverage of events.

In the spring of 1965 a group of fourteen faculty members, greatly concerned about warfare in Vietnam, announced through the newspapers that they would cancel their classes on March 24 in protest against United States policy in Vietnam and hold instead a "conference" on the subject. They urged other professors to join them in their protest, and three others immediately did. Sharp-eyed faculty noticed at once two omissions from the names: there was no one from the History or Political Science departments among them, but ten of the seventeen were from the Sociology and Psychology departments, and certain well-known faculty liberals who frequently championed debate of unpopular causes were absent from the list. The public announcement caused Governor Romney to recommend disciplinary action against the professors, the state Senate to pass a resolution condemning the "work moratorium," President Hatcher to comment tersely that "dismissing classes is certainly not an acceptable" method of protest, and Dean Haber to indicate a more lenient disapproval of the arbitrary decision. These reactions were mild compared to what some other members of the faculty said about their colleagues.

The group was surprised at this reaction. They had not considered the dismissal of classes as a breach of contract with both the University and the students. The right of this group to protest and be heard on their own time was never disputed. After brave declarations that they would not give up their "moratorium" on classes, they backed down, announcing that instead they would hold an all-night "teach-in" on March 24. The dean permitted the use of four neighboring auditoriums. The original group was now joined by many others who saw an educational benefit in the proposed discussion, including members of the History and Political Science departments. The planners decided not to permit anyone to speak in favor of United States policy in Vietnam on the ground that this view had had ample forms of expression.

The "teach-in" attracted about 2500 students. After hearing several speakers, the audience was recessed at midnight for a rally on the Diagonal, but only part of the crowd turned out in the cold weather. More than a hundred supporters of the government position heckled the speakers. Returning indoors, the group, now reduced below 500, divided into seminars. The endless talk was broken by refreshments, movies, and folk singing. At the conclusion of the dwindling all-night session, irate custodians hurried to clean up an incredible litter before eight o'clock classes.

Student reactions were mixed even among the percentage of the student body who had heard part of the "teach-in." Although the academic critics sounded like the isolationists of 1935 and the neutralists of 1940, they resented such comparisons, just as they objected to charges that their stand might give comfort to the enemy. Plans were pursued for a national "teach-in" or debate in Washington, between Johnson administration defenders and selected professors. It was held on May 15 and televised; four Michigan professors attended. Results were uncertain since argument seemed to spring from differences of fact before those of policy. Further, the critics of government policy could not agree on desirable alternatives. In the next months several faculty members joined an Inter-University Committee for Debate on Foreign Policy that professed satisfaction with the debate on Vietnam in Congress in 1966 and proposed more "teach-ins." The anniversary observance in March 1966 of the original "teach-in" attracted so little attention on campus that the *Daily* commented on the fading interest.

In the fall of 1965 a group of thirty-two students and five faculty members felt obliged to demonstrate their objection to United States policy in Vietnam by sitting in the office of the Ann Arbor draft board. When warned of trespass and ordered to leave, they refused. All were arrested, as apparently they wished to be. Eight pleaded guilty or no contest; the rest were convicted in municipal court of trespassing. They appealed to the circuit court, where they expected to defend themselves by statements of their motives, but the judge ruled that their motives were irrelevant. Convicted a second time, they were given fines and jail sentences. It was a simple and hard lesson.

The University administration maintained the attitude that as citizens the students have the same freedom of speech, peaceful assembly, and right of petition guaranteed to all citizens by our Constitution, no matter how unpopular they may render themselves. On the other hand, if they violate a law it is the responsibility of the law enforcement agencies to take appropriate action. There is an important difference between actions that are offensive or distasteful, and those that are illegal. Rights of citizenship were not granted by universities, but guaranteed by the Constitution before most universities existed.

VIETNAM RALLY

4. Students and alumni

Amid the growing student activism of the late 1960s, campus life continued along more traditional lines. Sponsored by the United States State Department, the symphony band of ninety-four members under Conductor William D. Revelli toured Soviet Russia and the Near East for four months in the spring of 1961, during which time it presented seventy-one concerts. It was enthusiastically received everywhere, many audiences unbelieving that all the band members were not making a vocation of music, and the State Department acclaimed it the most successful of any amateur American musical organization going abroad. In consequence the band received the award of the National Federation of Music Clubs for the ensemble "which most effectively increases appreciation of American music abroad."

The Men's Glee Club toured Europe in the summer of 1962 and again in 1963 and entered the International Eisteddfod, or contest, in Wales, where both times it won the coveted Llangollen Choral Award. They were the only United States singing group ever to win. Then in the spring of 1965 the State Department selected the University's jazz band to tour Central America and the West Indies. It ended gloriously in Santo Domingo just as insurrection flared up. The student musicians, on their last stop, were quickly flown out.

In the Honors Program more than a thousand students distributed among the four classes were moving through the University with distinguished achievement. Most went on for advanced degrees. In 1966-67 the University had 244 National Science Foundation fellowship holders, ranking it fifth in the nation and second among state universities for this number. A Junior-Year-Aboard program was started with the University of Wisconsin at the University of Aix-en-Provence in 1962, and another at the University of Freiburg in 1964 with Wisconsin and Wayne State University.

In an effort to achieve a consistent philosophy of University student relations for an enrollment that had reached 25,000, a special committee of faculty and students under John W. Reed of the Law School was appointed by the president to investigate faculty expectations and student wants. Its report was issued in 1962. The basic recommendation was this: "Students must be active participants in the whole process [of attaining a University education] not merely because it is essentially fair to allow the 'governed' to participate in the 'government,' or because student participation helps bridge gaps in attitude, age, and insight into student needs, but especially because opportunities for participation are indispensable for individual educational growth."

Recognizing the transient nature of the student body, the Reed report noted that the consequent urgency on its part to contribute produces "conviction-charged, creative impatience." But granting students power to make decisions would be unwise, "for in the final analysis it is the faculty and administration that are held accountable by the Board of Regents and by society for the educational yield of the institution."

The report reminded everyone of the enormous variety in the student population. Out of the 25,000 in attendance, 40 percent were in graduate and professional schools, 48 percent were over twenty-one years of age, 28 percent were married, 12 percent were under nineteen, and 6 percent came from other nations. Their fields of interest were so widely variegated that the University cannot work toward a single purpose.

The Reed committee believed that substantial supervision and guidance should be offered freshmen, but that these should decline sharply thereafter. The University should make clear to students and their parents that maturity and a high degree of self-discipline are required of students. The report was implemented by restructuring the office of vice-president for Student Affairs. No longer was there a dean of men and a dean of women. The office was reorganized functionally without distinction for sex. Vice-President Cutler developed five functional units for counseling, financial aid, University residence halls, student-community relations (especially housing), and student activities. Two student convocations were arranged in 1964-65 for President Hatcher to address and answer questions about the changes. About 150 students turned out for the first one, and perhaps twice that number for the second. President Hatcher reminded them of their opportunities in the 1964 Convocation:

"At the University [the student] has a few years of latitude and leisure for self-cultivation. He has a supportive and tolerant or indulgent environment, favorable but not too tightly planned, where he may associate with his peers in a common mission individually pursued under diminishing supervision as he hastens toward maturity. He has available all the tools of learning we know how to provide. He may know and be guided by the wisest and most learned men in all fields. He has a chance to recognize the ongoing forces of our world, how they take on new forms and new directions, to learn how we preserve the good in the old while creating the new, and how to minimize crises, eruptions and neurotic tensions, through natural growth and creative evolution. He may construct a new and vivid pattern and style of life for himself."

Through the early years of civil rights and activism, the appeal of victorious athletic teams did not lose its magic. In the fall of 1964 the football team won the Big Ten title and was invited to play in the Rose Bowl on New Year's Day, 1965. There Coach Elliott's team defeated Oregon State 34 to 7. Approximately 3000 Michigan students attended the game. An All-American himself, Chalmers "Bump" Elliott, '48, became head coach in 1959 and produced two more All-Americans, Bob Timberlake, '65, and Bill Yearby, '66 (twice). The gymnastics team won the Big Ten title six years in a row. A resurgence of enthusiasm for basketball was aroused by Coach David Strack in 1964 as his team swept to the Big Ten championship, and repeated in 1965 and again in 1966. These were the years that Cazzie Russell, '66, starred. Now with the oldest and smallest of field houses, Michigan felt the need to provide something larger to accommodate student rooters satisfactorily. The consequence was a new sports building near the Stadium and names after football coach, Fritz Crisler. It seats about 15,000 and can be used for other special events as well.

Fraternities and sororities maintained a healthy liveliness at Michigan through the 1960s. Once, just before the Civil War, fraternities enrolled two-thirds of the student body, undoubtedly a record high. By 1897 the percentage of affiliated men was down to 25 percent of male students. During the so called jazz decade it rose, standing at 32 percent

of the men and 22 percent of the women in 1924. In 1966 there were forty-five general social fraternities on campus having a combined membership of 2926 and nineteen professional fraternities with 946 members.

HOMECOMING

The 3872 total membership was 20 percent of all men students, the 2926 members of the social fraternities made up 29 percent of undergraduate men. The twenty-three sororities had a total of 1714 members, or 22 percent of undergraduate women students. To maintain percentages comparable to 1924 in the growth of the University meant a doubling of most chapter memberships. Fraternity houses therefore could no longer accommodate their full membership. Sororities, however, managed to add to their houses to take in all members, becoming small dormitories in the process.

Continuing enrollment pressures--total enrollment (including credit extension courses) passed 36,000 in the fall of 1966--raised the question of how additional students in the Literary College might be accommodated in better fashion. The College's curriculum committee suggested a separate small residential college within the Literary College. Next to a dormitory complex would be a classroom building containing also faculty offices, laboratories, and library. Some counselors or teaching fellows would live in. A common core of courses would be required, with some independent study and comprehensive examinations. The similarity to the Mason Hall setup in the 1840's was pronounced. Besides a community in residence and study, there would be community recreation, arts, and faculty relations. The overall purpose was to combine the advantages of a small college with the benefits of a large university. Associate Dean Burton D. Thuma was appointed director during planning. Funds could not be found for a separate building, so room was made in East Quadrangle for the new Residential College, which admitted its first students in 1968, with James Robertson of the English Department serving as the first director.

Despite the appearance of affluence in student spending and the thousands of cars registered on campus, approximately half the student body held jobs. (If summer jobs were counted, the percentage of students earning part or all their expenses rose to about seventy.) Some students needed cars for their jobs; others found jobs to support a car. Monies available for scholarships, grants-in-aid, graduate fellowships, and loans reached the whopping total of $11,000,000, including $1,000,000 from federal funds under the National Defense Education Act. Approximately 6,100 loans were made in 1964-65.

The national office on campus of the Michigan Alumni Association moved aggressively in the 1960's to make alumni more aware of their University and to try new programs for group interest, since the traditional class reunions and the focus on athletics were fading. Professors were taken to address alumni clubs, not on the University in general and not on reminiscences, but on what kind of research they were doing. These intellectual stimulations aroused some excitement about the learning that was taking place at their alma mater. Robert G. Forman was made the new executive director of the Association. In conjunction with the office of University Relations, President Hatcher and several of the vice-presidents visited alumni and civic leaders in several cities of Michigan to tell of University plans and answer questions. In a reverse move, on several week ends each year leading alumni and citizens were invited to Ann Arbor for two days of visiting classes, hearing from students and faculty.

By far the most successful innovation in alumni affairs in the 1960's was the founding of an alumni family summer camp. It made use of the Biological Station at Douglas Lake in 1961 and 1962, and then the Alumni Association bravely bought a large summer camp with buildings on Walloon Lake near Petoskey. It was opened for ten weeks each summer and accommodated fifty to fifty-five families for one or two-week periods. It has been sold out every summer since its establishment. Known as Camp Michigania, it carried on an educational as well as recreational program under Glen R. Williams, field secretary of the Alumni Association. In the old Chautauqua Lake tradition, different faculty members appeared every couple of days to lecture at night and lead discussions the next morning.

Two distinguished alumni came back to campus in June 1965: Lieutenant Colonel James A. McDivitt, '59 BSE, and Lieutenant Colonel Edward H. White, '59 MSE, just after their sixty-two orbits around the earth. They helped dedicate the new Space Research building on North Campus, made possible by funds from the National Aeronautics and Space Administration. Honorary degrees of doctor of astronautical science were conferred on both of them. Six of the forty-nine original astronauts held degrees from Michigan after studying in the Department of Aerospace Engineering.

The biggest undertaking involving alumni in the 1960s was the Sesquicentennial campaign to raise $55,000,000 for new academic programs, fellowships, and buildings "to insure the vital margin" between state support for operations and the University's capacity to achieve and explore. No tax-assisted university had ever attempted to raise such an amount, and professional counsel was used starting in 1964. But with perhaps the largest alumni body in the nation—225,000 at the time—the effort seemed worth making as the birthday anniversary celebration. Regent Paul Goebel served as national chairman and worked with district chairmen in a broad solicitation.

On campus Professor Charles Joiner was chairman of the Central Sesquicentennial Committee, with Richard L. Kennedy as executive director. They and their committees mounted a year-long series of events that focused national and international attention on the University throughout 1967; Howard Peckham's contribution to the celebration was the first University history written in over half a century, the *Making of the University of Michigan*.

CAMPUS, 1970

CHAPTER FOURTEEN

MAINTAINING THE EDGE OF EXCELLENCE

Looking back during the Sesquicentennial celebrations in 1967, the University understandably took pride in its accomplishments. One hundred and fifty years of growth and innovation, including the post-war expansion orchestrated by Harlan Hatcher, had admirably positioned the University for continued leadership in higher education. Yet the anniversary year in which the University reflected on its past was also one that bode an uncertain future: the tensions of the Vietnam War undermined the sense of community; students

ROBBEN W. FLEMING

challenged the authority of the administration; the Civil Rights movement had reached a point of frustration; and radical politics found ready adherents among a generation of students ill-at-ease with their parents' values, a paternalistic University, and a government waging an unpopular war. Although there was a great deal to celebrate, by 1968 the *status quo* was under siege.

Student protest was not the only problem, however. Though difficult to perceive at the time, the post-WWII University was coming to an end, and a re-defined institution was in the making. In 1970, financial resources would begin to decline, threatening the steady growth to which the University had become accustomed. In a worst case scenario, the years of activism were followed by declining federal support and a recession in Michigan that impacted heavily on higher education. The University watched its state support for the General Fund seriously erode and its research budget stagnate, while high inflation and an energy crisis sent prices of essential goods and services soaring. Efforts to stretch available dollars would be hampered by increasing government regulation and attempts to meet the needs and expectations of students and society in an era of rapid social and economic change—all of which cost money. Maintaining excellence in this difficult decade would present as great a challenge to the tenth president of the University of Michigan as any predecessor had faced.

Robben W. Fleming, B.A., LL.B., brought to the office of President from 1968-1978 a unique combination of skills that seemed tailored for the times. A graduate of Beloit College and the University of Wisconsin Law School, Fleming had served as Director of the Industrial Relations Center at the University of Wisconsin, Director of the Institute of Labor and Industrial Relations at the University of Illinois, and professor of labor law at both institutions. From 1964 he had been Chancellor of the University of Wisconsin. This background as an academic, administrator, and experienced labor mediator would prove an invaluable asset in a tense era followed by a prolonged period of financial contraction. With great patience, tact, and an understanding of the art of negotiation, Fleming maintained the confidence of the University community through a difficult decade. A genuine sympathy with student concerns and a belief that faculty should play a meaningful role in the decision-making process were as important to his success as President, however, as were his skills as a mediator. Perhaps most important, Fleming understood what is essential to a university and what could be negotiated away without harm.

1. Student activism: Vietnam, student power, and BAM

Opposition on campus to the war in Vietnam increased after the March 1965 faculty-sponsored Teach-In. This technique for constructive consciousness-raising, widely copied on campuses across the country, established a mechanism via which U.S. government policy could be examined and criticized, when necessary, in a time of war. The Teach-In provided a model for respectable dissent. By 1966, students' insistence on control over their personal lives, which included draft status and anti-war protest activity, collided with requests to the Hatcher administration by the House Un-American Activities Committee for co-operation in investigating war protestors, requests from the Selective Service Bureau for the class rank of all males to determine eligibility for deferments, and the use of plain clothes police on campus during rallies. Administration building sit-ins and a sleep-in by members of Voice, the political party of SDS on campus, had led to a ban on sit-ins in November 1966. In a Student Government Council (SGC) referendum, students overwhelmingly opposed administration policy. In late November, 1,500 students held a one hour sit-in at the Administration [LSA] Building. The formation of a number of student-faculty-administration commissions to review present procedures relieved tension for the moment. When the Johnson administration ended student deferments in 1967, anti-war activity re-focused away from the University administration and toward the national anti-war effort. However, it was clear that the University's involvement in the war effort would continue to be a target of student protest.

As the war escalated so did tensions on campus. By 1968 and for the next few years, anti-war rallies drew hundreds, even thousands of students. Sit-ins at the Ann Arbor Selective Service office led to arrests and town-gown confrontations, a reminder of how deeply devisive the war had become. Draft card

ANTI-WAR RALLY ON THE DIAG

burnings at rallies spurred the resolve of others to resist induction. Students, here as elsewhere, resisted the draft by refusing induction or leaving the country; by late 1968 the Selective Service would report 60,000 violations nationally. ROTC and classified military research acted as lightning rods to student anger and frustration, along with campus recruiting by the CIA, the military, and corporations involved in the war effort, particularly Michigan-based Dow Chemical, maker of napalm, a highly flammable chemical with devastating effects on humans. The Diag became the center of activity: SDS and other groups passed out leaflets, organized protests, and raised consciousness; crosses on the lawn symbolized the thousands killed; anti-war organizations rallied and recruited members; the Ann Arbor Resistance Committee put on dramatizations, such as mock killings and "die-ins"; the Michigan Council to Repeal the Draft and the Student Peace Union held marches and vigils urging students to resist the draft.

PEACEFUL DISSENT

Preventing violence and personal injury while keeping the University operating smoothly was Fleming's principal goal throughout this period. He knew that it was vital to maintain the trust and confidence of the faculty and students, to engage in genuine dialogue that would diffuse tensions and solve problems. Avoiding capricious decisions was crucial. He understood, and did not underestimate, the strength of individual convictions. As an experienced negotiator, Fleming was not one to take "flights of rhetoric" personally and was always willing to talk with students. In Fleming's view, it was the President's role to protect dissent and intellectual freedom, to defuse volatile issues, and to control those problems that would upset the flow of the great institution he knew the University of Michigan to be. Time and events proved this approach to be very effective. There were no take-overs of the president's office as at Columbia; no National Guard troops on campus as at Berkeley or Wisconsin; no fatalities as at Kent State or Jackson State; and the educational process went on with only minor interruptions.

SIMULATING A BOMB CRATER

Despite public criticism, Fleming refused to take inflexible stands on unimportant matters. When the Inter-Faith Council for Peace wanted to dig a large "bomb crater" on the Diag to symbolize the destruction of North Vietnam, Fleming found them a safe place to do it. His reaction to the crater affair was typical of his willingness to cooperate with peaceful dissent. "Why not let them dig one? Everybody else is digging holes for new buildings and so forth. It's not a big job to throw the dirt back in the hole after they get tired." In response to those who objected to his willingness to compromise, Fleming reasoned, "If you make an issue of activities that do no harm and don't interfere with the running of the University, you run the real risk of attracting a lot of other students who will then be sympathetic to their other demands."

Not provoking the majority of the student body into sympathy with the agenda of radicals was also important in navigating through the volatile situations of these years. To keep radical activity isolated he avoided confrontation when at all possible. Withdrawing the University from the highly controversial Institute for Defense Analysis helped lessen the emotion surrounding the issue of military research so that resolution of all issues associated with classified research became possible. Working with legitimate student organizations not controlled by the administration--particularly the *Michigan Daily*, the SGC, and the moderate wing of SDS--helped ensure that extremist efforts to provoke confrontation did not succeed. Civil authority was to be used only when actions destructive of the University's purpose or harmful to the rights of the community were involved--and only as a last resort.

Two examples will serve to demonstrate the attempts of radical students to provoke confrontation and Fleming's response: In March 1969 members of the Jesse James Gang, the militant wing of SDS, attempted to provoke a confrontation by locking themselves in the room with a military recruiter to prevent interviews from taking place, daring Fleming to call in the police. Fleming refused. He knew that "cracking heads" only makes others angry and gains sympathy for the offenders. After five hours the recruiter was released and the students disciplined through the campus judiciary system. In September 1969 anti-ROTC militants took over North Hall, again hoping to provoke a confrontation with police. With hundreds of students milling around, Fleming requested that police guard the building for safety, avoiding confrontation and leaving the back door unlocked and unguarded. As he expected, the protestors left quietly during the night, their images caught on videotape for later disciplinary action. The Regents did not change the University's fifty-year arrangement with the military.

The success of the administration's efforts to isolate radical activity but preserve peaceful dissent gave moderates within the anti-war movement the opportunity to influence public opinion. President Hatcher had expressed misgivings about the war in 1967. At an anti-war rally in Hill Auditorium in September 1969 Fleming expressed the view that the war was a "colossal mistake." Following a UofM football game the next day, 12,000 students marched from Michigan Stadium to the Diag in protest of the war. On October 15, 1969, a rally in support of a moratorium in the war was held in Michigan Stadium as part of the national moratorium effort. The Faculty Senate passed a resolution encouraging students and faculty to participate and with the administration's blessing cancelled or rescheduled classes. That night 20,000 people gathered in Michigan Stadium to protest the war. The visibility of such events, widely covered by the media, helped to demonstrate that the anti-war movement was not confined to a radical fringe.

It was an incident involving student power and not the war, however, that resulted in the only confrontation that Fleming was unable to resolve without calling in the civil authorities to remove protestors. Activist students had long been demanding a student-operated book store, and other Big Ten schools had established them by this time. Following a raucous Board of Regents meeting in September 1969, at which the Regents agreed to fund a book store but not to give students control, the Radical Caucus of SDS organized a student take-over of the LSA Building. Concerned about the security of faculty offices and student files in the building, Fleming sought a restraining order, which could not be served as students had the doors locked. At 4:00 a.m. state and city police forcibly evacuated the building, arresting 107 people who were charged and released on bail. The arrests, Fleming later recalled, "let students know that there were some things we would not let them do." A joint faculty-student committee eventually worked out an agreement to establish a student-operated book store that would not leave the Regents financially liable in the event of failure, and the University Cellar began operating in the Michigan Union.

The war in Vietnam and a desire for greater student autonomy were not the only causes of unrest during the years of activism. Low minority enrollment had been a concern on campus since the early 1960s. The University

STUDENT BOOKSTORE, MICHIGAN UNION

had expressed its intention of increasing the enrollment of African-American students, which still numbered only 1,000, by 1969. This snail's pace toward inclusion was one factor that had led various groups on campus to organize as the Black Action Movement (BAM), dedicated to assisting minority students and opening the University's traditionally white campus to wider minority participation. Unable to secure from the Regents the financial guarantees to meet its goals, BAM called for a campus-wide strike in March 1970.

The BAM strikers sought a number of guarantees from the administration and Regents including: increased financial aid, support services, and minority staff to address the needs of minority students; support for a Center of Afro-American and Africa Studies; and the increase of African-American enrollment from its existing 3% to 10%. The strike included a boycott of classes and the establishment of picket lines at crucial service facilities on campus, an astute move that was significant to the success of the strike.

The BAM strike, which raised the volatile issue of race, created more serious problems for the administration in terms of public relations and the potential for violence on campus than had any other protest activity. Fleming faced considerable pressure to call in the National Guard. He persuaded the Regents to bear with the unpleasantness, arguing that avoiding potential tragedy "calls for enduring a certain amount of damage, or intimidation, harrassment and insult, in return for more rational and sane means of dealing with the problem." As with anti-war protest, the

University president was prepared to be called gutless and worse in order to avoid the serious division of the campus over issues that deeply concerned the University community. The strike was widely supported. Some units, such as the Residential College and Social Work shut down, and LSA attendance dropped to as low as 25% as some 300 teaching assistants and faculty cancelled classes. More telling was the honoring of picket lines at the heating plant, food service building, and the dormitories by university employees; food was not delivered and waste piled up.

BAM I

Eight days after it began the strike was settled. The University gave approval to the essential BAM demands of increased minority aid, services and staff. It also agreed to work toward a goal of 10% African-American enrollment by 1973.

2. Finances, energy, and collective bargaining

A number of problems combined in the early 1970s to bring about a financial crisis in higher education. The end of the robust post-WWII economy, the Arab oil embargo, cut-backs in federal funding, and rising inflation wrecked havoc with general fund and research budgets nationwide. Federally and state-mandated initiatives for minorities, women, and the handicapped added financial commitments without supplying funds. Higher education dollars had been stretched to their limit by the expansion of public higher education in the 1950s and 1960s, creating competition for education dollars when financial resources began to shrink. In the State of Michigan, Wayne State University and Michigan State University now enjoyed equal status constitutionally with the University of Michigan, while the State's other four-year public colleges had been renamed and flourished as universities. All of these institutions were far more expensive to maintain than a decade before. In the short run it probably did not help the University's financial position that the Regents twice sued the State for interfering with the powers of the Regents. In the long run, such challenges were vital for maintaining the autonomy of the Regents.

While higher education in general faced a multitude of problems during the 1970s, Michigan colleges and universities faced an additional burden brought on by the decline of the automobile industry. As a state-

supported institution, the University of Michigan had grown and prospered with the State of Michigan during the preceding decades, in large
measure through America's love-affair with the automobile. It would now
also suffer when the Arab oil embargo and then foreign competition caused
automobile sales to plummet. Although Governor William Milliken was
highly supportive, the State had to face increasing demands for unemploy-
ment compensation, social services, and prisons as the depression deepened and urban problems increased. The years of abundant state support
for higher education had come to an end.

The first in a long series of economic shocks came in 1970 when the
state budget comittee ordered a 1% cut ($735,000) in the University's state-
appropriated annual budget *after* it had been approved. The cut reflected
both a shortfall in tax revenues to the State and the constitutional requirement of the governor to order reductions in the budgets of public agencies
when those budgets exceed available revenue. State support at the time
made up about 60% of the General Fund budget which covers teaching,
some research, library services, student aid administration, operating
expenses, and buildings and grounds operation and maintenance. The
dollars lost were real dollars, some of which had already been spent.

The decisions made to meet this first budget emergency became the
means for coping with financial stringency at the University for the rest of
the decade and beyond: delay maintenance and remodeling; delay filling
vacant positions; defer all but essential equipment requests; and plan a
reduction for the following budget year to free funds for innovation and
new initiatives. Unfortunately, the planned reductions for reallocation did
not result in the extra funds anticipated. Despite a self-imposed 3% cut in
the 1971-72 budget, rising expenses and inflation caused the gap between
state dollars and University need to reach 10%. In 1972-73 the
State appropriation for the University was $11 million less than
had been requested, on top of which another retroactive cut of 2%
was imposed as the year unfolded. Long a leader in state support
of higher education, by 1975 the State of Michigan had slipped to
19th. By 1980 it ranked 35th and was still falling.

Throughout his administration Fleming was assisted by respected
and highly capable executive officers who skillfully guided the University
through the years of unrest and then of financial contraction. The key
decisions on the University's response to the financial crisis of the 1970s
were given over to Vice President for Academic Affairs Allan Smith and
Vice President and Chief Financial Officer Wilbur Pierpont. "If you start
out as a President," Fleming later reflected, "with a Vice President for
Academic Affairs and a Vice President for Finance who are superb people,
you are about three quarters of the way down the path of success, because
those are your critical areas. You mustn't let yourself get into a position

financially where you can't get out, or where you are in such miserable shape that you can't do anything, and you mustn't let quality go on the academic side." In 1974 Smith was succeeded by Frank H. L. Rhodes, who left in 1977 to become the fifth University of Michigan faculty member or adminstrator to be President of Cornell University. In 1977 Pierpont was succeeded by James Brinkerhoff. University relations with the State had become far more complex in the 1960s, and the position of Vice President for State Relations and Planning had been created in 1968. Arthur M. Ross held the position until 1970 and Fidele Fauri briefly thereafter. For the remainder of Fleming's years this important role of liason with the governor and legislature would be filled by Richard L. Kennedy.

Faculty insistence on a role in the budgeting process during the crisis led in 1972 to the Office of Budgets and Planning within which three committees of executive officers and faculty were formed to deal with budget priorities, long range planning, and program evaluation. As faculty salaries began to lag behind those of peer institutions, a faculty task force on Budgetary Processes and Priorities and a Committee on the Economic Status of the Faculty (CESF) were formed to help make faculty more effective in this sometimes painful financial planning. Reallocation of funds from one unit to another and keeping premier faculty from being "raided" by more affluent institutions, particularly in the South and West, took careful planning.

Students and their parents were called on to shoulder a significant portion of the financial burden. Tuition increased 16% in 1971, bringing the cost of in-state tuition from $568 to $660 per year and out-of-state to $2,140. By 1973, tuition had jumped to $904 and $2,800, the highest among comparable institutions. Between 1973 and 1979, tuition would climb another 43%; in 1980 it was $1,536 and $4,426. The days when Michigan could pride itself on providing the highest quality education at an affordable price were over.

Just as the University was beginning to adjust to the decline in state support, a new financial burden was added—skyrocketing energy costs brought on by the 1972-73 Arab oil embargo. In January 1973 the University was informed by its suppliers that no more than a six-week's supply of oil and natural gas could be guaranteed. The situation became critical and reminiscent of World War I when Junius Beal pulled the University and the town through a similar fuel crisis. University pumps were completely dry for at least one day in March 1973, and rationing of gasoline was discussed. Along with the days of abundant state support and low tuition, the days of cheap, unlimited fuel were over.

Solutions to the economic burdens imposed by the energy crisis were sought in a number of ways. Alternative forms and sources of energy became the subject of study, at least as long as the energy crisis lasted and research funds were available. Measures were taken to conserve energy. An Energy Conservation Task Force was formed in January 1973 to work on lowering consumption as a means of cutting costs. Building temperatures were lowered to 65 degrees, and everyone bundled up. Fans and exhaust systems were shut down at night, and evening classes were rescheduled so that buildings could be locked early. University buses were rerouted; car pooling was encouraged. Air conditioning systems were left off that spring until May 1. Except for Baits 1 and 2, the University virtually shut down over winter break, a response to an emergency that would continue after the emergency passed. However, even with these efforts, utility bills continued to climb. In 1973-74 the University used 10% less fuel than the preceding year, but its energy costs were 12% higher. New electrical generators were installed which produced about 70% of electricity needs on campus. Nonetheless, by 1975, the cost of electricity had climed nearly 300% over 1969-70 figures. Cost reduction was not an option; the best that could be hoped for was to cut the angle of increase, an oft-stated goal of the '70s.

Higher energy costs had ripple effects on other necessary products and services. A severe paper shortage brought on by increases in manufacturing and transportation costs caused prices to rise 100% on some stocks. Recycling of paper products began. Reusable campus mail envelopes and cheaper paper for intra-University correspondence were among the changes that came and did not leave. Inflation, which was fueled in part by higher energy costs, added other burdens. The Consumer Price Index rose 50% between 1969 and 1975. Salaries did not keep pace. Increases for staff benefits, student aid and utilities far outstripped the rate of inflation. Budgets for books, equipment, supplies, and travel kept falling behind anticipated needs. Student enrollments were increased to raise tuition revenues, but practically all of the increase came at the graduate level where the educational costs were twice that of teaching undergraduates. Although tuition at the graduate level was greatly increased, tuition dollars failed to keep pace with the rate of inflation. From year to year, through most of Fleming's presidency, support for instruction and research barely escaped serious erosion.

The inevitable reductions that had to be made to accommodate the budget shortfalls went to the heart of the University's mission of teaching and research. Most departments cut faculty in the wake of the hiring freezes and some, such as Business Administration, increased teaching loads. The College of Engineering made no new appointments. Neither did the School of Education, which also reduced course offerings. Public Health eliminated faculty positions at the very time that enrollment demands were at an all-time high. Loss of federal funds left positions eliminated and programs threatene: Pharmacy lost 25% of its federal funds, while the University Library lost 37 staff positions, closed the education library, and reduced reference services. The Law School increased the student-faculty ratio 25 to 1, the highest among the nation's leading law schools. Although difficult in the short run, it allowed them to recruit one of the finest classes of new Law faculty in the country, enhancing their reputation for exellence. Difficult times forced difficult choices.

The areas on North Campus that were no longer mowed reflected the deep cuts experienced by the Physical Properties Office. Remodeling, sidewalk replacement, and elevator renovation were all delayed. Grass mowing and snow removal were less prompt. Even with the reduction in work and services, the plant department was maintaining 21% more floor space in 1975 than in 1969 with fewer engineers, custodians and tradesmen to carry out the work. It was not the fault of the buildings and grounds crews that the campus began to look seedy, but it did, and there was no money to do anything about it. Building maintenance like faculty raises had to be put off until another day, even though to do so was to mortgage the future.

Still the cuts went deeper. Another $1.6 million was cut from the General Fund budget in December 1975. The hiring freeze continued in order to cover the loss. All deans had to assume a further 3%-5% reduction. By 1976 the losses could no longer be made internally without cuts in existing programs. There was nothing left to cut. Fixed expenses comprised most of the University's operating costs from health insurance, social security, and salaries to utilities, litigation, and safety. New services and government mandates drove staffing upward: By the mid-1970s staff expenses outweighed the costs for instruction by some $2 million dollars; in the mid-1960s that ratio was reversed. The faculty was "graying" and becoming more expensive: Over the decade only 5% of the full and associate professorial staff retired or left while 27% of the assistant professors departed, some because it became more difficult to obtain tenure.

The financial stringencies resulting from recession and inflation both produced and were compounded by unionization and collective bargaining. The 1965 Public Employee Relations Act of Michigan established formal procedures for the organization of collective bargaining units at state institutions and gave responsibility for overseeing this process to the Michigan Employment Relations Commission (MERC). In 1968 there were two small unions operating. By 1974 the University was bargaining or in litigation with numerous newly organized union locals and bargaining agencies representing, among others, operating engineers at the heating plant, tradesmen, clerical workers, and technical staff. Striking employees became a new element of campus life. Carpenters, electricians and plumbers walked off the job in June, 1974, technical workers in 1977. Other strikes were averted through successful negotiations with newly unionized groups, such as the Hospital nurses. At a time of economic instability and accelerating cultural and technological change, the ever present picket signs, including "Boycott Word Processors," reflected the deep anxieties of these years.

While collective bargaining made it more difficult to control costs during an inflationary period, the process of unionization also changed the nature of the relationship between the University and important segments of the university community. In no area was this change as fundamental as in the relationship between the University and its trainees and graduate students. In January 1971 the Intern-Resident Association (I-RA) petitioned MERC to become the collective bargaining agent for the medical trainees. The MERC ruling in favor of the I-RA petition set a precedent for rulings on petitions from other student trainees, particularly the graduate student assistants (GSAs) responsible for teaching discussion and laboratory sections and for grading in large courses.

A SIGN OF THE TIMES

Assistantships and grading positions had traditionally been considered a way for individual departments to provide assistance to graduate students, who were viewed as students, not employees. In 1971 the Teaching Fellows Union petitioned for the right to act as the bargaining agent for the GSAs, arguing that the GSAs were employees. The petition was denied. The GSAs immediately began the process of compliance with the MERC requirements for a collective bargaining agency through the formation of the Graduate Employees Organization (GEO), an initiative the Regents chose not to contest. It took time and some unexpected help from the courts, however, before a broad-based interest in collective bargaining emerged among graduate students.

The GEO received a ground-swell of support from the 2,100 GSAs in the fall of 1974. The impetus for the change in attitude toward unionization was provided by an unrelated and successful court challenge to the University's interpretation of in-state residency. Anticipating a substantial loss of out-of-state tuition revenue from students as a result of the successful challenge—less than 1,000 were ultimately reclassified—

the University eliminated the in-state fee privilege or tuition waiver customarily accorded to all GSAs. Although fellowships were granted to cover the 1973-74 academic year, the threat of future large increases in the cost of a graudate education with no increase in salary or benefits compensation enabled the GEO to become the sole and exclusive bargaining agent for the GSAs by a 2-1 vote. Henceforth all terms of employment for GSAs would be negotiated with the University directly and not by individuals with their departments.

When the first round of contract talks became stalled in February 1975, the GSAs walked out of the classroom. Fleming understood that the GEO wanted more money and other benefits in a period of high inflation, "just as does every other group of employees." While he could sympathize with all those involved in collective bargaining, it was his job to hold the line on costs. Support for the strike varied with 0%-80% attendance at classes in LSA, Social Work, and the Residential College to nearly normal attendance elsewhere. Seniors missing classes due to striking GSAs were assured they would graduate. Before a contract was signed in March, fifty-five GEO pickets had been arrested, mostly for violating agreements on trespassing. The settlement included only a token 10% tuition waiver. In an early and vigorously debated victory for equal rights in the work place, particularly gay male and lesbian rights, it was also agreed that future contracts would be applied without regard to non-relevant factors such as sex, race, creed, color, religion, national origin, age, handicap, or sexual preference.

With the accumulation of cut-backs, demands, and pressures leading to relentless financial contraction, it was clear that the academic quality of the institution would become seriously affected unless long-range planning was given a high priority. In June 1977 Harold Shapiro, an economist who had served as chair of the Budget Priorities Committee, became Vice President for Academic Affairs. Shapiro proposed the Priorities Fund, a tax on all research and instructional units that would make money available for reallocation. It is the difficult choices that would be made and the vision that Shapiro brought to this task that would serve as the foundation for his own presidency beginning in 1979.

Through the years of economic retrenchment, the energy crisis, and collective bargaining, Fleming's goal was to maintain the stature of the University. Every survey over the preceding 50 years ranked the University of Michigan one of the top universities in America. A 1974 survey of professional school deans ranked it one of the five universities with the greatest number of top-ranked professional schools. However, with a diminished General Fund budget, small salary increases, and reductions in research budgets, the danger of a decline in quality was inevitably present. Overall, stature as a leading

University was maintained. Yet the strains were beginning to produce some cracks in its reputation. A highly regarded survey published in the *Chronicle of Higher Education* in 1979 indicated that while the University of Michigan remained strong in its traditional areas of strength, the social and behavioral sciences, its position in other areas, particularly chemistry, physics, and medicine, was eroding. Without improvement of existing facilities and strong initiatives at faculty hiring in the next decade, the stature of the University would clearly diminish.

3. Growth and major initiatives

Unlike Harlan Hatcher, President Fleming was faced with greatly reduced state and federal support for capital projects. Given the financial squeeze, it is not surprising to find that most new building and renovation occurred by 1973. Creativity was needed if growth were to continue and major initiatives pursued. Spurred by the 55 M Campaign that celebrated the Sesquicentennial, private and corporate philanthropy would now become crucial if Michigan were to meet its building needs and maintain its edge of excellence. By 1980 several projects had been successfully completed and the largest project ever undertaken had been initiated, while others had to wait until better economic times. These initiatives demonstrated the University's capacity for growth under difficult economic conditions, strengthened the educational and research base of the University, enhanced the quality of campus life, and provided vital services to the people of Michigan.

Several major capital projects completed in the early 1970s were planned and financed before 1968. The Graduate Library was extensively renovated and an eight-story South wing added that loomed above the President's House—the first high rise on the Diag. This building at the heart of the LSA campus was renamed the Harlan Hatcher Graduate Library. Crisler Center opened next door to Michigan Stadium for intercollegiate basketball and use as a multi-purpose arena in 1971, the culmination of Fritz Crisler's legendary career as Athletic Director. Power Center for the Performing Arts also opened in 1971, providing the University with a large professional theatre.

Capital projects dependent on state or federal funds were constructed almost entirely in the early 1970s. The last dormitory of the Hatcher expansion, Bursley Hall, opened in 1968, as did the Administration Building, which would become the Sally and Robben Fleming Administration Building after the new president's retirement. The Highway Safety Research Institute was housed on the northern perimeter of campus in 1969, and the new School of Dentisty building opened in 1970. The School of Public Health building (1971) was named for Thomas Francis Jr., whose career would always be associated with the conquest of polio. The

School   of Art and Architecture occupied its new building on North Campus in 1973. That particular University/State project provides an example of the change in state fortunes and available funds for capital improvement in the 1970s. When planners secured approval for the building in the late 1960s, members of the legislature suggested that the library be deleted from the plans as the legislature would provide funding for a general library on North Campus within two to five years. The library was deleted, but the promised funding was a casualty of diminished State revenues. President Duderstadt broke ground for the promised North Campus library, the ITIC Building, in the spring of 1994.

Construction of a much-needed classroom building was delayed due to a dispute with the State over who had the right to appoint the architect for buildings constructed on state university campuses. A compromise was reached that gave the University the right to recommend architects and the legislature the right to veto them with cause. Once this dispute was resolved, the Modern Languages Building was built in 1972. Its completion moved the central campus area one step closer to realization of the Ingalls Mall, a broad landscaped expanse stretching from Rackham to the Graduate Library. With parking lots and parking meters still cluttering the area, however, only the University planners could yet envision such an idyllic space.

The shrinking of state funds is best evidenced in the failure to transfer the College of Engineering to North Campus. The high visibility provided by University of Michigan astronauts greatly facilitated the completion of the Aerospace Engineering Building in 1972. The remainder of the move hinged on construction of three new buildings: one for aeronautical engineering that would connect the wind tunnel and Fluids Laboratory, a second for chemical engineering and its allied fields, and a third for electrical engineering and computer science. A capital fund campaign was launched by the College in 1974 to raise matching funds to build these facilities; however, the anticipated and necessary state support was no longer available. A more modest approach was taken through renovation of G. G. Brown Laboratory for mechanical and civil engineering and an addition to and renovation of the Cyclotron Building for naval architecture and marine engineering. Although the Naval Architecture and Marine Engineering Building was completed in 1978, most of engineering remained on central campus.

Activity on the medical campus was almost entirely confined to building projects and renovations planned before Fleming arrived. Medical Science II, C.S. Mott Children's Hospital, and the Towsley Center for Continuing Medical Education were completed in 1969; the Upjohn Center for Clinical Pharmacology in 1970; and the Holden Perinatal Research Laboratory, Mott Cardiac Care Study Unit, and an expanded

Outpatient building in 1971. After a hiatus during the economic doldrums of the early 1970s, the Hospital Administration Building was constructed in 1976. The Scott and Amy Prudden Turner Memorial Clinic opened in 1977 in a new building on Wall Street adjoining the small, original building of the Kellogg Eye Center. Dedicated to the study and healing of diseases affecting the elderly, the Turner Clinic was grounded in traditional Medical School missions of teaching, research, and patient care, plus a strong component of community outreach that reflected the social concerns of the time.

The first steps were also taken in 1976 to replace University Hospital, whose facilities were state-of-the-art in 1925 but by the 1970s were cramped and outmoded for patients and seriously out-of-date both for research and the training of physicians. In order to build a new hospital, people and services had to shift from some of their present quarters. That process began with the purchase of the old St. Joseph Mercy Hospital at 300/400 North Ingalls when the Sisters of Charity moved their health care facilities to a new complex on E. Huron River Drive. Medical administration, planning and support services were moved into the North Ingalls Building in order to keep all clinical services on the medical campus. Nursing obtained more space by moving to North Ingalls, leaving their old quarters in Medical Science I for Medical School expansion.

Planning the most expensive hospital ever built was a daunting task. After several plans for the Replacement Hospital Project (RHP) did not prove satisfactory, Fleming suggested that he become chair of the University Hospital executive committee. Once this was done, Fleming gathered all the information from the Executive Committee as to what was needed—number of beds, space allocations, equipment costs, and so forth. He then personally wrote the report to the Regents, secured Governor Milliken's commitment of state funds, determined the amount of money the Medical School needed to raise, submitted the report to the medical faculty for approval, and then sent the report to the Regents. Looking back on his actions, Fleming later commented: "If I did that to the LSA faculty, I'd probably be ridden out of town on a burning log." However, planning the new hospital was a very large project, and the expertise of an experienced administrator was necessary to help conceptualize the scope of what was needed and to secure the approval of the Medical School faculty, the State and the Regents. In retrospect Fleming considered his moving the hospital replacement project off dead-center and getting a commitment to something everybody could support one of the best things he ever did. It would take 10 years, the efforts of two more skillful chief executives, and a great deal more planning before the project would be completed.

As the State economy declined into severe recession, private support became increasingly crucial for maintaining growth. The 1970s was a transtition time for the concept of development as both central administration and individual units moved toward professional development officers. To keep the momentum going following the successful 55 M Campaign and to develop future programs for private giving, the old position of Vice President for University Relations was refocused to become the Vice President for University Relations and Development with Michael Radock assuming the office.

Several initiatives reflect the importance of private and corporate philantrophy in maintaining the edge of excellence in the University's academic and research base during these years, particularly the new libraries for research. The Bentley Historical Library was built on North Campus in 1972 to house the Michigan Historical Collections. In 1976 Fleming signed the deed of gift with the National Archives for disposition of the papers of Gerald R. Ford '35, 38th President of the United States. Private donations were raised to build the presidential library whose cornerstone was laid in 1979, next door to the Bentley Library on North Campus. In the later 1970s private

BENTLEY HISTORICAL LIBRARY

donors also made possible planning for the Alfred E. Taubman Medical Library and the addition to the Law Library. Private gifts for the Clayton G. Hale Auditorium (1971) and Paton Center for Accounting (1976) in the School of Business Administration were crucial at a time when the pressure was increasing for MBA programs. The William D. Revelli Band Building (1973), which honored the retiring dean of university band directors, was built with funds raised by loyal band alumni and supporters. The University's leadership in social science research was evident in the large addition to the Institute for Social Research completed in 1976.

The crucial decisions made in 1971 concerning the floundering campuses at Flint and Dearborn highlight the commitment of the Regents and Fleming to undergraduate education and the support these branches had acquired in Lansing. Flint College of the University of Michigan had been founded as a two-year, senior-level campus in 1956 and had become a four-year college in 1965. In 1970 it was stagnating with a student body of less than 2,000 and remained confined to the Curtice Building of Flint Junior College. Dearborn had not fared any better. In 1956 the Regents had accepted a gift of land from the Ford Motor Company, which included Fair Lane, the home of Henry Ford, for an upper-division and master's-level campus. In 1957 the Dearborn Center of the University of Michigan opened with co-operative work-study degree programs in engineering and business administration. Despite its name change from "Center" to "Campus" in 1963, the expectation of drawing on community college graduates did not materialize. By 1970 the enrollment was still under 1,000 students.

The Regents had the choice of abandoning the Flint and Dearborn campuses as having out-lived their original purpose of relieving pressure on the Ann Arbor campus during the height of the baby boom, or securing the resources and making the commitment to upgrade Flint and Dearborn to viable four-year institutions with graduate programs. With assistance from the Mott and Ford Foundations and support from the Michigan legislature, although not with the blessing of the State Board of Education, Fleming and the Regents chose commitment. 1971 was the watershed year for both campuses. The University of Michigan-Flint and the University of Michigan-Dearborn were created as four-year colleges. Chancellors were appointed, and each campus had a full administrative structure, increased autonomy, and fiscal support.

UNIVERSITY OF MICHIGAN-FLINT, CROB BUILDING

William E. Moran was appointed the first Chancellor of the University of Michigan-Flint in July, 1971. In an agreement reminiscent of that of the Ann Arbor Land Company, which gave the original 40 acres of land for the University in Ann Arbor, the Mott Foundation agreed to purchase 40 acres of land along the Flint River for a new campus. The move could not come soon enough as enrollment rapidly increased. By 1975 a campus of 3,500 students was overflowing the old Curtice Building into temporary outdoor modules. CROB, the first classroom/office building on the new riverfront campus, opened in 1977 with the library on the 5th floor. The campus and its curriculum grew rapidly. In 1977 the first graduate degree program,the Master of Liberal Studies Program, was offered through Rackham. Chancellor Moran resigned in 1979 and was succeeded by Acting Chancellor William W. Vasse. The Harding Mott University Center opened the same year and enrollment went over 4,000 students. Conny E. Nelson was named UM- Flint's second Chancellor in 1980.

UNIVERSITY OF MICHIGAN-DEARBORN LIBRARY

In 1971 the University of Michigan-Dearborn also became a four-year undergraduate institution but with a continued commitment to its master's-level graduate programs. Leonard E. Goodall became the first Chancellor. UofM-Dearborn grew rapidly from under 1,000 students in 1970 to over 6,000 in 1979. As at Flint, the Dearborn administration scrambled to accommodate this soaring student population. Afternoon and evening course offerings, internship and individualized learning programs were all expanded. New buildings, including the Library, the Fieldhouse and University Mall, were constructed south of the original four buildings. By 1977 the renovation of Fair Lane and a conference center were planned. There would be a price to pay for such rapid expansion, however. When William Jenkins became the second Chancellor in 1980, he acquired a debt burden that would coincide with another state recession and cuts in state aid to the campus. The set-backs were only temporary, however, as University of Michigan-Flint and University of Michigan-Dearborn flourished, providing increased access to the University in two additional urban settings.

The issue of access was important in another major initiative of the 1970s, the upgrading of recreational facilities for use by the entire University community. Recreational and intramural club sports were separated from Physical Education in 1974, and plans were made to add the first recreational buildings in 50 years. When it was apparent that no money would be forthcoming externally for new recreational facilities, creative financing was employed. Funds were borrowed internally, which would be paid back from user fees. Opposition to this scheme was expected, but when a university-wide meeting was held in the Union only six students showed up, and they were all in favor of it. People wanted new recreational facilities and were willing to pay to use them.

In 1976 the University opened its two new recreation facilities. The Central Campus Recreation Building (CCRB) was built adjacent to Margaret Bell Pool and conveniently accessible from the overpass that now connected the hill dorms with the Diag. North Campus Recreation Building (NCRB) provided the first recreation building and pool for the University community living and working on North Campus. Unlike the old rules that once governed the Intramural Sports Building, the passage of Title IX in 1975 assured that these facilities would be open on an equal basis to women and men, although no one by this date intended otherwise.

Growth continued on the athletic campus as well, signaled by removal of the old Ferry Field Bleachers in 1969. A Sports Service Building for football was built in 1971 and the Track and Tennis Building in 1973. When basketball moved to Crisler, Yost Arena was renovated for ice hockey. When hockey moved out of the Coliseum, that facility was refurbished as an additional intramural and recreational facility. There is little doubt that Athletic Director Don Canham will be remembered as the Athletic Director who hired "Bo" and introduced Astro Turf to Michigan Stadium. However, it was his support for first-rate recreational facilities that may have had the greater impact on campus life.

If one were observant, signs of growth and change were evident on campus even as maintenance was often delayed. A small Dance Building appeared in 1977. The University continued its relentless expansion throughout Ann Arbor with the purchase of 24 acres of land, most in house lot-sized parcels, and the removal of several dozen older homes and other structures. The building of three new parking structures and an addition on a fourth reflected several trends: the growth of Ann Arbor, the increase in staff, and soaring real estate prices; people were living increasingly further from campus and had to drive. Two more sections were added to Northwood Housing to accommodate the increase in married graduate students. When the Historical Society of Michigan was granted use of the historic Tuomy Property at 2117 Washtenaw for its state headquarters, it was a victory for preservation. When the Regents ordered in 1977 that the Barbour Waterman Gymnasiums be torn down, despite vocal campus protest, it was a defeat for preservation and for nostalgia.

The leadership of the Computing Center and computer science faculty in making computer services available to the entire academic community came to fruition in 1971 with the opening of the Computing Center Building. Since the purchase of the IBM 704 mainframe in 1959, the University of Michigan Computing Center had been one of the most active in the country. Co-operative work with IBM to produce a computer with virtual storage in the 1960s had resulted in production by IBM and purchase by the University of the 360/67. This new mainframe made it possible to introduce MTS (Michigan Terminal System) in 1968. MTS was a unique operating system at the time and made it possible for hundreds of users to access the computer simultaneously from remote stations around campus. With MTS the University of Michigan set the standard among universities for computer access and would serve as a model throughout the decade for future development of remote user systems on university campuses. The three-story Computing Center Building on North Campus was testimony to the state of computer technology in 1971. It was designed with no interior supports or columns, and stairs ran around the perimeter of the building. This reflected the belief that computers would continue to expand physically without limits. Although the size of mainframe computers began to stabilize around this time, the advanced computer chip with its enormous storage capability, which made possible the personal computer, was still several years in the future.

Unlike most universities of the era at which computers served the needs of the computing science department and administration, the guiding philosophy of the University of Michigan Computing Center was open access by the widest possible user base. This philosophy of open access was not as pervasive outside the realm of computers, however, and the 1970s proved to be a difficult decade as would-be "users" of the University demanded inclusion.

4. Access and values

The politics of dissent was symptomatic of a larger movement to reform American institutions more generally, including universities. Throughout the 1970s, efforts at reform thus spread throughout the University with changes sought in the limited access under-represented groups had to its academic community, the way business was done, and the goals of research.

Access to the University by under-represented minority groups was obviously the central concern that sparked the Black Action Movement (BAM I) strike in 1970 and BAM II in 1975. Although the Fleming administration had bargained in good faith during BAM I to work toward the goal of 10% African-American enrollment by 1973, that goal was not reached. African-American enrollment peaked in 1973 at 7.3% and then declined. Although the University did not meet its enrollment goals, other steps were taken to improve the environment for African-Americans on campus. Financial support was given to the Center for Afro-American Studies, which dates from 1970. Henry Johnson became Vice President for Student Services, the first African-American appointed as a vice-president in University of Michigan administration. Cultural lounges were approved by the Regents to expose students to different cultures. The Black Women's Caucus in Stockwell established the first cultural lounge, the Rosa Parks Lounge; Rosa Parks attended the formal opening. Project Awareness began in the dormitories to help co-ordinate programs and activities that ranged from racial sensitivity training sessions to cultural nights and programs on race awareness. A national precedent was set when the William Monroe Trotter House, a center for supportive services for minority students, opened in October 1972.

The concerns of other groups were raised and addressed in different ways. Native Americans were troubled by the University owned ancestoral skeleton on display at the Fort Wayne Military Museum in Detroit. Deeply resenting the treatment of the skeleton as an "artifact," they petitioned the Regents for its return for burial. The Regents agreed to give the skeleton to the Commission on Indian Affairs for proper burial. More courses on Native Americans also began to enter the curriculum at this time. Students with physical handicaps wanted the University to recognize their problems, and again the University responded, this time by securing a federal grant to implement a series of building renovations to eliminate architectural barriers to the handicapped, making buildings wheelchair accessible and bringing the University up to newly established state and local building codes for accessibility. Students of the Third World Coalition pressed goals similar to those of the Black Action Movement: financial aid, support services, and enrollment increases. With total minority enrollment dipping below the 10% mark, statistics confirmed the perception that minority students still felt on the outside of the mainstream university, looking in.

For women, numerically the largest under-represented group on campus, the doors began to open slowly in 1969 after a complaint was filed with the U.S. Department of Health, Education and Welfare (HEW) charging the University with discrimination against women. Although it had been 80 years since the Board of Regents had voted to end discrimination in hiring on the basis of sex, only 11% of the faculty and 5% of full professors were women. Faculty hiring was still done largely through the "old boy" network, and that network included few women or minorities.

In order to respond to the complaint, HEW needed information on the University's employment of women—information that at the time did not exist. It therefore had to be collected. The pioneering work of compiling employment data on women was done by PROBE (Probing the University), a group of women volunteers from every unit on campus. Their effort took courage and commitment. While PROBE had the support of the Fleming administration, some women found themselves facing angry supervisors when their participation in PROBE became known. Their findings, published in "Probe '70," left little doubt that there were inequities: the mean for women's salaries was lower than men's in every instructional department; 81% of women were in the bottom of their pay or salary classifications as opposed to 38% of men. This and other reports confirmed and gave statistical verification to the *status quo* of University life: chronic underutilization of women except in traditional female job groups, such as secretarial and clerical, coupled with discourage-ment of women at the graduate level in certain fields, driving an unending circle of hiring men for faculty positions because few women were avail-able. HEW ordered the University to develop an affirmative action program (AAP) to meet the federal guidelines for the employment of women and minorities.

Between 1971 and 1975 a variety of initiatives were undertaken to comply with the HEW directives. In 1971 the Center For Women (CFW) was established as a mechanism to inquire more deeply into the condition of women on campus. A Director of Affirmative Action Programs was hired to centralize initiatives on minorities and women and to draw up the affirmative action plan. A Commission on Minority Groups worked to assure racial equity in the AAP. The Director of AAP noted that it was necessary to take steps to "shake the procedures" as discrimination was endemic.

Fundamental steps were taken to redress discrimination in hiring and promotion. All available positions were required to be advertised. The Office of Professional and Administrative Staff Services was created in 1972 to oversee development of a new classification system that enabled the University to implement a uniform salary program and classification system for all professional and administrative staff. Once adopted, an equal pay review resulted in 118 upgrades, most of them for women. In 1974 a classification system for the growing primary research staff was established with two career ladders, one for primary research positions comparable to the instructional staff and one for supporting research staff. A new appeals procedure was introduced to handle discrimination claims, which led to salary adjustments for another 100 instructional, professional, and admin-istrative women. Instructional departments had to establish affirmative action goals and procedures for meeting them. Internships to promote recruiting minorities and women in primary research were instituted, and the Alumnae Council began a popular internship program to prepare women for administrative posts.

One of the first universities to come under a compliance review, the University of Michigan was also one of the few universities by 1976 to have an approved, five-year affirmative action plan. By the end of the decade substantial improvement had been made in non-instructional areas; however,

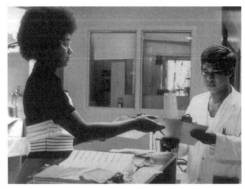

FROM "WOMEN'S INFORMATION NETWORK BULLETIN"

women and minorities made few gains in the instructional and administration ranks. At the end of the decade, of 434 administrative posts, 14% were held by women and 6% by minorities. The comparable figures for faculty were 17% women and 5% minorities. At the full professor rank, the increase for women had been negligible. While the more virulent forms of discrimination were gone, it was clear that full equality of opportunity and equal access to employment did not yet exist.

Women students fared better than women faculty, due primarily to the civil rights initiatives of the early 1970s, particularly in the area of women's athletics. In 1970 there were no women's varsity teams at the University, only clubs. This reflected both cultural attitudes over the preceding decades as well as a reluctance to share resources and sports facilities with women athletes. Title IX of the 1972 Education Amendments sought to correct on a national level this wide-spread imbalance by banning sex bias in any federally aided education program or activity. Title IX ushered in a new era in UofM women's athletics. In 1973 the University joined the Association for Intercollegiate Athletics for Women (AIAW) and fielded women's teams in volleyball, field hockey, swimming and tennis. An associate director of athletics responsible for women's sports was appointed in 1974, and all athletic facilities were opened to both men and women in September 1975. The first athletic scholarships for women were awarded in 1976 in what were by then seven varsity sports. Salary adjustments were made to provide equity between coaches of men's and women's varsity teams. Although Title IX regulations would be resisted, equal opportunity to participate, if not equal aggregate expenditures for male and female athletes, had begun.

As a result of these and other initiatives, all-male bastions began to fall throughout the University. In 1972 women students became eligible for membership in the Michigan Union on the same basis as men students. The Science Research Club, founded in 1902, voted to admit women, acknowledging that there was no longer a place for gender separation in academic and intellectual life on the campus. In 1972, the Marching Men of Michigan became the University of Michigan Marching Band. In the fall of 1974, the 94-year-old tradition of solely male cheerleaders at football games ended.

With the drive for access and greater diversity came questioning about the fundamental purpose of the University and the constituencies it served. The most obvious target for such questioning during the height of the war in Vietnam was the University's involvement in secret military research, most of which was conducted at the Willow Run laboratories. In October 1967, several hundred students occupied the Administration Building protesting the University's involvment in a Department of Defense project that helped the Royal Thai Armed Forces set up a full-scale military reconaissance system. The following year, the Research Policies Committee (RPC) took up the issue of secret research, eventually recommending that the University significantly limit the types of classified research contracts it accepted and refuse to accept "any classified research contract the specific purpose of which is to destroy human life or to incapacitate human beings."

The so-called "end use" clause and other provisions recommended by RPC were endorsed by Senate Assembly and the Regents the same year and incorporated into Regental policy in 1972 and 1976. In June 1972 the Regents also voted to divest the Willow Run Laboratories, which included the Infra-red Physics Laboratory and Institute for Defense Analysis, giving the entire facility to an independent, not-for-profit corporation later named the Environmental Research Institute of Michigan (ERIM). With the divestiture of Willow Run, the University's already shrinking classified research base dropped from 31 to 16 projects, reducing the University's research on such projects to less than 2% of its total research base. The following September, a Classified Research Panel made up of two faculty and one student was established to ensure the University's compliance with its new policies. Later, an independent board of trustees was established to supervise the Institute for Science and Technology (IST) on North Campus, where some classified research was also conducted.

The disenchantment with military research in the late 1960s and early 1970s, following the more pervasive attitudes of the Vietnam War era, was accompanied by an increased commitment to research that was seen as directly beneficial to society and addressed concerns about pollution, energy consumption, and a weak social infrastructure. A longitudinal study of the Huron River was begun that would become the longest running study of any river in the country. Faculty conducted research into drug abuse, desegregation training of school staff members, and urbanization and its effects on the family. Noted Fleming, "Whether we are talking of urban blight, environmental pollution, population control, resource allocation and conservation, mental health—name it—somewhere in the University of Michigan, someone is involved in the issue. Our task is to make that involvement as meaningful and beneficial to man and society as we can. We can do no more. Our purpose is to do no less."

From research, the concern with social issues spilled over into intellectual life more broadly, eventually having a significant impact on the curriculum as well. During the 1971-72 academic year, a "New Science Group" formed to coordinate the "long-standing concern on the Ann Arbor campus with urgent global problems such as population, environment, resources, and world order." A year later, the members of the group organized a conference on "Science, Technology, and Future Societies" and also published a list of 38 courses that dealt with human values, alternative social structures, the evaluation and control of technology, or the future more generally. Interestingly, the new social consciousness was not limited to campus; in 1972, University of Michigan faculty were serving as mayors in Ann Arbor and Ypsilanti, and as president of the Chelsea Village Council.

These efforts received an unexpected boost in October 1973 when Fleming discussed the importance of values in his annual State of the University address. A few months before, the University's Committee for Religious Affairs (CRA) had come to the conclusion that more emphasis needed to be placed on values in university education. Fleming's speech provided an opportunity to launch a major initiative. By February 1974, CRA had begun talking with Fleming about a values program. A few months later, $15,000 in support had been promised, which made it possible to designate 1974-75 the "University Values Year." Its purpose was to engage the entire community in a discussion of the consequences of the University's various efforts in research, teaching, and service, focusing particularly on issues relating to values and social impact.

As the University Values Year was beginning, a particularly difficult question relating to research emerged. A few years earlier, biomedical researchers had discovered how to engineer the basic blocks of life using recombinant DNA technology. Whether they could use this new technology safely was not yet known, a situtation that prompted microbiologists nationwide to adopt a rare, self-imposed moratorium on some types of research pending further study and the development of national guidelines. Michigan at the time had several researchers on its faculty who were familiar with the new technology and prepared to assume a leadership role in this important new area of research. However, before doing so, they asked Vice President for Research Charles Overberger to provide guidance on developing a university-wide policy to regulate recombinant DNA research. Overberger appointed a Committee on Microbiological Research Hazards in December 1974 to undertake this task. The Committee's report, submitted in April 1975, recommended that the University move quickly forward in this area, once it had constructed three specially designed laboratories to ensure safety and set up a new committee to monitor compliance with federal guidelines that were about to be issued.

At any other time in the University's history, the recommendations of the Microbiological Research Hazards committee would probably have been accepted without much discussion, allowing the researchers to go back to their laboratories to press on with work that unquestionably promised significant benefits. In 1975 and during a time when values and social consequences were on many minds, the report of a single committee was not sufficient. On the recommendation of the University's Biomedical Research Council, three additional committees were formed. Committee A looked at ways to improve the safety of the research and laboratories. Committee B discussed the social, political, and ethical implications of recombining genetic materials. Committee C, which was to be formed after Committees A and B had done their work, would serve as the permanent oversight body to ensure that if recombinant DNA research continued, it complied with the various rules and regulations that were in the process of being developed.

With this additional review process in place, the University embarked on a year of lectures, meetings, animated discussions, protests, and demonstrations in an effort to reach a consensus on a responsible policy toward the new research technology. Vice President Overberger engaged experts to talk with the Regents in meetings open to the public. The Ann Arbor City Council engaged in its own fact-finding, as did governing bodies in other university towns, such as Cambridge, Massachusetts. DNA, with its vast potential for good or evil, was a political as well as intellectual concern.

After all was said and done, the final policy adopted by the Regents in May 1976 differed little from the recommendations set out in the April 1975 report of the Committee on Microbiological Research Hazards. The University would go ahead with recombinant DNA research as long as it was "submitted to appropriate controls." Not everyone agreed with this decision, and efforts continued to end research that some believed delved into knowledge that humans were unprepared to use wisely. Many more felt that the University had at least made a good faith effort to act responsibly rather than rushing ahead without a community-wide debate. For the younger researchers whose careers depended on keeping up with a field in which the rate of change was measured in weeks or even days, a year was too long to wait. Several left for jobs in the new biotech industries that were being formed. Temporary set-back to the University's first initiative in the new field of molecular biology was the trade-off to responsible academic dialogue.

As all-consuming as the debates over classified and recombinant DNA research seemed to be at the time, they had very little effect on the University's total research effort, an effort that grew at a slow but steady pace through the 1970s, despite the economic hard times. In terms of actual dollars, research budgets nearly doubled during the Fleming years; however, adjusted for inflation they grew at less than 2%. Nonetheless, this modest growth was sufficient to keep the University's top-ten national ranking in research.

The lean budget times produced by the ripple effect of the energy crisis did affect research agendas as the 1970s wore on. With the flush days for federal funding coming to an end, the University increasingly looked to joint research ventures with industry, both to supplement its own resources and to help the State grapple with the depression in the auto industry. Topics singled out for further development included automotive research, computer assisted design (CAD) and the computer sciences, energy, image processing, macromolecular and recombinant DNA projects, robotics, and solid state electronics. The shift was particularly important for engineering, which had to redirect its efforts following the divestiture of the Willow Run laboratories and the decline in defense research. Between 1974 and 1979, engineering and social science research increased their share of the University's research budget a little more than one percent each, while the life sciences slipped about four percent to 42.6%—still by far the largest component of the University's research enterprise. Budgets and dollars, however, have never told the full story of the University's strength in research. Left out of these figures are the many scholars at the University who, in Vice President Overberger's words, need only "some books, manuscripts, perhaps a typewriter or a yellow legal pad, and a quiet place to exercise the critical intelligence or to follow the trained imagination." From time to time it may have been difficult to find quiet spots on campus in the 1970s, but critical intelligence and trained imaginations remained alive and well nonetheless.

5. *The experience*

The later 1960s produced the most distinct youth culture in collegiate history. It was anti-elitest, anti-establishment, and rejected the perceived materialism of its parents—except, perhaps, for guitars and stereos. Not everyone bought into the drug culture or Zen, but faded jeans (with bell bottoms after 1970), mini-skirts, long hair, and earth tones were the norm. The label "Hippie" stuck and was worn proundly, setting a generation apart from its elders. The changes wrought by rock music, political activisim, and co-ed dorms spelled the demise of "Joe College," the collegiate culture that had emerged in the later nineteenth century and

continued well into the
1960s. In an era of sit-ins,
rallies, and rock concerts,
campus traditions seemed
irrelevant—an establish-
ment legacy and thus re-
jected. When the era ended,
J-Hop, freshman hazing,
class plays, Cap Night, and
Saturday night dances at the
Union were gone. Like
single-sex dormitories, most
students in 1979 did not
know they had ever existed.

DIAG, MID-1970s

However, it was a long way from 1968 to 1979, from full employment
to 300 applications for every good job, from Underground Film 309 to cram
courses for the LSAT, GRE, and MCAT. Between these two collegiate
generations, the United States exited Vietnam, Watergate occurred, Student Affairs got out of students' lives, a code of conduct had been drawn up,
if not yet implemented, and a shrinking job market awaited graduates.
While students of 1968, like all students, thought their time and culture
would last forever, by the end of the decade ROTC enlistments were
picking up, and the Greek system had revived. The 60s, like Vietnam,
were history.

The Greek System was not a casualty of the 1960s, but it fell on very
hard times, endeavoring again to justify its existence as in the pre-Tappan
days. Students turned from it as too elitest and too social for a serious age.
In 1960, fraternities and sororities housed 12% of the student body. By
1973 it was 4.7%, with the largest drop occurring between 1968 and 1970.
15 fraternities and 5 sororities closed, some not to reopen. To keep large
houses operating in a time of declining enrollment, different houses tried
various routes to solvency. They took in boarders, went co-ed, co-opted the
prevailing drug culture, and sought help from their national organizations,
which pulled several of them through the lean years, on this campus and
elsewhere. Co-ops, however, resurged in popularity. Some students
thought they had started the co-op movement, which would have amused
the founders of the 1930s.

The cultural extremists of the time wanted a complete revolution in
American culture, with an emphasis on everything for everyone. The
principle counter-culture commune in Ann Arbor was the Trans-Love
Energies Tribe, housed on Hill St. and presided over by John Sinclair, UM-
Flint '64, a musical entrepreneur and publisher of a widely read alternative
newspaper of the day, *The Sun*. At attempt by the Trans-Love Tribe, the

White Panther Party, and the numerous hangers-on of the counter-culture in Ann Arbor to create a pedestrian mall on South U.—everyone get together—led to a nasty clash with the county sheriff's department in June 1969. President Fleming persuaded students to stay out of it, and most did. He opened his house as a refuge from the tear gas when the melee started.

Sinclair was sent to prison for possession of two marijuana cigarettes the next month, the government thinking he would be less trouble there. He used the time to lead a successful appeal against Michigan's harsh marijuana laws, which led to the decriminalization of marijuana, which in turn set the stage for the Ann Arbor $5.00 pot law--the most liberal in the nation--and the annual Hash Bash, a rite of spring on the Diag that quickly failed to endear itself to the Administration. The efforts to free Sinclair from prison led to the "Free John Sinclair Concert" in Crisler, the most memorable rock concert in Ann Arbor during these years, headlined by John Lennon, Yoko Ono, and Stevie Wonder. Sinclair was released three days later; he was clearly less trouble out of jail than in.

1970 was something of a turning point in the nature of student concerns. It was not that Vietnam, military recruiting, and the establishment went away or that students lost interest in national politics; they didn't. However, other threats were looming, and students added these to their agenda of problems that needed solutions. The nation's first Earth Day conference, sponsored by a new group on campus ENACT (Environmental Action for Survival), was held on March 12-15, 1970. Four days of workshops, films, and clean-up drives were held to heighten public awareness of environmental deterioration. To attract media attention, a gas-guzzling 1959 Ford Sedan was "hacked to death" on the Diag and thousands of non-returnable Coke bottles were dumped on the lawn of the Coca-Cola bottling plant. Wide press coverage carried this new message across the country adding Earth Day to the Teach-In as a UofM contribution to peaceful dissent.

The environmental movement spread quickly, and students were deeply involved. The Ann Arbor Ecology Center was founded and became one of the largest and most active in the country. The movement for a bottle bill requiring a 10 cent refundable deposit on soft drinks and beer cans became law in 1976. (The state estimated the bill reduced litter by 50%.) Bike

ADVERTISEMENT FOR A FOOD CO-OP

paths were laid out all around Ann Arbor; bike-a-thons became popular. The movement to protect endangered species of wildlife and concern with the number of species becoming extinct dates to this time. University activists joined in the campaigns to stop the use of alligator and crocodile skins and coats made of wild animal furs. Students began voluntarily contributing to PIRGIM through their tuition bills to protect the environment in Michigan.

Students became concerned about the food the nation ate—highly processed and sold in corporate super markets. How food was produced, harvested, and packaged led to boycotts of food products such as grapes and lettuce and even of super markets themselves—residence halls stopped buying lettuce unless it was either Michigan grown or United Farm Worker picked and met specific quality tests. Concern over additives, preservatives, coloring, and pesticides led to the formation of the Ann Arbor Food Co-op; other co-ops would follow. Stone ground bread flour, beans in bulk, organic, natural foods were in; processed food was out. The Community Organic Garden opened as a co-operative effort on North Campus to encourage people to practise back-yard ecology, skills a nation settled by farmers had lost. SGC voted down by one vote a proposal for a dope co-op: Buy in quantity; distribute free.

Disillusionment with national government, the assassinations of King and Kennedy, the de-escalating but continuing war , and the failure to achieve their political goals in 1968 all contributed to the reasoned conclusion that change has to begin in one's own community. A new political party was founded by students in Ann Arbor, the Human Rights Party (HRP). Two members of the HRP, committed to a variety of social reforms, were successfully elected to the Ann Arbor City Council in 1972. The line in one student polling area grew to over 700. A socially-conscious generation turned from picketing to voting, at least until the secret bombing of Cambodia and the Watergate scandal brought a return of disillusionment and a resurgence of individualism.

Social problems became more evident as the 1970s wore on, and the campus addressed them. Project Community, founded in 1962, grew to encompass a dozen major projects funded by the university to deal primarily with the community. They included a mental health halfway house, a day care project, and summer programs for children that provided free breakfasts. A campus branch of the Washtenaw Legal Aid Clinic helped clients with community problems. Students volunteered for Ozone House, an umbrella organization that offered help, a shelter, medical care, or drug help, free of charge, to the young transients and others who fell between the cracks in the existing health-care system. The Free People's Clinic provided walk-in health service, and Drug Help operated 24-hours a day.

Drugs were an accepted part of campus life, at least by most students. A University survey in 1968 indicated that 90% used alcohol and nearly 50% had smoked marijuana at least once. Although the use of hard drugs was slight on campus, young people who became hooked on drugs

TENANTS UNION SUCCESS STORY

were vulnerable to bad drugs and overdoses. Pharmacy undergraduates undertook a study of street drugs purchased in Ann Arbor, discovering only 16 of 55 drug samples purchased by students contained any amount of the substance they were supposed to contain. Marijuana use declined over the decade; however, abuse of alcohol continued to be a serious problem.

Acting Vice President for Student Services Barbara Newell (1968-1970), followed by Vice President Robert L. Knauss (1970-1972) had the responsibility of taking the University through the greatest change in student life since Tappan sent the boys off campus to live. In 1966 the first director of housing had been appointed, and 50 years of accummulated rules and regulations were dismantled. In 1967 hours for junior women were eliminated. In the tumultuous year of 1968, hours were eliminated for all other women students, first on an experimental basis and then permanently. Gone were the sign-out box and the race to get home by curfew. The live-in requirement was also eliminated in 1968 for students beyond their freshman year, despite fears that the the new Bursley and Baits dorms with 2,400 rooms would not fill. In 1968 Mosher-Jordan became the first truly co-ed dorm, followed by East Quad when it was remodeled to house the Residential College. West Quad went co-ed in 1970; all but Stockwell followed. The Regents insisted on keeping one all-female dorm, and Stockwell was chosen. It was immediately labeled the "Virgin Vault".

The fears of unfilled rooms lasted for a year. In the fall of 1969 dormitories were over-crowded with students living in temporary quarters in dining halls, linen rooms, and the janitors' workrooms. When the housing lottery replaced forced live-in in 1971, demand outstripped the number of rooms available, forcing students to look for rooms in the increasingly competitive Ann Arbor housing market and supplying a growing pool for members of the Ann Arbor Tenants Union. In 1972 there was at least one instance of desperate students breaking in and taking up residence in a vacant house when the landlady would not rent it to them. Now that there was little difference between dorm rooms and singles apartments, dormitory rooms became desirable. WCBN helped fill the vacuum created by diminishing paternalism when it became WCBN-FM in 1972, covering a two-mile radius of campus.

Students pressed for changes in the curriculum; faculty wanted to see graduation requirements updated. Graduation requirements were upgraded by reducing the number of transfer credits allowed from another institution and requiring 1/2 the credit hours toward a degree be taken in the last two years of study. Faculty agreed that it was time to make the curriculum more relevant. One vestige of paternalism in the curriculum was rooted out early--the physical education requirement for graduation was eliminated. Although the LSA faculty refused to drop the language requirement for the liberal arts degree, the Regents did add the Bachelor in General Studies degree in 1969—no language or concentration requirements. Advanced placement credit was accepted, up to 60 hours worth, and the number of hours for a concentration requirement were liberalized to a more flexible 24-48. Distribution credits were introduced by the requirement that at least 1/4 of the credit hours of work required for the degree be taken outside a student's field of concentration. For a few years an underground university flourished; students and faculty taught courses not offered in the regular LSA curriculum. The Pilot Program, Honors Program, and the Residential College were all popular alternatives to the traditional LSA curriculum. The Inteflex Program began in 1972 to shorten the time to an M.D. degree and to bring the benefits of the liberal arts degree more directly into medical training. In 1978 Chemistry began experimenting with TVs in the classroom to cut down on laboratory equipment and supplies. Students could not yet envision what computers would do to their lives.

Student demands for change in their relationship to the University were set against the problems these changes presented. Rights v.s. responsibilities were worked out. In 1970 the first version of a Code on University Conduct was drafted; there had been nothing quite like it before. The Code laid out the rules for living in the emerging non-paternalistic University. Over the next two years the Code was thrashed out and revised. The free speech aspect proved troublesome to resolve. We were still grappling with it in 1977, a legacy of the 1975 Honors Convocation at which non-University protestors shouted down the President of Israel. (They then left quietly.) When the first Code proved unworkable, a new Code was drafted, which students on the committee continued to veto for the rest of the decade. New rules were set on building use and rental as a result of what the administration called "massive violations of the law," particularly the smoking of marijuana at concerts and other events. A new judicial plan eliminated the old arbitrary system of justice under which the accused had few rights, although faculty and regental control were preserved. Public safety was a growing problem in this era of rapid social change. The Arboretum closed at night and motor vehicles were prohibited. Arson, theft, and vandalism all increased, reflecting national college trends. The University opted to maintain its relationship with the Ann Arbor police rather than establish its own police department, as many another university was doing. In 1976 Nite Owl bus service began as did security patrols in response to increased attacks on women. The campus, mirroring the city and nation as a whole, was becoming a less-safe place to be.

The end of the war, the aftermath of Watergate, increased crime in the dormitories and on campus, and worry about the job market all contributed to a difference in tone as the decade moved on. Activism did

PROFESSOR FORD, '35

not die but the focus changed. Racism, sexism and discrimination in the work place were of increasing concern to students whose consciousness had been raised on these issues and who knew there were fewer jobs waiting for them when they graduated. When his term was complete, President Gerald Ford '35 returned to teach a political science course to a generation more eager to work within the system than to fight it.

More traditional forms of campus life increased in popularity. After a decade of decline, students began the return to fraternities and sororities. The high cost of off-campus housing and dissatisfaction with the dormitories were cited as reasons. Some realized that in the heady days of student activism and rejection of tradition, the mechanisms of social life had been sacrificed and not a great deal that was permanent had replaced them. The Greek System had always offered an active social life and instant circle of friends, for which many students were now grateful. With Coach Bo Schembechler, football revived after the 1960s slump, and students helped fill Michigan Stadium with its bright green Astro-Turf. By 1979, Bo's teams had gone to the Rose Bowl twice. Michigan continued its tradition of having won more titles in more sports than any Big Ten school, and now women's teams were adding to the record count.

By the nation's Bicentennial in 1976, the anguish of the War and the exhilaration of challenging the system were passed. The system, after all, had responded, somewhat--18 year olds could vote; the draft had ended; Student Affairs was not there to organize your life for you, and a loyal alum

MOVING IN

was in the White House. Student interest in running the University had so declined that it was often difficult to fill the student slots on committees and boards their recent predecessors had worked so hard to infiltrate. By becoming a part of the system, the mystery had been taken out of it; long meetings could be very boring. MSA, having replaced the radical SGC as a more representative form of student government, was trying to improve voter turn out at its elections. The tone at mid-decade was decidedly more mellow. By the end of the decade, however, the stress and pressure relentlessly increased as the dislocation brought on by the post-industrial economy continued and the State scrambled to readjust. Competition from one's peers increased. The 80s loomed.

A President chosen to steer the University through a stressful era felt it was time to move on. Fleming always maintained that university presidents are not all that important. They are there to keep things running smoothly. Those who lived through that decade knew better. While other presidents floundered and many failed, the University of Michigan successfully weathered a painful period of transition. The University understood how important was presidential leadership and the calm under pressure that both Sally and Bob Fleming brought to a troubled campus. When Fleming bid farewell to the LSA faculty, the faculty applauded "and refused to stop," as one professor remembers it. There was well deserved praise from the Board of Regents. Perhaps it was the words of one Regent that best expressed the feelings of a grateful campus: "We shall be forever in your debt." The University had emerged from the period of unrest with no painful scars and from the years of economic retrenchment trimmer but with excellence maintained.

THE ART OF COMMUNICATION

CAMPUS, 1978

CHAPTER FIFTEEN

OPPORTUNITY FROM ADVERSITY

THE TRANSITION FROM THE 1970s to the 1980s—from the years of activism to the years of professionalism—was not punctuated by any single event. Many problems of the 1970s—declining State support, inflation, increasing government regulation, greater competition, more demands, and so on—only intensified in the 1980s. In addition, the roots of some of the major developments of the 1980s penetrated deeply into the 1970s or even the 1960s, in the case of the new University Hospital, which opened in 1986. The

HAROLD T. SHAPIRO

modern research university is a large, complex institution—by some accounts *the* most complex institution in the modern world. It is also an institution firmly grounded on tradition and therefore difficult to change. The 1980s did not dawn over night, as the sun set on the 1970s. "Yuppies" did not suddenly replace "hippies." Nonetheless, as the decade of the 1980s came to a close, the outline for a "new" University of Michigan once again was taking shape.

The new university of the 1980s, which became the university for the twenty-first century by the 1990s, outwardly looked much like the university of old. Teaching, research, and service still vied with one another for attention. Undergraduates, graduate and professional students enrolled in classes, demonstrated, and socialized on their way to becoming alumni and citizens of the world. New buildings replaced old or filled vacant spaces on an increasingly crowded campus. Within, however, a significant transformation was underway.

By the 1980s, the bedrock of public state support on which the institution of the nineteenth and early twentieth century had been built was no longer strong enough to support even the instructional component of the University. Federal funding also continued to weaken in the 1980s, as society turned its attention to mounting social and economic priorities. Being a "public university" could no longer be synonymous with being supported primarily by the public and therefore first and foremost serving the public. Thus, as the University changed leadership in 1979, under the interim presidency of law professor and former Vice President for Academic Affairs (1965-1974) Allan Smith, the search for new directions and a new University of Michigan began to take shape.

1. Transition from the 1970s to the 1980s

The year of Smith's acting presidency evidenced mixed signals for the future. There were signs that the hardest economic times and most vigorous days of student activism were behind. There were also ongoing problems that had yet to be resolved, and there were new problems emerging on the horizon. The country was also about to swing abruptly away from nearly two decades of growth in government programs and center-left politics toward the free-market, hands-off government of Republican President Ronald Reagan.

ALLAN SMITH

Signs of changing student attitudes emerged late in Fleming's presidency. After almost a decade of declining membership, the number of students joining sororities and fraternities rose in 1977-78. Greek Week revived in March 1978. The demand for football tickets increased markedly, making it necessary to institute a new, more restrictive ticket policy a month later. The following year and mirroring a national trend, ROTC units on campus reported increased enrollments. Engineering increased the ROTC credit hours that could be counted toward a degree and LSA reconsidered (but did not ultimately change) some of the limitations it had placed on ROTC courses in the early 1970s. At the same time, support for some organizations popular in the early 1970s began to erode. In January 1979 the Regents voted to lower the required support for PIRGIM (Public Interest Research Group in Michigan) from 33% to 25% of the student body so that it could continue to qualify for a special student assessment.

There were also signs in 1979 of the return of an active building program, after years of little growth in the mid-1970s. Following more than a decade of planning, in January 1979 the Regents approved a slightly scaled down plan for a massive new hospital, at an estimated cost of $254 million, and filed a certificate of need with the regional planning authority. The Replacement Hospital Project, as the new University Hospital was called, became the most ambitious building project ever undertaken at the University. Other projects approved or underway in 1979 included extensive renovations to the Michigan Union; the construction of a new Alumni Building, between Rackham and the Michigan League; and the Gerald Ford Library on North Campus—a privately funded federal building that was part of the National Archives' presidential library system but open to and quickly integrated into the life of the university community.

There were other signs of better economic times in 1979. The belt-tightening measures of the 1970s began to bear fruit by the end of the decade. The Priority Fund and the measures taken to cut energy consumption freed up limited resources for new programs, once inflation was brought under control. Instructional costs were kept in check by more rigorous promotion policies, which reduced the total number of annual promotions from a high of 260 in 1970 to 141 in 1979. (One result was that the number of new assistant professors entering the system declined over 50%, from 48 to 23.) On the development front, Vice President for University Relations and Development Mike Radock reported that the prospects for increased private giving looked good. While not yet a rosy picture, there were reasons to be optimistic during the year of Smith's acting presidency.

There were, of course, ongoing problems that needed to be solved as the 1970s came to a close. Internally, the University's stance on a number of public issues still troubled some members of the university community. South Africa remained a cause for protest that erupted in March 1979—prompting the adjournment of one Regents meeting. The University also continued to grapple with the problem of the graduate student union—GEO. Were GEO members employees, who could negotiate wage contracts, or students? This issue was in arbitration under the Michigan Employment Relations Commission when Smith took office. Moreover, as might be expected, every cutback caused some pain and usually protest, such as when Speech and Journalism were merged in 1979 to form the new Department of Communications, leaving Theatre split for a time between LSA and the School of Music. The disruption of a talk by Yigal Allon, former foreign minister and deputy prime minister of Israel, in Rackham in December 1978 also renewed calls for a better policy on free speech. The rules drawn up in 1975 in response to a similar incident and approved by the Regents in 1977 had not succeeded in finding a way to balance the right to free speech of speakers versus protesters.

Externally, the state and national government continued to exert pressures on the University as the decade of the 1970s came to a close. The State legislature demanded the release of specific information on faculty salaries, a step some felt would demoralize the faculty and complicate hiring. The Native American community's claim for the return of burial remains and relics was expanded in 1978 to a request for free admission for all Native Americans. This issue, too, was before the courts in 1979. The defeat of the Tisch-Headlee amendment in November 1978 did not end tax-cutting initiatives on the state level. New tax-cutting proposals began to surface immediately, with the same implications for the University's general-fund support from the State.

With the future thus uncertain, the Regents stressed leadership, economics, and imagination in their search for a new president and added stability by selecting an internal candidate—only the third in the University's history (fourth if former faculty member Erastus Haven is included). A Canadian by birth, Shapiro came to the University in 1964 after graduate studies at Princeton. He was widely known for his economic forecasts, based on models that grew out of the Research Seminar in Quantitative Economics he co-directed for many years. He served three years as Chair of the Department of Economics in LSA (1974-77) and two years as Vice-President for Academic Affairs (1977-79). In the later position he assumed responsibility for two key areas: budget, which he oversaw as Chair of the Committee on Budget Administration; and the Medical Center, where he served as Vice Chair of the University Hospital Executive Committee. He was thus well qualified and well positioned to take over the administration of a university that was about to construct one of the most expensive hospitals ever built under uncertain economic conditions. His appointment was announced in July 1979. After setting the affairs of the office of the Vice President for Academic Affairs in order, he took a brief, two-month sabbatical prior to assuming the presidency on January 1, 1980 as the University's tenth president.

If there was any hope that the State's financial condition and support for the University might improve as the 1980s rolled in (the *Record* published a short story in January 1980 announcing that the budget picture looked brighter), this hope was quickly dashed a few months

THE CAMPAIGN AGAINST PROPOSAL D'S TAX REDUCTIONS

after Shapiro took office. By March the University community was being warned of impending problems. In June the budget ax once again fell. The State's latest fiscal crisis translated into an immediate $1.8 million reduction for the 1979-80 budget, with warnings of more cuts to come.

Coming as it did on the heels of the cuts and austerity measures adopted in the 1970s, the budget crisis of the early 1980s presented the University with an intractable problem of increasing proportions. The budget shortfall in 1980-81 grew to $3.5 million, in 1981-82 to $12 million. Across-the-board cuts of 3% and 6% respectively were imposed on all general-fund budgets, but even these drastic measures fell $3 million short of the mark in 1981-82. Added to the immediate financial crisis was the painful fact that the days of generous support from the State were long over. In 1981, Michigan's growth rate for support for higher education slipped to 47th among the 50 states; a year later it fell to 50th (measured over two years; 49th if measured over a ten-year period).

The magnitude of the budget crisis of the 1980s decisively and irreversibly set the University on a course it had cautiously been exploring since the beginning of the century when research began to vie with education as the primary mission of the university. The "classic" state university of the nineteenth century received generous public support in return for which it provided broad general service at a reasonable price. Student fees were low and tuition was free well into the twentieth century. The hospital served mainly those who could not afford to pay. Michigan's faculty gave generously of their time in the cause of public service. The only area that depended some on private support was research, which began to build its own support base around the time of World War I and most significantly after World War II.

By the early 1980s, this "classic" image of the public university no longer conformed to reality, especially in Michigan. When Shapiro took office, state support accounted for only about 60% of the University's General Fund and 20% of its total operating budget. By the end of his presidency, state support slipped to below 50% of the General Fund and 15% of the total University budget. In name and through its governance structure, the University was still a "public" university; financially, it was not, although to be sure the State's component of the budget was still vitally important for many activities and especially for instruction. Moreover, since the change was not likely to be reversed anytime in the near future, it could not be ignored. It was against this background that the University under Shapiro rethought its goals and restructured its organization to reflect the social and economic realities of what was increasingly being called "post-industrial" America.

2. Agenda for a smaller university

The years of the Shapiro administration were driven above all else by the pursuit of excellence. As Provost he sent a strong message to this effect when he rejected some of the faculty promotion requests that needed his approval before going to the Regents. In his early talks and interviews as President, Shapiro focused on the need for improvement at all levels, pointing out examples such as the University's weakness in the natural sciences. He stirred discussion in his first talk before Senate Assembly by bringing to the attention of the faculty the less-than-sterling records of 100 marginal students who had recently been granted University of Michigan degrees. He was not content with the *status quo*, but improvement was vitally tied to resources. With State aid declining, the resources for improvement had to be found elsewhere. As in the past, the search for new funds began internally and talk once again turned to reduction, reallocation, and discontinuation.

The task of slimming an already trimmed university produced an uncertain future. The new Vice President for Academic Affair and soon-to-be-named Provost, Billy E. Frye, likened the situation to driving a nail in your foot: "it will hurt, ... but I don't know what that really means until I drive the nail into my foot." He and the rest of the University community soon found out. A few months after he assumed the Presidency, Shapiro began laying out plans for a "better paid, better supported, but smaller staff." The theme of quality over quantity, of "smaller but better," became the guiding principle of the budget reductions of the 1980s. Senate Assembly was briefed on the University's discontinuation policy early in the 1980-81 academic year. In December, the Regents authorized the review of four key support units: the Center for Research on Learning and Teaching (CRLT), Michigan Media, Extension Service, and Recreational Sports. A month later, news broke that LSA was reviewing the Geography Department and the Matthaei Botanical Gardens, with an obvious eye toward reducing budgets. The Center for the Continuing Education of Women, the Institute for Mental Retardation and Related Disabilities, the Phoenix Project, and the Professional Theatre Program were later added to the list of units being reviewed, along with the Schools of Art, Natural Resources, and Education. The University embarked on the road to a smaller, restructured, and hopefully better institution.

The prospect of yet more cuts and downsizing occasioned a great deal of uneasiness in the university community. Senate Assembly endorsed some reductions, provided the faculty was actively involved in all decisions. Others were less certain that reductions could be achieved without seriously damaging affirmative action, diversity, and other essential parts of the University. In an open letter signed by over 90 faculty from 21 programs, colleges, and schools, concern was raised about the possibility that more emphasis on research might adversely affect teaching. These same faculty were also not comfortable with closer ties with industry as a way of raising funds or with the prospect of putting the University financially out of the reach of middle-class students as a result of rising fees and tuition. They wondered, therefore, whether other ways could be found to weather the current budget crisis, such as increasing the enrollment of non-traditional students, borrowing on the University's endowment, or defering salary increases as a way of deficit spending.

The debate over ways to institute or delay the inevitable cuts that had to be made came to an end in April 1981 when plans for the 1981-82 budget were announced. As noted above, $12 million had to be cut to make up for anticipated declines in state support. The proposed budget called for $9 million of this to come from a 6% across-the-board reduction (following the 3% reduction in 1980-81) and $3 million in selective cuts, with the selective cuts coming from administration and programs that were not felt to be central to the academic mission of the University. Under this selective policy, two programs under review were elminated effective the coming academic year—Extension Services and the Institute for Environmental Quality. The former included adult education and credit-by-examination programs, which were said to be "inconsistent with the academic standards and goals of the University."

The other programs targeted for selective cuts included Recreational Sports ($130,000), the Center for Research on Learning and Teaching ($100,000), and Michigan Media ($250,000). Recreational sports compensated for some of its losses with increased user fees. The Center for Research on Learning and Teaching downsized and reorganized. Michigan Media was slowly dismantled, as its services and programs were transferred to other units or phased out. Most of the administrative cuts were implemented as staff reductions in the offices of Student Services, State Relations, and Business Affairs. Printing, Gift Receiving, and the Investment Offices gave up all general-fund support, beginning a trend to make other-than-academic units self-supporting.

With the immediate budget crisis solved, in February 1982 Provost Frye announced a new "Five-Year Plan" that not only balanced budgets but provided funds for building for the future. He proposed to reallocate 7% of the University's General Fund over the next five years. The savings, which amounted to $20 million, were to come from a combination of *smaller variable reductions* (less than 10%) spread across most of the University and *selective major reductions* (over 10%) from a few units targeted for major down-sizing. Reductions in non-instructional costs were emphasized over instructional costs. Frye was concerned that the University not undermine its academic strengths—especially in the "liberal arts," which he noted are "uniquely central to the well-being of the University as a whole." He also stressed the need to maintain "the collegial nature of the University" and the sense of being "engaged in a common endeavor." If the University was to emerge from the down-sizing effort a stronger institution, a sense of collegiality and common purpose had to be maintained.

The Five-Year Plan took effect in the 1982-83 budget year. For the units targeted for smaller variable reductions, it was simply a matter of continuing to chip away. Library Science, for example, saw its faculty numbers reduced by about one quarter between 1980 and 1984 as a result of the initial across-the-board cuts in 1980-81 and 1981-82 and its 9% (just under the 10% dividing line) obligation under the Five-Year Plan. Support staff in Library Science declined 40% during the same period. At the end of 1984, Russell Bidlack, the last of the deans with an open-ended appointment, retired, leaving his successor, Robert Warner, with debts that had to be paid and best wishes for successful negotiations with Central Administration. LSA had already reallocated over 50 positions in 1981-82 as its contribution to the 6% budget reduction that year. It now had to find an additional $200,000-$300,000 a year for five years to meet the goals of the Five-Year Plan. In units targeted for the largest variable cuts, positions became scarce, while vacancies due to retirement and faculty leaving were used to meet obligations to the Five-Year Plan. In this way, small pieces were taken from academic programs all over campus—a historian here, a sociologist there, an expert on libraries, and so on.

The smaller, across-the-board variable reductions produced some major cutbacks of their own as the schools and colleges adopted a strategy similar to the Five-Year Plan. Engineering stopped teaching basic humanities courses and instead required engineering students to take such basic courses in LSA, integrating them more into undergraduate education in general. As a result, the once pioneering Engineering Humanities program was downsized and transformed into the Program in Technical Communication, meeting new needs that had arisen in engineering. LSA as expected phased out the Geography Department, resulting in a very vocal but unsuccessful faculty protest. LSA also agreed to transfer its theatre program to the School of Music. Physical Medicine was eliminated from the Medical School and transferred to Flint. In this way, some larger gaps began to appear in the new, slimmer University.

However, the most significant changes were obviously reserved for the three academic programs—Art, Education, and Natural Resources—designated for selective major reductions (above 10%). Each was reviewed by a special committee, then by the University's Budget Priorities Committee, and finally, if major reductions were called for, by the Executive Officers and the Regents. Along the way, there were opportunities to respond. Hearings were held, demonstrations mounted, writing campaigns organized, as the University searched for ways to achieve major budget reductions.

After eight months of work, the committee reviewing the School of Art recommended 10%-15% cuts. These figures were passed to the Budget Priorities Committee, which increased the recommended cuts to 25%. The larger reduction was vigorously opposed at a public hearing held on North Campus on March 17, 1983 and at a demonstration in front of the

PRO-ART DEMONSTRATION AT THE MUSEUM

Museum of Art. During the demonstration, 25% of the assembled crowd, wearing "art" prominently displayed on dark shirts, were symbolically cut down with a large exacto knife. When the dust settled (and the bodies cleared away), the School of Art implemented a compromise 18% general-fund budget reduction. George Baylis, who was appointed Dean of the School of Art after its separation from Architecture in 1974, set the wheels in motion for the reductions and then took a new position at Temple University. His replacement, Marjorie Levy, a ceramics professor, administrator, and nationally recognized figure in the world of art, took over in August 1985.

The report for the School of Natural Resources when it was made public in January 1983 sketched out a course very similar to the recommendations for the School of Art. Undergraduate enrollments were to be reduced from 650 to 250; some programs, such as Forestry, were to be eliminated because they duplicated programs elsewhere in the State; graduate programs and research were to be strengthened; and the overall size of the School's General Fund was reduced 33%. Shortly after receiving these recommendations, the School's Dean, William Johnson, announced he would take an early sabbatical that filled his last six months in office. The task of implementing the cuts fell to his replacement, James Crowfoot, who was appointed Dean in January 1983.

The committee reviewing the School of Education issued its report in early March 1983. In addition to a 40% cut in the School's general-fund support, the Committee urged more emphasis on graduate education and research, the relocation and downsizing of Physical Education, and the elimination of all undergraduate programs. Dean Joan Stark completed her five-year term in office as these recommendations were being reviewed by the Budget Priorities Committee and the Executive Officers. Their implementation, once they were accepted, was seen through by the new Dean, Carl Berger, working with a transition team. Over the next five years, cuts totaling about $5 million were implemented, within but not following to the letter the review committee's recommendations. Undergraduate teacher training did continue, but more emphasis was placed on centers and interdisciplinary research. The School's administration and academic programs were streamlined considerably, including a reduction of doctoral specializations from 54 to 15 and masters specializations from 63 to 13.

The Five-Year Plan achieved the financial goals Shapiro and Frye had outlined in their agenda for a smaller university. Two years into the five-year reallocation process, Frye reported that the professorial staff of the University had been reduced about 3%, most of whom had been replaced by temporary instructors. Over the same period, the professional and administrative staff had been reduced 6% and the service and maintenance staff 26.5%. At the end of five years, the planned $20 million saving was achieved, at a significant cost in terms of the physical and mental energy that went into the reduction process.

As important as the success of the Five-Year Plan was, its overall impact on the University of the 1980s needs to be kept in perspective. $20 million represented less than 3% of the University's budget (7% of the General Fund), and the lion's share of these funds were reinvested in salaries. All of the $5 million reallocated the first year went to salary increases in an effort to keep up with inflation. (Throughout the 1980s, salaries at the University of Michigan slipped slightly in relation to peer institutions.) The second year's cuts went to salaries, graduate fellowships, instructional equipment, and the Library, with only $500,000 left for new programs. Overall, the Five-Year Plan resulted in a slightly smaller (in some units), better paid staff (better paid than if there had been no reallocations), with the cuts being concentrated in non-instructional areas. It did not produce the resources needed to recover from a decade of deferred maintenance, to initiate major new programs, or to construct the buildings needed to meet the professional and scholarly challenges that were at hand.

The second source of revenues tapped in the 1980s, as it had been in the 1970s—student fees, also failed to do more than compensate for inflation and declining state support. Between 1977-78 and 1987-88, tuition increased fourfold, raising annual tuition revenues from about $50 million to over $200 million. Students were also assessed for improvements in services that specifically benefited them, including the renovations of the Michigan Union and computer support services. Students were clearly being asked to pay for a greater percentage of their education, and did. However, the increase was offset almost completely by inflation and declining state support. Students were, in a word, being asked to pick up the portion of the bill the State could no longer afford to pay; they were not being asked to pay for nor could they afford the hundreds of millions of dollars the University invested in growth over the 1980s. For these funds, which fueled the opening phase of the University's journey toward the twenty-first century, more ambitious plans were needed that reconsidered the foundations of the University's financial support and its definition as a university.

3. "Opportunity from adversity"

The 1980s witnessed a burst in construction and new programs that hearkened back to the Burton building boom and the Hatcher period of expansion. Engineering nearly completed its move to North Campus. The Medical Center was transformed with the addition of the new hospital, new research facilities, and extensive renovations. Business Administration added new library and classroom facilities and its own hotel for executive conferences. A new chemistry building appeared where the Barbour and Waterman gymnasiums once stood. The entire campus was rewired as the University established its own phone company. Whole streets were replaced by flowered malls and campus landscaping in general was gradually but noticeably improved. By the end of Shapiro's administration, the face of the campus did not show the lines of wear brought on by close to two decades of budget crisis. As the University prepared in 1987 to celebrate its 150th anniversary in Ann Arbor, it was looking more and more like an institution gearing up for the twenty-first century and the challenges of the next 150 years.

The magnitude of the University's growth was most apparent on the medical campus and most clearly embodied in the single largest project of the 1980s, the Replacement Hospital Project (RHP). "Old Main," the symbol of growth in the 1920s, began showing obvious signs of age and inadequacy in the mid 1960s. Few doubted that it would one day have to be replaced; however, doing so proved to be a monumental task. Between 1964 and 1974, committees met, studies were published, but no clear plan for action emerged, so in 1975 the University hired a consultant, Dr. Douglas Sarbach, to carry through the planning of a new hospital.

The preferred plan was the construction of a single "replacement" hospital, but there were formidable obstacles that had to be overcome before it could be implemented. The costs were staggering and well beyond the University's ability to pay or raise funds. State aid was essential, at a time when the State and its major industry were in deep recession. The 1966 federal Comprehensive Health Planning and Service Act required public input and both regional and state approval. Seen from the perspective of Southeast Michigan, the need for a new hospital in Ann Arbor was questionable. Michigan had at the time a surplus of around 3,500 beds; the University was asking approval for a hospital complex with over 900 beds. Moreover, Ann Arbor was on the western edge of the Southeast region and the major regional population center—Detroit and its suburbs. The new facility also put strains on Ann Arbor's own resources in terms of roads, traffic, and parking. To sell a project of this magnitude and with as many potential obstacles took a decade of persistent effort by the Regents, three university presidents, their vice presidents, three Medical School deans, two Hospital directors, and a growing RHP staff.

Between 1976, when Sarbach arrived in Ann Arbor, and 1978, the earlier hospital plans were replaced by a new comprehensive plan drafted in final form by Fleming. Estimates of need ranged from about 500 beds to as many as 2,000, costing upwards of $500 million. In 1978, as Fleming was preparing to leave office, the Regents finally approved a proposal for a $254 million, 954-bed hospital complex. Under Smith and Shapiro, this plan was trimmed, modified, contested, threatened with court action, but eventually passed at the regional and state levels. The RHP team finally celebrated success, not at a gala picnic at Gallup Park as originally planned for August 1981, because a threat of court action still loomed, but in October 1981, when the official groundbreaking ceremony was held, complete with a giant RHP cake.

Since the State of Michigan and the University were forbidden to engage in deficit spending, a project of this size required creative financing. The State raised its portion ($173 million) through a combination of bonds issued by the newly created State Building Authority ($140 million) and funds from general revenues ($33 million). The University raised its portion (initially $112 million) through bond sales and gifts. Repayment of these debts came from several sources. The state bonds were to be paid off by a lease agreement between the University and the State Building

Authority, committing the University to $27 million annually for 30 years "to rent" the hospital. (The rent money in turn was covered by an additional annual State appropriation to the University of $27 million.) The University committed operating funds from the new hospital to service its bonds. The stakes were enormous, the risks not inconsequential. Given the financial uncertainties of the day, the University was gambling with its future.

Five years of construction (1981-86) followed the five years of intensive planning (1976-1981), as the RHP slowly rose on its new site, northeast of Old Main. Occasional strikes slowed construction. Parts of the project were trimmed, to lower costs, and then restored. Small and large modifications were made to meet the changing needs of a tertiary care teaching hospital. Two years of construction saw the building framed and topped off in June 1983. Two more years were required to complete and furnish the interior. By late 1985, some of the new facilities were opened for tours. Then on February 14, 1986 (Valentine's Day), moving day arrived. In an action reminiscent of wartime evacuations, 500 patients and 3,000 truckloads of equipment were moved into the new facilities in a single day. The Replacement Hospital sprang to life and the lights in Old Main went out. Three years later Old Main was taken down, not in a massive implosion as had once been contemplated, but brick by brick, making way for the future addition of the new clinical center growing up around the new hospital site.

As important as the construction of the Replacement Hospital was in the revitalization of the Medical Center, its success depended as much on the health-care network that supported it as on the building itself. This network was also revitalized in the 1980s. After earlier unsuccessful attempts, a new and this time successful effort began in 1979 to establish a health maintenance organization (HMO). The following year, one of many new pieces of diagnostic equipment was installed—a $1 million PET scanner. In 1982, a major gift from the Kellogg Foundation made possible the construction of the new, $12 million W. K. Kellogg Eye Center. When the new hospital was finally opened in 1986, it also had greatly expanded out-patient facilities in the A. Alfred Taubman Health Care Center. The University also opened a satellite clinic in Brighton the same year and instituted an emergency medical helicopter service to link the facilities in Ann Arbor with surrounding communities. New parking structures were added and the roads widened to make access to the complex—renamed the "University Hospitals"—more convenient. A new faculty track, called "clinical faculty," was created in 1985 to increase the number of University of Michigan physicians seeing and referring patients to the core tertiary care facilities. When the RHP opened in February 1986, the University had not only one of the most up-to-date hospitals in the world but also an up-to-date, health-care delivery system to support it. It had also created a new position to oversee activities at the Medical Center, the Vice Provost for Medical Affairs, which was filled by the head of surgery at Johns Hopkins and former University of Michigan faculty member, George Zuidema.

The basic medical sciences and clinical research experienced similar growth during the 1980s, spurred by the needs of the new clinical facilities and substantial growth of biomedical research budgets. In June 1982 the Regents gave approval for the design of a new $15.5 million Medical Science Research Building (number one), $14.5 million of which was funded by the Medical School and $1 million from general university funds. One floor was set aside for a new Center for Molecular Genetics, which was approved by the Regents in November of the same year. Two years later the construction of Medical Sciences Research Building II became possible when the Howard Hughes Medical Institute gave $8 million to the University to construct a Hughes Institute on campus, giving an additional boost to research on molecular genetics. The growth of these new programs rested heavily on the strong leadership of the Chair of Internal Medicine, William Kelley. The new hospital and the rapid growth of Michigan's biomedical research program played a major role in the Hughes decision. By 1985, research on the life sciences comprised nearly half (48.8%) of the University's annual research expenditures, up from 43.3% just five years earlier. By the time Shapiro left office in 1987, nearly $400 million had been awarded in building contracts on the Medical Campus, accounting for over half of all of the new building on campus started under his administration.

MEDICAL CAMPUS, 1988

The growth and revitalization of the Medical Campus was part of a general effort under Shapiro to strengthen all of the professional schools, focusing next on Engineering and Business Administration. In 1980, Engineering was still split between Main Campus and North Campus. It was also still adjusting to the divestment of the Willow Run laboratories and the steady decline in defense research on campus that began in the late 1960s. Ironically, the recession of the 1980s brought new opportunities, as politicians and business leaders across the country turned to engineering for solutions to the nation's economic woes. Michigan industry in particular was in dire need of retooling, which the new Dean of Engineering appointed in 1981, James Duderstadt, saw as challenges and opportunities.

First on the agenda was completing the move to North Campus, which had been ongoing for 30 years and was still counting. The opening of the privately funded Herbert H. Dow Building late in 1982 allowed chemical engineering and materials and metallurgical engineering to join aerospace, atmospheric and oceanic science, naval architecture and marine engineering, and nuclear engineering on North Campus. The Dow Building also contained space for badly needed instructional facilities. Between 1974 and 1980, the College of Engineering experienced a 33.5% jump in enrollments (1329 students), the largest increase of all of the schools and colleges. To accommodate these enrollments and to replace the facilities left behind on Central Campus, a small library, media center, and classrooms were built on the lower floors of the Dow Building.

Additional space was freed on North Campus by relocating some support services. Research Administration moved to Central Campus, freeing space for industrial and operations engineering. Printing Services moved to the old Hoover factory on Green Road, making room for the temporary placement of the new, state-funded Industrial Technology Institute. Engineering administration moved temporarily into the Chrysler Center and some vacated space in the North Campus stacks. Thus, little by little, the final pieces of Engineering were stuffed into spaces here and there on North Campus, filling the existing room to the bursting point.

The pressing need for space on North Campus finally convinced the State to provide $30 million for one more new building, the first fully state-funded university building in over two decades. Called originally Engineering Building I and later the Electrical Engineering and Computer

ELECTRICAL ENGINEERING AND COMPUTER SCIENCES (EECS)
NEARING COMPLETION

Sciences Building ("EECS" for short), the new facility housed not only electrical engineering and computer sciences but the College's administrative offices, student services, state-of-the art laboratories, and a four-storied, planted atrium that quickly became a gathering place for students and official receptions.

The new EECS building embodied more than a solution to space problems. It also symbolized and was an integral part of the College's new commitment to the State of Michigan. At the dedication, Governor James Blanchard called the building "a milestone in technological progress" that would serve the economic interests of the State. Duderstadt added that "this new facility will ... allow us to train engineers and industry leaders for the twenty-first century as well as to research technology critical to the future of Michigan industry." The new alliance, which harkened back to similar alliances in the 1920s and 1950s, joined the University, the State (and Nation), and industry in a common effort to stimulate economic development by putting university research to work.

Efforts to increase the economic spin-offs from University research intensified shortly after Shapiro took office. In 1981, planning began for a private corporation, called the Michigan Research Corporation, to commercialize ideas discovered at the University. The Regents also approved a new Robotics Center the same year, to help revitalize Michigan's weak industrial base. By 1982 the University was working closely with a new state initiative to found an Industrial Technology Institute and with the City of Ann Arbor to build an industrial park. The Michigan Research Corporation received Regental approval in 1983, along with $200,000 in seed funds to begin turning ideas into products, patents, and royalties. By 1986 the University owned outright about 75 patents with another 30 or so in process. Royalty income reached $500,000 a year and was predicted to reach $2 million by 1990. Engineering played a major role in the new commercialization effort, as did the Medical School and its growing core of molecular genetics researchers.

Given the importance of commercialization and economic development, which was embraced by both Michigan's Democratic Governor and the Reagan administration in Washington, the School of Business Administration logically became the third key player in the revitalization of the 1980s. During the last year of the Fleming administration, the School, under Dean Gilbert Whitaker, established its own Development Office to bolster support from alumni and friends. The goals were to increase annual giving and to raise funds for badly needed facilities. By 1980, annual giving reached the $1 million mark. A year later, the School launched a capital fund campaign to raise $15 million for three new buildings—a new library, a new building for computer facilities and executive classes, and an executive conference center. Ground breaking for the first two buildings took place in fall 1982; two years later Shapiro, Whitaker, and General Motors Vice President John Edman, chair of the Business School Development Advisory Board, led the dedication of the new Kresge Business Administration Library and the Computing/Executive Education Center. The three-day celebration that followed also included presentation of the 1984 Business Leadership Award to General Motors Chairman Roger Smith and the School's first alumni reunion. The same year the Burroughs Corporation (later the UNISYS Corporation) donated $12 million in computer equipment for the new Computing Center and the rest of the School.

While the State contributed its share to the growth of the 1980s, during very tight economic times the largest percentage of the funds for growth came from private donations and the University's own resources. With its large alumni—the largest in the country—the University had always benefited from substantial private giving. It was not, however, as active as other universities in seeking private support. In the late 1970s, Michigan's total, full-time development staff numbered less than 20; Harvard and Stanford, the schools with the greatest private support, had development staffs of 165 and 150. (Michigan at the time received about $30 million a year in private gifts, Stanford and Harvard about $60 million each.) Moreover, as Vice President for University Relations and Development Michael Radock looked to the future at a Regents meeting in 1979, he predicted more competition, especially from the "sun-belt" schools. Nonetheless, Radock was optimistic about the future, feeling that private support was there if only the University would, in the words of emeritus professor and long-time friend of the University, Dr. Harry Towsley, "go out and ask for it," which it increasingly did in the 1980s.

Shortly after his 1979 report to the Regents, Radock left the University to head the Charles Stuart Mott Foundation in Flint. His successor, Jon Cosovich, came from Stanford and brought with him the experience of a large, active development office. His experience was put to use immediately in a major capital campaign announced in May 1983 and formally launched in the fall, under the honorary leadership of Former President Gerald Ford and General Motors President Roger Smith. The Campaign for Michigan intended to raise $160 million, split roughly 50-50 between human and physical resources. $80 million was designated for endowed professorships, student fellowships, and related research and library resources. The remaining $80 million was for seven major building projects.

Most of the major building projects were well into the planning stages when the campaign began. Roughly $30 million was to go to the Medical Center for the Replacement Hospital and Kellogg Eye Center. Another $27 million was targeted for Engineering and Business Administration for the building programs discussed above. $1.4 was earmarked for a $2.3 million addition to Tappan Hall, begun a month before the Campaign was launched. Art History's nationally important collection of slides, photographs, and books was no long safe in the old Tappan Hall and desperately needed new quarters. The School of Music needed to raise $1.7 million to build two rehearsal halls that for budget reasons had been dropped from Saarinen's original 1964 design. The rehearsal halls were for a Vocal Arts Center and an Organ Teaching Studio and included space to display the Stearns Collection of historical musical instruments. This left $20 million for one more major project on campus, a new chemistry building.

The construction of a new chemistry building had significance well beyond chemistry itself. In the 1930s, the physical sciences were among the University's strongest programs. By the 1980s, the strength of the University depended heavily on the social sciences, humanities, and some professional programs. A detailed study of doctoral programs released in 1983 by the Associated Research Councils ranked four of the University's social science departments in the top five: anthropology (first among its peer departments), sociology (second), political science (third), and psychology (fifth). One more social science department (history) ranked in the top ten as did five humanities departments (art history, classics, French, Spanish, and philosophy). The three main physical science departments listed (chemistry, geology, and physics) ranked twentieth or below. Each was also housed in facilities that had been built well before the large increases in funding for science after World War II. Clearly, the time had come to undertake a major effort to strengthen the basic sciences, with the most visible first step being the new chemistry building. Similar efforts would also be undertaken in Physics, including the addition of several new faculty members, the renovation of the Randall Physics building, and the recruitment of a new chairman from Indiana University in 1987, Homer Neal.

Major steps were also undertaken to upgrade the University's computing and telephone facilities, beginning in 1983. A new optical-fiber telephone network was installed to form the backbone of the University's own phone system and communication network. With support from Apollo Computer, Apple Computer, and General Motors, Engineering installed the most advanced computing network (called CAEN or Computer Aided Engineering Network) that existed on any campus. A new IBM computer was added making it possible for the University to have two vast computer networks (UM and UB). Faculty and students were given the opportunity to purchase computers at reduced rates, and "computer clusters" began to appear all over campus. Computer Sciences moved from LSA to Engineering; the School of Library Science was renamed the School of Information and Library Studies, reflecting a new emphasis on information technology. With so much activity in this area, the University also created the new position of Vice Provost for Information Technology, which was filled by a computer specialist from Carnegie Mellon University, Douglas Van Howelling, in October 1984.

In these and many other ways, the "smaller but better" University of the 1980s took shape. The award winning Law Library addition, masterfully constructed below ground adjacent to the Law Quad, opened in 1981.

ECONOMICS, DECEMBER 26, 1981

A year later, astronomy became a partner with MIT and Dartmouth in the construction of a new $2.4 million telescope at the Kitt Peak, McGraw-Hill Observatory. Economics, which became homeless when its building (the original 1856 Chemical Laboratory with many additions) burned in December 1981, moved into the newly renovated Lorch Hall. Ruthven Museum added space. Renovations began in West Engineering and were planned for East Engineering as well.

The refurbishing of existing space and the construction of new buildings was particularly vital to the University's research effort, which experienced a decline in volume during the first few "smaller-but-better" years, although not in this case as a result of university policy. During Allan Smith's year as acting President, the University's research expenditures reached $98.7 million. Three years later, this figure had grown to $122.9 million in current dollars, but shrunk to $93.3. million when adjusted for inflation. A year later (1983), the comparable figures were $128.8 million in current dollars, $91.6 million in constant 1979 dollars. The decline in the purchasing power of the University's research dollars was most influenced by a decline in federal support for research, which now accounted for about three-quarters of the University's research expenditures.

The downward trend in the University's research budget reversed dramatically in 1984 and continued upwards through the remaining years of Shapiro's presidency, with the life sciences and engineering leading the way. By 1987-88 research in these areas comprised respectively 48.1% and 21.2% of the University's total research effort. However, the expansion of the University's research effort was not limited to these areas. Major growth also occurred in the research programs in Business Administration, Law, LSA, Natural Resources, Nursing, and Pharmacy. By 1986, the University ranked third among public universities and seventh overall in total research expenditures and was poised for continued growth, now under the direction of the first woman to head a major executive office at the University, Vice President for Research, Linda Wilson (appointed in July 1985).

Slowly, the decay that set in on campuses nationwide as a result of the economic and social turmoil of the 1970s was repaired and signs of growth once again appeared. Portions of Madison Street (by South Quad) and Ingalls Street (the block south of Rackham) were purchased in 1979 to create new malls and open spaces. Two years later, the Alumni Center opened on the newly created Ingalls Mall, between Rackham and the Michigan League. The same year, after more than a decade of rotating by the students and thousands of visitors to campus each year, the bearings on "The Cube" that stands in front of the renamed Fleming Administration Building were replaced. In 1985-86, the Frieze organ in Hill Auditorium was completely restored as it approached the hundredth anniversary of its move from the Chicago Columbia Exposition to the old University Hall in 1894. At the same time, the old, rusted bolts in the Baird Carillon (1936) were also replaced and a new keyboard built by John Taylor and Sons in England—the original bell founder—installed. The University had not only survived two decades of crisis, but seemed to have emerged an even stronger university, as its national rankings steadily improved. The University had in fact seized an extraordinary number of "opportunities from adversity," following the challenge Shapiro outlined shortly after taking office.

4. Issues of the 1980s

For those who experienced the turmoil of the 1970s, campus life appeared to quiet down during the early years of the Shapiro administration, to settle back to normal, as faculty went about the business of research and teaching and students the business of learning and finding jobs in an increasingly competitive world. After several years of decline, minority enrollments increased. Figures suggested that the number of women and minority faculty might be increasing as well. The University and GEO worked out agreements without major strikes. The tenth anniversaries of BAM I and Earth Day were celebrated peacefully. Federal affirmative action and Title IX reviews were passed with minimum problems.

This is not to say that there were no disagreements over major issues during the early years of the Shapiro administration, but initially they were talked out and settled with minimum protest. In 1978, the Regents had tried to set aside the controversial issue of the University's investments in companies doing business in South Africa by agreeing to sell holdings in companies that did not adhere to the Sullivan Principles. The latter provided a guideline for judging whether these companies were seeking to promote equal employment opportunities in their South African workplaces. Supporters of the 1978 policy believed that pressure exerted through investments was the best way to bring about an end to apartheid. Critics argued that any investments in South Africa necessarily prolonged the existence of apartheid and should be completely and immediately divested.

The 1978 investment policy had its share of critics, but it was not seriously challenged until late 1982. Then, attacks were mounted on two fronts. In December 1982, Governor William Milliken signed legislation introduced by Representative Perry Bullard that prohibited Michigan's public colleges and universities from investing in companies that did business in South Africa and the Soviet Union. The University's South African investments were, therefore, now against the law. Two months later, the Senate Assembly rejected a recommendation from its Senate Advisory Committee on Financial Affairs to continue the monitoring policy based on the Sullivan Principles and voted 40 to 3 in favor of immediate divestment.

The Senate vote presented problems, since it presumably indicated that the faculty were at odds with official university policy, but it did not bind the Regents to any course of action. Faculty committees can only advise, not legislate. The Regents were free to accept or reject the advice they received. However, the State legislation presented a different problem. As a direct order from the State to pursue a specific investment policy, it violated the constitutional autonomy of the Board of Regents. The Regents resisted all efforts to compromise their autonomy in the past, and they were not likely to accept any compromise now, however important the social issues.

"OUT OF SOUTH AFRICA"
RALLY

Thus, the April 1983 Regents meeting at which a final decision was to be made arrived with great anticipation. The meeting was moved to the Union ballroom to accommodate more than 200 observers. For two hours the Regents listened to a series of speakers, all of who recommended complete divestment. Then Regent Gerald Dunn introduced a resolution to solve what he said was "the toughest issue we've had to face in my 15 years on the Board." In a direct turn about from the 1978 policy, the Regents voted 6-2 to divest 90% of the University's investments in companies doing business in South Africa. The 10% retained was strictly in businesses headquartered in Michigan, to lessen the economic impact of the decision on the State and for the purpose of defying the State law so the issue of the University's constitutional autonomy could be tested in the courts. (The case took six years to resolve, with the major decision in favor of the University being made by the Michigan Court of Appeals on February 2, 1988. Ten months later, on October 21, 1988, the Regents passed a resolution approving 100% divestiture.)

As the debate over investments in South Africa was coming to an end, a second issue from the 1960s and 1970s—the University's policy on classified research—resurfaced. The so-called "end-use" provision ("the University ... [will] not enter into any classified research contract the specific purpose of which is to destroy human life or to incapacitate human beings"), which was incorporated into Regental policy in 1972 and 1976, surfaced again in the Research Policies Committee (RPC) in 1982 in response to a request to have the end-use provision applied more broadly to all university research. RPC favored such an extension, as did Senate Assembly in a recommendation to the Regents approved in April 1983. That June, the Regents voted 7 to 1 against the Senate Assembly resolution, throwing the debate back into the university community.

The debate over classified research continued off and on for the next three years. A small but very active student group, called the Progressive Student Network, organized periodic and decorous sit-ins in the laboratory of Engineering Professor Thomas Senior, who was reported to be doing research on the Stealth Bomber. Campus forums were organized. Groups, such as the faculty Collegiate Institute for Values and Science, were asked for guidance. In the midst of these debates, opponents of defense research, who now had the "Star Wars" program of the Reagan administration as their ultimate target, suc-

ceeded in getting a "nuclear free zone" proposal on the city ballot. Since "nuclear research" encompassed more than space-based weapons or weapons of mass destruction, the ballot proposal further divided the University community, before be-

RALLY AGAINST NUCLEAR WEAPONS RESEARCH

ing defeated in the November 1984 city election by a large majority.

New urgency was added to the debate in January 1985 when the Classified Research Review Committee, which had been charged in 1972 and 1976 to review all classified research contracts, voted not to approve two classified research projects—one submitted by Engineering Professor Theodore Birdsall on "Ocean Acoustic Tomography and Telemetry," the other by Political Science Professor Raymond Tanter on "Alternative Approaches to Arms Control." Vice President for Research Alfred Sussman overruled the Committee's advice on the Birdsall proposal but not the Tanter proposal, disapproving the latter because of apparent limitations on publication imposed by the funding agency. Tanter argued that the limitations would not interfere with his freedom as a scholar to publish; his colleagues on campus remained concerned about the basic principles involved.

One final effort to formulate an acceptable policy was attempted in the fall of 1985. In response to a request from the Regents, Shapiro established the Ad Hoc Committee on Classified Research, quickly called the Converse Committee after its chair, Institute for Social Research Professor Philip Converse. After more hearings and debate, the Committee issued a split report in July 1986. The majority favored the elimination of the end-use provision and the special review panel, while strongly endorsing the adoption of a comprehensive policy based on the rigorous enforcement of rules against publication restrictions. They were willing to allow reasonable publication delays to protect the proprietary interests of sponsors (patent and copyright interests), but favored openness as a way to allow the university community to monitor campus research. The minority worried that the new rules were too rigid and too focused on openness at the potential expense of the academic freedom of the individual researcher. After nearly a year of further deliberation, the Regents finally adopted a new research policy in May 1987. The new policy dropped the end-use clause, established rough guidelines for guarding against unreasonable publication restrictions, and placed the responsibility for monitoring all university research in the hands of the Vice President for Research and the Research Policies Committee. By this time, criticism of Star Wars was growing, large defense budgets were under attack, and the University's military research (classified and unclassified) had shrunk to a small fraction of the overall research budgets. (In 1967, the University received $12,358,160 for 69 classified research projects; in 1985 it received $366,827 for 2 classified research projects.) The times had changed, and so had the issues and concerns.

A third issue from the 1960s and 1970s that resurfaced in the 1980s— diversity—was not resolved as easily or as quickly as the debate over South African investments or classified research. In terms of numbers and representation, the University of 1980 was very different from the University of 1970. More under-represented minority students were enrolled, more women held faculty positions, and the university community in general had the appearance of greater diversity. However, as the drive for greater diversity struggled to maintain some momentum in the early 1980s (the percentage of African-American students declined from 7.7% in 1976-77 to 4.9% in 1982-83), new concerns arose about the University's overall commitment to diversity and the environment that all minorities faced on campus.

Nationally and locally the University was being seen more and more as an academic pressure cooker suited primarily for the professionally oriented students of the Reagan era. The 1982-83 *New York Times Selective Guide to Colleges* gave Michigan a top-ranked "5" for academics but only a "3" for social life, noting in particular the "intense pressure on campus." The consequences of intense academic and social pressure on minority students was verified by studies of the minority experience on the Michigan campus. Commenting on his national study of African-American students in March 1982, sociologist Walter Allen observed that while increased enrollments could be seen as "a positive trend," the fact remained that many African-American students fared "badly in terms of low academic achievement, feelings of isolation and alienation, and poor social adjustment." Since overall the African-American students of the 1980s had good academic backgrounds, Allen looked to the campus environment to explain their 10-15% higher dropout rate at Michigan and elsewhere. Similar concern about the experience African-American students had at Michigan was expressed two years later by Provost Frye when he asked in a memo to the University community: "what accounts for the inhospitable image of the University and of Ann Arbor in the eyes of minorities?" Frye candidly admitted that "while we cannot deny this image, we do not yet understand it well enough to improve and control it to the best advantage, and it remains a frustrating problem."

African-Americans were not the only ones who raised concerns about the campus environment in the early 1980s. Violent crimes against women and disappointing results in the recruitment of women faculty focused renewed attention on gender issues. The first "a

1981 RALLY ON THE LIBRARY STEPS

woman was raped here" signs appeared on campus sidewalks and streets during the 1980-81 academic year. Two years later the University instituted the "Tell Somebody" program to deal with increasing reports of sexual harassment. During the same period, groups representing lesbians and gays pressed for recognition and equal rights. Shapiro responded by issuing a presidential statement on sexual orientation in March 1984. His message was clear. Sexual orientation was to be treated similar to race, religion, sex, and national origin, none of which had any bearing on "academic abilities or job performance." LaGROC (Lesbian and Gay Rights on Campus) welcomed the statement as "the beginning of the end," when people would "be treated equally regardless of their sexual orientation."

While new rules, regulations, and programs helped change the environment on campus, one proposed rule, which had been in process since 1972, resulted in a storm of protest by a sizable proportion of all students and many faculty. That "rule" was the proposed "Student Code of Non-Academic Conduct." Drafted by a nine-member, faculty-staff-student committee formed at the request of the Executive Officers, its intent was to delineate the bounds of unacceptable behavior on campus. It covered acts such as intentional or reckless harm to other persons and property; threatening or harassing another person; unwelcome sexual advances and requests for sexual favors; interference with freedom of expression; the unauthorized possession of dangerous weapons; theft; and other miscellaneous intentional actions that disrupted normal campus life or interfered with the rights of others. However, the line between intentional disruptive behavior and protected political protest was one that the university community was not comfortable drawing in a detailed set of guidelines for behavior outside the classroom. The new Code was therefore vigorously protested and debated from its first publication in early 1984 through the rest of the Shapiro administration and into the early years of the Duderstadt administration.

As these events were unfolding, the University continued to implement changes aimed at strengthening under-represented minority recruitment and creating a more supportive environment on campus for all groups. More money was put into scholarship aid for under-represented minority students. The Admissions Office began special recruiting efforts in inner-city high schools. The Opportunity Program and the Coalition for the Use of Learning Skills were consolidated into a single Comprehensive Studies Program in an effort to provide more centralized support services for students. A new Associate Vice Provost for Academic Affairs, Niara Sudarkasa, Professor of Anthropology and a veteran of the earlier BAM protests, was appointed to coordinate the various recruitment and support programs being developed. By late 1986, the University could publish a special twenty-page supplement to the *Record* that included a directory of 20 support services and 29 organizations for minority students.

However, as in the 1960s and 1970s, change did not keep pace with expectations. By 1985, under-represented minority enrollment and graduation rates had increased, but not dramatically. By the end of the year, whatever progress had been made took a back seat to a new problem that emerged on campus, isolated episodes of overt racism. As the University prepared for a week-long commemoration of the birthday of Martin Luther King in early January 1986, Shapiro issued a personal message expressing his sense of grief and dismay over the episodes of racisim and asking for suggestions that would "articulate, emphasize, reinforce and build those values that support our diversity and our highest aspirations as a scholarly community." Creating a supportive environment was still proving to be an elusive problem. A year later and just after the special issue of the *Record* had been circulated, a racist flyer declaring "open season on Blacks" was slid under a dormitory lounge door where a group of African-American women students were meeting. The next week, a DJ on the campus radio station (WJJX) allowed a caller to tell a series of racist jokes on the air, complete with a laugh track supplied by the DJ. Within a few days, the combined United Coalition Against Racism (UCAR) was formed and BAM III was under way.

BAM III came to a head very quickly. UCAR organized its first major rally on March 4. On March 5, Representative Morris Hood of Flint convened a hearing of the Higher Education Subcommittee in the Michigan Union. University officials described the steps the University was taking to combat racism; students and staff from different backgrounds described the racism and harassment to which they had been subjected. UCAR and the coalition of students who called themselves "BAM III" organized another rally on March 18, followed by an overnight sit-in in the Fleming Administration Building on March 19. The sit-in moved to the Michigan Ballroom on March 20, where the Regents were meeting. On March 22, the Reverend Jesse Jackson came to Ann Arbor to meet with UCAR/BAM III students. The next day, Jackson, UCAR/BAM III leaders, and Shapiro reached agreement on a six-point plan of action, announced at a packed meeting in Hill Auditorium on the afternoon of the 23rd. After the plan was announced, Jackson delivered a passionate speech in which he confidently announced: "There may be darkness on campuses all around the country, but in Ann Arbor, a light is shining today."

The six-point plan included the appointment of a Vice Provost for Minority Affairs; the creation of a standing advisory committee on minority affairs and new grievance procedures; increased support for the Black Student Union (the Nelson Mandela House); and a greater commitment to attract and retain African-American students and faculty. (The Regents had earlier met one additional demand when they approved an honorary degree for Nelson Mandela, as first recommended by African-American faculty and students in 1985 but not then approved.) Beginning steps to initiate the plan followed immediately. The *Record* published a series of special editions outlining the different initiatives being undertaken. Nominations were solicited for the new advisory committee, and in early May, Professor of Education, Charles Moody, was nominated for the post of Vice Provost for Minority Affairs.

The adoption of the six-point plan once again (following the precedents of BAM I and BAM II) established an agenda for achieving greater diversity; it did not guarantee success. The latter rested on the University's commitment to change not only its image but also key elements of its culture. It required a commitment that would bring diversity to bear at every level of decision making within the University over the months and years needed to affect fundamental change. That commitment was already taking shape in the office of the Provost and would shortly move to center stage. Two months after the momentous meeting in Hill Auditorium, Shapiro accepted the Presidency of Princeton University, effective January 1988. The new President, former Engineering Dean and Provost, James Duderstadt, made diversity one of the hallmarks of his administration, as the six-point plan grew into an ambitious program called the "Michigan Mandate." With the transition to a new President and the slow shift to more centrist politics at the end of the Reagan era, the debates begun in the 1970s and carried into the 1980s slowly came to an end, as the University prepared for the 1990s and the coming of the twenty-first century.

5. *Tennis shoes or duckies and froggies?*

FRISBEE ON THE DIAG

Student bodies are never homogenous, but a majority sometimes follows noticeable trends. In the 1981 *Michiganensian*, section editors Lee Baker and Susan Blackman characterized their classmates as favoring pink and kelly green over maize and blue, Good Time Charlie's instead of the Pretzel-Bell (the P-Bell closed in 1985), and "plaid wool skirts in either pleats or kilts or a high-collared white turtle neck with the choice of duckies, froggies or strawberries (depending on the colors of the hairband and watchband). ... Optional, but strongly advised, are fraternity or sorority jewelry and Greek Week T-shirts." To this description was added the practical advice that "shopping in the Pendelton stores tends to be very expensive—so, if you still owe tuition from last term, it might be a good idea to stick with the old army jacket and beat up Adidas tennis shoes that were in a few years ago." Army jackets, tennis shoes, and all they represented did not disappear as the so-called Reagan-era yuppies moved on campus. They did take a backseat to the new interests and lifestyles of the 1980s, although not always to the extent that many observers described.

The less-serious side of campus life in the 1980s took the form of more parties, more drinking—with a corresponding decline in drug use—and more social life, strategically oriented around the academic week (said by some to end on Thursday and begin on Tuesday). If there

ESCAPING THE PRESSURES?

were excesses, increased pressures and higher expectations were often given as the excuse. Students saw the cost of their own education increase rapidly from year to year—increases driven by continuing inflation and declining state support. They also saw the number and variety of jobs open to them upon graduation dwindle, again reflecting the economic troubles of the world they were about to enter. Fields such as engineering and computer sciences offered the best prospects for jobs, professional careers the best opportunity to fullfil the expectation of living as well if not better than parents—the American dream. Success was less certain for students in the 1980s, or at least they thought it was, and so they dug in and tried harder. As noted above, the traditional college handbooks characterized this as "intense

MUDBOWL

pressure on campus." *A Black Student's Guide to College* described Michigan as "the pits." Students undoubtedly from time to time saw campus as both and much more, and sought diversion accordingly.

The pressures on students in the 1980s were felt in ways other than academics or economics. After a decade or more of loosening, efforts began to reimpose restrictions on students, with the Code being only the most obvious example. Nationally, Congress tied student financial aid—itself a constant target of the Reagan administration budget cuts—to draft registration. The Solomon Amendment, which went into effect in the fall of 1983, required male students receiving financial aid to sign a statement saying they had registered for the draft. Locally, officials began cracking down on under-aged drinking, driving students out of many of the traditional "student bars." The introduction of a "computerized registration

CRISP

and individual selection program" (CRISP) in fall 1981 reduced the time it took to register for classes, but closed courses and increased class size made registration more traumatic, especially for students in the most popular professional and pre-professional programs. In-state students felt the pressure of growing out-of-state enrollments; students on limited resources noticed signs of increasing wealth on campus. The days when a good, part-time job and a little aid from home paid the bills had long past, as students of the 1980s worried about preparing for jobs that would pay off mounting college debts.

More work and more play did not, as sometimes suggested, end activism, although students often sought to achieve their ends in ways different from their counterparts in the 1960s and 1970s. Students demonstrated against the Code, some of the reductions under the Five-Year plan, investments in South Africa, and classified research. Many students were deeply concerned about the racism, bigotry, and the violence against women that appeared to be growing on campus and took steps to create a more tolerant, supportive campus. "Out of El Salvador" marches and banners were much in evidence during the 1982-83 school year. Even after divestment, South

FRYE MEETING WITH STUDENTS

Africa remained a cause on many students' minds, as evidenced by the construction of the Diag "shanties" in March 1986. Planned by the Free South Africa Coordinating Committee, they were intended to stand only a few weeks as part of a national show of support for the African National Congress. They survived the 1980s, despite being repeatedly vandalized and from time to time totally demolished. The 1980s also saw the birth of a conservative student newspaper, the *Michigan Review*, and a weekly magazine, *Consider*, which endeavored to air opposing views on controversial campus and national issues.

Demonstration was not the only way students became involved in the 1980s. Funds for the United Way were raised during Homecoming in October 1983 by baking the "Ultimate Za." This world's largest pizza measured 2 1/2 by 312 feet and contained a half ton of mozzarella, 300 pounds of pepperoni, 200 pounds of bermuda onions, 80 pounds of green peppers and mushrooms, 48 gallons of tomate sauce, and nearly a ton of dough. This followed the record-breaking, 300-foot "Wolverine Sub" made the year before. From bucket drives, see-saw marathons, and jello baths on the Diag to fashion shows and charity balls, the students of the 1980s showed that the "me generation" often cared about more than themselves.

Students also took an interest in the Union and petitioned the University for changes. In response to these and other concerns, the Regents voted in January 1979 to transfer control of the Union from the volunteer board of directors to the Office of Student Services; to convert all but 12 of the 109 hotel rooms to student housing; to undertake a study of use and needs; and to assess students $2.65 per term to raise the funds needed for renovation and repairs. The room conversions were done immediately, further increasing the revenues for renovations. Then, over the next few years, new food malls, shops, and other services were installed on the ground floor, along with major renovations to the restaurant facilities on the first floor. The only casualty of these changes was the student book store, which chose to move off campus rather than contribute to the renovations—a decision that was in part responsible for its ultimate demise a few years later.

In sports, the other important focus of activity outside the classroom, Michigan continued its winning tradition in program after program. After five straight losses (for Bo Schembechler as well as the University), Michigan finally won the Rose Bowl again on New Year's Day, 1981, led by John Wangler at quarterback, Butch Woolfolk at running back, and the incomparable Number One, receiver Anthony Carter . Bud Middaugh took over as coach of the baseball team in July 1979 and led the team to a Big Ten Championship in his first year. Bill Frieder was hired to coach the basketball team the same year and would eventually recruit, train, and come within a month of coaching a national champion. Frieder was relieved of his coaching duties before the start of the NCAA championship when he announced that he would be moving to Arizona the next year. Men's tennis, women's volley ball, all won Big Ten championships, and other teams gathered awards as well during the 1980s.

Amidst the many championships, Michigan experienced some notable losses and near losses to its athletic program. In 1988, Michigan's athletic director of twenty years, Don Canham, retired, leaving behind as his legacy arguably the strongest athletic program in the country. His most successful recruit, football coach Bo Schembechler received offers from Texas A & M during the 1981-82 academic year but decided to remain at Michigan. The same year, sportscaster Bob Ufer died shortly after being honored at the Iowa game in October 1981. Between the opening of the football season in 1945 and the home opener against Wisconsin in September 1981, "Ufe," as he was known to his many loyal fans, broadcast 364 consecutive games, first for Ann Arbor's WPAG and then WJR in Detroit. He was known for his distinct prouanciation of "Meechigan," in a tradition said to go back to Fielding Yost's West Virginia drawl, and for his many "Uferisms": "the hole that Yost Dug, Crisler paid for, Canham carpeted, and Schembechler fills every Saturday afternoon with 100,000 fans;" "Schembechler, Ufer, and Elephants never forget;" and his game-ending, "That's all there is—there isn't any more."

While "smaller but better" provided an effective slogan for marshalling the resources and energies needed to cope with the financial crisis of the early 1980s, in one important way it did not accurately describe the transformation that took place during the Shapiro years. More than the new buildings and new programs discussed above were added in the 1980s. Between 1981-82, the beginning of the downsizing effort, and 1987-88, the General Fund and research budgets each increased about 70%, the instructional and non instructional staffs grew by 17% and 18% respectively, and student applications rose 50%, although student numbers remained roughly the same, growing only a modest 1%. Overall, the period of the Shapiro presidency is not one of downsizing but of growth.

The growth the University experienced in the 1980s was not spread evenly across campus. The path to a "better" university focused efforts on the parts and activities that were seen as the most vital to the University's mission. This meant emphasizing first and foremost research, graduate education, professional training, and professional service. If undergraduate education did not appear as prominently on this list as some felt it should, this was by design, not neglect. In times of financial crisis and dwindling public support, Shapiro turned first to the elements of higher education that society was willing to fund and stressed the one measure of higher education that Michigan had long championed and that most people seemed to understand—its academic reputation. A university that was recognized as a leader among its peers and that had financial strength and independence was one that could then afford and seek excellence in education.

More emphasis on education did follow once the worst of the financial times had passed and the reallocation of funds became possible. In January 1987, Acting President Duderstadt (Shapiro took a brief sabbatical in January-February 1987) announced a $5 million Undergraduate Initiative Fund aimed at enriching the undergraduate experience. A second initiative directed toward stimulating interdisciplinary research and cross-campus collaborations, the Presidential Initiatives Fund, had been launched a few months earlier with a $5 million grant from the Kellogg Foundation. With these and other initiatives, the University, Duderstadt noted, assumed "more control over its own destiny, to move it toward what it wishes to become." The years of austerity, of reallocation, and of diversifying the University's support base—years that extended well back into the Fleming presidency—began to pay off as Shapiro prepared to leave the University for Princeton in December 1987. For the first half of 1988, Robben Fleming returned as Acting President while the search for a new president continued. In the end, the decision was made once again to elevate the Provost and Vice President for Academic Affairs to the University's highest office. On September 1, 1988 James J. Duderstadt became the University's eleventh president in Ann Arbor.

CAMPUS, 1988

PREPARING FOR THE TWENTY-FIRST CENTURY

IN 1992, THE UNIVERSITY MARKED its 175th anniversary with a series of events that celebrated and took steps to preserve its past. An oral history of past presidents and other university leaders was initiated. A historical video and several historical publications were commissioned, including the revised edition of this book. Under the maize and blue banner of the "175th," events and lectures campus wide were drawn together to remind the university community of the strength and richness of its past. It was also in 1992 that the

JAMES J. DUDERSTADT

preservation of the University's heritage was placed in the hands of an official History and Traditions Committee appointed by the President and chaired by the University's newly appointed historian, Robert Warner.

As these events were unfolding, two powerful forces were also at work that increasingly turned the attention of the university community toward the future. One was the obvious approach of a new century, a time when individuals and institutions have traditionally heightened their interest in the world to come. The other was the vision of the University's eleventh President, James Duderstadt, who made preparing for the future one of the defining themes of his administration.

A nuclear engineer by training, Duderstadt brought to his administrative work, first as Dean of the College of Engineering (1981-86), then as Provost and Vice President for Academic Affairs (1986-1988), and finally as President (1988-), an infectious confidence in the ability of educated people to control their destinies and to build their own futures. Soon after taking office as Provost, he implemented an ambitious strategic planning process that challenged all concerned to anticipate the needs for higher education in the coming century and then to map out a strategy for meeting those needs. Inherent in this process was the opportunity to define the role the University wanted to play in higher education in the decades ahead.

From this process there emerged a clear and compelling strategic plan that had at its core one ambitious, all-encompassing goal—to become *the* university that set the standard for higher education in the twenty-first century, or as simply put in the *Victors*, the unofficial school song of every Wolverine, to become the "leaders and best."

The heart of the new strategic plan was its vision of the future. In countless talks before the University's extended family, which spread from students and faculty on campus to alumni, to legistators in Lansing, and more broadly to the citizens of Michigan, now President Duderstadt described a future in which three crucial elements—knowledge, globalization, and pluralism—would dominate. Knowledge was becoming increasingly important as the key to growth and change. Change through knowledge was quickly breaking down barriers between nations and economies, producing one inter-dependent global community that had to live and work together. As barriers disappeared and new groups entered the main stream of life, particularly in America, isolation, intolerance, and separation had to give way to pluralism and diversity. A new, dynamic world was emerging. If the University wanted to maintain the leadership position it had enjoyed for now close to two centuries, it had to adapt to life in that world.

With this vision clearly articulated, under the leadership of Duderstadt; his new Provost and Vice President for Academic Affairs, former Dean of Business Administration Gilbert Whitaker; and the other members of the new leadership team, the University set out to build for the future—physicially, financially, intellectually, and culturally. Beginning in 1987, an ambitious program know as the "Michigan Mandate" was implemented to increase the number of students, faculty, and staff in all under-represented groups on campus and to encourage increased community commitment to diversity. Internationalization was fostered through new overseas educational initiatives, greater emphasis on international co-operation in research and, in 1990, the creation of a new associate vice president for international academic affairs. Information, which has always been central to both research and teaching, increasingly merged with and became dependent on technology, through the various "nets" that link the University to the international world of higher education, business, and government. One sign of the new focus of some traditional fields was the appointment of a specialist in information technology and associate dean in Engineering, Daniel Atkins, to be the new Dean of the School of Information and Library Studies in 1992. Another was the 1991 selection of Garry Brewer, a Yale professor with interests in corporate America, to head the School of Natural Resources.

Over time, the areas for leadership grew into a more ambitious list of goals for the University in the 1990s. These goals targeted specific strategies for financial management, achieving excellence, helping American society rebuild its infrastructure, and creating an environment on campus that could change and embrace change more easily and more quickly. Leading higher education into the twenty-first century now included, among other activities: building more "spires of excellence," making Michigan "the university of choice for women leaders," developing "a new paradigm for undergraduate education," increasing the University's endowment to $2 billion, improving the quality of our facilities, making the "Ann Arbor area the economic engine of the Midwest," helping "to implement a plan for 'restructuring' the State of Michigan," and building "more of a sense of pride in ... respect for ... excitement about ... and loyalty to the University of Michigan."

As this revised edition of the University's history goes to press, the new strategic plan, "Vision 2000," is being implemented and carefully monitored under the watchful eye of an evaluation known as "Michigan Metrics." A new capital campaign, the Campaign for Michigan, was launched in the fall of 1992 with the goal of raising $1 billion. East Engineering was recently stripped bare to its structural skeleton in preparation for major renovations. Reminiscent of the earlier remodeling of the Angell-era main library in the 1920s, when the present north wing was erected around the original stacks, a "new" library is being constructed around the 1950s Undergraduate Library, which will be connected with walkways to the Hatcher Library and West Engineering, now the home of Physics, Women's Studies, the Center for AfroAmerican and African Studies, and the School of Library and Information Studies. The Diag will also soon have an entirely new Physics building, filling a space just south of Natural Resources and west of Randall Physics. The Medical Campus is about to dedicate a third Medical Sciences Research Building and is well along on a new Cancer and Geriatric Center. The new library and information technology center currently under construction on North Campus will complete Engineering's move to its new campus, a move that began nearly fifty years ago. These, and the hugh physical plant that has become the University of Michigan, will be home to the 36,000 students, 3,400 faculty, 14,000 staff, and 300,000 plus alumni who make up the university community, spending over $2 billion annually to run seventeen schools and colleges and hundred of programs, centers, and institutes.

As large and complex as the University is or promises to become, there is still one over-riding activity that not only binds it together but that binds it firmly to both its past and its future. However we go about our various activities, we are still a community and an institution that exists "to create, preserve, and disseminate knowledge." This seemingly simple task carries with it great responsibilities, responsibilities that can both challenge and overwhelm. After spending the afternoon reading in the

University's small library of only a few hundred books one day in October, 1844, George Pray wrote in his diary: "It is discouraging to an ambitious and ardent-minded student to enter a large library and see how much there is to be learned and how impossible it is to learn all things." His favorite teacher and later friend, physician Silas Douglas, expressed similar sentiments a few years earlier in a letter to his future wife when he wrote:

> *Our profession is one of a progressive character, and it requires all our energies to keep pace with its advancement. I have had a lot of periodicals for some time on my hands, calling loudly for perusal.... Oh' what a mass of <u>stuff</u> there is to learn. The futher we progress, the more we find ... which we should learn.*

Michigan's students, faculty, administrators, staff, alumni, and supporters have consistently risen to the challenge—the challenge to be at the cutting edge of creating, preserving, and disseminating knowledge. Assuming they continue to do so in the future, the chapters in the University's history that are yet to be written will be as rich and rewarding as those that have already been part of *The Making of the University of Michigan*.

BIBLIOGRAPHIC NOTE

FROM ITS FOUNDING IN 1817 through the era of President James B. Angell, the history of the University of Michigan remained a manageable whole that could be and was from time to time the subject of short essays and a few longer books. The earliest of these histories is Henry Philip Tappan's *Review by Rev. Dr. H.P. Tappan of his connection with the University of Michigan* (Detroit, MI: Detroit Free Press Steam Book and Job Printing Establishment, 1864), the bitter tone and personal nature of which made it impossible for him to be rehired by a new Board of Regents after his firing in 1864. Other works that cover all or parts of the University's early history include: Andrew Ten Brook, *American state universities, their origin and progress; a history of congressional university land-grants, a particular account of the rise and development of the University of Michigan, and hints toward the future of the American university system* (Cincinnati, OH: R. Clarke, 1875); Charles K. Adams, *Historical sketch of the University of Michigan* (Ann Arbor, MI: The University, 1876); Elizabeth M. Farrand, *History of the University of Michigan* (Ann Arbor, MI: Register Publishing House, 1885); *University of Michigan, 1837-1887: The semi-centennial celebration of the organization of the University of Michigan, June 26-30, 1887* (Ann Arbor, MI: The University, 1888); Noah W. Cheever, *Stories and amusing incidents in the early history of the University of Michigan* (Ann Arbor, MI: Register Publishing Co., 1895); Andrew Ten Brook, *The story of our city & its schools: with a survey of the settlement & school system of the West* [1895]; Charles K. Adams, *The University of Michigan, the sources of its power and its success* (Ann Arbor, MI: The University, 1896); *The quarter centennial celebration of the presidency of James Burrill Angell, June 24, 1896* (Ann Arbor, MI: The University, 1896); Burke A. Hinsdale, *History of the University of Michigan*, ed. by Isaac N. Demmon (Ann Arbor, MI: Published by the University, 1906).

More recent histories of the University and anniversary volumes include: Wilfred B. Shaw, *The University of Michigan* (New York: Harcourt, Brace and Howe, 1920; 2d ed., Ann Arbor, MI: G. Wahr, 1937) and *A short history of the University of Michigan* (Ann Arbor, MI: G. Wahr, 1934); *The 1937 celebration and commencement, University of Michigan, Ann Arbor, Michigan, June 14-19, 1937* [Ann Arbor, 1937]; and Kent Sagendorph, *Michigan, the story of the university* (New York: Dutton, 1948). Sagendorph's work should be read with caution, since the line between "good stories" and history is not always clearly drawn. Other works that cover important aspects of the University's history include: Richard R. Price, *The financial support of the*

University of Michigan (Cambridge, MA: Harvard University, 1923); Earl D. Babst and Lewis G. Vander Velde, eds., *Michigan and the Cleveland era: sketches of University of Michigan staff members and alumni who served the Cleveland administrations, 1885-89, 1893-97* (Ann Arbor, MI: University of Michigan Press, 1948); David B. Laird, *The Regents of the University of Michigan and the Legislature of the State, 1920-1950* (Ann Arbor, MI: University of Michigan School of Education [1972]); Alan Creutz, *Piety and intellect in the western wilderness : the first decade of the University of Michigan* (Ann Arbor, MI: Historical Society of Michigan, 1987); *Intellectual history and academic culture at the University of Michigan : fresh explorations*, Margaret A. Lourie, ed. (Ann Arbor, MI: Horace H. Rackham School of Graduate Studies, University of Michigan, 1989); Nicholas H. Steneck, *Faculty governance at the University of Michigan, principles, history, and practice : a report for the university community* (Ann Arbor, MI: University of Michigan, Senate Advisory Committee on University Affairs, 1991).

For researchers interested in pursuing the University's history in depth, the most comprehensive although dated source of information is Wilfred B. Shaw, editor, *The University of Michigan, an encyclopedic survey* (Ann Arbor, MI: University of Michigan Press, 1941-), with supplemental volumes published in by the Bentley Historical Library (Ann Arbor, MI: Bentley Historical Library, University of Michigan, 1977-). Topics not covered in the *Encyclopedic survey* or in the more specialized works discussed below can be researched in the University's rich archives, which are preserved in the Bentley Historical Library. Marjorie R. Barritt and Mary E. Arnheim, compilers, *Guide to the archives of the University of Michigan* (Ann Arbor, MI: Bentley Historical Library, University of Michigan, 1988; rev. ed., Ann Arbor, MI: Bentley Historical Library, University of Michigan, 1992) provides a comprehensive overview of the collections in the Bentley. More detailed guides and catalogues are available at the Bentley or can be accessed through the University's online catalogue — MIRLYN.

Biographical information on the University's early presidents and their administrations can be found in Charles M. Perry, *Henry Philip Tappan, philosopher and university president* (Ann Arbor, MI: University of Michigan Press, 1933); Erastus O. Haven, *Autobiography*, edited by C.C. Stratton, with an introduction by J.M. Buckley (New York: Phillips & Hunt, 1883); James Burill Angell, *From Vermont to Michigan* (Ann Arbor, MI: University of Michigan Press, 1936), and *The reminiscences of James Burrill Angell* (New York: Longmans, Green, and Co., 1912); Shirley W. Smith, James Burrill Angell: An American Influence (Ann Arbor, MI: University of Michigan Press, 1954), and *Harry Burns Hutchins and the University of Michigan* (Ann Arbor, MI: University of Michigan Press, 1951); Alexander G. Ruthven, *Naturalist in two worlds: random recollections of a university president* (Ann Arbor, MI: University of Michigan Press, 1963); and Peter E.

Van der Water, *Alexander G. Ruthven of Michigan : biography of a university president* (Grand Rapids, MI: Eerdmans Pub. Co., 1977). Additional information on the University's most recent presidents and acting presidents can be found in the oral histories collected by the University of Michigan History and Traditions Committee, *Interviews, 1991-1992*, Bentley Historical Library, University of Michigan. Among the many deans and faculty who have served the University over time, only a few have been the subject of major (auto)biographies, including Ruth B. Bordin, *Andrew Dickson White, teacher of history* (Ann Arbor, MI: University of Michigan, [1958]); Mortimer E. Cooley, with the assistance of Vivien B. Keatley *Scientific blacksmith* (Ann Arbor, MI: University of Michigan Press, 1947); Victor C. Vaughan, *A doctor's memories* (Indianapolis: The Bobbs-Merrill Company, [c1926]);

Over the years, numerous short articles and a few books covering aspects of the University's schools, colleges, programs, and campus life in general have appeared in a wide variety of sources. The early issues (through the 1960s) of the *Michigan Quarterly Review* provide the richest source for articles on the history of the University. The University's early library and fine arts collections are covered in Russell E. Bidlack, *"The University of Michigan General Library: A history of its beginnings, 1837-1852,"* dissertation, University of Michigan, 1954; and Alvah Bradish, *Remarks on the Fine Arts Department in the University of Michigan, with a history of the art lectures in that institution* (Ann Arbor, MI: 1868). Ruth B. Bordin, *The Michigan Historical Collections: the Vander Velde years: twenty-five years of leadership* (Ann Arbor, MI: University of Michigan [1961]) documents the growth of the University's archives. The growth of the law and medical schools have been the subject of two book-length studies: Elizabeth G. Brown, *Legal education at Michigan, 1859-1959* (Ann Arbor, MI: University of Michigan Law School, 1959); and Horace Davenport, *Fifty Years of medicine at the University of Michigan: 1891-1941* (Ann Arbor, MI: The University of Michigan Medical School, 1986). Joel Howell, editor, *Medical lives and scientific medicine at Michigan, 1891-1969* (Ann Arbor: University of Michigan Press, 1993) provides additional information on the growth of the Medical School. For an interesting discussion of the University's early leadership in the sciences, see: Howard Plotkin, "Henry Tappan, Franz Brünnow, and the founding of the Ann Arbor school of astronomers, 1852-1863," *Annals of science.* 1980; 37: 287-302.

Of the many works published on athletics at the University, the more comprehensive include: John R. Behee, *Fielding Yost's legacy to the University of Michigan* (Ann Arbor, MI: Distributed by Uhlrich's Books, [1971]); and *Hail to the victors* (Ann Arbor, MI: Distributed by Ulrich's Books [1974]); Philip C. Pack, *100 years of athletics, the University of Michigan; a review in words and pictures covering the University's athletic prowess and progress*

1837-1937, planned, prepared and published for the "M" club and the Michigan athletic managers' club by Phil Pack (Ann Arbor, MI, [1937]); Sheryl M. Szady, *The history of intercollegiate athletics for women of the University of Michigan* (1987); and Bo Schembechler and Mitch Albom, *Bo* (New York, NY: Warner Books Inc., 1989).

Information relating to the history of women and under-represented minorities at the University can be found in: Ruth B. Bordin, A*lice Freeman Palmer: the evolution of a new woman* (Ann Arbor, MI: University of Michigan Press, 1993); Elizabeth G. Brown, "The Initial Admission of Negro Students to the University of Michigan," *Michigan Quarterly Review*, 1963; 2: 233-236; Dorothy G. McGuigan, *A dangerous experiment; 100 years of women at the University of Michigan* (Ann Arbor, MI: Center for Continuing Education of Women, 1970); Madelon L. Stockwell, *A Michigan childhood : the journals of Madelon Louisa Stockwell, 1856-1860* , edited and annotated by Leslie Dick (Albion, MI: Albion College Library, Albion Public Library, 1988); and Bertha Van Hoosen, *Petticoat Surgeon* (Chicago: Pellegrini & Cudahy, 1947).

Campus life is best approached through the succession of newspapers and yearsbooks written and edited by students since their first publications appeared immediately after the Civil War. These include: *Castalian* (Ann Arbor, V. 1-11, 1866-96); *Michigan Daily* (Ann Arbor, V. 1- , 1890-); *Michiganensian, being a consolidation of the Palladium, Castalian, and Res gestae* (Ann Arbor, MI: Senior literary, law, and engineering classes, V .1- , 1897-); *Nia (purpose), the Black yearbook, University of Michigan* (Ann Arbor, MI: Black Yearbook Association, University of Michigan, V. 1- , 1976-); *Panorama* (Ann Arbor, MI, V. 1-5, 1937); *Res gestae* ([Ann Arbor, MI]: Senior law class, Vol. 1- 2 , 1896); *The Chronicle-Argonaut* (Ann Arbor, MI: The Chronicle-Argonaut Association, V. 1-2, 1891); *The Chronicle* (Ann Arbor, MI: The Chronicle Association, V. 1-2, 1890); *The Michigan Chimes* (Ann Arbor, V. 1-5, 1919-1924); *The Palladium, the senior annual of the secret societies of the University of Michigan* (Ann Arbor, The Inland Press, V. 1-27, 1858-1896); *The Tempest* ([Ann Arbor, MI]: University of Michigan, V. 1-5, 1923); and *The Wolverine* (Ann Arbor, MI: V. 1- , 1901-). The later recollections of alumni and other historical publications can be found in *The Michigan alumnus* (Ann Arbor, MI, V.1- , 1894-); and *Our Michigan: an anthology celebrating the University of Michigan's sesquicentennial,* edited by Erich A. Walter (Ann Arbor, MI: University of Michigan, 1966).

Finally, the many novels that revolve in one way or another about campus life provide enjoyable reading about the University and, if read with a bit of caution, some important insights into history. The following list, extracted from letters in *Michigan Today,* provides a starting point for the truly dedicated reader of fiction: Olive S. Anderson, *An American girl and her four years in a boys' college* (New York: D. Appleton and company,

1878); Katharine H. Brown, *Philippa at the Halcyon*. (New York: Scribner's, 1910); Lloyd C. Douglas, *Magnificent Obsession* (Boston: Houghton Mifflin, 1929); Richard Ford, *The Sportswriter* (New York: Random House, 1986); John K. Galbraith, *Triumph* (Boston, MA: Houghton Mifflin, 1968); Herbert Gold, *The Optimist* (Boston: Little Brown, 1958); Leonard Greenbaum *Out of Shape* (n.p., n.d); Jean H. Hoyte, *Wings of Wax* (New York: J.H. Sears & Company, 1929); Paul C. Jackson, *Rose Bowl Linebacker* (n.p, n.d.); Donald H. Haines, *Blaine of the Blackfield* (New York: Farrar and Rinehart, 1937); Hersilia A. Keays, *The Road to Damascus* (Boston: Small, Maynard & Co., 1907); Terry Lawrence, *Before Dawn* (New York: Silhouette, 1989); Richard Lees, *Parachute* (New York: Bantam Books, 1988), and *Out of Sync* (Farrar, Straus & Giroux, 1988); Sinclair Lewis, *Arrowsmith* (New York, P. F. Collier & Son Corp., 1925); Edmund G. Love, *Hanging on; or, How to get through a depression and enjoy life* (New York, W. Morrow, 1972; Detroit: Wayne State University Press, 1987); Richard Meeker, *Better angel* (New York: Greenberg, 1933; Boston: Alyson Publications, Inc., 1987); Kenneth Millar (Ross A. MacDonald), *The Dark Tunnel* (New York: Bantam Books, 1944); Walter F. Murphy, *The Vicar of Christ* (New York: Macmillan, 1979); Joyce Carol Oates, *Wonderland* (New York: Vanguard Press, 1971); Saul Parker, *Inevitable* (New York: Vantage Press, 1975); Marge Piercy, *Braided Lives* (New York: Ballantine Books, 1984); Allan Seager, *Equinox* (New York: Simon and Schuster, 1943); George Stewart, *A Doctor's Oral* (New York, Random House, 1939); Al Slote, *Denham Proper* (New York: Putnam & Sons, 1953); Betty Smith, *Joy in the morning* (New York: Bantam Books, [1964]); Danielle Steel, *Fine Things* (n.p, n.d.); Michael Thall, *Let Sleeping Afghans Lie* (New York: Walter & Co., 1990); Elizabeth Urh, *Cloudy and Cooler* (New York: Harcourt, Brace & World, 1968); Nancy Willard, *Things Invisible to See* (New York: Alfred A. Knopf, 1984); and Cristopher Zenowiel, *The Cost of Living* (n.p, n.d.).

PHOTO CREDITS

All photographs are located in the Michigan Historical Collections, Bentley Historical Library, University of Michigan unless otherwise noted

Abbreviations:

UM=University of Michigan

PVF=University of Michigan. Photographs Vertical File

CA=University of Michigan. Class Albums, 1861-1887

AA=University of Michigan. Alumni Association

NIS=University of Michigan. News and Information Service

UC=Unit Collection

Cover photo: Jasper Francis Cropsey, The University of Michigan Campus, 1855; original in the Bentley Historical Library, University of Michigan

Chapter 1: xii, *Michigan Terrmitory*, Fielding Lucas, Baltimore 1824, William L. Clements Library, University of Michigan; p. 1, John Montieth photographic series; p. 4, Early views collection; p. 8, PVF, D3 [130]; p. 14, Issac Edwin Crary photograph collection.

Chapter 2: p. 16, UM, Class of 1849, Records, 1889 & 1899; p. 17, Alvah Bradish, oil on canvas, original in Bentley Historical Library; p. 22, Jaspar Francis Cropsey visual materials collection, 1855-1856, Sketchbook, 1855-1856; p. 23, UM, Class of 1849, Records; p. 30, CA, Class of 1861, Box 1.

Chapter 3: p. 34, Robert Legget,1856, engraving after painting by J. F. Cropsey; p. 35, CA, 1861, Box 1; p. 41, *Ibid.*, Class of 1858; p. 42, *Ibid.*, 1861; p. 47, *Ibid.*, 1858; p. 51, PVF, E27 [358]; p. 55, Alexander Winchell papers, 1833-1891, Box 22, 1855-1864.

Chapter 4: p. 58, PVF, D2 [120]; p. 59, CA, Class of 1871, Box 16; p. 64, UM, Medical School, Box 136; p. 65, Department of Engineering, Scrapbook on Engineering history; p. 69, PVF, D2 [106]; p. 71, CA,1871, Box 16; p. 74, PVF, D13 [298].

Chapter 5: p. 76, PVF, D2 [121]; p. 77, James Burill Angell papers, 1845-1916, Box 22; p. 80, PVF, D13 [165]; p. 81, UM, Law School, Box 64; p. 85, CA, Class of 1875, Box 30; p. 86, UM, Department of Physical Education for Women, Box 9; p. 90, PVF, D13 [221]; p. 92, PVF, F1 [374]; p. 95, Wilfred Shaw photograph series., Box 8.

Chapter 6: p. 98, Maps: Ann Arbor, 1860-1899, Survey of Ann Arbor, 1890; p. 99, James Burill Angell papers, 1845-1916, Box 22; p. 102, UM, School of Nursing, Box 32; p. 105, UM, Medical School, Box 136; p. 107, PVF, F84

[469]; p. 114, *Ibid.*, D13 [322]; p. 117, Harry O. Potter photograph collection; p. 119,Louis P. Jocelyn photograph collection; p. 122, UM, Alumnae Council photograph collection, Box 1; p. 122, Mabel A. J. Livingston, Livingston family photograph collection; p. 125, Angell, Box 14.

Chapter 7: p. 126, Richard Rummell, Photogravure, Boston, A. W. Elson & Co., c. 1908; p. 127, Harry Burns Hutchins visual materials series; p. 133, PVF, D13 [204]; p. 136, *Ibid.*, [137]; p. 138, UM, Michigan Union, Box 9; p. 142, Bernice Bryant Lowe photograph album; p. 144, UM., *Michiganensian*, 1918; p. 145, *Ibid.*; p. 146, *Ibid.*; p. 148, Paul C. Wonderly photograph collection; p. 152, AA, Box 137.

Chapter 8: p. 154, PVF, D2 [100]; p. 155, AA, Box 139; p. 157, PVF, D13 [327]; p. 158, UM, Law School, Box 64; p. 163, AA, Box 135; p. 164, Robert Frost photograph collection; p. 167, Private collection; p. 168, UM, Men's Glee Club photograph series, Box 5; p. 171, AA, Box 137; p. 172, Private collection.

Chapter 9: p. 176, PVF, D2 [100]; p. 177, AA, Box 143; p. 180, Biomedical Communications, slide collection; p. 183, UM, Sesquicentennial Celebration; p. 184, PVF, D13 [244] ; p. 184, UM, *Michiganensian*, 1926; p. 186, PVF, D13 [252]; p. 187, UM, *Michiganensian*, 1926; p. 189, AA, Box 138.

Chapter 10: p. 192, AA, Box 135; p. 193, Alexander Grant Ruthven photograph series, 1920s-1960s, Box 64; p. 200, AA, Box 136; p. 201, PVF, D2 [105]; p. 202, Michigan Union, Box 17; p. 209, AA, Box 138; p. 214, John Beehee, *Hail to the Victors*, p. 59; p. 215, Inter-Cooperative Council, Box 3.

Chapter 11: p. 224, PVF, D2 [105]; p. 225, Ruthven, Box 64; p. 230, Law School, Box 64; p. 231, Harry A. Towsley photograph series, 1940-1952; p. 231; PVF, E27 1 [370]; p. 232, AA, Box 137; p. 237, *Ibid.*, Box 135; p. 238, *Ibid.*; p. 240, *Michigan Daily*, May 21, 1948.

Chapter 12: p. 244, PVF, D2 [105], p. 245, Harlen H. Hatcher photograph series, Box 66; p. 247, AA, Box 135; p. 248, *Ibid.*; p. 249, *Ibid.;* p. 249, AA, Box 135; p. 253, PVF, E25 [354]; p. 255, UM, NIS, Box 1; p. 257, AA, Box 138; p. 258, AA, Box 135; p. 260, *Ibid.*; p. 263, James T. Wilson photographic series; p. 264, Hatcher, Box 66.

Chapter 13: p. 266, LSA Office Services, Angell Hall; p.267, Hatcher, Box 66; p. 268, AA, Box 135; p. 269, James T. Wilson photograph series; p 269, AA, Box 135; p 271, AA, Box 135; p. 278, NIS, Box 1; p. 279, *Ibid.*, Box 135; p. 279, *Ibid.*, Box 136; p. 281, *Daily*, Box 12; p. 284, AA, Box 137.

Chapter 14: p. 288, NIS, UC; p. 289, UM, Office of the President, Box 259; p. 291 NIS, Box E; p. 291, *Daily*, Box 12; p. 292, Inter-Faith Council for Peace photograph collection, Box 13; p. 294, University Cellar photograph collection, Box 5; p. 295, NIS, Box 1; p. 300, NIS, UC; p. 305, Private collection; p. 306, *Michiganensian*, 1977; p. 307, UM-Dearborn, Office of Development; p. 312, Office of Affirmative Action, Box 12; p. 317, NIS,UC; p.318, *Ibid.*; p.320, *Daily*, Box 12; p. 322, NIS, UC; p. 323, *Ibid.*; p. 323, *Ibid.*

Chapter 15: p. 324, NIS, UC; p. 325, UM, Office of the President, Box 259; p. 326,

UM, Faculty Staff Photographs, Box 4; p. 328, NIS. UC; p. 332, *Ibid.*; p. 337, V.P. for Development, Box 33; p. 338, *Ibid.;* p. 342, Ann Arbor News, December 26, 1981; p. 344, *Daily*, Box 12 ; p. 345, NIS, u.c.; p. 347, AA, Box 135; p. 350, NIS, UC; p. 350, *Ibid.*; p. 351, *Ibid.*; p. 351, *Ibid.*; p. 352, *Ibid.*

Epilogue: p. 356, UM, Vice President for Development, Box 33; p. 357, UM, Office of the President, UC.

UNIVERSITY OF MICHIGAN REGENTS
1967-1994

Frederick C. Matthaei, Sr. (1960-67)
Allan R. Sorenson (1962-1967)
Paul G. Goebel (1962-1970)
Robert Peter Briggs (1964-1968)
William B. Cudlip (1964-1972)
Alvin M Bentley (1966-1969)
Frederick C. Matthaei, Jr. (1967-1968)
Otis M. Smith (1967-1970)
Robert J. Brown (1967-1974)
Gertrude V. Huebner (1967-1974)
Lawrence B. Lindemer (1968-1975)
Gerald R. Dunn (1969-1984)
Robert E. Nederlander (1969-1984)
Paul Walker Brown (1971-)
James L. Waters (1971-)
Deane Baker (1973-)
David Laro (1975-1980)
Sarah Goddard Power (1975-1987)
Thomas A. Roach (1975-1990)
Nellie M. Varner (1981-)
Neal D. Nielsen (1985-1992)
Veronica Latta Smith (1985-1992)
Philip H. Power (1987-)
Shirley M. McFee (1991-)
Laurence B. Deitch (1993-)
Rebecca McGowan (1993-)

NAME, BUILDING, AND CAMPUS INDEX

Regents

Adam, John J. 19
Adams, Paul 265
Anderson, John 11
Baits, Vera B. 235, 265
Barbour, Levi 107, 123
Barnard, Henry 37, 54
Baxter, Benjamin 44, 54, 66
Beal, Junius E. 123, 128, 158, 174, 197, 297
Beal, Rice 82, 83
Bentley, Alvin M. 276
Biddle, John 11
Bishop, Levi 44, 45, 46, 47, 54
Blair, Austin 89
Boilvin, Nicholas 11
Bonisteel, Roscoe O. 235, 265
Brablec, Carl 265
Bradley, George 54
Briggs, Robert P. 276
Brown, E. Lakin 44, 54
Brown, William 11
Bulkley, Harry C. 129
Burt, Hiram A. 78
Butterfield, Roger W. 123
Cass, Lewis 3, 5, 8, 9, 10, 11, 12, 26
Chapin Lucius D. 62
Clemens, Christian 11
Clements, William L. 113, 128, 133–135, 152, 157–158, 162, 174, 197
Connable, Alfred B. Jr. 172, 235, 265
Cook, Franklin M. 197
Cram, Esther Marsh 196
Crowley, David 197
Cudlip, William B. 276
Cutcheon, Byron 89
Dean, Henry S. 123
Denoyers, Peter 11
Doan, Leland I. 265
Duffield, George Jr. 89
Dunn, Gerald 344
Eckert, Otto E. 235, 265, 276

Ely, Elisha 36
Farnsworth, Elon 36
Felch, Alpheus 88
Ferry, William M. 54
Fletcher, Frank W. 111, 123, 133
Gilbert, Thomas D. 59
Goebel, Paul 276, 286
Gore, Victor M. 129, 196
Grant, Claudius B. 78, 104
Hanchett, Benjamin S. 128, 151, 196
Hemans, Charles F. 197
Herbert, J. Joseph 197, 235
Hill, Arthur 113, 133
Hoffman, Michael 19
Hubbard, Lucius L. 128, 135, 196
Hunt, Henry 11
Hunt, John 11
Johnson, J. Eastman 53, 54, 60
Jones, De Garmo 11
Joy, James F. 89
Kearsley, Jonathan 19, 30, 31
Kennedy, Charles S. 235, 265, 276
Kiefer, Herman 103, 123
Kingsley, James 36
Kipke, Harry 197, 235
Knappen, Loyal E. 125
Larned, Charles 11
LeRoy, Daniel 11
Lecuyer, John 11
Leech, Gurdon C. 19
Leib, John 11
Leland, Frank B. 128, 166
Lovejoy, Elijah 18
Lynch, John D. 197
Lyon, Lucius 19
Mason, Stevens T. 13–15, 19–22, 24
Matthaei, Frederick C. 261, 265, 271
McClelland, Robert 19
McGowan, Jonas H. 78, 82
McInally, William K. 265, 276
McIntyre, Donald 44, 47, 54, 59
Moore, Edward S. 36
Murfin, James O. 129, 197, 212, 218
Murphy, Irene 265

Faculty and Staff

Students and Alumni

Buildings and campus

GENERAL INDEX

B